Mass Media and American Politics

Sixth Edition

Doris A. Graber

University of Illinois at Chicago

CQ PRESS

A Division of Congressional Quarterly Inc.
Washington, D.C.

CQ Press
A Division of Congressional Quarterly Inc.
1255 22nd Street, N.W., Suite 400
Washington, D.C. 20037

(202) 822-1475; (800) 638-1710

www.cqpress.com

Printed and bound in the United States of America

05 04 03 02 01   5 4 3 2 1

∞ The paper used in this publication meets the minimum requirements of the American National Standard for Information Sciences—Permanence of Paper for Printed Library Materials, ANSI Z39.48-1992.

Cover design: Laurie Williams
Cover photo: © Todd Buchanan (All Rights Reserved)

Library of Congress Cataloging-in-Publication Data

Graber, Doris A. (Doris Appel).
    Mass media and American politics / Doris A. Graber.— 6th ed.
        p. cm.
    Includes bibliographical references and index.
    ISBN 1-56802-635-8 (pbk. : alk. paper)
    1. Mass media—Social aspects—United States. 2. Mass media—Political aspects—United States.   I. Title.
    HN90.M3 G7 2001
    302.23'0973—dc21

                                                                2001005557

Mass Media
and
American Politics

To
Jack, Jim, Lee, Susan, Tom —
my very special students

Contents

Tables, Figures, and Boxes

Tables

Figures

Boxes

Preface

AS I WRITE THIS, THE SCREEN OF MY TELEVISION displays horrifying scenes of death and destruction in New York City and the nation's capital in the wake of terrorist attacks. I have already been inundated with e-mail messages from friends and colleagues from across the globe who have been stirred by the same appalling images. I have gained important insights into the situation from the Web sites to which they have alerted me and from Web sites that I discovered on my own.

Do these pictures and the verbal messages that accompany them tell me and others enough? Are we getting the truth, the whole truth, and nothing but the truth? What is the effect of these news stories on my fellow citizens, on friends and foes abroad, and on my government? Are people abroad seeing and hearing a different truth? All of these questions, and many more swirling around my head, drive home the important role that news media play in the lives of average citizens and their leaders worldwide. If these events had happened in 1996, when the previous edition of *Mass Media and American Politics* was published, would the flood of images have been different? If so, in what way?

To answer these questions we must identify the stable foundations of the American mass media system as well as the political and technological developments that generate change. The sixth edition of *Mass Media and American Politics* does just that. It features up-to-date information about the fundamentals of the current media scene and the ongoing developments that are modifying its contours. The book recognizes that we have entered a period of transition where narrowcasting and broadcasting exist side by side and where the boundaries between print and broadcast media have become porous. What mix of information sources will ultimately prevail and how that mix will change the political as well as the media scene remain intriguing and fateful mysteries.

The data featured in this new edition come from the rich crop of current political communication studies, including my own research on television's bearing on politics. Fresh examples have replaced older ones throughout. The book's approach continues to be interdisciplinary and objective, offering a variety of viewpoints on controversial issues. From this evidence and the ample citation of additional information sources, readers should be able to form their own opinions and evaluations. The approach is direct and clear to suit the needs of novices in this area of knowledge, without sacrificing the scholarly depth, documentation, and precision that more advanced readers require.

The primary focus of the book is on news disseminated by television and newspapers because these media are still the chief sources of current information for people in public and private life. In addition, each chapter features analysis of the impact of the Internet and cable television on the available information stream and on politics. I have also made a concerted effort to discuss the public policy issues raised by the new media scene and the battles over regulatory policies. In these policy matters, average citizens must understand what is at stake for their vital sources of information so that they can make their voices heard in Congress and elsewhere. If they remain mute, narrow economic interests are likely to prevail over broad public interests.

Although the scope of research continues to broaden, most political communication research still concentrates on the relationship between media and politics during elections. The sixth edition of *Mass Media and American Politics,* like prior editions, takes a much broader approach. It encompasses the entire media landscape because media scholars cannot afford to ignore how all the pieces of the media–government puzzle fit together. Understanding these complex interrelationships requires a comprehensive, up-to-date text that provides an overview of the entire media field from a political perspective, yet is steeped in an intimate knowledge of the U.S. media system.

Chapters 1 and 2 examine the mass media as institutions in the U.S. political system and contrast the situation in the United States with that in other societies. The chapters show how the media are influenced by governmental structures and functions and how the media, in turn, influence government. I discuss the wave of media consolidations, as well as new developments in regulatory policies in the wake of the 1996 Telecommunications Act. Chapter 3 completes the analysis of the legal and political framework in which American media operate. It describes the legal rights of citizens, public officials, and newspeople to obtain and publish information and to seek protection from damaging publicity.

Chapter 4 deals with newsmaking under ordinary circumstances, with a focus on media structures, personnel, and operations. I also report on "public journalism," which remains a significant media reform movement. Chapter 5 describes news patterns under extraordinary circumstances, such as natural disasters and wars. It has proved to be a highly useful guide in understanding the role of the media in the weeks following the September 11, 2001, terrorist strikes against the United States. Chapter 6 focuses on what happens when newspeople take an exceptionally active role in politics—such as when they investigate business scams or misbehaviors by public officials—and the influence this type of investigative reporting has on public policy. In Chapter 7, I explore the wealth of information about political learning and opinion formation, along with theories about media-induced asocial and prosocial behavior. Much of this material is based on my own ongoing research.

The powerful influence of the media in a variety of political situations is the subject of Chapters 8–11. These situations include media coverage of elections (Chapter 8) and the interplay between the media and major political institutions such as the presidency and Congress (Chapter 9). The media's role in the judicial system and at state and local levels is set forth in Chapter 10. Chapter 11 details the growing impact of news media on the conduct of foreign policy. The book concludes with a discussion of policy trends and the new technologies and political forces shaping them (Chapter 12). Boxed vignettes exploring compelling media issues add a bit of spice to individual chapters.

The changes in this new edition reflect the political and technological events that have transpired since 1996, the treasure trove of new mass media studies, and much-appreciated suggestions from colleagues and students who have used the book. I am indebted to my research assistants, especially Shikha Jain and Adam Stretz, who played major roles in generating new, up-to-date tables and tracking down elusive references and other data. The editorial team at CQ Press provided their usual strong support that greatly eased the many chores entailed in book production. Among them, special thanks must go to Gwenda Larsen whose magical touch managed to squeeze an incredible amount of editorial work into a far too tiny time slot. The concern and friendship of the CQ Press crew and its freelance helpers have been real morale boosters. My husband, as always, has tolerated with grace and good humor my time-consuming dalliance with yet another revision. His loving support is legendary. I thank him for being a major partner in all I do.

Doris A. Graber

Mass Media
and
American Politics

chapter   one

Media Power
and Government Control

"CAPITAL PUNISHMENT IN ILLINOIS IS A SYSTEM so riddled with faulty evidence, unscrupulous trial tactics and legal incompetence that justice has been forsaken."[1] So reported the *Chicago Tribune* in late 1999, basing its judgment on an investigative report titled "The Failure of the Death Penalty in Illinois." Reporters for the *Tribune* had plowed through trial records, court opinions, and lawyers' disciplinary records to discover how 285 men had been sentenced to die during a twenty-two year period. The investigators found that 127 of the 285 death sentences pronounced since 1977—nearly 45 percent—had been reversed on appeal for egregious errors. Problematic procedures included the use of outdated crime laboratory procedures and the failure to include members of the defendant's racial group in the jury. In 33 cases the accused was represented during his trial by an attorney who had either been disbarred or suspended for incompetent, unethical, or even criminal conduct. In at least 46 cases evidence against the accused was questionable because it had come from a notoriously unreliable source—a fellow prisoner who could hope to reduce his own sentence by supplying the evidence. By 1999, 115 of the 127 reversed cases had been reviewed. For 12 defendants (nearly 10 percent), the death sentence was upheld, but 13 men (11 percent) were exonerated entirely. In the remaining 90 cases (78 percent), the death penalty was set aside in favor of a less severe penalty.

The shocking facts brought to light by the *Tribune* stories attracted worldwide attention, especially from opponents of capital punishment. In Illinois, legislative and judicial committees began to explore reform

1

measures, including special competency standards for prosecutors and attorneys serving in death penalty cases. Shortly after the publication of the *Tribune* report, Illinois governor George Ryan halted all further executions until a specially created panel could investigate the badly flawed death penalty system. Illinois became the first among the thirty-eight U.S. states practicing capital punishment to introduce such a moratorium.[2] The governor's action received broad acclaim in Illinois and throughout the nation. It sparked steps toward reform of the death penalty justice system in other states and at the national level. Public opinion support for death sentences fell.[3]

Political Importance of Mass Media

The impact of news stories on political leaders and on the average citizen's views about the merits of public policies and the performance of public officials demonstrates how mass media, in combination with other political factors, can influence American politics. News stories take millions of Americans, in all walks of life, to the battlefields of the world. They give them ringside seats for space shuttle launches or basketball championships. They provide the nation with shared political experiences, such as watching presidential inaugurations or congressional investigations, that then undergird public opinions and unite people to decide when political action is required.[4]

Print, audio, and audiovisual media often serve as attitude and behavior models. The images that media create suggest which views and behaviors are acceptable and even praiseworthy in a given society and which are unacceptable or outside the mainstream. Audiences can learn how to conduct themselves in ordinary social and work situations, how to cope with personal crises, and how to evaluate major social institutions like the medical profession or grocery chains. Media stories also indicate what is deemed important or unimportant by various groups of elites, what conforms to prevailing standards of justice and morality, and how events are related to each other. In the process the media present a set of cultural values that their audiences are likely to accept in whole or in part as typical of American society. The media thus help to integrate and homogenize our society.

The mass media also serve as powerful guardians of political norms because the American people believe that a free press should keep them informed about the wrongdoings of government. Media images are especially potent when they involve aspects of life that people experience only through the media. The personal and professional lives of politicians, political events in distant lands, frenzied trading at stock exchanges, tornadoes in the Middle West, or earthquakes in California are not generally experienced firsthand. Rather, popular perceptions of these aspects and crises of life are shaped largely by the images portrayed in news and in fictional stories in print and electronic media. Like caricatures, media stories often create skewed impressions because they cannot report stories in detail and in full context. For example, thanks to a heavy focus on crime news and fiction stories, television exaggerates the likelihood of an individual becoming a victim of crime. Heavy viewers, therefore, fear crime to a greater extent and take more protective measures than do light viewers.[5]

Attention to the mass media is all-pervasive among twenty-first-century Americans. The average high school graduate today has spent more time in front of a television set than in school, particularly during his or her preschool and elementary school days. Even in school much learning about current events is based on information provided by the media. An average adult American spends nearly half of her or his leisure time watching television, listening to the radio, or reading newspapers and magazines. Averaged out over an entire week, this amounts to more than seven hours of exposure per day to some form of mass media news or entertainment. Television, relayed over the air, via cable, through the Internet, or through a videotape recorder, occupies three-fourths of this time. Despite considerable reported dissatisfaction with the quality of television programs in all of these modalities, television remains the primary source of news and entertainment for the average American. It is also the most trusted source of information.[6]

A total of 75 percent of the people responding to a national survey in late spring 2000 said that they regularly watched some form of television news. Additionally, 63 percent claimed to read a daily newspaper regularly, and 46 percent said that they paid regular attention to radio news.[7] The ability to attract such vast audiences of ordinary people, as well as political elites, is a major ingredient in the power of the mass media and makes them extraordinarily important for the individuals and groups whose stories and causes are publicized. Table 1-1 shows the attractiveness of various types of news venues for average Americans.

Politically relevant information is often conveyed through stories that are not concerned explicitly with politics. In fact, because most people are exposed far more to nonpolitical information, make-believe media, such as movies and entertainment television, have become major suppliers of political images. The Center for Media and Public Affairs, which, among other things, keeps track of political jokes on late-night comic shows, recorded 771 jokes involving Gov. George W. Bush in 2000 compared to

TABLE 1-1   News Consumption Patterns: 2000

Medium	Percentage
Local TV news	56%
Newspapers "read yesterday"	46
TV news magazines	31
Nightly network news	30
Online news "three or more days"	23
CNN	21
Network morning shows	20
Fox News Cable	17
National Public Radio	15
CNBC	13
News magazines	12
MSNBC	11
Business magazines	5
NewsHour	5
C-Span	4

SOURCE: Adapted from the Pew Research Center for the People and the Press, "Internet Sapping Broadcast News Audience," http://www.people-press.org/media00sec1.htm; http://www.people-press.org/media00sec2.htm (June 13, 2000).

NOTE: Based on national telephone sample of 3,142 adults reporting "regular" use of a news medium.

494 for Vice President Al Gore.[8] That made Bush look less presidential and more deserving of ridicule than his rival. Other entertainment shows on television portray social institutions, such as the police or the schools, in ways that convey esteem or heap scorn on them. These shows also express social judgments about various types of people. For instance, television in the past often depicted African Americans and women as socially inferior and limited in abilities. This type of coverage conveys messages that audiences, including the misrepresented groups, may accept at face value, even when the portrayals distort real-world conditions. Audience members may also think that social conditions and judgments shown on television are widely accepted and socially sanctioned and therefore ought to be maintained.[9]

Not only are the media the chief source of most Americans' views of the world, but they also provide the fastest way to disperse information throughout the entire society. Major political news broadcasts by twenty-four-hour services like CNN spread breaking stories throughout the country in minutes. People hear them either directly from radio or

YOUR TAX DOLLARS AT WORK: CONGRESS STARTS THE DAY WITH THE PLEDGE.

Reprinted by permission: Tribune Media Services.

television or secondhand from other people who had received mass media messages.

All of the mass media are politically important because of their potential to reach large audiences. However, their impacts vary, depending on the characteristics of each medium, the nature and quantity of the political messages that it carries, and the size of the audience that it reaches. Print media of various kinds, including media featuring printed text on the Internet, generally supply the largest quantities of factual political information and analysis. They need readers who are literate at appropriate levels. Electronic media, especially television broadcasts, provide a greater sense of reality, which explains why audiences find electronic media more credible than print media. Moreover, large segments of the U.S. population have limited reading skills and find it far easier to capture meanings from pictures and spoken language. Electronic media also convey physical images, including body language and facial expressions, much more effectively than print media. They are especially well suited to attract viewers' attention and arouse their emotions. Many people find it easier to gather insights on events and issues through audiovisual media.

The nature of each technology has implications for the political purposes for which it is useful.

Functions of Mass Media

What major societal functions do the mass media perform? Political scientist Harold Lasswell, a pioneer in media studies, mentions (1) surveillance of the world to report ongoing events, (2) interpretation of the meaning of events, and (3) socialization of individuals into their cultural settings.[10] To these three, a fourth function must be added: deliberate manipulation of politics. The manner in which these four functions are performed affects the political fate of individuals, groups, and social organizations, as well as the course of domestic and international politics.

Surveillance

Surveillance involves two major tasks. For the political community at large, surveillance throws the spotlight of publicity on selected people, organizations, and events. This publicity then may make the issues or individuals matters of concern to politicians and to the general public. It may determine which political demands are exposed and which are kept hidden. It also may force politicians to respond to situations on which their views would not have been aired otherwise. In contrast with such *public* surveillance, surveillance for their "private" purposes informs individual citizens about current events. Although it may lead to political activities, its primary functions are gratification of personal needs and the quieting of anxieties. The media, as Marshall McLuhan, another pioneering media scholar, observed, are "sense extensions" for individuals who cannot directly witness most of the events of interest to them and their communities.[11]

Public Surveillance.   Newspeople determine what is *news*—that is, which political happenings will be covered and which will be ignored. Their choices are politically significant because they affect who and what will have a good chance to become the focus for political discussion and action.[12] Without media attention the people and events covered by the news might have no influence, or reduced influence, on decision makers. Conditions that may be tolerated if these people or events remain obscure may become intolerable quickly in the glare of publicity. The death penalty situation in Illinois is a perfect example. Without the public airing of the situation, reforms would have been unlikely. Politicians are keenly aware of the media's agenda-setting power. This is why they try mightily to time and structure events to yield as much favorable publicity as possible and to forestall damaging coverage.

Not all media surveillance spurs beneficial reactions, of course. Misperceptions and scares created by media stories have undermined confidence in good policies and practices, good people, and good products on many occasions. The human and economic costs have been vast. For example, stories of dubious validity that questioned the safety of bioengineered foods caused millions of dollars of losses in the affected industries.

If media stories overemphasize crime and corruption in the inner city, scared residents may move to the suburbs, leaving the inner city deserted and even less safe and deprived of tax revenues. Speculation that international conflicts or economic downturns are in the offing may scare investors and produce fluctuations in domestic and international stock markets and commodity exchanges. Serious economic (and hence political) consequences may ensue.

Fear of publicity can be as powerful a force in shaping action as actual exposure. Politicians and business leaders know what damage an unfavorable story can create and act accordingly, either to avoid or conceal censurable behaviors or to atone for their misdeeds by public confessions of guilt and regret. President Bill Clinton, whose eight-year term was pockmarked with allegations of scandals, tried valiantly to keep some of them out of the public eye by forceful denials of the truth of the allegations. But whenever proof made the charges undeniable, as was the case in his affair with White House intern Monica Lewinsky, he escaped much public wrath by publicly apologizing for his misbehavior.[13]

The media can doom people and events to obscurity by inattention as well. When the information supply exceeds the media's capacity to transmit it, many stories remain untold. Constraints are most stringent on television and radio newscasts. Newspeople also ignore matters that do not seem "newsworthy" by accepted journalistic criteria or that fail to catch their attention. Conscious attempts to suppress information for ideological or political reasons are another, less frequent reason for lack of coverage.

For many years left-wing social critics have faulted mainstream American journalists for using their news selection power to strengthen white middle-class values and suppress socialist viewpoints. These critics claim that these choices are made deliberately to perpetuate capitalist exploitation of the masses, in line with the ideological preferences of media owners. Critics also claim that the media have intentionally suppressed the facts about dangerous products, such as alcohol and tobacco, and about the socially harmful activities of large corporations, which may be responsible for water and air pollution or unsafe consumer goods.[14] By the same

token, right-wing critics complain that the media give undue attention to
the views of the enemies of the established social and political order in
hopes of undermining it. Each camp can cite a long list of stories to support its contentions.[15]

Media people deny these charges. They disdain political motives in
news selection and defend their choices on the basis of the general criteria of newsworthiness (treated more fully in Chapter 4). They can muster
a lot of evidence from news stories to support their claims. At the heart of
controversies over the ideological bias of the media lie two basic questions
that cannot be answered conclusively. The first concerns people's motivations. How can one prove what motivates journalists to act in certain ways?
And is it fair to ascribe motivations to them in the face of their denials?
The second question relates to story effects. To what degree can media
stories produce the goals that owners of print and electronic media and
news professionals are allegedly seeking?

Besides calling attention to matters of potential public concern, the
media also provide cues to the public about the degree of importance of
an issue. Important stories are covered prominently—on the front page
with big headlines and pictures or as a major television or radio feature.
Less important matters are buried in the back pages or given brief exposure on television or radio. However, nearly all coverage, even though it is
brief and comparatively inconspicuous, lends an aura of significance to
publicized topics. Through the sheer fact of coverage the media can confer status on individuals and organizations. They "function essentially as
agencies of social legitimation—as forces, that is, which reaffirm those
ultimate value standards and beliefs, which in turn uphold the social and
political status quo."[16]

Television made African American civil rights leaders and their
causes household names. Martin Luther King Jr. and Jesse Jackson
became national figures in part because television showed them giving
speeches and leading marches and protests. In King's case, television
captured the riots following his assassination. A political candidate
whose efforts to win an election are widely publicized, a social crusader
whose goals become front-page news, or a convicted murderer or terrorist who wins a hearing on radio or television often becomes an instant celebrity. Their unpublicized counterparts remain obscure and
bereft of political influence.

Because the attention of the media is crucial for political success,
actors on the political scene deliberately create situations likely to receive
media coverage. Daniel Boorstin has labeled events arranged primarily to
stimulate media coverage "pseudo-events."[17] They may range from news
conferences called by public figures even when there is no news to

announce, to physical assaults on people and property designed to drama-tize grievances. Newspeople who must cover such events may feel manipu-lated and resent their assignments. But they are loath to allow competing media to scoop them.

When events are exceptionally significant or have become widely known already, or when the story is reported by competing media, deci-sions about what to publish and thereby put on the agenda for public dis-cussion and possible action are beyond the discretion of media personnel. For example, professional considerations demand the reporting of news about prominent persons and major domestic or international events.[18] Beyond such unavoidable events, there remains an extremely wide range of persons and events for which coverage is discretionary.

The power of the media to set the agenda for politics is a matter of concern because it is not controlled by a system of formal checks and bal-ances as is power at the various levels of government. It is not subject to periodic review through the electoral process. If media emphases or claims are incorrect, remedies are few. Citizens can be protected from false advertising of consumer goods through truth in advertising laws, but there is no way in which they can be protected from false political claims or improper news selection by media personnel without impairing the cru-cial rights to free speech and a free press. Media critic Jay Blumler ex-pressed the dilemma well:

> Media power is not supposed to be shared: That's an infringement of editor-ial autonomy. It is not supposed to be controlled: That's censorship. It's not even supposed to be influenced: That's news management! But why should media personnel be exempt from Lord Acton's dictum that all power cor-rupts and absolute power corrupts absolutely? And if they are not exempt, who exactly is best fitted to guard the press guardians, as it were?[19]

Private Surveillance. Average citizens may not think much about the broader political impact of the news they read, hear, and watch. They use the media primarily to keep in touch with what they deem personally important. The media are their eyes and ears to the world, their means of surveillance. The media tell them about economic conditions, weather, sports, jobs, fashions, social and cultural events, health and science, and the public and private lives of famous people.

The ability to stay informed makes people feel secure, whether or not they remember what they read or hear or see. Even though the news may be bad, at least they feel that there will be no startling surprises. News reassures them that the political system continues to operate despite constant crises and frequent mistakes. Reassurance is important for people's peace of mind. But it also tends to keep them politically quiescent because there is no need to act if political leaders seem to be doing their jobs. For good or ill, the public's quiescence helps to maintain the political and economic status quo.[20]

Other significant private functions that the mass media fulfill for many people are entertainment, companionship, tension relief, and a way to pass the time with minimal physical or mental exertion. The mass media can satisfy these important personal needs conveniently and cheaply. People who otherwise might be frustrated and dissatisfied can participate through the media vicariously in current political happenings, in sports and musical events, in the lives of famous people, and in the lives of families and communities featured in the news.[21]

Interpretation

Media not only survey the events of the day and make them the focus of public and private attention, but they also interpret their meanings, put them into context, and speculate about their consequences. Most incidents lend themselves to a variety of interpretations, depending on the values and experiences of the interpreter. The kind of interpretation that is chosen affects the political consequences of media reports. For example, since 1962 the way in which the media interpret the legal and social significance of abortions has changed considerably. Abortion almost universally used to be considered murder. The abortionist was the villain and the pregnant woman was an accomplice in a heinous crime. Now abortion is often cast into the frame of women's rights to control their bodies in order to protect their physical and mental health.

The situation that spawned the switch in media interpretation and eased the change in public attitudes toward abortion involved television personality Sherri Finkbine, hostess of *Romper Room,* a popular children's television show in the 1960s. She had taken thalidomide during her pregnancy before the drug's tragic effects on the unborn were known. Once she learned of the potential harm, she feared giving birth to a severely malformed baby and underwent an abortion in 1962.

Instead of reporting the action as murder, as had been the custom, news media throughout the country defended the popular Finkbine's decision to terminate her pregnancy. To steer clear of the negative connotations of the word *abortion,* journalists used a new vocabulary. They talked of "surgery to prevent a malformed baby," of "avoiding the possibility of mothering a drug-deformed child," and of the necessity of inducing a miscarriage to spare a child from loathing "its own image and crying out against those who might have spared it this suffering."[22]

Numerous circumstances influenced the type of interpretation that the Finkbine story received. In the end, it hinged on journalists' decisions, made independently or in response to pressures, to frame the story in a specific way and to choose available informants accordingly. Journalistic concerns play a large role in determining how the news will be framed, which in turn determines its likely impact.

By suggesting the causes and relationships of various events, the media may shape opinions even without telling their audiences what to believe or think. For example, linking civil strife in Central America to the activities of Soviet and Cuban communist agents during the cold war era ensured that the American public would view the situation with considerable alarm. Linking the hostilities to poverty and social oppression would have put the problems into a far less threatening light.

There are countless ways in which news presentations can predetermine the conclusions that people are likely to draw.

> We [journalists] can attribute any social problem to official policies, the machinations of those who benefit from it, or the pathology of those who suffer from it. We can trace it back to class or racial inequalities, to ideologies such as nationalism or patriotism, or to resistance to the regime. We can root the problem in God, in its historic genesis, in the accidental or systematic conjuncture of events, in rationality, in irrationality, or in a combination of these or other origins. In choosing any such ultimate cause we are also depicting a setting, an appropriate course of action, and sets of virtuous and evil characters, and doing so in a way that will appeal to some part of the public that sees its own sentiments or interests reflected in that choice of a social scene.[23]

The items that media personnel select to illustrate a point or to characterize a political actor need not be intrinsically important to be influential in shaping opinions and evaluations. They do not even need exposure in respected media outlets. This is why House Speaker–designate Bob Livingston resigned from Congress in 1998, when he learned that the publisher of the pornographic *Hustler* magazine was about to publicize charges of adultery about him. Livingston had confessed extramarital liaisons to his colleagues in Congress but feared that adverse media publicity would seriously harm his party and his career.

Socialization

The third function of major mass media mentioned by Lasswell is political socialization (discussed more fully in Chapter 7). It involves the learning of basic values and orientations that prepares individuals to fit into their cultural milieu. Prior to the 1970s, studies largely ignored the mass media because parents and the schools were deemed the primary agents of socialization. Research in the 1970s finally established that the media play a crucial role in political socialization.[24] Most information that young people acquire about the nature of their political world comes directly or indirectly from the mass media. The media present to the young specific facts as well as general values, teaching them which elements produce power, success, and dominance in society, and they provide young people with models for behavior. Because young people lack established attitudes and behavior patterns, they use such information to develop their opinions.

Research indicates that most of the new orientations and opinions that adults acquire during their lifetime also are based on information supplied by the mass media. People do not necessarily adopt the precise attitudes and opinions that may be suggested by the media. Rather, mass media information provides the ingredients that people use to adjust their existing attitudes and opinions to keep pace with a changing world. The mass media must be credited, therefore, with a sizable share of continuing adult political socialization and resocialization. Examples of resocialization—the restructuring of established basic attitudes—are the shifts in sexual morality and racial attitudes that the American public has undergone since the middle of the last century and the changing views on relations with mainland China and with Russia.[25]

Manipulation

In the wake of President Richard Nixon's resignation from office in 1974, following the Watergate scandals, direct manipulation of the political process by the media has become increasingly common. Many journalists are major players in the game of politics; they do not just play their traditional role as chroniclers of information provided by others. Political manipulation often takes the form of investigative journalism. Major print and electronic media now operate their own investigative units. Television shows such as *60 Minutes* and *20/20,* and feature stories in print media that focus on revealing the results of investigations, are very popular.

The purpose of such investigative shows is to *muckrake.* President Theodore Roosevelt was the first to apply the term to journalists who conducted their own investigations into corruption and wrongdoing in order to stimulate governmental action to clean up the "dirt" they had exposed. The term comes from a rake designed to collect manure. Muckraking today may have several different goals.[26] The journalist's primary purpose may be to write stories that expose misconduct in government and produce reforms. Or the chief purpose may be to present sensational information that attracts large media audiences and enhances profits. Other manipulative stories may be designed primarily to affect the course of politics in line with the journalist's political preferences. The various forms that manipulation can take are discussed in Chapter 6.

Effects of Mass Media

The public believes that the media have an important impact on the conduct of politics and on public thinking. Politicians act and behave on the basis of the same assumption. But many studies conducted by social scientists fail to show substantial impact. Why is there such a discrepancy between many social science appraisals of mass media effects and the general impression, reflected in public policies, that the mass media are extremely influential?

There are three major reasons. First, many studies, particularly those conducted during the 1950s and 1960s, have taken a narrow approach to media effects, looking for only a few specified effects rather than all possible effects. Second, theories about the ways in which people use newspapers, television, radio, and other mass media have enhanced the belief that media have minimal effects because people are disinclined to learn from the media. Third, social scientists have encountered great difficulties in measuring effects because media make their impact as part of a complex combination of social stimuli.

Early Studies

American social scientists began to study the effects of the mass media primarily in one narrow area: vote change as a result of media coverage of presidential elections. Among these early studies, several are considered classics. *The People's Choice* by Paul Lazarsfeld, Bernard Berelson, and Hazel Gaudet, all of Columbia University, reported in 1944 how people made their voting choices in Erie County, Pennsylvania, in the 1940 presidential election. Sequels to the study followed in short order. The best known are *Voting: A Study of Opinion Formation in a Presidential Campaign, The Voter Decides,* and *The American Voter.*[27]

Focus on Vote Choices. The early studies on voting were based on the assumption that a well-publicized campaign presumably changed votes. If it did not, this indicated that the media lacked influence. Subsequent studies have shown that this reasoning is faulty. There may be measurable media influence even when vote choice remains stable. Besides, media effects vary, depending on the office at stake and the historical period. At the time of the early voting studies, change of vote choice was quite uncommon because most voters adhered closely to party lines, regardless of media coverage. In recent years party allegiance has weakened substantially among many voters, so that the opportunities for media influence on vote choice are far greater.

Had the investigators concentrated on other settings, such as judicial or nonpartisan elections (for which few voting cues outside the media are available), they might also have discovered greater media-induced change in attitude. Substantial media influence might have been found even in presidential elections if changes in people's trust and affection or knowledge about the candidates and the election had been explored. The early studies largely ignored all media influences that did not result in easily measurable behavior and attitude changes. Yet such changes constitute important media influences that are crucial components of a variety of political behaviors aside from voting decisions.

The early voting studies focused almost exclusively on effects at the individual level and failed to trace effects on the social groups to which individuals belong and through which they influence political events. Gay men might not change their votes after hearing a candidate attack their lifestyle. But they might urge their association to testify against legislation favored by the candidate. They might even participate in violence in the wake of news stories reporting hate crimes against the gay community. In turn, these activities may have major political repercussions. Yet the early studies of media effects totally ignore such sequential impacts on the entire political system and its component parts.

The findings that media effects were minimal were so pervasive in early research that social science research into mass media effects fell to a low ebb after an initial flurry in the 1940s and 1950s. Social scientists did not want to waste time studying inconsequential effects. Despite the seemingly solid evidence of media importance, they did not care to swim against the stream of established knowledge. As a consequence, in study after study dealing with political socialization and learning, the mass media were hardly mentioned as important factors.

Learning Theories. The early findings were all the more believable because they tied in well with theories of persuasion. Mass media messages presumably miss their mark because they are impersonal. They are not tailored to the interests of specific individuals, as are the messages of parents, teachers, and friends. They do not permit immediate feedback, which then allows the sender to adjust the message to make it more suitable for the receiver. Furthermore, there is no compulsion to listen to mass media messages and no need to answer. Hence it is easy to ignore them.

Although there is a lot of truth to these claims, they fail to consider that television can be a very personal medium. Audiences frequently interact with the television image as if what appears on screen were actually present in front of them. They may look on television commentators and actors as personal friends. Children often imitate people and situations on television, just as if they were part of what they saw.

Further support for the minimal-effects findings come from various cognitive consistency theories. They postulate that average individuals dislike being presented with information that is incompatible with cherished beliefs. To avoid a painful experience that might require changing established beliefs, people expose themselves to the media selectively. Social scientists have evidence that people are indeed selective in their use of the media and search for information that reinforces what they already believe and know. But, as will be discussed more fully in Chapter 7, the phenomenon is limited.

Recent Research

When researchers resumed their investigations of mass media effects in the wake of persistent evidence of strong media impact, they cast their net more broadly. They began to look beyond media effects on voting to other effects during elections and in other types of political situations. In this vein, researchers have examined media impact on factual learning, on opinion formation, and on the satisfaction of a variety of other human needs. They also have looked beyond the individual to effects on political systems and subsystems, a search that promises to be highly rewarding. But despite improvements in research designs and techniques, research into mass media effects has remained hampered by serious measurement problems.

Measuring Complex Effects. Mass media effects are difficult to measure, both at the level of the individual and at the societal level, because they are highly complex and elusive. The most common measuring device at the individual level—self-assessment of impact elicited during interviews—is notoriously unreliable. Researchers lack tools to measure human thinking objectively. Even when people engage in overt behavior, one cannot judge accurately what messages may have prompted the behavior. Actions spring from a variety of motivations, so that it is difficult to isolate the part played by media.

Assessing the impact of particular news stories is especially difficult because mass media audiences already possess a fund of knowledge and attitudes that they bring to bear on new information. Because researchers rarely know precisely what this information is, or the rules by which it is combined with incoming information, they cannot pinpoint the exact contribution that particular mass media stories have made to an individual's cognitions, feelings, and actions. To complicate matters further, the impact of the mass media varies depending on the subject matter. For instance, media impact is greater on people's perceptions of unfamiliar issues than on their perceptions of familiar issues especially when they have faced them personally.

It is even more difficult to establish effects at the societal level. A good example is the *CNN effect,* which was widely credited as propelling President George Bush to dispatch U.S. troops to Somalia in 1992. The term *CNN effect* refers to the belief that news media, particularly as exhibited by the extensive news coverage of breaking events by the Cable News Network (CNN), directly inflame public opinion by showing gripping pictures. The public's clamor for action then forces government to take hasty action. Media coverage becomes the dog that wags the public policy tail.

In the Somalia case, reports and pictures of widespread starvation and devastation had been aired widely by CNN and other television networks in the summer months of 1992. These pictures presumably inflamed the public and aroused pressure groups that forced members of the Bush administration, against their better judgment, to airlift relief supplies and later to dispatch American troops to Somalia. The rescue effort ultimately failed, and American lives were lost.[28]

Political scientists Steven Livingston and Todd Eachus reached a different conclusion about the respective roles of the news media and the Bush administration in determining U.S. policy in Somalia. After examining a variety of sources, including *New York Times* and *Washington Post* stories about U.S. humanitarian relief policies and after interviewing key government decision makers and long-term relief personnel in Somalia, they concluded that plans for relief efforts had been under way for more than a year prior to CNN coverage of the tragedy. Government officials, including concerned members of Congress who had traveled to Somalia, rather than television news stories, had been the spur to action.

Despite persuasive evidence that extensive media coverage of the tragedy followed, rather than preceded, President Bush's announcement of the military airlift and other relief measures on August 14, 1992, many observers still argue that media mobilization of public opinion was an essential prerequisite for the Somalia intervention. It is impossible to prove definitively that the administration would have abstained from relief measures in the absence of media coverage of the tragedy. Inability to prove the scope of mass media impact beyond a doubt has made social scientists shy away from assessing media influence on many important political events. Some social scientists even go to the other extreme and deny that effects exist simply because the effects defy precise measurement. This is unfortunate because many elusive effects can be observed in the field and studied in the laboratory.

Measurement of media effects also has suffered because unanticipated effects are frequently ignored. For example, the stock market is highly sensitive to news reports even when the reports do not have a readily discernible link to the country's economy. A brief story about one patient's "miracle cure" from an unusual disease may have a strong, unrecorded effect on drug companies even though the story is barely a blip on the audience's attention screen.

Statistical versus Political Significance. Social scientists often underestimate media impact because they falsely equate statistical significance with political significance. Media impact on a statistically insignificant number of individuals can still have great political consequences. For example, during an election, only 1 or 2 percent of the voters may change their votes because of media stories. That is a statistically negligible effect. From a political standpoint, however, the impact may be major, because many important elections, including several presidential elections, have been decided by a tiny margin of the voters. In the 2000 presidential race, the ultimate outcome was decided by a fraction of less than 1 percent of the vote in the state of Florida. Overall, more than 105 million votes were cast for president. An "insignificant" 1 percent of that total would still represent more than one million people.

On a smaller scale, if a broadcast of details of a race riot attracts a few listeners to the riot site and stimulates some to participate, the situation may escalate beyond control. In the same way, the impact of a single news story may change the course of history if it induces one assassin to kill a world leader or convinces one world leader to go to war.

Influencing Elites. Another major problem with social science research on mass media effects is that it has concentrated on measuring the effects on ordinary individuals rather than on political elites. The average individual, despite contrary democratic fictions, is fairly unimportant in the political process. Mass media impact on a handful of political decision makers usually is vastly more significant than similar impact on ordinary individuals. In addition, the impact on decision makers is likely to be far more profound because mass media information relates more directly to their immediate concerns. News that President Clinton had pardoned hundreds of convicted offenders without seeking the customary Justice Department consultation during his last days in office caused few ripples among the American public. But it roiled members of Congress and sparked efforts to curb the president's unlimited pardoning powers. Political elites may pay closer attention to stories in which the public is not interested and that the public often fails to understand. And they may spend considerable time and effort to generate media coverage that promotes their interests.

In light of what we have discussed thus far, it seems totally unrealistic to deny that the media are important in setting the stage for ongoing political developments, in shaping the views and behaviors of political elites and other selected groups, and in influencing the general public's perception of political life. As Theodore White put it, albeit with some exaggeration:

> The power of the press in America is a primordial one. It sets the agenda of public discussion; and this sweeping political power is unrestrained by any law. It determines what people will talk and think about—an authority that in other nations is reserved for tyrants, priests, parties, and mandarins.
>
> No major act of the American Congress, no foreign adventure, no act of diplomacy, no great social reform can succeed in the United States unless the press prepares the public mind.[29]

Even if one argues that the media are nothing but conduits of information over which they have no control, one cannot deny that people throughout the world of politics consider the media to be powerful and behave accordingly. This is why governments everywhere, in authoritarian as well as democratic societies, try to control the flow of information produced by the media lest it thwart their political objectives.[30]

Who Should Control News Making?

Attempts by governments to control and manipulate the media have been universal because public officials everywhere believe that media are important political forces. This belief is based on the assumption that institutions that control public information can shape public knowledge and behavior and thereby determine the support or opposition of citizens and officials to the government and its policies. That is why Emperor Napoleon complained that "Four hostile newspapers are more to be feared than a thousand bayonets."

Although control occurs in all societies, its extent, nature, and purposes vary. There are several reasons. Political ideology is a major one. In countries in which free expression of opinion is highly valued and in which dissent is respected, the media tend to be comparatively unrestrained. The right of the press to criticize governments also flourishes when the accepted ideology grants that governments are fallible and often corrupt and that average citizens are capable of forming valuable opinions about the conduct of government. Finally, freedom of the press, even when it becomes a thorn in the side of the government, is more easily tolerated in governments that are well established and politically and economically secure. In developing nations, for instance, where governments are often unstable and resources limited, it may be difficult to tolerate press behavior that is apt to topple the government or retard its plans for economic development.

Nowhere are the media totally free from formal and informal government and social controls, even in times of peace. On the whole, authoritarian countries control more extensively and more rigidly than nonauthoritarian ones, but all systems represent points on a continuum of control. There are also gradations of control within nations, depending on the current regime and political setting, regional and local variations, and the nature of news. The specifics of control systems vary from country to country, but the overall patterns are similar.[31]

Authoritarian control systems are based either on a totalitarian ideology and are designed to control and use the media to support ideological goals or they are nonideological and simply represent a desire by the ruling elites to control media output tightly so that it does not interfere with their conduct of government. Examples of nonideological authoritarian control can be found in states ruled by military governments or in which constitutional guarantees have been suspended. Examples of control based on communist ideology are found in Cuba and the People's Republic of China.

There are also two types of *nonauthoritarian approaches to control,* linked to differences in philosophies about the role that the media ought to play in countries in which they enjoy a great deal of freedom. The two types have been labeled *libertarian* and *social responsibility.* When journalists in democratic societies subscribe to the libertarian philosophy, they feel free to report whatever they wish so long as public tastes are satisfied. By contrast, when social responsibility philosophies prevail, newspeople expect to contribute to the betterment of society, spurring media audiences to behave in socially responsible ways. Journalists in the United States and Western Europe furnish examples of both these philosophies. Often libertarian and social responsibility journalism occur simultaneously, or they may alternate during successive historical periods.[32]

In today's world, fully or partially authoritarian systems of media control prevail in the majority of countries, although many governments profess a desire for democratization and are struggling to move in that direction. Nonetheless, their attempts to control internal and external news flows persist. Several members of the United Nations Educational, Scientific, and Cultural Organization (UNESCO) have opposed freedom of reporting about their countries in foreign media. They contend that only news that supports the established regime should be permitted and that

TABLE 1-2   Contrasting Assumptions about Press Mission

Authoritarian regime assumptions	Democratic regime assumptions
Government knows and respects people's best interests	Governments are fallible and often corrupt
Press should not attack the government and its major policies	Press should attack the government when officials and policies seem flawed
News should engender support for major policies	News should stimulate critical thinking about major policies
News and entertainment programs should be selected for their social values	News and entertainment programs should be selected for audience appeal

SOURCE: Compiled by author.

all newspeople should be subject to supervision by officials of the country whose affairs they report. This story is told more fully in Chapter 11.

Role of Media in Authoritarian Regimes

What basic assumptions underlie authoritarian and nonauthoritarian philosophies of media operation, and what types of governmental structures and practices have been invented to implement these philosophies? As Table 1-2 suggests, authoritarian systems operate on the assumption that the government knows and represents the best interests of the people. Therefore, the mass media must not interfere with the operations of the government or endanger its survival. The press may point out minor deficiencies or corruption of low-level officials and suggest adjustments in line with prevailing policies, but criticism of the basic system or its rulers is considered destructive.

In most authoritarian political systems the mass media are expected to take positions that firmly support the government. News must engender support for major policies and must echo official stands about who the country's domestic and international friends and enemies are. Beyond that, the media are free to choose the stories they wish to publish, so long as government officials agree that these stories do not interfere with public policies.

In totalitarian societies the role of the media is more stringently defined. The likely political and social effects of a story—rather than its general significance, novelty, or audience appeal—determine what will be published and what will be buried in silence. For instance, news about accidents, disasters, and crimes is often suppressed because it does not contain socially useful information that is apt to strengthen people's allegiance to the political system. Even entertainment programs, such as music and drama performances and even cartoon shorts in movie theaters, must carry appropriate social messages or have historical significance. The government supports such entertainment financially because it serves the important public purpose of shaping people's minds in support of the system.

Role of Media in Nonauthoritarian Regimes

The basic assumptions underlying mass media control in democratic countries contrast sharply with those of authoritarian societies, as Table 1-2 indicates. In democracies, governments are viewed as fallible, potentially corrupt servants of the people. Therefore, they must be watched constantly to detect mistakes and misbehaviors and spur remedial action.

Journalists are regarded as the public's eyes and ears. They must scrutinize government performance and report their findings. In that way, they provide the feedback that democratic systems need to remain on course. If, as the result of their scrutiny, governments fall and public officials are ousted, this is as it should be.

While this is the theory behind the role of media in democratic societies, the practice is less clear-cut. In the United States, for example, neither newspeople nor government officials are completely at ease with the media's watchdog role. The media limit their criticism to what they perceive as perversions of fundamental social and political values or noteworthy examples of corruption and waste. They rarely question the fundamentals of the political system. Because journalists depend heavily on the established elites as their sources of news, their links to the existing power structures are strong. They may even share information with government agencies, including law enforcement bodies such as the Federal Bureau of Investigation and the Central Intelligence Agency. When disclosure might cause harm, reporters in a democratic society occasionally withhold important news at the request of the government. This has happened repeatedly during terrorism incidents when the lives of hostages were at stake and in the preparation stages of military interventions. In an effort to keep their images untarnished by media attacks, government officials may try to control the media through regulatory legislation or through rewards and punishments. These tactics are described more fully in Chapter 9.

The chief obligation of the news media in free societies is to provide the general public with information about significant current events and with entertainment. According to the *libertarian* philosophy, anything that happens that seems interesting or important for media audiences may become news. It should be reported quickly, accurately, and without any attempt to convey a particular point of view. Subjects with the widest audience appeal should be stressed, even if that means heavy doses of sex and violence. Audience appeal is then expected to translate into good profits for media owners either through fees paid by audience members or through advertising revenues. Although audiences may learn important things from the media, libertarians believe that teaching is not the media's chief task. Nor is it their task to question the truth, accuracy, or merits of the information supplied to them by their sources. Rather, it is left to the news audience to decide what to believe and what to question.

By contrast, adherents to the tenets of social responsibility believe that news and entertainment presented by the mass media should reflect social concerns. Media personnel should be participants in the political process, not merely reporters of the passing scene. As guardians of the public welfare, they should foster political action when necessary by publicizing social evils, such as the dumping of nuclear waste or child abuse. In a similar vein, undesirable viewpoints and questionable accusations should be denied exposure, however sensational they may be. If reporters believe that the government is hiding information that the public needs to know, they should try to discover the facts and publish them.

Social responsibility journalism and totalitarian journalism have some philosophical resemblances. Both approaches advocate using the media to support the basic ideals of their societies and to shape people into more perfect social beings. They are convinced that their goals are good and would not be achieved in a media system dominated by the whims of media owners or audiences.

But the similarities should not be exaggerated. Social advocacy in nonauthoritarian systems lacks the fervor, clout, and single-mindedness it has in systems in which media control is monopolized by the government. Social responsibility journalism rarely speaks with a single uncontested voice throughout the entire society. Nevertheless, it frightens and antagonizes many news professionals and news audiences. If one agrees that the media should be used to influence social thought and behavior for "good" purposes, it becomes difficult to determine which purposes deserve to be included in that category. Critics of social responsibility journalism point out that journalists do not have a public mandate to act as arbiters of social values and policies in a society that has many disparate visions of truth and goodness. Newspeople lack the legitimacy that in a democracy comes only from being elected by the public or appointed by duly elected officials.

Whatever the merits or faults of these arguments may be, at the present time social responsibility journalism is popular with a sizable proportion of the news profession.[33] Pulitzer prizes and other honors go to journalists who have successfully exposed questionable practices in the interest

Enticing the Media Watchdog to Bark

Throughout the political life of the United States, the mass media have been considered a watchdog. This watchdog "barks" by telling stories that alert the public to wrongdoing by government officials so that remedial steps can be taken. Many public-spirited citizens have used their resources to support journalists who act as watchdogs. For example, the annual $25,000 Goldsmith Prize for Investigative Reporting was endowed by Berda Marks Goldsmith to reward journalists "whose investigative reporting in a story or series of related stories best promotes more effective and ethical conduct of government, the making of public policy, or the practice of politics."[1]

The Pulitzer Prizes for journalism, valued at $7,500, were endowed by newspaper publisher Joseph Pulitzer in 1904. They have been awarded annually since 1917 and are the most prestigious recognition of journalistic excellence. This is why there were 1,516 entries competing for the prize in 2000, a typical year. Pulitzer himself was a courageous and successful fighter for the causes of good government. His efforts to curb corruption in government and business contributed mightily to the passage of antitrust legislation and regulation of the insurance industry.

Pulitzer articulated his vision of the role that can be played by good journalism in a 1904 article in the *North American Review:*

> Our Republic and its press will rise or fall together. An able, disinterested, public-spirited press, with trained intelligence to know the right and courage to do it, can preserve that public virtue without which popular government is a sham and a mockery. A cynical, mercenary, demagogic press will produce in time a people as base as itself. The power to mould the future of the Republic will be in the hands of the journalists of future generations.[2]

That's quite a challenge! How well is the American press meeting it?

---

1. Shorenstein Center Goldsmith Awards Program,
   http://www.ksg.harvard.edu/presspol/goldsmith/goldprize.htm.
2. http://www.pulitzer.org/History/history.html.

of social improvement. The most prominent "villains" targeted for exposure are usually big government and big business.[34]

Models of the News-Making Process

Beyond the basic concerns reflected in the philosophies of libertarians and social responsibility advocates, there are many other guiding principles for reporting events. For example, the news-making process can be described in terms of five distinct models: *the mirror model, the professional model, the organizational model, the political model,* and *the civic journalism model.* Each represents judgments about the major forces behind news making that shape the nature of news and affect its political impact.

Underlying Theories

Proponents of the *mirror model* contend that news is and should be a reflection of reality. Newspeople observe the world around them and report what they notice as accurately and objectively as possible. "We don't make the news, we merely report it," is their slogan. The implication is that newspeople reflect whatever comes to their attention; they do not shape it in any way.

Critics of the mirror model point out that this conception of news making is unrealistic. Millions of significant events take place daily, forcing journalists to choose which items they wish to observe and report. Events that are publicized inevitably loom larger than life, distorting the picture that the real world presents. Events that are ignored routinely vanish into nothingness. Even films and photographs deceive the eye. A small group of demonstrators may look like an invading army when cameras zoom in on them.

In the *professional model,* news making is viewed as an endeavor of highly skilled professionals who put together an interesting collage of events selected for importance, attractiveness to media audiences, and balance among the various elements of the news offering. There is no pretense that the end product mirrors the world. Because audience appeal is a crucial consideration for economic reasons, the audience becomes the ultimate judge of which stories pass scrutiny and which will be ignored.

The *organizational model,* sometimes called *the bargaining model,* is based on organizational theory. Its proponents contend that the pressures inherent in organizational processes and goals determine which items will become news. Pressures spring from interpersonal relations among journalists and between them and their information providers, from professional norms within the news organization and from constraints arising from technical news production processes, cost–benefit considerations, and legal regulations.

The *political model* rests on the assumption that news everywhere reflects the ideological biases of individual newspeople, as well as the pressures of the political environment in which the news organization operates. High-status people and approved institutions are covered by the media; people and events outside the dominant system or remote from the centers of power are generally ignored. Supporters of the prevailing system are pictured as good guys, opponents as bad guys.

In the 1990s *public journalism,* or *civic journalism,* became popular, spurred by widespread concern that average citizens shun participation in public affairs and are distrustful of government and the news media. Proponents of the civic journalism model believe that the press can ascertain citizens' concerns and then write stories that help audiences play an active and successful role in public life.[35] Journalists must articulate and explain available public policy choices in readily understandable language. They must facilitate a public dialogue that encourages and respects diversity of views. After consensus has been reached among the clients of a particular news channel, that enterprise then must vigorously champion appropriate public policies.

None of these models fully explains the news-making process; rather, the process reflects all of them in varying degrees. Because the influences that shape news making fluctuate, one needs to examine individual news-making situations carefully to account for the factors at work. Organizational pressures, for instance, vary depending on the interactions of people within the organization. Audience tastes change or are interpreted differently. Perceptions of "facts" differ, depending on reporters' dispositions. Moreover, the precise mix of factors that explains news making in any particular instance depends to a large degree on chance factors and on the current needs of a particular news medium.

Control Methods

Four types of controls of the press are widely used: *legal, normative, structural,* and *economic.* All governments have laws to prevent press misbehavior such as the publishing of deliberate falsehoods. All societies also have social norms that the press generally heeds. For example, in a conservative country, ridiculing sacred concepts or widely accepted beliefs, behaviors, institutions, and individuals would lead to social condemnation. The way media organizations are structured and operated also shapes their product, as is clear when one compares the policy discretion enjoyed by publicly and privately owned media. Russia's government-controlled media, for example, dare not criticize the government's war against rebels in Chechnya. Privately owned media in Russia have no such hesitation. Finally, economic support in the form of direct and indirect subsidies can be used to influence media performance.

The combination of methods by which governments control the media varies, and so do the major objectives of control. To ensure that news stories remain supportive of most government policies, authoritarian societies use legal, structural, and economic means to restrict access to mass communications to voices friendly to the regime. By contrast, nonauthoritarian regimes rarely make *formal* attempts to deny foes of the regime access to the media. However, they often use normative pressures to avert potentially disastrous political news or news that violates widely cherished social norms.

Many authoritarian societies establish control over media content by limiting entry into the media business. For example, the government may require franchises for entry and grant them only to people who fully support the government. Franchises often bestow monopoly control. Control through franchise is quite common for electronic media, even in democratic countries, because the capacity of the broadcast spectrum is limited. But democratic countries use this power less frequently to shut out political opponents. Entry to the mass media business is usually open to people representing a wide spectrum of political views. Newspapers generally need no licenses in democratic societies and access to the Internet has remained equally unrestricted. In the United States, for instance, anyone with sufficient money can start a newspaper or newsletter or create a Web site.

Authoritarian countries frequently control publications through subsidies to favorite publishers or favoritism in the allocation of tightly controlled paper stocks for printing newspapers and magazines. Newspaper publishers whose activities displease the government may find themselves out of business because they cannot obtain paper. These types of economic controls may be imposed informally on disliked publishers or they may be invoked through formal rationing and subsidy schemes.

Media also may be controlled through the manipulation of access to news. For instance, the government may release information only to favored publications, in effect putting less favored ones out of business. Although such practices are common in authoritarian societies, they occasionally happen on a smaller scale in more open societies. In 1993 President Clinton barred reporters from easy access to the White House communication office by closing off a connecting hallway to the press room.[36]

In addition to controlling the news business through franchises and restraints on access to news, authoritarian governments often limit what information may be published. In some countries, nothing can be printed or broadcast until it has been approved by the government censor, who can suppress any story deemed objectionable. At times, deletions are made after papers or magazines have been prepared for printing or are already printed. This leaves tantalizing white spaces or missing pages.

Television and radio scripts often are written or edited directly by government officials and must be broadcast without editorial changes.

Authoritarian societies frequently use treason and sedition laws to control media output. *Treason* and *sedition* usually are defined broadly in these countries so that anything that is critical of the government is potentially treasonable or seditious. People judged guilty of these crimes may be removed from the media business, sentenced to prison, or even executed. Such severe punishments are extremely strong deterrents to publishing stories that attack the government. Accordingly, disobedience is rare. Most journalists avoid difficulties with official censors and with treason and sedition laws by refraining from using material that is likely to be objectionable. Government censorship then becomes replaced largely by self-censorship.

In totalitarian regimes, media control is simplified because the government owns and operates all mass media, and fully determines their output. In the past, totalitarian countries could frequently block out all unapproved communications from abroad. Practices included jamming foreign broadcasts and prohibiting the import of foreign printed materials. In the Internet age, tight controls have become well-nigh impossible. The strictness with which the controls are applied waxes and wanes, depending on the country's relations with other powers and the level of its fear that information might undermine the political system. Such censorship is viewed as an intellectual quarantine that must be imposed to keep evil influences from undermining a beneficial political system.

In democratic societies official control of the content of mass media is deemed largely unnecessary. The First Amendment to the U.S. Constitution, which provides that "Congress shall make no law . . . abridging the freedom of speech, or of the press," has given the media an exceptionally strong basis for resisting government controls in the United States. The courts have ruled, however, that the protection is not absolute. On occasion, it must give way to social rights that the courts consider to be superior.

Competition among privately owned papers, magazines, and television and radio stations presumably generates a variety of viewpoints. If some media attack the government, other media will support it. The underlying, intriguing, but questionable assumption is that positive and negative as well as correct and incorrect information will somehow balance out and that the audience will be able to extract the truth from these conflicting reports.

A limited number of controls, such as regulatory laws, court decisions, and informal social pressures, guard against excesses by the media. In the United States the courts generally have ruled that these controls may be enforced only after media misbehavior has occurred. Courts have been loath to impose prior restraint such as the granting of injunctions that would stop publication of information on the grounds that it would cause irreparable harm. But informal social and political pressures and the fear of indictments after publication have restrained presentation of potentially disturbing stories.

Controls in nonauthoritarian societies generally fall into four categories: guarding state survival through treason and sedition laws, shielding sensitive governmental proceedings, protecting individual reputations and privacy, and safeguarding the prevailing moral standards of the community. All societies find it necessary to have treason and sedition laws that prohibit publication of information that would endanger the nation's survival. The difficulty is to determine the point at which secrecy is so essential that freedom to publish must give way. In democratic societies, media and the government are in perennial disagreement about the exact location of this point. Governments lean toward protection; the media lean toward disclosure.

There is little argument that treason and sedition are beyond the boundaries of unrestricted publication, even in an open society. More controversial are curbs on publication of government secrets—so-called classified information. Governments try to establish controls over the publication of material that they deem harmful to themselves or to individuals. For instance, confidential reports about the performance of government agencies, records of bidding on public jobs, and conversations during closed meetings generally are shielded from publicity. Finally, most governments also have laws protecting the reputations of individuals or groups and laws against obscenity. The merits of these controls on publication are discussed more fully in Chapter 3.

Defining the limits of government control over information dissemination raises difficult questions for democratic societies. Does official censorship, however minimal, open the way for the destruction of free expression? What guidelines are available to determine how far censorship should go? What types of material, if any, can harm children? Or adults? Should prejudicial statements be prohibited on the ground that they damage the self-image of minorities? The answers are controversial and problematic.

In addition to formal control of potentially damaging news in authoritarian and nonauthoritarian societies, many informal restraints control the actual production and flow of news. As we shall see in Chapter 9, all governmental units, and often many of their subdivisions, have their own information control systems by which they determine what news to conceal or release and how to present it.

The limitations on the freedom of publication in democratic societies raise questions about the actual differences in press freedom in nonauthoritarian and authoritarian societies. Is there really a difference, for example, in the independence of government-operated television networks in France and in North Korea? The answer is a resounding "yes." The degree of restraint varies so sharply that the systems are fundamentally different. In authoritarian societies the main objective of controls is to support the regime in power. In democratic societies the media are usually free to oppose the regime, to weaken it, and even to topple it. Although they rarely carry their power to the latter extreme, the potential exists. It is this potential that makes the media in nonauthoritarian societies a genuine restraint on governmental abuses of power and a potent shaper of governmental action.

Summary

The mass media are an important influence on politics because they regularly and rapidly present politically crucial information to huge audiences. These audiences include political elites and decision makers, as well as large numbers of average citizens whose political activities, however sporadic, are shaped by information from the mass media.

Decisions made by media personnel about whom and what to cover determine what information becomes available to media audiences and what remains unavailable. By putting stories into perspective and interpreting them, media personnel assign meaning to the information and indicate the values by which it ought to be judged. At times, newspeople even generate political action directly through their own investigations or indirectly through their capacity to stimulate pseudo-events.

Although social scientists remain skeptical about claims of large-scale media impact on politics, politicians and their governments everywhere are keenly aware of the political importance of the media. Therefore, they have developed philosophies about the political role to be played by the media in their societies and about the proper ways to control the impact of the media on government activities. These philosophies have been implemented by constitutional and legal rules as well as by a host of informal arrangements. In this chapter we have described briefly how the basic philosophies, constitutional arrangements, and legal provisions differ in authoritarian and nonauthoritarian regimes.

Notes

1. Ken Armstrong and Steve Mills, "Death Row Justice Derailed," *Chicago Tribune,* Nov. 14, 1999.
2. Ken Armstrong and Steve Mills, "Ryan: 'Until I Can Be Sure,'" *Chicago Tribune,* Feb. 1, 2000.
3. Ken Armstrong and Steve Mills, "Death Penalty Support Erodes," *Chicago Tribune,* March 7, 2000.

4. For a brief overview of current knowledge about mass media effects, see W. Lance Bennett, *News: The Politics of Illusion*, 4th ed. (White Plains, N.Y.: Longman, 2001); and Leo W. Jeffres, *Mass Media Effects*, 2d ed. (Prospect Heights, Ill.: Waveland Press, 1997).

5. George Gerbner, Larry Gross, Michael Morgan, and Nancy Signorielli, "Charting the Mainstream: Television's Contributions to Political Orientation," *Journal of Communication* 32 (1982): 106–107. Also see Richard Campbell, *Media and Culture* (New York: St. Martin's Press, 1998), esp. Part I.

6. Pew Research Center for the People and the Press, "Internet Sapping Broadcast News Audience," June 13, 2000, http://www.people-press.org/media00sec4.htm.

7. Ibid., http://www.people-press.org/media00sec1.htm.

8. Center for Media and Public Affairs, "Dubya Dethrones Clinton as Late-Night Laugh Target," http://www.cmpa.com/pressrel/electpr14.htm. The data are based on monitoring *The Tonight Show, The Late Show with David Letterman, Late Night with Conan O'Brian,* and *Politically Incorrect* from January 1 to December 15, 2000.

9. Robert M. Entman and Andrew Rojecki, *The Black Image in the White Mind: Media and Race in America* (Chicago: University of Chicago Press, 2000).

10. Harold D. Lasswell, "The Structure and Function of Communication in Society," in *Mass Communications,* ed. Wilbur Schramm (Urbana: University of Illinois Press, 1969), 103.

11. Marshall McLuhan, *Understanding Media: The Extensions of Man* (New York: McGraw-Hill, 1964).

12. Chapter 4 gives a more detailed definition of news. Evidence that the media set the agenda for national issues is presented in David L. Protess and Maxwell McCombs, eds., *Agenda Setting: Readings on Media, Public Opinion, and Policymaking* (Hillsdale, N.J.: Erlbaum, 1991). For a more recent discussion of agenda setting for news consumers, see Wayne Wanta, *The Public and the National Agenda* (Mahwah, N.J.: Erlbaum, 1997).

13. Larry J. Sabato, Mark Stencel, and S. Robert Lichter, in *Peep Show: Media and Politics in an Age of Scandal* (Lanham, Md.: Rowman and Littlefield, 2000), discuss the appropriate ways to deal with scandal stories.

14. Examples of such criticism can be found in Bennett, *News: The Politics of Illusion;* Robert W. McChesney, *Rich Media, Poor Democracy* (New York: New Press, 1999); and Michael Parenti, *Inventing Reality: The Politics of the News Media,* 3d ed. (New York: St. Martin's Press, 1993).

15. An example of a conservative Washington-based media analysis group is Accuracy in Media (AIM), which publishes periodic reports of its media investigations. For claims that journalists in the elite media are ultraliberal, see S. Robert Lichter, Stanley Rothman, and Linda S. Lichter, *The Media Elite* (New York: Adler and Adler, 1986).

16. Jay G. Blumler, "Purposes of Mass Communications Research: A Transatlantic Perspective," *Journalism Quarterly* 55 (summer 1978): 226.

17. Daniel Boorstin, *The Image: A Guide to Pseudo-Events* (New York: Atheneum, 1971).

18. Criteria of what constitutes *news* are discussed fully in a historical context in Kevin G. Barnhurst and John Nerone, *The Form of News* (New York: Guilford Press, 2001). Also see Samuel P. Winch, *Mapping the Cultural Space of Journalism* (Westport, Conn.: Praeger, 1997).

19. Blumler, "Purposes of Mass Communications Research," 228.

20. The results of reassuring publicity are discussed by Murray Edelman, *The Symbolic Uses of Politics* (Urbana: University of Illinois Press, 1964), 38–43, reprinted 1985.

21. Robert Kubey and Mihaly Csikszentmihalyi, *Television and the Quality of Life: How Viewing Shapes Everyday Experience* (Hillsdale, N.J.: Erlbaum, 1990), chaps. 5 and 7.

22. Marvin N. Olasky and Susan Northway Olasky, "The Crossover in Newspaper Coverage of Abortion from Murder to Liberation," *Journalism Quarterly* 63 (1986): 31–37.

23. W. Lance Bennett and Murray Edelman, "Toward a New Political Narrative," *Journal of Communication* 35 (1985): 156–171.

24. The early writings include David Easton and Jack Dennis, *Children in the Political System: Origins of Political Legitimacy* (New York: McGraw-Hill, 1969); Fred I. Greenstein, *Children and Politics* (New Haven: Yale University Press, 1965); Richard Dawson and Kenneth Prewitt, *Political Socialization* (Boston: Little, Brown, 1969); and Robert D. Hess and Judith Torney, *The Development of Political Attitudes in Children* (Chicago: Aldine, 1967). Examples of the studies in the 1970s are Sidney Kraus and Dennis Davis, *The Effects of Mass Communication on Political Behavior* (University Park: Pennsylvania State University Press, 1976); Steven H. Chaffee, "Mass Communication in Political Socialization," in *Handbook of Political Socialization,* ed. Stanley Renshon (New York: Free Press, 1977). Also see Ellen Wartella, ed., *Children Communicating: Media and Development of Thought, Speech, and Understanding* (Beverly Hills, Calif.: Sage, 1979).

25. Benjamin I. Page and Robert Y. Shapiro, *The Rational Public: Fifty Years of Trends in Americans' Policy Preferences* (Chicago: University of Chicago Press, 1992); Shanto Iyengar and Donald Kinder, *News that Matters: Television and American Opinion* (Chicago: University of Chicago Press, 1987); and Doris A. Graber, *Processing the News: How People Tame the Information Tide,* 3d ed. (Lanham, Md.: University Press of America, 1993).

26. David L. Protess et al., *The Journalism of Outrage: Investigative Reporting and Agenda Building in America* (New York: Guilford Press, 1991), 8–12. Also see Sabato, Stencel, and Lichter, *Peep Show.*

27. Paul Lazarsfeld, Bernard Berelson, and Hazel Gaudet, *The People's Choice* (New York: Columbia University Press, 1944); Bernard Berelson, Paul Lazarsfeld, and William McPhee, *Voting: A Study of Opinion Formation in a Presidential Campaign* (Chicago: University of Chicago Press, 1954); Angus Campbell, Gerald Gurin, and Warren E. Miller, *The Voter Decides* (Evanston, Ill.: Row, Peterson, 1954); and Angus Campbell, Philip E. Converse, Warren E. Miller, and Donald Stokes, *The American Voter* (New York: Wiley, 1960).

28. This account is based on Steven Livingston and Todd Eachus, "Humanitarian Crisis and U.S. Foreign Policy: Somalia and the CNN Effect Reconsidered," *Political Communication* 12 (1995): 413–429.

29. Theodore White, *The Making of the President, 1972* (New York: Bantam, 1973), 327.

30. Jeffres, *Mass Media Effects,* presents an excellent overview of the media effects literature.

31. The discussion is modeled on Fred Siebert, Theodore Peterson, and Wilbur Schramm, *Four Theories of the Press* (Urbana: University of Illinois Press, 1963).

32. For a brief account of media history in the United States, see Timothy E. Cook, *Governing with the News: The News Media as a Political Institution* (Chicago: University of Chicago Press, 1998), 17–60. Also see Kevin G.

Barnhurst and John Nerone, *The Form of News* (New York: Guilford Press, 2001), which traces changes in form and substance of news delivered by U.S. media.

33. David H. Weaver and G. Cleveland Wilhoit, *The American Journalist in the 1990s: U.S. News People at the End of an Era* (Mahwah, N.J.: Erlbaum, 1996). See also Edmund D. Lambeth, Philip E. Meyers, and Esther Thorson, eds., *Assessing Public Journalism* (Columbia: University of Missouri Press, 1998); Michael Schudson, "The Public Journalism Movement and Its Problems," in *The Politics of News, The News of Politics*, ed. Doris Graber, Denis McQuail, and Pippa Norris (Washington, D.C.: CQ Press, 1998).

34. See, for example, Dean Alger, *Megamedia: How Giant Corporations Dominate Mass Media, Distort Competition, and Endanger Democracy* (Lanham, Md.: Rowman and Littlefield, 1998).

35. Lambeth et al., *Assessing Public Journalism*; Schudson, "The Public Journalism Movement and Its Problems."

36. John Anthony Maltese, *Spin Control: The White House Office of Communication and the Management of Presidential News*, 2d ed. (Chapel Hill: University of North Carolina Press, 1994), 232–233.

Readings

Aufderheide, Patricia. *Communications Policy and the Public Interest: The Telecommunications Act of 1996*. New York: Guilford Press, 1999.

Bennett, W. Lance. *News: The Politics of Illusion*. 4th ed. White Plains, N.Y.: Longman, 2001.

Cook, Timothy E. *Governing with the News: The News Media as a Political Institution*. Chicago: University of Chicago Press, 1998.

Graber, Doris A., ed. *Media Power in Politics*. 4th ed. Washington, D.C.: CQ Press, 2000.

Hess, Stephen. *News and Newsmaking*. Washington, D.C.: Brookings Institution, 1996.

Lichter, S. Robert, Linda S. Lichter, and Stanley Rothman. *Prime Time: How TV Portrays American Culture*. Washington, D.C.: Regnery, 1994.

Patterson, Thomas E. *Out of Order*. New York: Knopf, 1993.

Schudson, Michael. *The Power of News*. Cambridge: Harvard University Press, 1995.

Smith, Leslie, Milan Meeske, and John W. Wright II. *Electronic Media and Government: The Regulation of Wireless and Wired Communication in the United States*. White Plains, N.Y.: Longman, 1995.

Thomas, Erwin K., and Brown H. Carpenter, eds. *Handbook on Mass Media in the United States: The Industry and Its Audiences*. Westport, Conn.: Greenwood, 1994.

Ownership, Regulation, and Guidance of Media

LIN HAI, A TWENTY-YEAR-OLD COMPUTER EXECUTIVE, went on trial in 1999 in Shanghai for "inciting subversion of state power." His crime, according to the prosecutor, was that Lin Hai had undermined the government's control over the minds of the Chinese people by making it easy for Chinese computer users to gather news from foreign media rather than exclusively from media controlled by their own government.

The accused man had supplied thousands of Chinese e-mail addresses to foreign publications, including an electronic newsletter compiled by Chinese democracy advocates located in Washington, D.C., and distributed to more than 250,000 computer users in China. Although the Chinese government has succeeded in using an electronic firewall to block access to Web sites it deems objectionable, e-mail has been virtually uncontrollable. The Chinese authorities feared that the newsletter, which features debates about democracy and news about the activities of Chinese dissidents, may incite its citizens to overthrow communism.[1] China's strenuous effort to keep full control over all media, including the Internet and e-mail, is a contemporary version of the classic battle for control of the information communicated to political elites and the general public.

Concern about who will wield media power has been a central issue in American politics since colonial days. In this chapter, we will weigh the pros and cons of government and private sector control of the mass media. We will also assess the impact of internal and external pressures on the industry, including those arising from economic constraints and from citizen lobbies. The public policy issues involved in media control are so complex, so intertwined with political predispositions and preferences, that no ownership and control system stands out clearly as "best." All have major advantages and drawbacks. It therefore is no wonder that attempts to legislate about media ownership and control have produced clashes of views, litigation, and little agreement on what the laws should be.

Control and Ownership:
Public and Semipublic

The various forms of control and ownership of the media affect not only media economics but also the substance of media output, in line with the old adage, "He who pays the piper calls the tune." People who fear government are likely to disapprove of government ownership and operation of the media. They also are apt to be leery about extensive government regulation of privately owned and operated media. By contrast, people who are afraid of the business ethics of private individuals and corporations, especially when corporations are very large, would not want unfettered media control in private hands.

The Crux of the Debate

The debate over the merits of public versus private ownership of television illustrates the pros and cons. When governments own and operate major television channels, programming tends to support governmental policies, even in democratic countries. However, Britain's experience with operating radio and television through the British Broadcasting Corporation (BBC) shows that governments can keep programming reasonably free from direct political interference.

Business control of television, if it is divided among many owners, is likely to bring more conflicting interests into play than control by a central government. Even in the world of big business, a conglomerate heavily involved in export industries will not share the same views on tariffs as another conglomerate interested primarily in domestic manufacturing. Within conglomerates, the interests of various components may clash, thus moderating the stands of the general management and lessening the chances that specific business interests will dominate programming. Nonetheless, the prevailing values reflected in the choice of broadcasts are likely to be mainstream and middle class.

Although there is more chance for diversity of political outlooks when multiple businesses, rather than governments, control programming, the pressures springing from profit considerations lead to the types of offerings that yield high financial returns. Mass appeal, rather than any social or cultural concerns, becomes the primary goal. Advertisers and other sponsors want to attract large numbers of viewers, particularly the eighteen- to forty-nine-year-old age group, which holds the bulk of purchasing power. Governments are free from such pressures because they can use tax money to finance whatever programs they believe to be in the public interest. They must consider intragovernment power struggles, but they do not need to concern themselves with the economic consequences of the size of their audiences.

At present, when distrust of government is at a higher level than distrust of business enterprises, private ownership control of the mass media is the option preferred by most Americans. Thanks to this choice, the bulk of television fare is geared to simple, emotion-laden programming that attracts large, diverse audiences. It also means shying away from controversial or troublesome issues that may antagonize and deplete media audiences and diminish advertising revenues.

Although "lightweight" programming draws the wrath of many people, particularly intellectual elites, one can argue that their disdain constitutes intellectual snobbery. Who is to say that the mass public's tastes are inferior to those of elites? The contention that people would choose educational programs over fluffy entertainment, if they had the chance, is false. Proof is plentiful that the mass public does indeed prefer light entertainment to more serious programs.[2] In 1998, for example, President Clinton's State of the Union message attracted 53 million viewers. Some months later, a broadcast in which he promised to discuss an inappropriate sexual relationship with a White House intern attracted 68 million. Later that year, the finale of the popular *Seinfeld* show on NBC drew 76 million viewers, topping the audience for the president's yearly report by more than 40 percent. In print news, magazines featuring sex or violence far outsell journals that treat political and social issues seriously. In fact, scholarly political journals frequently require subsidies to remain in print. Huge crowds are willing to pay heavily in time and money to see movies featuring heinous crimes and explicit sex. The most popular pay television channels show what is euphemistically called "adult entertainment," whereas channels devoted to highbrow culture languish and often perish.

Related to the concerns about domination of the media by government or powerful private business interests is the fear of undue concentration of influence if a few giant organizations control the nation's media. Diversity of media ownership presumably encourages the expression of a great variety of views, which, to many Americans, is the essence of democracy. The marketplace into which ideas and opinions flow must be wide open. But there is no agreement on exactly how diverse ownership must be to ensure sufficient diversity.[3] Americans appear to be more concerned about the concentration of media ownership in comparatively few hands than about control of the media by business. Social reformers, however, are more concerned about business control, claiming that it caters to the lowest levels of taste and suppresses discussion of pressing social problems.

How the Public and Semipublic System Works

In the United States outright government ownership and control over media has been comparatively limited. However, it is growing as more and more local governments own cable television systems or operate channels on privately owned systems. Government ownership raises serious unresolved questions about the limitations, if any, to be placed on the government's rights to use these outlets to further partisan political purposes.[4]

The federal government currently is most heavily involved in broadcasting, with local governments in second place. The federal government controls broadcasts to American military posts throughout the world and owns various types of foreign propaganda outlets. Most programs broadcast by these propaganda agencies, such as the Voice of America, are barred from the domestic airwaves because Congress has been reluctant to expose American audiences to deliberate propaganda.

A substantial proportion of the radio broadcast spectrum, ranging from 50 percent in the pre-Carter years to 25 percent thereafter, belongs to the federal government, which uses it for radio services supplied by the executive branch. Another 40 percent of the space is shared by the government and private interests, leaving only 35 percent for the exclusive use of the private sector.[5] Altogether, foreign and domestic federal broadcasts equal the volume of commercial broadcasts produced in the United States.

Media operation by semipublic institutions is another control option. The public broadcasting system is one example. It represents a mixture of public and private financing and programming and public and private operation of radio and television stations. Created through the Public Broadcasting Act of 1967, the public broadcasting system supports educational and public service television stations whose programs generally do not attract large audiences. These stations usually cannot find enough commercial sponsors to pay for their shows.

Roughly one-fourth of American television stations participate in the public broadcasting system. In 2000, members included 348 noncommercial television stations and 560 noncommercial radio stations, the latter linked together as National Public Radio (NPR).[6] The administrative arrangements for the public broadcasting system have been complex. The Corporation for Public Broadcasting (CPB), staffed by political appointees, has handled the general administration, but it has been kept separate from the programming side of the operation to insulate public broadcasting from political pressures. A separate Public Broadcasting Service (PBS) has produced television programs, often in collaboration with state-supported foreign broadcast systems, like Britain's BBC or France's Antenne Deux or Japan's NHK. The Independent Television Service, created by Congress in 1991, has awarded grants to independent producers for "programming that involves creative risks and addresses the needs of underserved audiences."[7]

The attempt to keep the CPB from influencing programming has failed. The corporation does not tell public television stations what specific programs they should feature. Instead, it has guided programming by paying for some types of programs and refusing to pay for others. This has constituted effective purse-string control of programming by government. In the field of radio, NPR was created both to produce and distribute programs. Because cost considerations made it impossible to include all noncommercial radio stations, only the largest, best-organized ones were included and are eligible for CPB funding grants and participation in NPR programs.

Private foundations and big business enterprises and large corporations have poured money into the public broadcasting system. Table 2-1 lists their contribution as 20 percent of total income. During the Reagan years PBS was authorized to engage in some commercial broadcasting of economic news and to accept a limited amount of advertising. All of these changes have enhanced corporate influence over programming. The general public also has influenced public broadcasting through donations that constitute one-quarter of the income of public broadcasting systems and through community advisory boards. Nevertheless, securing adequate financing is an enduring problem. Even at a time of budget surpluses, the CPB budget for 2001 topped out at $340 million. Dependence on public funds, even when these funds constitute less than 20 percent of total funding, may mean subservience to government control, despite barriers to direct government influence.

Public television broadcasts are distinguished from commercial television primarily by an emphasis on experimental programs, cultural offerings such as plays, classical music, and ballet, and a stress on high-quality news and public affairs programs. The nature and quality of programming varies widely because public television represents a decentralized bevy of local stations. The audience for public television, except for its children's programs, has been small, rarely comprising more than 2 percent of the viewers. Even minority groups, to whom a number of public broadcast programs are targeted, prefer the entertainment provided by commercial

TABLE 2-1   Income Sources of Public Broadcasting System: 1997
(includes nonbroadcast income)

Income sources	Millions of dollars	Percentage of budget
Federal government	$322	17%
State/local government and colleges/universities	537	28
Subscribers and auction/marathons	493	25
Business and industry	280	14
Foundations	111	6
Other	192	10
Total income	1,935	100

SOURCE: Bureau of the Census, *Statistical Abstract of the United States, 1999,* found at http://www.census.gov/prod/99pubs/99statab/sec18.pdf (Washington, D.C.: U.S. Government Printing Office, 1999), 585.

NOTE: Public broadcasting system includes 694 Corporation for Public Broadcasting-qualified public radio stations and 352 public television stations.

stations. Because of the limited appeal of public broadcasting and pressures to reduce public expenditures, there has been some pressure to disband the system completely and reallocate its frequencies to commercial channels. Some of its programs then might be shown on commercial cable stations, possibly with federal subsidies.[8]

Supporters of the system contend that it should be viewed as a provider of needed special services that are neglected by commercial television precisely because they lack mass appeal or are commercially unattractive. They point out that innovations pioneered by public broadcasting have spread to commercial broadcasting. For example, public broadcasting played a leading role in developing captions for individuals with hearing impairments. At the turn of the century, it led in pioneering digital television, including interactive news and feature programs. Public radio and public television also were among the first to move to satellite distribution that made it possible to deliver multiple national programs to communities. Nonetheless, the future of public broadcasting seems precarious.

Patterns of Private Ownership

The overarching feature of media ownership in the United States is that it is predominantly in private hands. Arrangements vary from individual ownership, where one person owns a newspaper or radio or television station, to ownership by huge corporate conglomerates. Owners include small and large business enterprises, labor groups, religious and ethnic organizations, and many other types of interests represented in American society. The facts about private media control patterns are relatively simple to explain, but there is much disagreement about their consequences.

Business Configurations

Independents—individuals or corporations that run a single media venture and nothing else—are a vanishing breed in the media business. The publisher who owns one newspaper or one radio or television station is an example. *Multiple* owners have become the norm. These are individuals or corporations who own several media of the same type—mostly radio or television stations or cable channels or newspapers. Because there are fewer than 1,500 daily newspapers in the entire United States and fewer than 2,000 commercial television stations, one might question whether society is well-served when a vast majority of these media are held by group owners.[9] Nevertheless, this has been the trend.

Crossmedia ownership has been less common than multiple ownership. It occurs when an individual or corporation owns several types of media, such as newspapers *and* television stations or newspapers *and* radio stations. Crossmedia ownership is most worrisome when one owner controls all media in the same region. Such monopolies have been prohibited since 1975, except where they were already established. However, crossmedia ownership dispersed over various locations is thriving. Gannett Company, for example, now owns ninety-three daily newspapers, sixteen television stations, and nineteen radio stations following its merger with Multimedia Company in 1995.

A fourth pattern encompasses *conglomerates*—individuals or corporations own media enterprises along with other types of businesses. The General Electric Company (GE) is an example. Figure 2-1 illustrates the diversity of GE's interests. Conglomerates raise fears that their nonmedia business interests may color their news policies. If, for instance, there is a soundly based demand to reduce the size of the military or to oppose construction of a missile system, the management of a conglomerate such as GE, which holds many defense contracts, may not examine these questions open-mindedly.

In major urban centers most media fall into the multiple-owner, crossmedia, and conglomerate classifications. For instance, the Tribune Company's *Chicago Tribune* owned eleven daily newspapers in 2000, twenty-two television stations, four radio stations, and a 25 percent stake in the WB television network. It could reach nearly 80 percent of U.S. households after its merger with the *Los Angeles Times* in 2000.[10] All major television and radio stations in Chicago are owned by the national television networks and

FIGURE 2-1   The Diverse Holdings of the General Electric Company

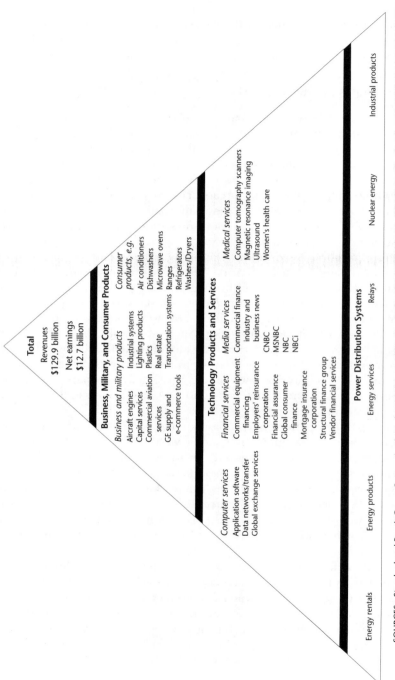

Total

Revenues
$129.9 billion

Net earnings
$12.7 billion

Business, Military, and Consumer Products

Business and military products
Aircraft engines
Capital services
Commercial aviation
services
GE supply and
e-commerce tools

Industrial systems
Lighting products
Plastics
Real estate
Transportation systems

Consumer products, e.g.
Air conditioners
Dishwashers
Microwave ovens
Ranges
Refrigerators
Washers/Dryers

Technology Products and Services

Computer services
Application software
Data networks/transfer
Global exchange services

Financial services
Commercial equipment
financing
Employers' reinsurance
corporation
Financial assurance
Global consumer
finance
Mortgage insurance
corporation
Structural finance group
Vendor financial services

Media services
Commercial finance
industry and
business news
CNBC
MSNBC
NBC
NBCi

Medical services
Computer tomography scanners
Magnetic resonance imaging
Ultrasound
Women's health care

Power Distribution Systems

Energy rentals   Energy products   Energy services   Relays   Nuclear energy   Industrial products

SOURCES: Standard and Poor's Corp., *Corporation Records*, 1999; General Electric, *Annual Report*, 2000.

conglomerates or members of conglomerates. Radio and television stations that remain under single ownership for the most part are small with comparatively weak signals. The number of media outlets controlled by various entrepreneurs ranges widely and fluctuates considerably, especially in an era of widespread consolidation. For instance, in 1995 Capital Cities/ABC, the American Broadcasting Company Network, owned seven television stations, seven radio networks serving more than three thousand affiliated radio stations, eighteen radio stations, and seventy-five weekly newspapers, as well as numerous magazines and trade publications. It grew even larger after merging with the Walt Disney Company in 1995, which, in 2001, was looking towards further enlarging its media holdings.[11] Since the turn of the century, many companies have added Web sites to their holdings. Knight Ridder, for example, now controls forty Web sites located in various regions of the United States. But one cannot judge the sweep of control exercised by any group merely by looking at the number of its outlets. Three additional factors need to be considered: *market size, competition within the market,* and *prestige of each media supplier.*

Market Size

For the purposes of assessing mass media performance and regulating electronic media, the country is divided into markets rather than cities or regions. A *market* is the area in which a medium reaches a substantial audience. For instance, each television station has a signal that can be received clearly by people living within a certain radius of the station. All of the people within that radius who can receive the signal are considered to be within the market. This means that they can be exposed to sound and advertising for products and services provided by program sponsors.

Altogether, there are 208 newspaper markets and 210 broadcast markets in the United States. These sizes vary widely. In major metropolitan areas such as New York, Chicago, or Los Angeles, a market within a fifty-mile radius may have a population of several million people. The same radius for a station in Wyoming might cover more than a few people.

The FCC has considered market size both in shaping its regulations designed to prevent concentration of ownership. It has specified that one owner may reach no more than 35 percent of the audience in a market. Such limits are under attack, however, by the industry, and lower court decisions portend that they may be abandoned. FCC regulations also set top limits for the numbers of stations that can be under the same ownership. Additional restrictions are imposed on multiple and crossmedia ownership.

The Telecommunications Act of 1996 limits an owner to a total of eight commercial AM and FM stations in a radio market with forty-five or

Radio Is Alive and Well

Importance

Radio continues to be an immensely important source of public information. Although 75 percent of the public watched television news in 2000, and 63 percent sought news from daily papers, a hefty 46 percent tuned in to radio news. Even larger numbers used the radio to listen to music. Most listeners tune in on car radios, primarily during the morning and evening commute to and from work.

Concentration

In the wake of the 1996 Telecommunications Act, which eliminated most restrictions on buying and selling stations, there has been a wave of concentration of radio station ownership. The largest chain, Clear Channel Communications, owns more than 1,140 stations, including 381 engaged in Internet broadcasting. Fewer than 30 percent of the stations remain independently owned and operated.

Consolidation has encouraged national programming so that major talk radio stars like Rush Limbaugh, Howard Stern, Don Imus, and Dr. Laura Schlessinger are heard throughout the country. But most programming remains locally produced and tailored to the tastes of local listeners. More than 12,000 radio stations currently operate in the United States, compared with barely 1,000 just fifty years earlier. Most large markets feature more than 40 stations. Chicago, for example, has 33 AM and 48 FM stations within the metropolitan area's hearing range. Eight of these feature talk radio and 5 specialize in news, including sports reports. Fourteen stations provide ethnic programs, and ten concentrate on religion. The rest offer a large variety of musical formats. Although fans of classical music may complain that only a single station features their "high quality" music, diversity certainly prevails.

(Box continues, next page)

Rules for Survival

Radio is a perfect example of the chameleon-like ability of American mass media to adapt to new technologies and new types of competitors. Predictions that television and its spin-off technologies would kill radio and movies have been utterly wrong. Radio has boomed, thanks to new technologies like the transistor and FM and thanks to the targeting of its programs. It offers more than twenty radio formats, often in various types of incarnations, that cater to distinct demographic groups. News-talk formats, both political and personal, have been growth leaders. Age, income, gender, race, and ethnicity are major programming cleavage lines that appeal to advertisers who like to target their products to likely customers. Ten percent of the billions of dollars spent on advertising across the nation goes to radio stations.

SOURCE: Much of the information about radio comes from Richard Campbell, *Media and Culture*, 3d ed. (Boston: Bedford, 2002), chap. 4.

more commercial stations, with lower limits set for smaller markets. There must be a rough balance between the number of AM and FM stations under a single owner's control. For television stations, the top limit, established in 1992, is twelve television stations in a single market, but Congress has directed the FCC to reexamine the appropriateness of this number. Lifting previous restrictions with the declared aim of using deregulation to enhance competition, the 1996 act permits owners of a broadcast network to own a cable system as well. It also permits owners of cable systems to offer many services that were previously provided only by telephone companies. Although limitations on building media empires have been eased, the government has imposed strict antimonopoly controls on merging companies.[13] Regulations to enforce social policies also have been enhanced. For example, the 1996 act provides for special services for hearing- and vision-impaired audiences and puts curbs on the display of obscenity and violence in television programs accessible to minors.

Newspapers can enter an unlimited number of markets. As a result, newspaper chains can expand at will, up to the limits allowed by antitrust and antimonopoly laws. Antitrust regulations become operative when the eight largest firms in a particular type of business control more than half of the market and the twenty largest firms control three-quarters or more. By 1997 more than 80 percent of America's daily papers were controlled by national and regional chains.[14] The twelve largest groups controlled more than four hundred dailies with a circulation of nearly 35 million. Gannett was the leader in circulation in the United States with ninety-two daily papers followed by Knight Ridder (thirty-five), Advance/Newhouse (twenty-five), and Dow Jones (twenty).[15] Most of these newspaper groups also own papers published less frequently, as well as radio and television stations. Although ownership figures are changing constantly as papers are bought and sold, the relative rankings remain fairly stable. The proportion of circulation controlled by chain-owned papers has been growing over the decades, but not by leaps and bounds. Although individual papers within chains generally enjoy editorial-page autonomy, they tend to be more uniform in political endorsements than are independently owned papers.[16] Table 2-2 shows circulation figures for the largest U.S. newspapers.

Influence is even more concentrated for television. Four conglomerate-owned networks—National Broadcasting Company (NBC), Columbia Broadcasting System (CBS), American Broadcasting Company (ABC), and Fox Broadcasting Corporation—dominate the television households in the nation. The networks have full control over stations they own—35 for CBS, 33 for Fox, 13 for NBC, and 10 for ABC. But they also dominate programming on their affiliates, thereby reaching nearly all of the nation's television households. ABC and NBC each have 217 affiliates, CBS has 213, and Fox 187.[17] In the past, the networks produced only a limited number of television and radio entertainment programs for their own use. The bulk of entertainment programming came from other sources. That has changed drastically in the 1990s with the removal of FCC prohibitions, which previously barred the merger of program production enterprises with distribution enterprises.

To keep figures on media concentration in proper perspective, however, one must keep in mind that the major television networks compete vigorously with each other for public favor and that they do not dominate programming completely for their affiliates. Further competition comes from cable and satellite television and programs on the Internet. Cable television's share of the audience has been rising steadily. By 2000, 67 percent of the public was served by various cable channels in addition to over-the-air television, and 18 percent had satellite television.[18] More than 10 million households had satellite television.[19]

The capstone to the picture of oligopoly control (or limited competition) over information outlets is supplied by the wire service companies. A huge share of the news stories appearing in nearly every newspaper in the country and featured on television or radio news originates from the wires of the Associated Press (AP). The roots of this organization go back to

TABLE 2-2   U.S. Newspaper Circulation: October 2000–March 2001

Daily		Sunday	
Newspaper	Circulation	Newspaper	Circulation
Wall Street Journal	1,819,528	*New York Times*	1,698,281
USA Today[a]	1,769,650	*Los Angeles Times*	1,391,343
New York Times	1,159,954	*Washington Post*	1,070,809
Los Angeles Times	1,058,494	*Chicago Tribune*	1,001,662
Washington Post	802,594	*New York Daily News*	821,080
New York Daily News	716,095	*Dallas Morning News*	782,748
Chicago Tribune[b]	676,573	*Philadelphia Inquirer*	762,194
Newsday	576,692	*Detroit News/Free Press*	738,248
Houston Chronicle	545,066	*Houston Chronicle*	737,626
San Francisco Chronicle	527,466	*Boston Globe*	710,256

SOURCE: Audit Bureau of Circulation.

[a] Numbers are based on best days only—Monday–Thursday.

[b] Numbers are based on best days only—Wednesday–Friday.

1848, when six New York newspapers formed a cooperative association to share the cost of collecting foreign news. Out of this initial effort grew large organizations that employ reporters scattered throughout the world to collect and report news. News stories and bulletins are transmitted electronically to subscriber newspapers and radio and television stations. A handful of other wire services, such as those operated by the *New York Times, Los Angeles Times,* and *Chicago Tribune,* serve their own papers, along with a large array of subscribers.

News stories and bulletins supplied by the wire services are used either verbatim or are rewritten by their clients. Depending on the resources available to a particular news organization for gathering and writing its own news, the proportion of wire service stories used directly or in rewritten form may vary from less than 10 percent to 80 percent or more of all stories. For many newspapers, a look at the mix of stories carried by wire services on any particular day will foretell accurately the mix of stories carried by the paper. Wire service stories tend to predominate for foreign news and even for national news for smaller papers and stations that cannot afford their own correspondents. This means that a large share of news production in the United States is dominated by a small number of companies.

Despite efforts by the FCC to increase intramarket competition, oligopoly conditions prevail in the majority of markets. Electronic media generally are owned in pairs, limiting the total number of media owners in the community. Intramarket newspaper competition also has become rare. Ninety-eight percent of all American cities have only one daily newspaper.[20] Newspaper competition is rare outside the largest cities. Suburban dailies, which flourish in a few major cities, do not alter the situation substantially because their coverage of major news stories usually is limited. However, none of the situations of limited competition that have been discussed involve monopoly controls. Even in one-newspaper towns, there is intermedia competition from various types of television and radio outlets. As Robert Picard has noted:

> Compared with other Western nations, the United States tends to have less ownership concentration in communications industries. In the United States, the largest newspaper group has only about 10 percent of circulation, the top radio station owner has about 3 percent of commercial stations, the top TV networks each attract on average less than 20 percent of viewers at any one time, and the largest cable system operator serves about 20 percent of households. In France the largest newspaper group has about 25 percent of newspaper circulation. In Canada the largest radio station owner has 8 percent of the commercial stations. In Sweden the top private television network gains about 45 percent of viewers at any one time. In Finland the largest cable system operator has about 75 percent of households.[21]

Prestige Leadership

Another reason for homogeneity in news supply is the consensus among journalists about the nature of news and the elements of good reporting. There are widely accepted standards of professionalism in journalism, just as there are in law or medicine or engineering. As part of this system of norms, certain members and products are accepted widely as models whose influence reaches far beyond their own organization. Critics call this the "jackal syndrome" or "pack journalism." In the political news field, the *New York Times* is the lion whom the jackals follow. In television, major anchors like Dan Rather and Tom Brokaw are models for the profession. Other news professionals in the traditional media watch what information these sources present, how they present it, and what interpretations they give to it; they then adjust their own presentations accordingly. The upshot is that the multiplication of voices in much of the media marketplace—aside from the huge, hard-to-scan Internet universe—has contributed relatively little to meaningful diversity in news. Newcomers quickly join the old chorus and hum the prevailing tunes.

The Dangers of Big Business Control

The steady trend toward consolidation in the media industry increasingly has left control of information in the hands of a limited number of very large organizations. Concentration generally has stopped short of infringing antitrust and antimonopoly laws; consequently, these laws have been of little help in halting or reversing consolidation. As will be pointed out in Chapter 4, economic factors are largely responsible for consolidation. Production of television programs and worldwide news gathering are expensive. Only large, well-financed organizations, which are able to spread the costs over many customers, can provide the lavish media fare that attracts ample audiences.

Is it sound public policy to allow the rapid pace of consolidation of media enterprises to continue? Is there a danger that centralized control will bring undesirable uniformity and lead to neglect of local needs? Does the absence of newspaper competition in American cities prevent diverse viewpoints from reaching the public? Although there have been some troubling cases, the fears underlying these questions have proven largely groundless. There has been little change in the uniformity of news in the wake of media mergers; cable, satellite, and Internet television have diversified the media marketplace in one-newspaper towns.[22] Neither is there solid evidence that the media giants routinely squelch antibusiness news in the news outlets under their control. In fact, there has been an upswing of antibusiness news that has tarnished business giants like Microsoft, Nike, Nestle, Walmart, and Firestone.[23] It is true that many important stories are not published, including some that would be poor publicity for big business, but there is no hard evidence that the choices that are necessary to cope with an oversupply of news conform predominantly to conservative political orientations.[24]

The charge that media owners pressure journalists into supporting the existing political system also is not borne out. American journalists in large organizations, like their colleagues in small, independently owned enterprises, are interested in appealing to their audiences. This is why their stories usually reflect the values of mainstream American society, regardless of the journalists' personal political orientations.[25] However, there is a real danger that serious news increasingly will be overwhelmed by "infotainment" programs in the wake of the mergers of news enterprises with entertainment giants, especially when the public prefers such shows to hard-news offerings. Still, an ample supply of hard news remains available on cable stations, on news radio, and on the Internet.

Compared to offerings by small, individually owned enterprises, large enterprises have been able to offer qualitatively superior programs. They are able to absorb the losses that are often incurred in the production of expensive documentaries and public service programs. They also can spend more money on talented people, research, investigations, and costly entertainment shows. They can afford to send their reporters to all parts of the world to cover breaking stories firsthand. When FCC rules have forced small stations to offer non-network programs, cost considerations have forced them to fill their non-network hours with cheap canned movies or syndicated quiz or talent shows. Obviously, current policies designed to reduce media concentration and encourage local programming have failed to meet their objectives. These policies must be reconsidered, keeping in mind the media's mandate to serve the public interest of a democratic society. This is difficult to accomplish because large business enterprises maintain close and friendly ties with high-level politicians, giving them considerable clout when policies are drafted and enforced.

Government Regulation of the Media

The federal government regulates private electronic media primarily through the FCC, a bipartisan body appointed by the president and confirmed by the Senate.[26] The FCC was a seven-member body until the summer of 1984, when for financial reasons it was downsized to five commissioners. In 1986 the appointment term was shortened from seven to five years, ensuring faster turnover of commission personnel and greater control by the president. In theory, the commission is an independent regulatory body. In practice, congressional purse strings, public and industry pressures, and presidential control over appointment of new members, including the responsibilities of naming the chair, have greatly curtailed its freedom of operation. The commission's independence is weakened also because its rulings can be appealed to the courts, which frequently have overturned them. Conflicting political pressures from outside the agency as well as internal political pressures further limit FCC policymaking so that it tends to be "a reactive rather than an innovative system sluggish to respond to change in its environment, particularly to technological change . . . . Clearly there are problems with this kind of policy-making system." [27]

FCC Rules

Its vague mandate under the Communications Act of 1934 and its 1996 counterpart to "serve the public interest, convenience, and necessity" has made it difficult for the FCC to identify the objectives that should guide its regulatory powers. It has had to determine which social, economic, and technical goals the communications industry should achieve. It also has had to deal with conflicts over the adoption of various technologies and with the philosophical issue of regulation versus deregulation. On balance, the FCC's record of setting goals and enforcing its rules has earned it the reputation at best of being an ineffective watchdog over the public interest and at worst an industry-kept, pressure-group-dominated lapdog.

FCC control is limited to electronic media that reach large audiences, with the exception of cable television, which has been treated largely as a carrier of broadcast messages rather than a broadcaster. Similarly, interactive computer broadcasting systems, such as the Internet and the World Wide Web, have been excluded from regulation. The Computer Decency Act passed in 1996 to protect minors from obscenity in cyberspace was declared unconstitutional in 1997.[28] The print media essentially are uncontrolled except for antitrust and monopoly laws. Despite these laws the Justice Department has permitted economically weak newspapers to combine their business and production facilities, free from antitrust and monopoly restraints, as long as their news and editorial operations are kept separate.

FCC control has taken four forms: (1) rules limiting the number of stations owned or controlled by a single organization, (2) examinations of the goals and performance of stations as part of periodic licensing, (3) rules mandating public service and local interest programs, and (4) rules to protect individuals from damage caused by unfair media coverage. Although none of these rules prescribe specific content, all of them were designed to increase the chances that content would be diverse and of civic importance.

Rules Limiting Station Ownership.   As explained earlier, to prevent high concentrations of media ownership and to ensure diversity of information sources, the FCC limits the number of stations that television and radio owners may control. It also limits the size of the audience that may be within the range of any one group of owners, allowing over-the-air television no more than 35 percent and cable television no more than 30 percent of the market share. Nonetheless, networks such as ABC, CBS, NBC, and Fox, through their many affiliates, are within reach of more than 90 percent of the nation's audiences.

Television station ownership has been enormously profitable. This is why the Viacom Company was willing to spend more than $37 billion in 1999 to acquire and run CBS. The mushrooming of broadband outlets since the 1990s has increased competition and slashed profitability, especially for television news units. Consequently, news budgets have been slashed and many units have been forced to downsize, often at the expense of quality of coverage. The network audience's share of prime time viewers dropped from 71 percent in 1996 to 58 percent in 2000, producing a drop in advertising rates. Advertising revenues also declined because the pool of large advertisers shrank in the wake of business mergers.

Thus far, no initial investment has been required to get a license from the government, although pressures to change this are mounting. The FCC estimates that auctioning licenses to the highest bidder could yield the federal government billions of dollars, considering that licenses of profitable stations—with their profit margins of up to 50 percent—currently trade for millions of dollars because the demand exceeds the supply.

Licensing as Performance Control. By granting or refusing to grant a radio or television license initially or renewing it after eight years, the FCC determines who may own valuable communication properties. What performance standards does it use for license decisions? Communication law mandates that television and radio must "serve the public interest, convenience, and necessity."[29] But beyond requiring broadcasters to ascertain community needs and interests by talking with community leaders, there are no guides for interpreting these rules. Even the requirement to keep in touch with community leaders was dropped in 1984. In the absence of specific performance requirements, it has been nearly impossible to use the power to grant licenses initially and to renew them as a tool to foster high quality. When processing licenses, the FCC usually looks at the mix of programs, the proportion of public service offerings, and the inclusion of programs geared to selected groups. It does not scrutinize the subject matter of broadcasts in detail. This hands-off attitude has applied to both program inclusions and exclusions. However, the FCC has set limits on the amounts of advertising permitted in children's shows. Ads may not exceed twelve minutes per hour on weekdays and ten and a half minutes on weekends.

The FCC has used its power to grant new licenses to ensure service geared to the information needs of socioeconomic groups different from those already served by existing stations in a given area. When there are several qualified applicants for new broadcasting stations, the FCC may use a lottery that is tilted to favor applications by women, minorities, labor unions, and community organizations that are underrepresented in the ownership of telecommunications facilities. Once a license has been granted, owners hold it for good unless they engage in discriminatory or fraudulent practices or receive many complaints about poor programming. Owners may sell their licenses at will, earning huge profits on the sale.

Since the 1970s numerous civic groups have entered renewal hearings to protest the type of programming offered or omitted by a particular station. As a result of such pressures, the FCC reluctantly has withdrawn licenses from a few stations over the years. For example, a Chicago station lost its license in 1990 for neglecting informational programs and presenting obscene movies.[30] However, the 1996 Telecommunications Act makes license withdrawal more difficult. It specifically forbids the FCC from continuing its practice of comparing the merits of new applicants with those of existing license holders in license renewal applications.

Compared with regulatory agencies in other countries, even in Western Europe, Canada, and Australia, the FCC controls the electronic media with a very light hand. The members of the FCC could, if they wished, rigorously define what constitutes "programming in the public interest." They could enforce the FCC rulings more strictly and verify station performance records at license renewal time. The threat of license withdrawal for rule violations could be used as a much more powerful deterrent to misbehavior and as a much stronger lever to guide programming. That does not happen because political cross-pressures are strong and the FCC staff is much too small to cope with all the duties assigned to the agency. In fact, it is chronically behind schedule, even for routine matters such as the publication of its annual reports.

Public Service and Local Programming. In the past the FCC stipulated the minimum time that ought to be devoted to public service programs on television. Under the 5-5-10 rule, which is no longer enforced, 5 percent of programming had to be devoted to local affairs, 5 percent to news and public affairs, and 10 percent to nonentertainment programs. Beyond checking a television station's log to ascertain that it recorded the minimum amount of public service programming, the FCC did not examine the nature and quality of programs labeled "public service." In 1991, as part of its regulations of children's television, the FCC directed stations to maintain a record of educational and informational programs for children. But it set no quality standards, even though the record is a requirement for license renewal.[31] A year later, Congress passed the Cable Television Consumer Protection and Competition Act, requiring cable television systems to dedicate some of their channels to local broadcast television stations. The Supreme Court has upheld these "must carry" rules as content-neutral measures to assure that over-the-air broadcasters have access to publics that they might otherwise be unable to reach.[32]

Fair Treatment Rules. The FCC also has made rules about access to the airwaves for candidates for political office and for people who have been subjected to media attacks. These types of controls are discussed in Chapter 3.

Control by Industry Associations and Advertiser Pressures

Industry lobbies are another means of controlling the mass media. Radio and television interests, especially the networks and their affiliated stations, are active lobbyists. Most belong to the National Association of Broadcasters (NAB), a powerful Washington lobby despite the diversity and often clashing interests of its members. A number of trade associations and publications, such as *Broadcasting* magazine, also engage in lobbying, often at cross-purposes to each other. For newspapers the American Newspaper Publishers Association (ANPA), now merged with several other press associations, has been one of the most prominent groups. These organizations try to influence appointments to the FCC and to guide public policies affecting new technologies that may threaten established systems or practices. For instance, the network lobbies for many years tried to stifle cable television and to acquire control over domestic satellites. The National Cable Television Association and the National Association of Broadcasters have used members' stations to urge support for their policy recommendations. On other occasions, such as the passage of the Telecommunications Act of 1996, they have tried to de-emphasize coverage that might arouse unwanted opposition.

To forestall regulation by outside bodies, the industry has developed mechanisms for self-control. The NAB has had a radio code since 1929 and a television code since 1952 that set rules on program content and form. Both codes have been modernized periodically. Industry-wide codes have been supplemented and often are superseded by individual codes in major broadcast enterprises and by codes adopted by the Council of Better Business Bureaus. Print press self-policing has developed along similar lines. Scholars, too, have set forth codes of journalism ethics. Most codes are quite vague, mandating honesty, fairness, independence, and concern for the public's interests. What these principles mean in practice is left for decision in specific cases. Overall, the impact of industry-wide codes always has been limited. Typically, they apply only to an organization's members who explicitly subscribe to them. Penalties for code violations have been minimal. The codes have been useful in blunting demands by pressure groups for government intervention to set and enforce standards. For instance, congressional leaders lifted a threat to pass laws limiting excessively violent and sexually explicit shows on programs available to children in return for industry promises to develop a rating system to guide parents.

In the 1970s advertisers began to influence program content by actually withdrawing their commercials from programs they considered to be obscene or excessively violent. Sears Roebuck was one of the earliest and largest advertisers to do so. McDonald's, American Express, and AT&T refused to place commercials on such shows. Other large advertisers, such as Procter and Gamble, retained consultants to seek out acceptable programs for their advertisements and avoid unacceptable ones. With advertisements on top-rated shows such as *Sixty Minutes* yielding $250,000 for a thirty-second spot, threats of withdrawal constitute significant economic

By permission of Mike Luckovich and Creators Syndicate.

pressures that have had some impact on programming. While reductions in programs featuring sex and violence have been welcome, other changes have been problematic.

There is deep concern that advertisers, spurred by pressure groups, may become unofficial censors. For instance, General Motors's sponsorship of an Eastertime program on the life of Jesus was canceled because evangelical groups objected to the content. There were crippling withdrawals of advertising from a CBS documentary on gun control, opposed by the gun control lobby. Fearing similar punishments from fundamentalist religious groups, the networks have refused advertising designed to instruct viewers about the use of condoms for protection against unwanted pregnancies and acquired immune deficiency syndrome (AIDS). Such unofficial censorship at the behest of advertisers is worrisome.

Citizen Lobby Control

Citizens' efforts to affect the quality of broadcasting began in earnest in 1966, when the Office of Communication of the United Church of

Christ, a public interest lobby, challenged the renewal of a TV license for WLBT-TV in Jackson, Mississippi, accusing the station of discriminating against African American viewers.[33] African Americans then constituted 45 percent of Jackson's population. The challenge failed, but it was the beginning of efforts by many other citizens groups to use pressure tactics to challenge license renewals.

A major victory was won in 1975, when the FCC refused to renew licenses of eight educational television stations in Alabama and denied a construction permit for a ninth station because citizen groups had charged racial discrimination in employment at these stations. There also had been complaints that programs dealing with affairs of the African American community had been unduly excluded.[34] Since then, numerous stations have yielded to pressure for increased minority employment and programming rather than face protracted legal action.

During the 1980s many citizens' groups were formed to lobby for better programming and tighter government controls. Typical ones were Accuracy in Media (AIM), a well-financed conservative media-monitoring organization, and its counterpart, Citizens for the American Way (CAW), a liberal media organization intent on blocking conservative lobbies; the Coalition for Better Television (CBTV), representing fundamentalist religious groups; Action for Children's Television (ACT), which disbanded in 1992; the National Black Media Coalition (NBMC); and the National Latino Media Coalition (NLMC).

Despite the substantial impact of such groups on FCC rule-making and licensing procedures, citizens' national lobbying efforts declined in the 1980s and have never regained their original vigor.[35] One reason has been the difficulty of sustaining citizen interest over long periods of time; another was lack of financial support and loss of leadership. The broadcast lobby defeated efforts to obtain public funding for citizens' lobby groups, and foundation support has dried up. Many groups also were discouraged when the appeals courts reversed substantial victories won in the lower courts and when the 1996 Computer Decency Act was voided by the U.S. Supreme Court (see note 28). Some of the energies of citizens groups have been redirected into lobbying at the local level to ensure that cable systems serve the interests of various publics at reasonable prices to consumers.

In addition to the more than sixty organizations concerned exclusively with media reform, other organizations, such as the Parent Teacher Association (PTA), the National Organization for Women (NOW), and the American Medical Association (AMA), have lobbied on a variety of media issues. They have shown concern about stereotyping, access to media coverage and to media employment and ownership, advertising on children's programs, and enforcement of FCC program regulations. The groups' tactics include monitoring media content, publicizing their findings, and directly pressuring broadcasters, advertisers, media audiences, and government control agencies. Protest by PTA members has pressured advertisers, who, in turn, have succeeded in reducing the number of violent programs shown in the early evening hours. Legal maneuvers have ranged from challenges of license renewals to damage suits for the harmful effects of media content.

It is difficult to assess the precise influence of these organizations because many of their goals overlap with other forces that affect media policy. Some of the causes for which they have worked, such as for measures fostering good programming for children, have prospered over the years, however, and part of the credit undoubtedly belongs to them. Yet these groups have a long road to travel before they can match the influence enjoyed by the broadcast lobby in protecting its interests even when they run counter to the concerns of large numbers of citizens.

Summary

In this chapter we have examined the most common types of ownership and control of the media. The national government owns and operates vast overseas radio and television enterprises. At home it partially controls a far-flung system of public television and radio broadcasting that provides an alternative to commercial programming.

For the average American, these government-controlled systems are peripheral compared with privately owned print and electronic media enterprises. The major political problem in the private sector is concentration of ownership of media and concentrated control over news and entertainment programs. There has been great concern that the American public is ill-served because much of the media output is controlled by large business conglomerates, and newspaper competition is limited in most cities. Comparatively few potentially biased minds shape the news and entertainment supply that undergirds public perceptions of political issues.

We have looked into the structure of the media business and government regulations designed to avert the potential dangers of concentration. We also have tried to evaluate the impact of the existing system on the form and slant of news and entertainment. Many prevailing views about the interrelation between media structures and functions appear to be wrong. Business ownership has not led to programming dominated by business perspectives, although it has enhanced the focus on soft news and entertainment. It has not shielded big business from harsh criticism often in the form of investigative reports. Coverage of local news has not withered, and large, rather than small, enterprises have excelled in providing news and entertainment. Because fears about the ill effects of the current structure seem misdirected, further research is needed to provide a sounder basis for public policies intended to ensure that American media serve the public interest.

Media operations and products are shaped not only by who owns them but also by industry lobby groups and citizens' lobbies. Given the diversity of influences that are brought into play when news and entertainment are produced, it is as yet impossible to assess the precise impact that each of these influences has on media content in general or even on a particular story. In the next chapter we will focus on legal aspects of news production for additional clues to the mystery of the mix of influences shaping the news.

Notes

1. Erik Eckholm, "A Trial Will Test China's Grip on the Internet," *New York Times,* Nov. 16, 1998.
2. Examples of the types of shows that attracted the largest audiences in 2000 are *The Sopranos* (dark comedy), *E.R.* (drama), and *Sixty Minutes,* a popular investigative series that shares many qualities with popular detective shows. In addition, there are the ever-popular sports events such as the Super Bowl, entertainment industry awards presentations, and competitions such as *Who Wants to Be a Millionaire?* and "reality" shows like *Survivor.*
3. Ben H. Bagdikian, *The Media Monopoly,* 5th ed. (Boston: Beacon Press, 1996); Dean Alger, *Megamedia: How Giant Corporations Dominate Mass Media, Distort Competition, and Endanger Democracy* (Lanham, Md.: Rowman and Littlefield, 1998); and Robert Picard, "Media Concentration, Economics, and Regulation," in *The Politics of News, The News of Politics,* ed. Doris Graber, Denis McQuail, and Pippa Norris (Washington, D.C.: CQ Press, 1998). For a negative view of the "marketplace of ideas" concept, see Benjamin Ginsberg, *The Captive Public: How Mass Opinion Promotes State Power* (New York: Basic Books, 1986), 98–148.
4. "Despite the expressed insulation of public broadcasters from federal editorial domination, case law specifically allows broadcast program decisions to be dictated by political officials when the state is licensee. Therefore, potential conflict exists between First Amendment and political interests." William Hanks and Lemuel Schofield, "Limitations on the State as Editor in State-Owned Broadcast Stations," *Journalism Quarterly* 63 (winter 1986): 798.
5. Erwin G. Krasnow, Lawrence D. Longley, and Herbert A. Terry, *The Politics of Broadcast Regulation,* 3d ed. (New York: St. Martin's Press, 1982), 23, 74.
6. http://www.cpb.org/about/partner/
7. Ibid.

8. For an impassionate analysis of the trials and tribulations of U.S. public television, see James Ledbetter, *Made Possible By ....The Death of Public Broadcasting in the United States* (London: Verso, 1997).

9. U.S. Census Bureau, "Industry Quick Report," http://factfinder.census.gov. . .lt/

10. In addition to media holdings, the Tribune encompasses the fields of energy, mining, trucking, paper, finance, and a major league baseball team.

11. Seth Schiesel, "Where the Message Is the Medium," *New York Times,* July 2, 2001.

12. www.USMarkets.com, The Newspaper Index, 2000.

13. Stephen Labaton, "F.C.C. Approves AOL-Time Warner Deal, with Conditions," *New York Times,* Jan. 12, 2001.

14. Alger, *Megamedia,* 31.

15. Ibid., 92.

16. Media critic Dean Alger claims that quality deteriorates when papers are acquired by a chain. Ibid., 180–182.

17. Bill Carter, "A Struggle for Control: Local TV Fears the Networks' Power," *New York Times,* April 23, 2001.

18. Furthermore, nearly 79 million households owned videocassette recorders (VCRs) that permitted them to supplement over-the-air television fare. *Television and Cable Fact Book,* 2000.

19. http://www.fcc.gov/csb/shva/

20. Alger, *Megamedia,* 31, 130–134.

21. Picard, "Media Concentration, Economics, and Regulation," 201.

22. Ibid., 208–212; David Pearce Demers, *The Menace of the Corporate Newspaper: Fact or Fiction?* (Ames: Iowa State University Press, 1996); W. Lance Bennett and Timothy E. Cook, "Journalism Norms and News Construction: Rules for Representing Politics," *Political Communication,* special issue (winter 1996). For contrary views, see Alger, *Megamedia,* 153–194; and Robert W. McChesney, *Rich Media, Poor Democracy* (New York: New Press, 1999).

23. Jarol B. Manheim, *The Death of a Thousand Cuts: Corporate Campaigns and the Attack on the Corporation* (Mahwah, N.J.: Erlbaum, 2001).

24. Bennett and Cook, "Journalism Norms and News Construction."

25. For a discussion of journalists' political orientations and professional values, see chap. 4.

26. In decisions about media mergers, the Federal Trade Commission also plays a major role.

27. Krasnow, Longley, and Terry, *The Politics of Broadcast Regulation,* 284.

28. *Reno v. American Civil Liberties Union,* 521 U.S. 844 (1997).

29. 47 U.S.C.A. §307(a), 1934.

30. Steven Morris, "FCC Denies WSNS-TV New Broadcast License," *Chicago Tribune,* Sept. 20, 1990.

31. Many contradictory bills have been introduced in Congress to deal with news and public service programming requirements. Most of them die early in the game. The *CQ Weekly* (formerly *Congressional Quarterly Weekly Report*) is an excellent source for tracking these legislative developments.

32. *Turner Broadcasting Systems v. FCC,* 520 U.S. 180 (1997).

33. *Office of Communication of the United Church of Christ v. FCC,* 359 F.2d 994 (D.C. Cir. 1966).

34. Krasnow, Longley, and Terry, *The Politics of Broadcast Regulation,* 54–62.

35. Ibid., 56–57.

Readings

Alger, Dean. *Megamedia: How Giant Corporations Dominate Mass Media, Distort Competition, and Endanger Democracy.* Lanham, Md.: Rowman and Littlefield, 1998.

Aufderheide, Patricia. *Communications Policy and the Public Interest: The Telecommunications Act of 1996.* New York: Guilford Press, 1999.

Bagdikian, Ben H. *The Media Monopoly,* 5th ed. Boston: Beacon Press, 1996.

Bennett, W. Lance. *News: The Politics of Illusion.* White Plains, N.Y.: Longman, 2001.

Compaine, Benjamin, and Douglas Gomery. *Who Owns the Media: Competition and Concentration in the Media Industry.* 3d ed. Mahwah, N.J.: Erlbaum, 2000.

Demers, David Pearce. *The Menace of the Corporate Newspaper: Fact or Fiction?* Ames: Iowa State University Press, 1996.

Graber, Doris, Denis McQuail, and Pippa Norris, eds. *The Politics of News, The News of Politics.* Washington, D.C.: CQ Press, 1998.

Hoynes, William. *Public Television for Sale: Media, the Market, and the Public Sphere.* Boulder: Westview, 1994.

Krasnow, Erwin G., Lawrence D. Longley, and Herbert A. Terry. *The Politics of Broadcast Regulation.* 3d ed. New York: St. Martin's Press, 1982.

c h a p t e r   t h r e e

Press Freedom and the Law

HOW PREVALENT IS PRESS FREEDOM? The disappointing answer is "not very." Thirty-six percent of the world's people, living in sixty-two countries, do not enjoy a free press at all, and another 43 percent, living in fifty-three countries, enjoy only partial press freedom. That leaves just 21 percent of the world's people in seventy-two countries benefiting from full press freedom.[1] These ratings are based on four sets of criteria: laws and regulations that influence media content; political pressures and controls over media content; economic influences over media content; and repressive actions such as various types of censorship and physical violence, including the killing of journalists.

The United States, along with most Western democracies, ranks among the countries where, according to Freedom House's 2001 survey, print and broadcast media and the Internet are essentially free, though most fall considerably short of a perfect score. Why and how has the United States maintained its high press-freedom rankings for more than sixty years? What does press freedom, guaranteed by the U.S. Constitution, mean in practice? How can the freedom of privately controlled institutions to choose, frame, and report all news be reconciled with protection of society from irresponsible news stories that damage public interests? How can an unfettered media establishment be kept responsive to the many voices that should be heard? These questions are difficult to answer because keeping the press unfettered poses perplexing dilemmas.

We will begin to shed light on these puzzles by probing problems that arise when a free press claims the exclusive right to decide what to publish and, in the process, often clashes with demands by citizen groups for newspaper space and air time to publicize social and political causes. Then we will turn to difficulties the press faces in gaining access to information needed for a story when the government claims the right to conceal this information. Finally, we will examine barriers to publication that have been imposed by legislators and courts to safeguard private and public interests.

The First Amendment is the constitutional basis for press freedom in America. The amendment guarantees that "Congress shall make no law . . . abridging the freedom of speech or of the press." This makes the press the only private enterprise in America that is granted a privileged status by the Constitution. The interpretations of the scope of this privilege, however, have fluctuated since the First Amendment was ratified in 1791, and similar clauses in state constitutions often have been construed in ways that differ from interpretations at the national level.[2]

America's founders granted this special status to the press because they considered the right to express opinions and to collect and disseminate information free from government controls as the bedrock of a free society.[3] If restraints are needed to protect society from harmful publicity, they must come through the deterrent effects of fear of punishment after publication, not through "prior restraint." Publication can be prevented only if it "will surely result in direct, immediate, and irreparable damage to our nation or its people."[4] The belief in the political importance of a free press has stood the test of time and remains a cornerstone of American democracy. Therefore, any factor that affects the interpretation or the scope of this basic right is a matter of major political significance.

Access to the Media

The notion of government "by the people" implies that the people have a right to make their voices heard. Practically speaking, this means that they must have access to the mass media to advocate their beliefs. Ralph Nader's consumer protection movement or the various environmental protection crusades that have swept the country periodically, for example, never could have gathered widespread support without mass media publicity. Did the reformers have a *right* to mass media publicity for their views and for their organizing activities?

The answer is "no." In fact, it is difficult for most people, other than journalists or major public figures, to gain access to the media. In a book on the right of access to the mass media, Jerome Barron, a lawyer interested in civil liberties, accused journalists of fighting for broad rights of free expression for themselves while denying these same rights to the public.[5] Media personnel decide what stories to publicize and whose views to present, leaving many who want to proclaim their views without a suitable public forum.

Barron argued that the First Amendment right to publish freely should extend to all individuals and groups, not only to news professionals. If individuals have a special cause or think that mass media stories have been inaccurate or inadequate, they should have an opportunity to use the mass media to state their views. Without this right, citizens may be doomed to political ineffectiveness.

Uncontrolled Media

What rights of access to the mass media do individuals in private and public life have? To answer this question accurately, a distinction must be made between uncontrolled and controlled media. American courts usually have held that the freedom of the print media to determine what they will or will not print, and whose views they will present, is nearly absolute. Cable television and the Internet thus far enjoy the same freedom, although this issue remains contested because many legislators and large numbers of the American public favor controls, especially to protect children from unsavory information. As long as uncontrolled media stay clear of deliberate libel and slander and do not publish top-secret information, their publishing decisions are unhampered by legal restraints. They may even publish false or misleading information, such as pronouncing the wrong candidate as the winner, as happened during the 2000 presidential election.

The U.S. Supreme Court defined print press rights in the case of *Miami Herald Publishing Company v. Tornillo* (1974).[6] At issue was the constitutionality of a Florida statute that gave a right to immediate reply to candidates for public office who had been personally attacked by a newspaper. The rebuttal had to match the format of the original attack, and it had to be placed in an equally prominent spot in the newspaper. The law had been passed to deal with the problem of personal attacks published very late in a campaign, giving candidates little time to respond. The consequence might be loss of the election.

The case arose in 1972 when Patrick Tornillo, Jr., leader of the Dade County Teachers Union, was running for the Florida state legislature. Just before the primary the *Miami Herald* published two editorials objecting to Tornillo's election because he had led a recent teachers' strike. Tornillo demanded that the paper print his replies to claims made in the editorials. The paper refused. After Tornillo lost the primary decisively, he sued the paper.

When the case reached the U.S. Supreme Court in 1974, the Court ruled unanimously that newspapers can print or refuse to print anything they like. No one, including a candidate whose reputation has been damaged, has the *right* to obtain space in a newspaper. Therefore, the Florida right to reply statute was unconstitutional. The decision reaffirmed what had been the thrust of the law all along. Private citizens may request that a story or response to a personal attack be printed and that request may be granted, but they have no right to demand publication.[7]

Controlled Media

The rules are different for the broadcast media, because limited spectrum space makes them semi-monopolies. Besides, entry into the broadcast media business requires a license from the government. In return for the privilege of broadcasting over the public airwaves, license holders are subject to government regulations. These include rules ensuring that the license holders respect the public's limited rights of access to the airways. The freedoms granted to print media were later extended to cable television because it initially served only as a carrier of media content that originated elsewhere. Like the telephone, it was a "common carrier" open to all who requested that it carry their messages. Similarly, the Internet has been likened to a common carrier that accepts messages from anyone.

To halt the deleterious effects on programming, many members of Congress and many broadcasters and communication scholars have urged ending differential treatment of various types of media. Broadcast media no longer are semi-monopolies. In fact, print media face less competition in the age of one-newspaper towns than do broadcast media. Besides, the distinctions between various types of media are becoming increasingly blurred because they use a mixture of technologies to disseminate their messages. Therefore, the argument goes, all media should be free from government interference in making publishing decisions.

Based on Section 315 of the Communications Act of 1934 and its many subsequent amendments and interpretations, the public's access rights to broadcast media fall under three categories: the *equal time provision,* the *fairness doctrine,* and the *right of rebuttal.* All of these rights arise only after a station has broadcast the information in question.

The Right to Equal Time. If a station gives or sells time during an election campaign to one candidate for a specific office, it must make the same opportunity available to all candidates for that office, including those with few backers. However, if the station refuses time to all candidates for the same office, none of them has a right to demand access under the campaign coverage provisions of Section 315. The rules exclude coverage provided through regular news programs and specifically exempted talk shows.

Stations constrained by the all-or-none equal time rule often opt for "none," particularly for state and local offices and when many candidates are competing for the same office. This keeps many viable candidates off the air who might otherwise have gained exposure. But it saves stations from cluttering their programs with numerous campaign broadcasts that would be of little interest to their listeners and costly to the station in lost advertising revenues.

To make it possible to stage lengthy debates among mainline candidates for major offices without running afoul of the equal time provisions, Congress suspended these provisions in 1960 so that Kennedy and Nixon could debate. A different tactic was used in 1976 and 1980. To facilitate the Carter–Ford and Carter–Reagan debates, the FCC permitted them to be staged as public meetings, which could be covered by the news media like regular news, exempting them from the equal time rule. This was obviously a subterfuge to avoid the intent of the law.

Several minor party candidates, eager to be included in the debates, sued in 1976, claiming that this circumvention of equal time provisions was illegal. But the courts ruled against them. Finally, in November 1983, the FCC lifted its previous restraints, allowing radio and television broadcasters to stage political debates at all political levels among a limited array of candidates chosen in a nondiscriminatory way. Candidates who feel that they have been unfairly shut out may appeal to the FCC. The ruling applies even to public television stations.[8]

The curbs on political dialogue other than debates remain and have led to widespread dissatisfaction with the equal time rule. Their unintended effect has been to block the public from receiving many important messages by current and prospective public officials. Even presidential speeches about projected policies have been blocked when the media feared that audiences would not be interested. Critics are also unhappy about public sanction of subterfuges to evade the rule such as allowing the League of Women Voters to sponsor debates so that the event can qualify as regular news. They believe the Equal Time rule should be abandoned, rather than continuing the current practice of piecemeal legalized exceptions.

The Right to Fair Treatment. The fairness doctrine, cherished by Democrats and reviled by Republicans, has had a broader reach than the equal time provision because it is not limited to candidates for political office. It mandates free air time for the presentation of issues of public concern and the expression of opposing views whenever a highly controversial public issue, including the candidacy of a named official, has been discussed on television. Like the equal time provision, the fairness doctrine has impoverished public debate by suppressing controversy, because the media frequently shy away from programs dealing with controversial public issues to avoid demands to air opposing views in place of regular revenue-producing programs. It has also been difficult to decide who, among many claimants for airtime, has the right to reply to controversial programs. In October 2000 the U.S. Court of Appeals for the District of Columbia, which routinely handles FCC cases, ordered the FCC to repeal the fairness rule immediately because of its adverse effects.[9] Considering that a Republican president, with the consent of a Republican Senate, appointed a Republican (Michael Powell) to head the commission, the death sentence for the fairness rule may be final. But one can never be sure about the demise of federal regulations that, like the proverbial cat, seem to be blessed with nine lives.

Pressures and litigation produced by the fairness rule have made the media more receptive to featuring opposing views. For example, it has become traditional to allow spokespersons for the opposition to offer rebuttals after presidential, gubernatorial, and mayoral speeches covering major policy issues. The temper of the times has thus curbed editorial freedom, even though legal rights remain unchanged. In fact, in a 1999 survey of reporters and news executives, 41 percent reported exercising some kind of self-censorship in terms of the news they presented or ignored. Their goal was to please their audiences or their colleagues or the desire to protect their news organization's interests.[10]

Is there a right of reply to contentious statements made in business commercials? The oil industry, environmentalists, and the drug industry, among other groups, have used commercials to raise questions about controversial public policies. Commercial firms and public interest groups have asked for time to respond. The question about response rights arises because First Amendment protections do not extend automatically to commercial messages. In fact, free expression in such messages has been constrained severely through truth-in-advertising laws administered by the Federal Trade Commission. If the media must make time available to respond to commercial messages, must the time be free of charge? The answer is unclear because the courts have spoken with forked tongues and media willingness to allow replies has been quite mixed.

The Right of Rebuttal. Individuals who are assailed on radio or television in a way that damages their reputations have the right of rebuttal. The landmark case *Red Lion Broadcasting Co. v. Federal Communications Commission* (1969)[11] established a rather broad scope for the right of reply. The case arose because a book about a conservative senator was attacked on a program conducted and paid for by the ultraconservative

Christian Crusade. Fred Cook, the book's author, asked for rebuttal time, free of charge. The station was willing to sell him reply time but refused free time, disclaiming responsibility for the content of programs prepared by private parties.

The courts sided with Cook, who was granted the right of rebuttal, at station expense, on the grounds that maligned individuals deserve a right to reply and that the public has a right to hear opposing views. The decision proved to be a hollow victory for supporters of free access to the airways, however, because stations sharply curtailed air time available for controversial broadcasts, fearing rebuttal claims.

The *Red Lion* case is also noteworthy as an example of political manipulation of the regulatory process. Cook's protest had been paid for and orchestrated by the Democratic National Committee as part of an effort to generate an avalanche of demands for rebuttals to conservative radio and television programs. The hope was that stations then would cancel these programs to avoid the costs of free rebuttal time.[12] This did, indeed, happen. By 1975 the Christian Crusade had been dropped by 300 of its 350 stations. Since 1969 the courts have retreated somewhat from their broad support for the right of rebuttal at station expense because of its chilling effects on controversial broadcasts. The flood of rebuttal requests also mired the FCC in a morass of claims and counterclaims that it could not process with its limited resources. Easing of the rules has been a boon to the many interactive radio and television talk show programs that have mushroomed in recent years.

Problems of the Status Quo

Apart from the right to reply to a personal attack and the right of rival candidates to have equal broadcast time, there are no access rights for individuals. Aside from using advertisements, e-mail, or a Web site or chat room on the Internet, there is no way to bring messages to public attention through the most widely disseminated mass media if the media are unwilling. Public television enjoys complete editorial freedom as well. When the film *Death of a Princess* was canceled by public television in Alabama in response to protests by Saudi Arabia's royal family and threats of economic boycott, a group of citizens charged unfair denial of their right of access to information. The federal district court disagreed.[13] The station, *not* the public, had the right to decide what to feature and what to censor.

Single networks or stations often secure exclusive broadcast rights to popular events, such as major baseball and basketball games. This practice is another restraint on information dissemination. News outlets aside from the contract holder are precluded from covering the event. Exclusive contracts have been negotiated even for public spectacles such as the rededication of the Statue of Liberty during its centennial and the Olympic Games in Sydney, Australia, in 2000. The television networks also have been very restrictive in allowing professionals outside their own organizations to air public information programs. In the same way, professional organizations frequently restrain the flow of news to the general public. For instance, when scientists discovered a treatment that could cut pneumonia deaths by AIDS patients by half, they felt constrained to withhold the news for five months until the *New England Journal of Medicine,* a highly regarded professional publication owned by the Massachusetts Medical Society, had first published its reports. The power of the journal to act as the gatekeeper for major medical news springs from the fact that scientists prize the prestige derived from publication of their work in the journal. If they violate journal rules by releasing data to the lay public prior to publication in a medical journal, their story may be rejected for publication.[14]

People in public office who want access to the mass media to explain their views face problems quite similar to those of private individuals. Although the media are likely to be more sympathetic to their requests, on many occasions coverage is denied or granted only outside prime time when audience size peaks. Several speeches by Presidents Nixon, Ford, Reagan, Bush, and Clinton were not broadcast at all because the media considered them partisan political statements or claimed that they contained nothing new. Others were carried by only a few stations, forcing the president to compete against regular broadcasts, reducing his audience sharply. Presidents prevent access problems by tailoring their requests for media time to the needs of the media. In particular, they avoid schedule conflicts with major sports events.

The question of access rights to the airwaves also has been raised in connection with interest groups. Several groups have asked for more children's programs, even though they would be of little interest to the majority of adult listeners and viewers. The FCC has concurred that children constitute an important special audience whose needs for distinctive programming must be met. It has pressured stations to increase programming, often with a veiled threat that failure to oblige would lead to mandatory rules. Stations have been reluctant to add children's programs because revenues from them are comparatively low, particularly after the FCC shortened the time allowed for advertising to spare immature viewers from temptations.

Other audiences whose right of access to special programs has been recognized sporadically include African Americans, Hispanics, and lovers of classical music, to name a few. Occasional rulings have forced the electronic media to set aside time for broadcasts geared to such groups, whose needs might be ignored if the forces of the economic marketplace were allowed full rein. The FCC has further protected the interests of these groups by giving preference in license applications to stations whose output is likely to serve neglected clienteles. In light of the growing number of cable, television, and radio outlets, making access easier for everyone, government protection of special interest groups is declining. In 1981 the Supreme Court freed the FCC from any obligation to weigh the effects of alternative program formats on various population groups when making licensing decisions. The Court's ruling arose from a series of cases in which radio stations had changed their format, for instance, from all news to all music.[15]

Other Approaches to Media Access

Attempts to gain access to the mass media through independently produced programs, individual requests for air time, and FCC rulings that support the interest of minority audiences have been only moderately successful. Other routes to access are even less satisfactory. Letters to the editor and op-ed essays are examples. Because of lack of space, most papers publish few letters and opinion pieces. The *New York Times,* for instance, receives more than 60 thousand letters a year and publishes 4 to 5 percent of them, limiting length strictly. Even with these stringent controls, space devoted to letters equals the space allotted for editorials in the *Times.* Editors select the letters and op-ed essays to be published, using a variety of criteria that disadvantage average people. Messages that are unusual or that are sent by someone well known are most likely to be printed.

Another avenue to access is through the use of paid advertisements. Labor unions, business enterprises, lobby groups, and even foreign governments have placed advertisements on the air or in major newspapers to present their side of disputes and public policy issues. Usually only large companies can afford the steep purchase price, which may run into thousands of dollars for full-page advertisements and national broadcast exposure. Print and electronic media occasionally have refused to publish advertisements or sell airtime when messages seemed to them too controversial—on topics such as the energy crisis and the Arab–Israeli dispute, for example. Public concern about the denial of advertising space has lessened in the wake of creation of the Internet where Web sites can be used to disseminate messages to computer users around the world. However, access to that message system is still regarded as a less effective way to reach the public than the daily papers and major over-the-air broadcasts.

When people who are eager to publicize their views cannot afford the high cost of paid messages, they may try to gain attention by creating a sensational event and inviting the media to witness it. A young Chinese dissident used the tactic in 1992, when he invited the media to watch his display of posters commemorating the brutal suppression of China's pro-democracy movement in Beijing's Tiananmen Square. The ensuing free publicity reached millions of people all over the world. Few publicity seekers meet with such success and many fail miserably, as happened to a man who invited the media to a self-immolation to protest unemployment in 1983. Camera crews filmed the action while the protester suffered life-threatening burns. The story received nationwide coverage, but the emphasis was on the callousness of the film crew that did not stop the burning. The unemployment issue was well-nigh ignored.[16]

The rise of lobby groups eager to ensure broad access rights to people with minority viewpoints, and the FCC's sympathy with their pleas, have made broadcasters more sensitive to pressures for access by political activists. But even if radio or television station management is willing to grant access to such people, especially when they have engaged in newsworthy activities, there still is the problem of insufficient time to air every claimant's views. Despite the multiplication of television and radio channels in the wake of technological advancements, there will never be enough channels or even newspaper pages to publicize all important views to large audiences. Even the creation of the Internet does not guarantee everyone wide public exposure. Concerned citizens have neither the time nor the capacity to listen to all significant views and put them into proper perspective. In fact, the capacity to broadcast and publicize already far exceeds the audience's capacity to listen and assimilate. Studies of cable system users have shown that regardless of the number of channels available and the important stories that they may feature, the average viewer rarely taps into more than six.

Access to Information

Access to information involves two major issues: *who* shall have access and *what* information must be open for public inspection.

Special Access for the Media?

The right to publish without restraint means little if journalists are denied access to places where they wish to gather information. Supreme Court decisions have denied that the media enjoy special rights in this regard. The U.S. Supreme Court has ruled that neither ordinary citizens nor media personnel have a constitutional right to gather information.[17]

In fact, "the First Amendment does not guarantee the press a constitutional right of special access to information not available to the public generally."[18] This even includes such mundane matters as the addresses of people who have been arrested.[19] The Court rejected the argument that surveillance of the political scene on behalf of the public entitled the press to special rights of access.

Without special access rights, journalists can be barred from many politically crucial events, thus depriving the public of important, albeit sensitive, information. Closed White House and State Department meetings provide examples. The media often are excluded from pretrial hearings and grand jury proceedings that determine the sufficiency of evidence of wrongdoing to justify indictments. Because grand jury proceedings frequently involve high political stakes, participants often leak news about them to newspeople. The press also has no right to attend conferences of the Supreme Court at which the justices reveal why they decided to hear certain cases and refused to hear others. Media people may be barred from attending sessions of legislative bodies closed to the general public. Such sessions ordinarily deal with confidential information that may require protection or with matters that might prove embarrassing to legislators.

Newspeople have no right to be admitted to sites of crimes and disasters when the general public is excluded. Nor do they have the right to visit prisons or to interview and film inmates, even for the purpose of investigating prison conditions and checking out rumors of brutality. In many cases in which access has been denied, the Supreme Court has stressed that reporters could get the information they needed without special access privileges.[20] This may indicate that the Court is willing to grant access in situations in which information about prison conditions is totally lacking. Many of the Supreme Court's decisions in the early 1970s regarding access to information were highly controversial, as shown by 5 to 4 divisions among the nine justices. This clash of views has made media access rights a fluid and exciting area of legal development.

In wartime, military officials often bar news personnel from combat zones. They keep them out by denying transportation to these areas or by keeping invasion plans secret. That was the case during the buildup to the Persian Gulf War in 1990–1991 and during the war itself. Despite press protests and a suit filed by news outlets against President George Bush and the Department of Defense (DOD), the government effectively throttled free access to news. Such news blackouts clearly exemplify denial of access to news without any legal recourse. Following the Gulf War, the DOD issued new regulations to ease media access in similar future situations. Past experience suggests that the regulations will make little difference in practice because of the military's culture of secrecy.

By custom, although not by law, newspeople often receive preferred treatment in gaining entry to public events. Press passes ensure media access to the best observation points for inaugurations of chief executives, space shuttle landings, and political conventions. In many instances the media are admitted to the scene of events, such as accidents and crimes, while the general public is kept out. Access, however, is purely at the discretion of the authorities in charge. It remains moot whether it is legal for police to invite journalists to accompany them and take pictures during a raid.[21]

Access to Government Documents

Government documents are another extremely important source of political information to which access frequently is obstructed. The Freedom of Information Act, signed by President Lyndon B. Johnson on July 4, 1966, and amended in 1974 to make the act more enforceable, ostensibly opened many government files to the news media and the general public.[22] Burdensome application requirements and the costs of duplicating information, however, have limited its usefulness for news personnel. In recent years, the intricacies of scanning computerized records that were programmed in unfamiliar ways have raised additional access hurdles. Nonetheless, the act has led to important disclosures such as CIA involvement in political affairs in Chile and Cuba; illegal financial dealings by members of Congress; and the failure of the government to protect the public from unsafe nuclear reactors, contaminated drinking water, and ineffective drugs. Most reporters, however, are content to cover readily available current news rather than use the Freedom of Information Act to dig into government files to unearth past misdeeds. Only 5 percent of the requests for information filed under the act come from reporters.[23]

The act has also been abused. Organized crime and narcotics traffickers have used it to spot threats to their activities, and business firms have used it to spy on competitors. To cope with these and other abuses, the act has been amended repeatedly. Fees charged to businesses for information have been raised to cover the full costs of inquiries. Fees have been lowered for media enterprises to encourage their search for information. Although most of the changes have garnered widespread approval because they attempted to resolve acute problems, most have also been criticized as either an undue expansion of First Amendment rights or as an unsavory contraction.

General Rules.   Many types of public documents remain unavailable to reporters despite the pervasiveness of freedom of information laws at all levels of government. Most laws provide for access to public records, but various political jurisdictions define *public records* differently. Laws obviously constitute a public record, but are citizens entitled to inspect the minutes of the meetings that preceded passage of a law, or tapes of the proceedings, or exhibits that a legislative committee considered before passing the law? In many states the term *public record* does not include any information about the genesis of laws and regulations.

The computerization of governmental records is raising many new issues about access. The courts have acknowledged that information stored in government computers constitutes a public record, but they have yet to decide definitively what access rights exist. For example, it is unclear whether journalists have the right to ask for specific data within a database, or whether that entails the creation of a new "record" that public agencies are not required to supply. Must government agencies facilitate computer access by installing user-friendly programs? The *Congressional Record,* for example, could not be searched effectively until full text-searching facilities were developed. What about data stored in now obsolete files that current personnel cannot retrieve? It will take many years to find satisfactory answers to such questions and to develop reasonably uniform policies.

Applicants for information often must demonstrate a special need for a particular set of data. A journalist or private citizen cannot go into a record center and request to examine all records on public health matters or public housing or road repairs. Applicants must specify precisely what information they want, which is difficult to do without knowing what is available. Administrators determine how specific the request must be and whether and how applicants must demonstrate that they truly need the information.

A widely used rule of thumb about access to information is that disclosure must be in the public interest and must not do excessive harm. Access should be denied if the harm caused by opening records is greater than the possible benefit. Accordingly, a reporter's request for the records of welfare clients for a story on welfare cheating probably would be denied because it is embarrassing to many people to have others know that they need public assistance. Because there are no precise guidelines for determining what is in the public interest and what degree of harm is excessive, the judgments of public officials who control documents are supreme.

Many state legislatures are unwilling to leave access policies to the discretion of administrative officials. Therefore, they construct detailed lists of the kinds of records that may or may not be disclosed. That approach is unsatisfactory, too, because legislators cannot possibly foresee all types of requests. Release of records may then be forestalled simply because their contents are not mentioned specifically in the legislation.

Certain types of documents are barred routinely from disclosure. For example, examination questions and answers for various tests given by government agencies usually are placed beyond public scrutiny. If they were published, the value of these examinations might be totally destroyed. However, if the fairness and appropriateness of examination questions for public jobs are in doubt, public scrutiny of questions and answers might be beneficial. Favoritism in grading exams of the protégés of the powerful is a common abuse that also is difficult to expose without access to graded exams.

Other data frequently kept from media personnel are business records that could give advantage to competitors, such as bids for government contracts. Because corruption is common in awarding government contracts, reporters often are very interested in what has been bid or what promises have been made in return for contract awards. Without access to the records, investigative reporting of suspected fraud or corruption is impossible. However, secrecy is warranted because publicizing the details of a bid could give an unfair advantage to another firm to underbid the lowest bidder by a few dollars and clinch the contract.

Clearly, some restraints on access are essential to protect individuals and business enterprises, especially now when access to computerized government information can make even the average citizen's life an open book with deleterious consequences for exposed individuals. Yet restraints may make betrayals of the public trust easier. The cloak of secrecy may conceal vast areas of corruption. Finding the right balance between protection of individuals and their business ventures and protection of the interests of the public through media access is an extremely difficult and controversial task.

Historical and National Security Documents. Access to the official and private records of major public officials is limited. They are usually unavailable to the media and the general public until twenty-five years after the death of the public official. The lengthy limit was selected to spare possible embarrassment to people whose private and public lives were entangled with that of the official.[24] Exceptions to the twenty-five-year rule are frequently contested in court, as happened when former president Richard Nixon unsuccessfully sued to recover control of many of his records about the Watergate affair that had been released to the media.

The closure of the private records of public officials is part of the privacy protection afforded to all individuals, but it serves a public purpose as well. For uninhibited discussion in policy making, assurance of confidentiality is essential. Without it, people will posture for an audience rather than freely address themselves to the substance of the issues under consid-

eration. The danger of inhibiting free discussion also explains why deliberations prior to legislative or judicial decisions are generally closed to
public scrutiny.

Documents concerning matters of national security usually cannot be
published. Examples are CIA intelligence data and information about prospective negotiations or sensitive past negotiations. News about specific new
weapons adopted by the United States or stories indicating that security
devices are not operating properly may be restricted also. In some cases,
however, such information is available in open files, in traditional media, or
on the Internet so that it can be pieced together into a coherent story. This
is how a Wisconsin magazine, *The Progressive*, was able to piece together and
publish directions for making a hydrogen bomb. Government efforts to
stop the publication of this kind of story have been unsuccessful in recent
years, except when prohibitions about publication have been a matter of
law. In 1982, for instance, it became a crime to publish the names of covert
intelligence agents, even when they were taken from public documents.

Of course, most instances of security censorship never reach the lawsuit stage, leaving an enormous number of documents concealed from
the public. The National Archives estimated that they have 300 million to
400 million classified documents dating from the World War I era to the
mid-1950s. That is a tiny fraction of the total body of classified information. More than 1 million documents are labeled as *classified* annually.
Many more are placed beyond easy access because they contain information taken from previously classified documents. Added to these staggering statistics at the federal level are massive numbers of documents withheld by state and local officials. The Clinton administration attempted to
unblock the jams in information flow at the federal level by putting the
burden of proof on the government that secrecy was essential, rather than
requiring applicants to prove otherwise. Still, while somewhat eased, the
problems of access to classified documents remain staggering.[25]

The most difficult aspect of security censorship is to determine which
information is truly sensitive and must be protected and which information
should remain open to media personnel and the public. The media and, to
a lesser degree, Congress have been trying to expand the range of information that is made available for publication. The president and executive
agencies, charged with protecting national security, generally have bent
over backward to protect information that might compromise security.

A graphic illustration of this perennial battle is the *Pentagon Papers*
case. Daniel Ellsberg, a former aide to the president's National Security
Council, claimed that foreign policy information contained in a DOD
study of America's gradual entrapment in the Vietnam War had been classified improperly as top secret. Its release, he thought, would turn people

against the war. He copied the information surreptitiously and gave it to prominent newspapers for publication. Because the war was still in progress, the executive branch considered his actions a criminal breach of security and sued Ellsberg and the media that printed the information.

In *New York Times Co. v. United States* (1971), the Supreme Court absolved the media, ruling that the government had been overly cautious in classifying the information as top secret.[26] In the Court's view publication did not harm the country. The government's case against Ellsberg for leaking the information was dismissed also because prosecutors had collected evidence through illegal means. Although the case cleared Ellsberg and the media of the specific charges brought against them, it left the government's contention unchallenged that officials may be prosecuted when they jeopardize national security by disclosing classified information to the press. Accordingly, Samuel Loring Morison, a naval intelligence analyst, was convicted in 1985 on espionage charges for providing a British military magazine with intelligence satellite photographs.[27]

The Supreme Court decision in the *Pentagon Papers* case and subsequent lower court rulings did not end the public controversy. Analysts still disagree about whether the disclosures from the *Pentagon Papers* damaged national security of the United States. Those who concur with the Court point out that much of the information released had been available already. Dissenters counter that the information had never been compiled in a single document and published in prominent sources such as the *New York Times* and the *Washington Post*. They also refer to the dismay expressed by many European leaders about spotlighting events that they had deemed confidential.

Prior to the Nixon years, if a government agency decided that certain information needed to be kept from the media, the courts usually went along with the decision on the assumption that the agencies charged with guarding national security are infinitely better qualified to assess such matters than are judges whose training is narrowly legal. This has changed. Wise decisions about disclosure of national security information are particularly difficult because both the clamor of the media to obtain access and the government's contention that the information requires protection are often self-serving. What is dubbed "the public interest" may be simply the reporters' interest in furthering their careers, or the publishers' interest in making money, or the government's interest in shielding itself from embarrassment.

At times, security issues, such as information about hostage situations, are resolved through informal cooperation between the government and the media or through self-censorship. For instance, news organizations worldwide voluntarily withheld news for twenty days about an Associated Press reporter who had been kidnapped in Somalia. The story was published only after the reporter's release.[28] In a similar way, media have refrained from pro-

"WELL IF YOU ASK ME, THE FIRST AMENDMENT SHOULD ONLY PROTECT UNCONTROVERSIAL EXPRESSION."

Reprinted with special permission of King Features Syndicate.

viding the public with details in a number of kidnapping incidents when news stories could have jeopardized delicate negotiations between kidnappers and the would-be rescuers of the victims. Information about these instances is hard to obtain because neither the media nor the government want to publicize their collaborative efforts to suppress news. If the information leaks out, it is often denied by all the collaborators.

Executive Privilege. The doctrine of executive privilege is deeply intertwined with the question of the limits of secrecy. Chief executives have the right to conceal information that they consider sensitive. This privilege extends to all of their personal communications to their staffs about public matters. Prior to the Nixon years the courts usually upheld executive privilege, but decisions since then suggest that the scope of the privilege is waning.

Silence by various government departments and agencies also sharply restricts political news available to the media. Undisclosed information frequently concerns failures, incidents of malfeasance, malfunctions, or government waste. Agencies guard this type of news zealously because disclosure might harm the agency or its key personnel. Chief executives at all levels of government often issue directives restraining top officials from talking freely to journalists. President Reagan even ordered lie detector tests for officials to check compliance with disclosure rules but the directive was later rescinded. Although not usually enforceable, directives that muzzle public officials tend to reduce the flow of information to the press and the public.

Except for the ever-present opportunity to get information through leaks, reporters find it difficult to penetrate the walls of silence erected by publicity-shy agencies. It is far easier to rely on press handouts or publicity releases supplied by the agency or on secondary reports from agency personnel. Handout information, however, usually reflects the sources' sense, rather than the reporters', of what is news.[29]

Private Industry Documents

Although the problem of government secrecy as a restraint on information collection is formidable, it is small compared with the problem of access to news stories covering the private sector of society. Numerous enterprises whose operations affect the lives of millions of Americans as much as or more than many government agencies shroud their operations in secrecy. If asbestos companies or major tobacco companies want to exclude reporters from access to information about their business practices, they can do so with impunity. So can drug companies, repair shops, or housing contractors. Fear that a company may sue a media organization for millions of dollars is also a powerful deterrent to airing questionable business practices. Even *60 Minutes,* renowned for its fearless investigative reports, has occasionally caved in to such pressure. That happened in 1995, when an interview with a tobacco industry whistle blower was temporarily shelved because exceptionally high legal expenses loomed.[30]

The Freedom of Information Act does not cover unpublished records of private businesses, except for the reports made to the government about sales or inventory figures or customer lists. As noted earlier, many of these reports are withheld from the public on the ground that business cannot thrive if its operational data are made available to its competitors. Moreover, the chances that withheld information will be disclosed through leaks are infinitely less in business than in government. Employees can be pledged to secrecy as a condition of employment and summarily dismissed if they break their vow.

Individual Rights Versus the Public's Right to Know

Thus far we have mainly considered barriers to the free flow of information imposed by the mass media to protect editorial freedom or by government or industry to shield potentially sensitive information. Next we will discuss barriers to circulation of information imposed by individuals or on behalf of individuals for the purpose of protecting the right to privacy, the right to an unprejudiced trial, the right to gather information freely, and the right to a good reputation.

Privacy Protection

How much may the media publish about the private affairs of people in public and private life without infringing on the constitutionally protected right of privacy? How much is excluded from public scrutiny because of privacy rights? The answers depend on the status of the people involved. Private individuals enjoy broad, though shrinking, protections from publicity; people who have become public figures because their lives are of interest to the public or because they are public officials do not enjoy such protections.

In general, state and federal courts have been fairly lenient in permitting the media to cover details about the personal affairs of people whose lives have become matters of public record. The right to publish has been upheld more often than the right to privacy. This trend is epitomized by a 1975 Georgia case involving a young woman who had been raped and murdered. To protect their privacy, the family wanted to keep the victim's name out of stories discussing the crime. Nonetheless, the news media published the victim's name and gruesome details of the crime. The family sued for invasion of privacy, claiming that there was absolutely no need to disclose the name and that Georgia law prohibited the release of the names of rape victims. The U.S. Supreme Court disagreed and overturned the Georgia law. It held that crime was a matter of public record, making the facts surrounding it publishable despite protests by victims and their families.[31]

Circumstances may turn private individuals into public figures. This happened to Oliver Sipple, a young man in a crowd of people watching a public appearance by President Ford. Sipple prevented an assassination attempt on the president by grabbing the would-be assassin's gun. When newspeople checked his background they discovered that he was homosexual and included this information in subsequent stories. Sipple brought suit for invasion of privacy, but the courts denied his claim, saying that he had forfeited his right to privacy. By seizing the gun, he had become an "involuntary public figure." Individuals also may lose their right to privacy when they grant interviews to reporters. Reporters are free to round the story out with "newsworthy" observations that were not part of the interview. Reporters are also free to publish those facts that were told to them in confidence, though they usually honor their pledge of keeping an interviewee's name confidential.[32] If reporters, without malice, misrepresent some of the facts, this, too, is tolerated. The rationale is that the public is entitled to a full story, if it gets any story at all, and that reporting should not be unduly inhibited by fears of privacy invasion suits.

Many privacy invasion cases involve unauthorized photographs of people in public life. Jacqueline Kennedy Onassis, the widow of President John F. Kennedy, sued one particularly obnoxious photographer for taking photographs of her in her private life. The court ruled that even though she was no longer the first lady, she remained a public figure. Therefore, pictures could be taken and printed without her consent. The court, however, ordered the photographer to stop harassing her.[33] The courts have also permitted reporters to keep the homes of relatives of murder suspects under photographic surveillance and to film police officers during compromising sting operations.

To strengthen privacy protection, the courts in recent years have permitted subjects of unsolicited investigative reports to use trespass laws to stop the media. An example is the trespassing judgment won by the owners of a fashionable New York restaurant against CBS after reporters had entered the premises and filmed a story showing violations of the city's health code.[34] The courts also have been increasingly willing to protect people against willful inflictions of emotional pain by news media. However, the Supreme Court ruled unanimously in 1988 that the work of satirists and cartoonists enjoyed full First Amendment protection.[35] It denied a plea for privacy protection and for compensation for emotional injury inflicted by a salacious attack on Rev. Jerry Falwell against the publisher of *Hustler* magazine.

Because relatively few cases of invasion of privacy are taken to the courts for decision, privacy protection rests primarily on the sensitivity of the news media. In recent years, it has not been finely honed. Even mainstream newspapers now feature columns devoted to celebrity gossip, and tabloid papers and television shows of the same genre revel in this type of journalism. When Rev. Jesse Jackson learned in 2001 about an impending story about a daughter that he had fathered out of wedlock, he knew that efforts to protect his privacy would be futile. Therefore, he chose to announce the story himself. In the current news climate it has become impossible to protect newsworthy individuals from the "feeding frenzy" of print and electronic tabloid journalists. Once the proverbial cat is out of the bag, all join the chase, including serious news professionals who do not want to ignore stories that draw large audiences.[36] Efforts by several states to prohibit privacy invasion when the news lacks "social value" are currently under judicial scrutiny to determine whether they violate the First Amendment.[37]

Fair Trial and the Gag Rule

The courts favor a broad scope of disclosure for most people in public life, but they insist on a limited scope of disclosure in their own bailiwick. The courts have guarded the right of accused persons to be protected zealously against publicity that might influence judge and jury and harm their cases. This has been true even though scientific evidence demonstrating that media publicity actually influences the parties to a trial is scant and contradictory.[38]

The stern posture of the courts in censoring pretrial publicity is weakening, however. In 1983 two Supreme Court justices refused to block a nationwide television broadcast about a sensational murder case scheduled for trial three weeks later. The trial involved seven white New Orleans police officers accused of the revenge slaying of four African American men suspected of participating in the murder of a white police officer. In the same vein, a federal court refused to prevent television stations from showing tapes of a cocaine transaction incriminating John DeLorean, a well-known automobile maker and jet-set celebrity. DeLorean's attorneys had argued that the pretrial publicity would make it impossible to impanel an impartial jury. In another case the courts ruled that incriminating tapes used in a corruption trial of several members of Congress could be shown publicly, even though some of the defendants had not been tried as yet and the convicted defendants were appealing the case.[39] When prominent national political figures have asked to have their trials moved out of Washington because of prejudicial pretrial publicity, their requests almost invariably have been refused.[40] However, Timothy McVeigh's lawyers were able to have his 1997 trial moved away from Oklahoma City, the scene of his deadly bomb attack, when publicity about the trial was overwhelming.

The question of the permissible scope of media coverage of court cases was brought to wide public attention by two murder cases, *Shepherd v. Florida* (1951) and *Sheppard v. Maxwell* (1966).[41] In these cases the Court held that the defendants, convicted of murder, had not had a fair trial because of widespread media publicity. As Justices Robert H. Jackson and Felix Frankfurter stated in *Shepherd v. Florida,* "The trial was but a legal gesture to register a verdict already dictated by the press and the public opinion [it] generated."[42] The convictions therefore were overturned.

Judges have the right to prohibit the mass media from covering some or all of a court case before and during a trial, even when the public is allowed to attend courtroom sessions. *Gag orders* interfere with the media's ability to report on the fairness of judicial proceedings. They also run counter to the general reluctance of American courts to condone prior censorship. Nonetheless, the courts have upheld gag laws as a necessary protection for accused persons. As discussed in Chapter 10, judges may make rules restraining filmed coverage or may bar it completely without presenting evidence that the information covered by the gag order would impede a fair trial. Gag orders may extend even to judges' rulings that tell the media to refrain from covering a case. Thus the fact of judicial suppression of information may itself be hidden.

Numerous reporters have gone to jail and paid fines rather than obey gag rules because they felt that the courts were overly protective of the rights of criminal suspects and insufficiently concerned with the public's right to know. A 1976 decision, *Nebraska Press Association v. Stuart,* partly supports the reporters' views.[43] In that case the Supreme Court reversed a gag order in a murder trial. The Court declared that careless reporting that interferes with the rights of defendants should be forestalled by judicial maneuvers short of gag laws. For instance, trials can be moved to different jurisdictions if there has been excessive local publicity. Suits also can be brought against media enterprises or individual reporters who act irresponsibly, such as publicizing testimony from closed sessions of the courts, taking unauthorized pictures, or bribing court personnel to leak trial testimony.

The policy on gag laws is still unclear, however. Some lower courts have failed to comply with Supreme Court directives or have evaded the spirit of decisions. For example, instead of gagging the press, judges have placed gags on all the principals in a case, including the plaintiffs and defendants, their lawyers, and the jury, to prohibit them from talking about the case, particularly to members of the press. In an increasing number of cases, judges have barred access to information by closing courtrooms to all observers during pretrial proceedings as well as trials. However, this has not stopped legal personnel, including prosecutors, from leaking information to the press when that seems advantageous.

During the 1980s the Supreme Court struck down a number of these restrictions or limited their use by specifying the circumstances under which media access may be denied. In *Richmond Newspapers v. Virginia* (1980), the Court ruled that the public and the press had an almost absolute right to attend criminal trials.[44] In the same vein, the justices declared in 1984 that neither newspeople nor the public may be barred from observing jury selection, except in unusual circumstances.[45] The Supreme Court appears to be moving closer to the notion that the public's access to judicial proceedings is part of the First Amendment rights guaranteed by the Constitution. However, a change in direction is possible following adverse public reaction to televising the 1995 murder trial of O. J. Simpson as if it were a soap opera serial. In fact, during the trial, network blow-by-blow coverage averaged 50 percent more time than coverage given to President Clinton. Almost two-thirds of the audience watched on a daily basis, but complained nonetheless that "the trial of the century" was covered excessively.

Shield Laws

Digging into the affairs of public officials and other prominent citizens or exposing the activities of criminals or dissidents often requires winning the confidence of informants with promises to conceal their identities. Newspeople contend that they are hampered in their research if a court or legislative body has the right to know the identity of their sources, to examine unpublished bits of information, and to issue subpoenas for them. If reporters disclose such information, they break their word. Their sources are likely to dry up, whether these sources are public officials who have leaked confidential information or underworld informers. This is why reporters want laws to shield them from subpoenas.

However, failure to disclose information may allow criminals to go unpunished and innocent victims to be denied justice. Law enforcement agencies may find it difficult to penetrate dissident and terrorist groups. Shield laws are needed also to protect the physical safety of sources who disclose the activities of organized criminals or terrorists. This is why media organizations at times agree to comply with subpoenas fully or partially. For instance, CBS agreed to surrender portions of unused filmed scenes from the hijacking of a TWA airliner that it deemed relevant for the prosecution of the hijackers.[46] In 1992 seven local television stations, the *Los Angeles Times,* and a *New York Times* photographer received federal grand jury subpoenas to produce unpublished pictures of crimes committed during the Los Angeles riots. They were expected to refuse; however, they were willing to surrender pictures that had been published already and did so.[47] A 1999 survey of four hundred news organizations by the Reporters Committee for Freedom of the Press showed that 36 percent of the print media and 77 percent of the broadcast media had received one or more subpoenas.[48]

The Supreme Court has ruled that newspeople generally do not have a common law right to protect their sources in the face of a subpoena. Nor may they shield records or editorial deliberations from judicial scrutiny if these records are needed to prove deliberate libel, unless the needed information is available from unshielded sources.[49] However, more than half of the states have passed shield laws to protect reporters from forced testimony. Shield laws give journalists most of the rights enjoyed by lawyers, doctors, and clergy to shield their sources' identity and information. Shield laws also may bar searches of news offices to discover leads to crimes.

Shield laws do not ensure absolute protection. For example, when the right of reporters to withhold the names of their sources clashes with the right of other individuals to conduct a lawsuit involving serious matters (such as gathering evidence for a murder or conspiracy trial or a libel suit), state shield laws and common law protections must yield. In 1983 the Maryland Supreme Court ruled that Loretta Tofani, a *Washington Post* reporter, had to testify about prisoners in a suburban jail who had told her about committing rape and being rape victims. The reporter's articles had won a Pulitzer Prize.[50] Likewise, CBS News was required to give Gen. William Westmoreland the text of its in-house investigation of a 1982 television documentary that allegedly had libeled him. The documentary on the Vietnam War had charged Westmoreland with falsifying enemy troop figures. In his libel suit, Westmoreland contended that the producers of the documentary had deliberately omitted information that exonerated him.[51]

Some journalists advocate a federal shield law to protect all newspeople throughout the country and to reduce the costs of litigation when they resist forced disclosure. Others, fearing that such a law would provide conditional shielding only, prefer to do without shield laws of any kind; they contend that the First Amendment constitutes an absolute shield. These differences of opinion have taken steam out of the pressure for a federal shield law. Members of the judiciary also deny that shield laws are needed, but for different reasons. In the words of Justice Byron R. White, "From the beginning of our country, the press has operated without constitutional protection for press informants and the press has flourished." Hence the absence of shield laws has "not been a serious obstacle to either the development or retention of confidential news sources by the press."[52]

Libel Laws

Libel laws are designed to provide redress when a person's reputation has been tarnished unjustly by published information. To win a libel suit, a plaintiff must prove that the defendant's negligence or recklessness led to the publishing of information that exposed the plaintiff to hatred, ridicule, or contempt. For years, libel suits, even when they were lost in court, had a dampening effect on investigative reporting. That changed substantially in 1964 for cases involving public officials. The police chief of Montgomery, Alabama, brought an action for libel because an advertisement in the *New York Times* had charged him with mishandling civil rights demonstrations. The Supreme Court absolved the newspaper, ruling in *New York Times v. Sullivan* that a public official who claims libel must be able to show that the libelous information was published "with knowledge that it was false or with reckless disregard of whether it was false or not."[53] The *Sullivan rule* has made it very difficult for public officials to bring suit for libelous statements made about them. Malicious intent and extraordinary carelessness are hard to prove, especially because the courts give the media the benefit of the doubt. By the same token, the Sullivan rule has made it much easier for media to publish adverse information about public officials without extensive checking of the accuracy of the information prior to its publication.

The best protection for public figures from unscrupulous exposure by the media comes from the informal and formal codes of ethics by which most journalists generally abide. The increasing number of suits by public figures against media people also have become a damper on careless reporting because these suits are costly in time and money, even when the media are exonerated, which happens nearly half the time. The average initial awards in the ten to twenty cases that go to trial each year total more than $5 million. These awards are often sharply reduced if the case is appealed. Nonetheless, financially weak institutions cannot afford to risk multi–million-dollar judgments against them that might force them out of business.[54]

Since its 1974 decision in *Gertz v. Robert Welch,* the Supreme Court has narrowed the "public figure" category.[55] In that case the Court held that a person who had not deliberately sought publicity would be deemed a public figure only in exceptional—as yet unspecified—circumstances. Therefore, a prominent lawyer, whose name had been widely reported in the news, was not a public figure and could sue for libel.[56]

The battle between freedom of the press and the right of individuals to be protected from harmful publicity is full of confusing developments. The courts have pulled back from the position that individual rights are largely subordinate to press freedom, except for the right to a fair trial. They have done so by distinguishing the rights of private individuals from those of public figures and by construing the category of public figures more narrowly. This leaves private individuals with substantial rights to bar the media from publishing potentially libelous or embarrassing facts, so long as those facts are not matters of public record. It remains unclear whether libel suits may be brought to challenge expressions of demonstrably false opinions.[57] The emergence of the Internet has raised several new issues in libel law that remain to be settled. Most important, who bears responsibility for publishing libels? Early decisions suggest that message carriers, such as America On Line (AOL) or Netscape, are not responsible for screening content for libels and other illegal content such as foul language or obscenity.

Other Restrictions on Publication

As discussed in Chapter 1, all governments prohibit the publication of certain information on the ground that the public interest would be harmed. The United States is no exception. Censorship is most prevalent

Three Cheers for Chaos on the Internet

June 12, 1996, was a day of victory for the First Amendment. A three-judge panel in Philadelphia, home of the Liberty Bell, extended full First Amendment protections to the Internet. The Communications Decency Act of 1996 (CDA), designed to censor Internet content to protect minors from indecent messages, was declared unconstitutional. Although supporters hailed the decision as "a benchmark, establishing a First Amendment for the 21st century," opponents complained that a "judicial elite is undermining democratic attempts to address pressing social problems . . ." The Supreme Court was accused of "purposely disarming the Congress in the most important conflicts of our time."[1]

Excerpts from the Opinions

U.S. Circuit Court of Appeals "[T]he Internet may fairly be regarded as a never-ending world-wide conversation. The Government may not, through the C.D.A., interrupt that conversation. As the most participatory form of mass speech yet developed, the Internet deserves the highest protection from government intrusion.

True it is that many find some of the speech on the Internet to be offensive, and amid the din of cyberspace many hear discordant voices that they regard as indecent. The absence of government regulation of Internet content has unquestionably produced a kind of chaos. . . . The strength of the Internet is that chaos. . . the strength of our liberty depends upon the chaos and cacophony of the unfettered speech the First Amendment protects."[2]

U.S. Supreme Court "It is true that we have repeatedly recognized the governmental interest in protecting children from harmful materials. But that interest does not justify an unnecessarily broad suppression of speech addressed to adults. As we have explained, the Government may not 'reduc[e] the adult population . . . to . . . only what is fit for children.' '[R]egardless of the strength of the government's interest' in protecting children, '[t]he level of discourse reaching a mailbox simply cannot be limited to that which would be suitable for a sandbox.'

[T]he Government asserts that in addition to its interest in protecting children its '[e]qually significant' interest in fostering the growth of the Internet provides an independent basis for upholding the constitutionality of the C.D.A. The Government apparently assumes that the unregulated availability of 'indecent' and 'patently offensive' material on the Internet is driving countless citizens away from the medium because of the risk of exposing themselves or their children to harmful material.

We find this argument singularly unpersuasive. The dramatic expansion of this new market place of ideas contradicts the factual basis of this contention. The record demonstrates that the growth of the Internet has been and continues to be phenomenal. As a matter of constitutional tradition, in the absence of evidence to the contrary, we presume that governmental regulation of the content of speech is more likely to interfere with the free exchange of ideas than to encourage it. The interest in encouraging freedom of expression in a democratic society outweighs any theoretical but unproven benefit of censorship."[3]

1. John M. Broder, "Clinton Readies New Approach to Smut," *New York Times,* June 27, 1997.
2. Judge Stewart Dalzell in *Reno v. American Civil Liberties Union,* 25 Media L. Rep, 1833 (1996).
3. Justice John Paul Stevens in *Reno v. American Civil Liberties Union,* 521 U.S. 844 (1997).

in matters of national security involving external dangers, national security involving internal dangers, and obscenity. In each category there is general agreement that certain types of information should not be publicized. There is very little agreement, however, about where the line ought to be drawn between permitted and prohibited types of material. We have already discussed the controversy surrounding the release of the *Pentagon Papers* as well as the government's efforts to prohibit publication of a magazine article detailing, on the basis of available but dispersed information, how a hydrogen bomb might be manufactured. Additional examples involving external security will be presented in Chapter 11.

Internal security news primarily entails investigations of allegedly subversive groups and reports on civil disturbances. Several relevant cases are discussed in Chapter 5. Such news also involves media portrayal of asocial behavior that might lead to imitation. Various attempts to limit the portrayals of crime and violence, either in general or on programs to which children have access, are examples. They are discussed in Chapter 7.

Closely related to restraints on the depiction of crime and violence are restraints on publication of indecent and obscene materials and broadcasts that include offensive language or that portray sexual matters or human excretion. Censorship advocates fear that such broadcasts may corrupt members of the audience, particularly children, and lead to imitation of undesirable behavior. They contend that publication of indecent and obscene materials, particularly in visual form, offends community standards and therefore should be prohibited by law. This argument rests on the notion that the public should have the right to prohibit the dissemination of material that offends the sense of propriety of local citizen groups.

Despite the huge popularity of pornography, as shown by the millions of citizens who buy pornographic magazines, pay for pornographic movies and stage shows, rent pornographic videos, and visit pornography sites on the Internet, laws in many places bar free access to such information. FCC rules require that indecent programming be featured only between midnight and 6:00 a.m., when children are unlikely to be watching television. Obscene programming is barred at all times. Indecent material has been defined by the FCC as "material that depicts or describes, in terms patently offensive by contemporary community standards for the broadcast medium, sexual or excretory activities or organs." Obscenity has been defined by the Supreme Court as "something that, taken as a whole, appeals to the prurient interest; that depicts or describes in a patently offensive way sexual conduct; and that lacks serious artistic, political and scientific value."[58] Congress has repeatedly tried to pass laws that would make it difficult for children and adolescents to view pornography. The 1996 Communications Decency Act and the 2000 Children's Internet Protection Act are examples. Ultimately, the Supreme Court declares most such measures unconstitutional.[59]

Another example of protective censorship is the ban since 1971 on cigarette advertising on radio and television. It is designed to protect susceptible individuals from being lured into smoking by seductive advertisements. Pressures for additional areas of protective censorship have been considerable and range from pleas to stop liquor, sugared cereal, and casino gambling advertisements to requests to bar information dealing with abortion or drug addiction. Legislatures and courts have rejected most of them except when advertising on children's programs was involved.[60]

So-called hate broadcasters also remain a gray area in broadcast law, which has achieved new prominence because hate messages abound on the Internet. Indeed, the Internet had more than two thousand racial hate Web sites at the end of the year 2000.[61] Contrary to the expressed public policy of the nation, many small over-the-air and cable stations or individual programs routinely attack racial, ethnic, and religious groups. As with broadcasts using obscene language, these attacks violate the sense of propriety of many citizens. Nevertheless, the FCC has been reluctant to withhold licenses from the offending parties because genuine freedom of expression includes "freedom for the thought we hate," as Supreme Court Justice Oliver Wendell Holmes said long ago. Although formal restraints remain few, informal restraints have mushroomed. Television and radio stations have disciplined or dismissed reporters and commentators who made comments offensive to groups such as African Americans, women, and homosexuals.

Summary

In a democratic society, citizens have the right and civic duty to inform themselves and to express their views publicly. The press, as the eyes and ears of the public, shares these rights and must be protected against restraints that could interfere with its ability to gather information and disseminate it freely. In this chapter we have seen how these important basic principles have been adapted to meet the realities of political life in the United States. Despite legislation such as the Freedom of Information Act of 1966, a great deal of information about government activities remains unpublished. Either it has been classified as secret for security reasons or it has not been released to the public because it could embarrass individuals or lead to undesirable business practices. The public and press also are excluded from many executive sessions of legislatures, grand jury sessions, pretrial proceedings in the courts, and other official meetings if the participants so desire.

Nearly all of these exclusions have been challenged in the courts because they constitute restrictions on the right of access to information that may deserve publication. The courts have ruled that most of them are compatible with constitutional guarantees of free speech and press. They also have ruled, for the most part, that news professionals enjoy neither greater rights of access to information than does the general public nor, in the absence of shield laws, greater freedom to protect their access to information by refusal to disclose their sources.

The right to publish information is also limited. Here the public is most seriously restricted because newspeople claim the exclusive right to determine what to publicize and what to omit. The power of print media to exclude stories is nearly absolute, except for the presence of social pressures to report issues that are clearly vital to the public. Under current rules and regulations television must grant equal access to the air to political candidates for the same office. The fairness rule requiring exposure of opposition views and the right of rebuttal are in limbo. Either death is in the cards or a reincarnation in the form of legislation.

Even when access to a media forum is ensured, the right to publish is not absolute. News has been suppressed because of public policy considerations, such as the need to safeguard external and internal security and the need to protect the moral standards of the community. The scope of permissible censorship has been the subject of countless inconclusive debates and conflicting decisions by the courts in a perennial contest between legislators eager to censor objectionable messages and judges equally eager to wave the banner of First Amendment rights.

The right to publish also conflicts on many occasions with the rights of individuals to enjoy their privacy, to be protected from disclosure of damaging information, true or false, and to be safe from publicity that might interfere with a fair trial. The courts have been the main forum for weighing these conflicting claims, and the scales have tipped erratically from case to case. Two trends stand out from the haze of legal battles: The right to a fair trial generally wins out over the freedom to publish, and private individuals enjoy far greater protection from publicity than do people in public life. Shifting definitions of what turns a private person into a public person have blurred this distinction, however.

When one looks at the massive restraints on the rights of access to information, the rights of access to publication channels, and the right to publish information freely, one may feel deep concern about freedom of information. Is there cause for worry? Taking a bright view, one can point out, as Justice White did in a 1972 case, "the press has flourished. The existing constitutional rules have not been a serious obstacle" stopping the press from investigating wrongdoing.[62] The press as watchdog may be chilled by legal restraints, but it is not frozen into inaction. From the perspective of champions of First Amendment rights, this may be small comfort. Many current political trends, including pressures by private organizations to enforce the norms of "political correctness," point toward greater restraints and greater public tolerance for restraints, especially when social and national security are involved. Constant vigilance is the price that will have to be paid to preserve the heritage of freedom of thought and expression.

Notes

1. Freedom House, "Press Freedom Survey 2001," www.freedomhouse.org/.
2. Robert F. Copple, "The Dynamics of Expression under the State Constitution," *Journalism Quarterly* 64 (spring 1987): 106–113.
3. For an analysis of how well these rights have been used, see Doris A. Graber, "Press Freedom and the General Welfare," *Political Science Quarterly* 101 (summer 1986): 257–275.
4. Justice Potter Stewart in *New York Times v. United States,* 403 U.S. 713 (1971).
5. Jerome Barron, *Freedom of the Press for Whom? The Right of Access to the Mass Media* (Bloomington: Indiana University Press, 1973).
6. 418 U.S. 241 (1974).
7. For a full discussion of the case, see Fred W. Friendly, *The Good Guys, the Bad Guys, and the First Amendment: Free Speech vs. Fairness in Broadcasting* (New York: Random House, 1977), 192–198.
8. *Arkansas Educational Television Commission v. Forbes,* 523 U.S. 666 (1998).
9. Stephen Labaton, "Court Rejects F.C.C. Mandate to Broadcast Political Replies," *New York Times,* Oct. 12, 2000.
10. Pew Research Center for the People and the Press, "Self Censorship: How Often and Why?" http://www.people-press.org/jour00rpt.htm, 1999.
11. 395 U.S. 367 (1969).
12. Friendly, *The Good Guys,* 32–42.
13. *Muir v. Alabama Educational Television Commission,* 688 F.2d 1033 (5th Cir. 1982). First Amendment problems encountered when governments own media are discussed by William Hanks and Lemuel Schofield, "Limitations on the State as Editor in State-Owned Broadcast Stations," *Journalism Quarterly* 63 (winter 1986): 797–801. The right of public broadcasters to editorialize was upheld in *League of Women Voters v. FCC,* 731 F.2d 995 (D.C. Cir. 1984).
14. "AIDS Panel Delayed News of Treatment," *New York Times,* Nov. 14, 1990.
15. *FCC v. WNCN Listeners Guild,* 450 U.S. 582 (1981).
16. W. Lance Bennett, Lynne A. Gressett, and William Haltom, "Repairing the News: A Case Study of the News Paradigm," *Journal of Communication* 35 (spring 1985): 50–68.
17. *Zemel v. Rusk,* 381 U.S. 1 (1965).
18. *Branzburg v. Hayes,* 408 U.S. 665 (1972).
19. *Los Angeles Police Department v. United Reporting Publishing Corporation,* 528 U.S. 32 (1999).
20. See, for instance, *Pell v. Procunier,* 417 U.S. 817 (1974); *Saxbe v. Washington Post Co.,* 417 U.S. 843 (1974); and *Houchins v. KQED,* 438 U.S. 1 (1978).
21. *Wilson v. Layne,* 526 U.S. 603 (1999).
22. The act was an amendment to the 1946 Administrative Procedure Act—5 U.S.C.A. 1002 (1946)—which provided that official records should be open to people who could demonstrate a "need to know" except for "information held confidential for good cause found" (Sec. 22). The 1966 amendment stated that disclosure should be the general rule, rather than the exception, with the burden on government to justify the withholding of a document (5 U.S.C.A. Sec. 552 and Supp. 1, February 1975).

23. Ken Armstrong, "The Trickle of Information Act Is Closer to the Truth," *Chicago Tribune,* July 4, 1997. Suits have mushroomed as have damage awards and lawyers' fees.
24. Douglas Jehl, "Clinton Revamps Policy on Secrecy of U.S. Documents," *New York Times,* April 18, 1995.
25. Neil A. Lewis, "New Policy on Declassifying Secrets Is Debated," *New York Times,* Jan. 4, 1994.
26. 403 U.S. 713 (1971).
27. *United States v. Morison,* 844 F.2d 1057 (4th Cir.), *cert. denied,* 488 U.S. 908 (1988).
28. William Glaberson, "Somali Kidnapping: Should Press Be Mum?" *New York Times,* July 12, 1994.
29. Doris A. Graber, *Public Sector Communication: How Organizations Manage Information* (Washington, D.C.: CQ Press, 1992), 49–61.
30. William Glaberson, "'Sixty Minutes' Case Illustrates a Trend Born of Corporate Pressure, Some Analysts Say," *New York Times,* Nov. 17, 1995.
31. *Cox Broadcasting Corp. v. Cohn,* 420 U.S. 469 (1975).
32. *Cohen v. Cowles Media Co.,* 501 U.S. 663 (1991).
33. *Gallella v. Onassis,* 487 F.2d 986 (2d Cir. 1973).
34. *Le Mistral Inc. v. Columbia Broadcasting System,* 402 N.Y.S.2d 815 (1978).
35. *Hustler v. Falwell,* 485 U.S. 46 (1988). See also Robert E. Drechsel, "Mass Media Liability for Intentionally Inflicted Emotional Distress," *Journalism Quarterly* 62 (spring 1985): 95–99.
36. Larry J. Sabato, *Feeding Frenzy: Attack Journalism and American Politics* (New York: Free Press, 2000).
37. Linda Greenhouse, "National Enquirer Forces Trial on Invasion-of-Privacy Issue," *New York Times,* Dec. 5, 1995.
38. Although judges often command jurors to strike improper information presented in court from their memory, they disclaim the ability to wipe out media information that jury members might have received outside the courtroom.
39. For examples of the court's reasoning, see *U.S. v. Alexandro,* 459 U.S. 835 (1982); *U.S. v. Jannotti,* 457 U.S. 1106 (1982).
40. An example is Michael K. Deaver, a Reagan White House aide indicted for perjury. In his request for a change of venue, he presented the court with 471 hostile news clips from Washington, D.C., papers.
41. 341 U.S. 50 (1951) and 384 U.S. 333 (1966).
42. 341 U.S. 50 (1951), at 69.
43. 427 U.S. 539 (1976).
44. 448 U.S. 555 (1980).
45. *Press-Enterprise v. Riverside County Superior Court,* 464 U.S. 501 (1984). The controversy arose because the Riverside County, California, Superior Court closed jury selection in a rape and murder case. The Press–Enterprise Company of Riverside sued to gain access to the court proceeding and to the relevant transcripts.
46. Alex S. Jones, "CBS Compromises on Subpoena for Videotapes of Hostage Crisis," *New York Times,* July 27, 1985.
47. "Tapes and Photos of Riots Are Focus of Legal Struggle," *New York Times,* May 22, 1992.
48. Reporters Committee for Freedom of the Press, "Agents of Discovery," 2001, http://www.rcfp.org/agents/

49. *Anthony Herbert v. Barry Lando and the Columbia Broadcasting System Inc.*, 441 U.S. 153 (1979).
50. *Tofani v. State of Maryland*, 297 Md. 165 (1983).
51. "Westmoreland/CBS Controversy," *Historic Documents of 1983* (Washington, D.C.: Congressional Quarterly, 1984), 401–412. See also *Westmoreland v. CBS, Inc.*, 596 F. Supp. 7170 (S.D.N.Y. 1984).
52. *Branzburg v. Hayes*, at 699.
53. 376 U.S. 254, at 279–280 (1964).
54. Libel Defense Resource Center, "Press Release, Feb. 26, 2001," http://www.ldrc.com/damages01.html.
55. 418 U.S. 323 (1974).
56. *Time Inc. v. Firestone*, 424 U.S. 448 (1976); *Hutchinson v. Proxmire*, 443 U.S. 111 (1979); *Wolston v. Reader's Digest*, 443 U.S. 157 (1979).
57. Hughes, "Rationalizing Libel Law"; Linda Greenhouse, "Ruling in Libel Case, High Court Says Some Opinion Isn't Protected," *New York Times*, June 22, 1990.
58. *Miller v. California*, 413 U.S. 5, at 15 (1973). Definition quoted in Tim Jones, "Broadcasters Get Long-Awaited Indecency Guidelines," *Chicago Tribune*, April 7, 2001.
59. See, for example, *Reno v. American Civil Liberties Union*, 521 U.S. 844 (1997). For an editorial opinion about such censorship laws see "Congress Quietly Censors the Web," *Chicago Tribune*, Dec. 23, 2000.
60. *Greater New Orleans Broadcasting Association v. U.S.*, 527 U.S. 173 (1999); *44 Liquormart, Inc. v. Rhode Island*, 517 U.S. 484 (1996).
61. Lisa Guernsey, "Mainstream Sites Serve as Portals to Hate," *New York Times*, Nov. 30, 2000.
62. *Branzburg v. Hayes*, at 699.

Readings

Carter, T. Barton, Marc A. Franklin, and Jay B. Wright. *The First Amendment and the Fourth Estate: The Law of Mass Media*. 8th ed. Westbury, N.Y.: Foundation Press, 2000.

Godwin, Mike. *Cyber Rights: Defending Free Speech in the Digital Age*. New York: Times Books, 1998.

Heins, Marjorie. *Not in Front of the Children: Indecency, Censorship, and the Innocence of Youth*. New York: Hill and Wang, 2001.

Hemmer, Joseph J. *Communication Law: The Supreme Court and the First Amendment*. Lanham, Md.: Austin and Winfield, 2000.

Martin, Shannon E. *Bits, Bytes, and Big Brother: Federal Information Control in the Technological Age*. Westport, Conn.: Praeger, 1995.

Teeter, Dwight L., and Don R. LeDuc. *Law of Mass Communications: Freedom and Control of Print and Broadcast Media*. 8th ed. Westbury, N.Y.: Foundation Press, 1995.

Tillinghast, Charles H. *American Broadcast Regulation and the First Amendment*. Ames: Iowa State University Press, 2000.

News Making and News Reporting Routines

WHAT IS "NEWS"?[1] OLD-TIME JOURNALISTS WILL TELL you that when a man bites a dog, that's news, but when a dog bites a man, that is not. Why not? Why are some events chosen for extensive nationwide coverage whereas others that seem as politically significant or even more so are slighted? What explains the uniformity of story types in America's print and electronic media? What stories should the media cover, and how should they cover them? This chapter focuses on how routine news is usually selected and reported. News making during various types of crises is left to the next chapter. Speaking about news "making" does not mean that journalists concoct the events they report. It does mean that they decide which of a myriad of events happening in a particular time period will become news stories. The way they present these events shapes their meaning and likely impact. News stories are therefore manufactured creations rather than natural growths that journalists merely harvest.

No magical quality makes something "news." What is publishable in one setting for one medium is not necessarily appropriate for another. Newsworthiness of individual stories will vary from country to country, audience to audience, and time to time. Thus, in 1903, when Orville and Wilbur Wright invited the press to Kitty Hawk, North Carolina, to cover their attempts to fly an airplane, not a single reporter came. Only seven American newspapers considered the first controlled and sustained flight newsworthy enough to print stories about it, and only two papers gave the feat front-page play. Now all facets of aviation fascinate the public. Flocks of reporters came in 2001 to watch the first American space tourist leave for his journey on a Russian spacecraft. The story received worldwide press and television coverage.

Profile Sketch of American Journalists

What determines journalistic choices and thus shapes the flow of news and entertainment? The question can be answered from three perspectives. *Personality theory* explains professional behavior in terms of personality and social background factors. *Organization theory* focuses on the impact of organizational goals and pressures on the behavior of members of news production organizations. *Role theory* maintains that stories will vary, depending on the professional role conceptions that media personnel adopt. For instance, journalists who see themselves as impartial reporters of the news will behave differently from those who see themselves as partisan reformers.

Background and Personality Factors

Factors known to influence occupational performance include features of social background such as level of education, race, and gender as well as idiosyncratic factors such as artistic tastes, emotional outlook, and intellectual interests. Idiosyncratic factors explain why newspeople who have similar backgrounds will nonetheless prefer different stories or will give a different emphasis to the same news story or entertainment plot. Personality factors and organizational logic intertwine with organizational factors to set the broad boundaries of what is acceptable news.

What are some of the personality and background factors that influence the substance and shape of news? Data collected by G. Cleveland Wilhoit and David H. Weaver for their study *The American Journalist in the 1990s* are helpful in answering this question. These authors' findings are based on telephone interviews with 1,410 randomly selected newspeople in the United States working for 574 diverse daily and weekly newspapers, radio and television stations, and news services and magazines.[2]

Wilhoit and Weaver found that the social profile of newspeople resembled the profile of other professionals in the United States. Ninety-two percent of the participants in their study were white, 66 percent were male, 54 percent were Protestant, and 82 percent had graduated from college. Education appears to be the single most important background characteristic that shapes newspeople's general philosophy of reporting. Most American journalists are college-educated, though many did not major in journalism. Like most people with a college degree, they tend to be socially more liberal than the general population and tend to have a keener sense of social responsibility.

Journalists were more likely to be Democrats and less likely Republicans than the general population at the time of Wilhoit and Weaver's 1992 poll, and that trend grew even stronger over the ensuing decade. Forty-one percent of the respondents claimed to be Democrats, compared with 34 percent of the public; 16 percent called themselves Republicans, compared with 33 percent of the public; and 34 percent considered themselves independents, compared with 31 percent of the general population. The overall tone of stories selected is in tune with the political orientations of media personnel, albeit leaning a bit more toward the moderate middle of the political spectrum. Economic and social liberalism prevails, especially in the most prominent media organizations. So does a preference for an internationalist foreign policy, caution about military intervention, and some suspicion about the ethics of established large institutions, particularly big business and big government. However, despite perennial complaints about partisan bias in election campaign coverage, most studies show that media personnel treat the major parties fairly.[3] Such evenhandedness is encouraged by anticipation of scrutiny and criticism on that score. Media bias has rarely been investigated outside the election context. Hence the extent to which biased reporting based on party preferences is a problem in American media is not fully known.[4]

Minority journalists and women present a slightly different demographic profile. For example, African American, Hispanic, and Asian journalists are more likely to be women. Among Hispanic journalists, Catholicism is the prevailing religion. Even though the proportion of nonwhite journalists has risen, the proportion of women has remained steady at roughly one-third of the total. It is lowest in the wire services and television and highest in weekly newspapers and news magazines. By contrast, nonwhites have their highest representation in radio and television and their lowest representation in weekly newspapers. Minorities and women are much more likely to call themselves Democrats than are white journalists, and they are less likely to claim to be independents. Overall, nonwhite journalists constitute a far smaller proportion of the journalism workforce than that of the total population.

What effect do demographic characteristics have on the news product? The evidence is inconclusive, making it debatable whether adequate coverage of the nation's problems requires media organizations that are a microcosm of the larger society.[5] If demographically distinct groups are uniquely qualified to assess their own needs, then racial, ethnic, and gender underrepresentation in the media is harmful. Most general media emphasize established white middle-class groups and values while neglecting the concerns of minorities and poor people. The media also stress urban rather than rural affairs and focus heavily on male-dominated sports. These patterns suggest either that news output reflects reporters' backgrounds and interests or that the patterns cater to the tastes of the kinds of audiences that advertisers find most attractive.[6] Reporters' unique life experiences are also important in shaping their stories. For instance, Washington-based reporters routinely use friendships with well-connected government officials to get important scoops. As a result of close personal ties with these officials, the reporters are apt to become captives of their Beltway sources' perspectives on the world.

Organizational Factors

Colleagues and settings strongly influence newspeople. Every news organization has its own internal power structure that develops from the interaction of owners, journalists, news sources, audiences, advertisers, and government authorities. In most news organizations today, the ideology of working journalists is slightly to the left of middle America, quite similar to that of liberal Democrats. Still, most journalists support the basic tenets of the current political and social system.

By and large, print and broadcast journalists believe that many of the structural changes in the news business in the twenty-first century have harmed the quality of journalism. Surveys of national and local print, television, and radio journalists show that 73 percent believe that the buyouts of local newspapers by large newspaper chains and of news organizations by diversified corporations damage the news.[7] They also deem some format changes mandated by organizational pressures harmful but by far smaller margins. For example, 53 percent of the respondents called television's shift toward magazine formats an undesirable trend. They believe that reporters should be news announcers, rather than storytellers.

Some organizational changes are deemed beneficial. For example, three out of four journalists praised the establishment of newspaper and television Web sites, and 58 percent thought that the emergence of online-only news pages and magazines was good. Fifty-two percent believed the same about the increasing number of cable news outlets. Half of the national journalists thought that the public's ability to bypass the news media and go directly to information sources is splendid. Local journalists were more skeptical; 38 percent thought it was a bad idea, 30 percent liked it, and the rest thought it made little difference.

In spite of being part of ever larger business organizations, 70 percent of the journalists surveyed thought that advertising concerns had little or nothing to do with news choices, and 58 percent thought that corporate

TABLE 4-1   News Selection Criteria: Reasons for Rejecting Newsworthy Stories (in percentages)

Reasons for rejection	National executives	National journalists	Local executives	Local journalists	Blood-hound	Totals
News too dull						
Common/sometimes	79%	85%	62%	76%	77%	77%
Rarely/never	21	14	33	23	19	20
Don't know/refuse	0	1	5	1	4	3
News too complicated						
Common/sometimes	63	61	41	45	59	52
Rarely/never	34	38	54	48	31	42
Don't know/refuse	3	1	5	7	10	6
Alienate good source						
Common/sometimes	34	42	32	48	57	42
Rarely/never	63	56	60	51	38	54
Don't know/refuse	3	2	8	1	5	4
Be subjected to ridicule/scorn by peers						
Common/sometimes	42	32	38	39	32	38
Rarely/never	55	66	54	60	62	58
Don't know/refuse	3	2	8	1	6	4

Damage journalist's career

Common/sometimes	39	42	38	34	37	38
Rarely/never	58	53	57	65	59	55
Don't know/refuse	3	5	5	1	4	7

Hurt owner's finances

Common/sometimes	42	28	32	44	50	35
Rarely/never	58	72	60	55	44	61
Don't know/refuse	0	0	8	1	6	4

Embarrass/hurt advertisers

Common/sometimes	34	19	24	39	40	29
Rarely/never	66	80	65	60	54	66
Don't know/refuse	0	1	11	1	6	5

Magnify community problem

Common/sometimes	8	13	27	23	27	19
Rarely/never	89	82	68	76	69	77
Don't know/refuse	3	5	5	1	4	4

SOURCE: Adapted from Pew Research Center for the People and the Press, http://www.people-press.org/jour00que.htm.

NOTE: Based on a survey of 100 print and broadcast executives and journalists, including investigative reporters. Respondents were drawn from national and local media samples representing a cross-section of news organizations and their personnel. They were interviewed in February and March 2000.

owners put minimal pressures on their news operations. Table 4-1 lists several other concerns that, journalists believe, could potentially suppress coverage. The most potent barriers turn out to be related to the content of stories rather than to pressures by influential business interests. Journalists claim to skip otherwise newsworthy stories if the content is too dull or too complex. Sometimes they reject a story if its publication would alienate a good source. Three of four regard journalism as a regular business enterprise that is accountable to its shareholders; at the same time, they call it an essential public service that provides citizens with the information that they need for self-governance. Journalists are fairly evenly split about whether increased bottom-line pressures hurt the quality of news coverage or merely are changing the ways in which news organizations function.

Organizational pressures begin to operate even before the job starts. Most journalists join news organizations and remain with them only if they share the organization's basic philosophy. To win approval from their colleagues, professional recognition, and advancement, reporters learn quickly which types of stories are acceptable and which are likely to be squelched—and they learn to react in ways that maximize receptiveness. Relationships with colleagues are particularly important within large, prominent news enterprises in which newspeople receive their main social and professional support from coworkers rather than from the community at large.[8] The opposite holds true in small towns, where newspeople often interact freely with community leaders and receive their support.

Despite the substantial evidence of media influence on American politics, most newspeople deny that they should be concerned about the real-life impact of their stories. Journalists insist routinely and appropriately that government and business must take responsibility for the intended and unintended consequences of their actions. Yet journalists reject responsibility for the consequences of their own work even while claiming to subscribe to social responsibility journalism. Journalists commonly argue that journalism is a craft and not a profession. Eschewing candor to protect their flanks, they allege that they simply report the news found in the marketplace—nothing more.

Role Models

Although editors and reporters throughout the country take many cues and follow interpretations about stories from the Eastern elite media—such as the *New York Times, Wall Street Journal,* and *Washington Post*—they shape their basic news policies according to their own views about the role that media should play in society. The effects of the social responsibility role compared with libertarian stances have already been considered (see Chapter 1).

News products also vary depending on whether newspeople see themselves largely as objective observers who must present facts and diverse views voiced by others or as interpreters who must supply meanings and evaluations.

There are major differences on that score among reporters in Western democracies and among proponents of traditional and *civic* or *public* journalism.[9] The advocates of civic journalism believe that reporters must tailor the news so that it not only informs citizens about important happenings but also helps them to take collective action to resolve problems.[10] Beyond turning reporters into interpreters of what the news means or should mean, this approach also turns them consciously into participants in the political process. Although this may be laudable in many instances, civic journalism may sacrifice journalists' role as neutral observers. When journalists are asked about the core values of their calling, 76 percent acknowledge neutrality as a core value that serves their audience's interests. Other highly rated values to which 75 percent or more journalists subscribe are getting the facts right, avoiding rumors, maintaining distance between themselves and the people covered by their stories, listening to counterarguments in controversial stories, and confirming anonymous news tips.[11]

Journalists' perceptions of the proper roles of reporters and media obviously shape news and are politically significant. Table 4-2 presents journalists' answers to questions about the importance of various journalistic roles. It shows that journalists, irrespective of the demographic differences noted earlier, take a broad view of their responsibilities. Informing the public and playing the watchdog role are designated as their primary obligations.

Readers who live in large cities or subscribe to out-of-town papers often can select the papers with the type of focus they want. They may choose a paper like the *Wall Street Journal,* which tailors its news to the tastes of business people, or like the *New York Times,* which emphasizes broad general coverage. In Chicago, citizens can subscribe to the conservative *Tribune,* the sensational *Sun Times,* or more specialized papers such as the *Herald,* which serves the southern part of the metropolitan area, or the *Defender,* which caters to African Americans. Aside from the still limited number of people who read newspapers on the Internet, most people cannot pick and choose news sources representing particular role models easily. They have only a single print source readily available, along with radio and television stations. They are therefore limited to the role models represented by these sources.

Gatekeeping

A small number of journalists have final control over story choices. They are often called *gatekeepers.* Included are wire service reporters, Web editors

TABLE 4-2 Roles Deemed "Very Important" by Journalists (in percentages)

Role	National print	National TV and radio	Local print	Local TV and radio	National executives	National all[a]	Local all[a]
Provide needed information	67%	73%	74%	78%	77%	(96%)	(99%)
Uncover wrongdoing	56	44	58	46	48	(93)	(95)
Witness to history making	50	60	34	38	59	(93)	(87)
Contribute to society reform	34	18	36	17	34	(65)	(79)
Foster community spirit	23	13	32	27	28	(57)	(75)
Become famous/well known	6	9	2	17	7	(43)	(38)

SOURCE: Adapted from Pew Research Center for the People and the Press, http://www.people-press.org/press99rpt.htm.

NOTE: Based on a survey of 552 print and broadcast executives, producers, and working reporters and editors. Respondents were drawn from national and local media samples representing a cross-section of news organizations and their personnel. They were interviewed between November 20, 1998, and February 11, 1999.

[a] Numbers in parentheses combine "very" and "fairly" important categories.

and other reporters who initially choose stories, the editors who assign the reporters and accept or reject what they submit, disc jockeys at radio stations who present five-minute news breaks, and television program executives. In general, fewer than twenty-five people within a large newspaper or television organization are involved in the *final* decision of what news is used.

These few, particularly those who make news choices for nationwide audiences, wield a tremendous amount of political power because their choices determine what will be widely available as "news." This is why in public opinion polls that rank the political influence of various American institutions, the news media routinely rank among the top ten. When pollsters asked a national sample of Americans which telephone call the president should answer first if a topnotch editor, business leader, church figure, and educational leader called simultaneously, most chose the newspaper editor.[12] As we saw in Chapter 1, news stories influence what issues ordinary people as well as political elites will think about.[13] Of course, media gatekeepers are not entirely free in their story choices. Coverage of major events, such as wars, assassinations, and airline hijackings, is almost mandatory. Other events can be included or omitted at will, within the limits set by news conventions. On an average evening, somewhat more than half of the stories on each major television network represent unique choices. The figures are slightly lower for print media.

Gatekeepers also select the sources through whose eyes the public views the world. As Table 4-3 shows, government officials are the main source of most political stories reported by the wire services and national and local media. This gives public officials an excellent chance to influence the slant of the news. However, when highly controversial issues are at stake, gatekeepers usually turn to unofficial sources as well.[14] Table 4-3 also shows that private individuals rarely are sources either domestically or abroad.[15] Basing the news on a narrow spectrum of sources can lead to biased reporting. Reporters may give the widest publicity to the views of "celebrity" authorities in tangentially related fields and ignore important specialists. Reporters' choices of sources have led to one-sided presentations in stories about genetic engineering research, the swine flu vaccination program, and the development of an artificial heart.[16]

A study of sources used for stories about welfare reform, consumer issues, the environment, and nuclear energy concluded that journalists favor sources that reflect their own inclinations.

> On welfare reform, liberal sources predominate over conservative ones. On consumer issues they look to Ralph Nader, the public interest movement, and liberal activist groups. On pollution and the environment, they select activist environmental groups and, once again, liberal leaders. On nuclear

TABLE 4-3   Sources of Front-Page News Stories (in percentages)

Source	*Times/Post* staff stories	*Tribune* staff stories	Wire services staff stories	Total stories
Government officials	56%	54%	60%	56%
U.S.	34	14	38	28
State	7	17	6	10
Local	5	17	4	9
Foreign	10	6	12	9
Group-linked person[a]	25	34	18	25
Private person	4	6	4	5
Foreign person	4	5	8	7
Other	11	1	10	7

SOURCE: Author's research.

NOTE: Based on content analysis of news stories attributed to staff or wire services writers and published in the *New York Times, Washington Post,* and *Chicago Tribune* from 1994 to 1995. $N = 2,362$ for *Times/Post* stories, 801 for *Tribune* stories, and 2,032 for wire service stories, for a total of 5,195 stories.

[a] "Group-linked" persons are identified as members of a group but are not necessarily official spokespersons for the group.

energy, anti-nuclear sources are the most popular.... Journalists by no means depend exclusively on liberal viewpoints. They cite a mixture of public and private, partisan and nonpartisan, liberal and conservative sources. But the liberal side consistently outweighs the conservative.[17]

Sources who have gained recognition as "experts" through media publicity tend to be used over and over again. Newspeople may neglect other, less publicized sources.

When a variety of media cover the same story, as happens routinely, they often use sources representing different elites. When that happens, the thrust of the story may vary widely even though the underlying facts are the same. For example, when researchers looked at 167 stories about a major stock market crash in 1987, they found that the causes and effects of the crash were assessed in quite diverse fashion by the *CBS Evening News, Newsweek,* the *New York Times,* and the *Wall Street Journal.* The three print media had relied most heavily on experts from the financial sector as primary sources, drawing 38, 52, and 65 percent of their sources, respectively, from this sector. Government sources and academics took second and third place but were used far less frequently. For CBS, government sources came first, followed by sources from the business sector and the financial sector. CBS was also unique in drawing heavily (44 percent) on unnamed sources.[18]

The use of different sources led to disparate appraisals of the meaning of the crash and hence different impressions about needed remedies. In

Newsweek, the national debt and presidential policies were cited as the chief causes; in the *New York Times,* it was the debt and computerized trading. *Wall Street Journal* sources emphasized computerized trading and the foreign trade deficit. On the *CBS Evening News,* the national debt was the chief villain, with twice the emphasis it had received in other sources. Presidential policies and partisan politics were other important causes. When it came to estimating the effects of the crash, all but the *Wall Street Journal* mentioned improved cooperation between president and Congress as a likely outcome. Beyond that, speculations about probable effects diverged widely, presenting media audiences with clashing images about the country's economic problems.

A few highly respected national newscasters also are extraordinarily influential in putting their versions of news events on the political agenda. By singling out news events for positive or negative commentary, these media figures may sway public and official opinions. If anchors Peter Jennings, Tom Brokaw, or Dan Rather declare that health care legislation will lower the quality of medical care or that an American military presence along the coast of China will risk war, popular support for these policies may plunge.[19] A sixty-second verbal barrage on the evening news or a few embarrassing questions can destroy programs, politicians, and the reputations of major organizations.

Because Americans like to view their media as effective guardians of the public interest, the positive consequences of news story choices are usually stressed. Negative or questionable consequences should not be overlooked, however. For example, Peter Braestrup, chief of the Saigon bureau of the *Washington Post* during the Vietnam War, argued in his book *Big Story* that unwise story choices and interpretations about the conduct of the war misled the public and government officials.[20] Walter Cronkite and other commentators had used available information to construct a picture of defeat for the South Vietnamese and American forces, ignoring data that indicated a defeat for the North Vietnamese. These erroneous interpretations heightened antiwar pressures and contributed to the collapse of public support for the war. They produced a speedup of troop withdrawal and prompted President Lyndon B. Johnson to abandon a second-term race.[21] The economic collapse of the Soviet Union in the 1980s, which led to the abrupt end of the cold war, is another example. American journalists had largely ignored Soviet economic news, leaving policymakers and the public uninformed about momentous developments.[22]

General Factors in News Selection

As mentioned earlier, what becomes news depends in part on the *demographics, training, personality,* and *professional socialization* of news personnel. In the United States this means, by and large, upwardly mobile, well-educated white males whose political views are liberal and who sub-scribe in ever larger numbers to the tenets of social responsibility journal-ism (discussed in Chapter 2). News selection also hinges on the *intraorga-nizational norms and professional role conceptions* of newspeople and on *pressures of internal and external competition.*

Within each news organization, reporters and editors compete for time, space, and prominence of position for their stories. News organiza-tions also compete with each other for audience attention, for advertisers, and, in the case of the networks, for affiliates. If one station or network has a popular program, others often will copy the format and try to place an equally attractive program into a parallel time slot to capture their competitor's audiences and advertisers. Likewise, papers may feel com-pelled to carry stories simply because another medium in the same mar-ket has carried it.

News personnel operate within *the broad political context of their societies* in general and their circulation communities in particular. Most have internalized these contexts so that they become their frames of reference. As media scholar George Gerbner observed long ago, there is "no funda-mentally non-ideological, apolitical, non-partisan news gathering and reporting system."[23] For example, if a reporter's political context demands favorable images of religious leaders, news and entertainment will reflect this outlook most of the time. If adverse criticism of the clergy is encour-aged, news events will be framed accordingly.[24]

Political pressures also leave their mark. Media personnel depend on political leaders for much of their information and are therefore vulnera-ble to manipulation by these sources. Powerful elites flood the media with self-serving story materials that are often hard to resist. Intensive, frequent contacts between journalists and leaders and the desire to keep associa-tions cordial may lead to cozy relationships that hamper critical detach-ment. Wooing reporters to elicit favorable media coverage is the mark of the astute politician. Reporters often succumb to the blandishments of politicians for fear of alienating powerful and important news sources.

Economic pressures are even more potent than political pressures in molding news and entertainment. Newspapers and magazines need suffi-cient income to cover their production costs and earn profits. Except for publications that are subsidized by individual or group sponsors, media enterprises must raise most of their income from subscriptions and adver-tisers. Therefore, media offerings must appeal to large numbers of sub-scribers or potential customers for the products that advertisers sell. This means that programs and stories must be directed either to general audi-ences in the prime consumption years of life (roughly twenty-five to forty-five years of age) or to selected special audiences that are key targets for particular advertiser appeals. For instance, toothpaste, laundry detergent, and breakfast cereals are best marketed to the huge nationwide audiences who watch the regular nighttime situation comedies or detective stories; expensive cameras, fancy foreign sports cars, and raft trips down the Amazon are most likely to find customers among a select few. Advertisers for such products are attracted to journals with well-to-do subscribers such as *National Geographic* or the *Wall Street Journal* as well as to specialized cable channels and television documentaries.

Producers of television and radio programs that are directed to nationwide audiences try to maintain a smooth flow of appealing programs throughout the prime evening hours to keep audiences from switching channels. As long as a program is unobjectionable, most audiences will remain with the station. If boring or controversial programs come on, a sizable part of the audience will defect to another station and remain tuned to it for the rest of the evening. Such considerations deter producers from mixing serious audience-losing programs with light entertainment in prime time. The fear of losing the audience for an entire evening has also been a major reason for opposing the expansion of the nightly network news to a full hour.

The desire to keep audiences watching a particular station even affects the format of news and public service programs. Newscasters are selected for their physical attractiveness. Informal banter is encouraged, and nearly every newscast contains some fascinating bits of trivia or a touching yet inconsequential human-interest story. The news becomes *info-tainment*—a marriage of information and entertainment values. Complicated stories are avoided for fear of confusing audiences. "Dull" stories, such as those that are about budget negotiations, are slighted despite their importance. However, media people occasionally underestimate the public's tastes for serious presentations, as shown by the popularity of the televised congressional debates about American involvement in the Persian Gulf War in 1991 and by the massive attention given to presidential news conferences and addresses. But these instances of audience attentiveness are the exceptions rather than the rule. H. L. Mencken was probably right when he said that "nobody ever went broke by underestimating the public's taste."

Criteria for Choosing Specific Stories

In addition to deciding what is publishable news, gatekeepers must choose particular news items to include in their mix of offerings. The motto of the *New York Times,* "All the News That's Fit to Print," is an impossible myth; there is far more publishable news available to any

Reprinted with special permission of King Features Syndicate.

paper than it can possibly use. Gatekeepers also must decide how they want to frame each item so that it carries a particular message. For instance, when journalists cast stories about controversial policies like health care reform as games of strategy, as they are wont to do, the policy issues blur and lose importance.[25] In 1993 and 1994, for example, 67 percent of the health news coverage was framed as political gaming with stories focusing on who was winning and losing supporters for their favorite policy. Only 25 percent of the stories addressed substantive issues in health care reform.

The criteria newspeople use in story selection relate primarily to audience appeal rather than to the political significance of stories, their educational value, their broad social purposes, or the newspeople's own political views. This holds particularly true for television, where viewer numbers, demographic characteristics, and viewer attitudes are constantly monitored by rating services, such as A. C. Nielsen and the American Research Bureau (ARB). For both radio and television, advertising rates are based on audience size. An increase in audience size of just 1 percent can mean millions of dollars in additional advertising income. Newspaper advertising rates are also based on paid circulation, which is monitored by an independent agency, the Audit Bureau of Circulation. Audiences are rarely asked if they would prefer different programs to the existing fare. The fact that they watch or listen to or purchase papers in large numbers is assumed to certify that they like what they get.

The emphasis on audience appeal, and the economic pressures that mandate it, needs to be kept in mind when the totality of media output is evaluated. They explain why the amounts and kinds of coverage of important issues often are not commensurate with their significance in the real world at the time of publication. For instance, television news coverage of crime reached record highs in 1995 because journalists believed that the public wanted extensive coverage of the O. J. Simpson murder trial and several other sensational cases. The combined story totals for health issues, the economy, and federal budget talks fell substantially below crime story totals, leaving the impression that these stories mattered less than the various crime sagas.[26] Stories like the Clinton sex scandals, the death of Britain's Princess Diana, or the custody fight over Cuban child refugee, Elian Gonzalez, receive inordinate amounts of coverage at the expense of more significant events. News also projects distorted images when peaks in coverage of events like urban riots or terrorist attacks do not match peaks in actual happenings. Peaks in news about street crime typically do not coincide with peaks in street crime as recorded by police.

Discrepancies between the frequency of newsworthy events and their coverage are especially well illustrated by crime news reporting (see Table 4-4). In 2000, 31 percent of the local crime stories reported by the *Chicago Tribune* dealt with murder and 12 percent with sexual assaults. These crimes constituted just slightly over 1 percent of all crimes recorded in police statistics. Another 43 percent of the stories cover crimes like robbery, burglary, theft, and arson, the total of which constituted 86 percent of all officially recorded crimes. Even considering that murder and sexual assaults are more serious than these other crimes, the huge discrepancy in coverage seems unwarranted. Compared with a decade earlier, crime in Chicago had dropped roughly 12 percent by the turn of the century. Surprisingly, crime coverage had been cut in half, creating an exaggerated impression about the scope of the drop in crime.

Five criteria are used most often for choosing news stories. First, stories must be likely to have a *strong impact* on readers or listeners. Stories about health hazards, consumer fraud, or pensions for the elderly influence people more than do unfamiliar happenings with which they cannot identify. To make stories attractive, newspeople commonly present them as anecdotes that have an effect on average people. Inflation news becomes the story of the housewife at the supermarket; foreign competition becomes the story of laid-off workers in a local textile plant. In the process

TABLE 4-4　Police Versus Newspaper Crime Reports: Chicago, 2000

Crime	Police reports of Chicago crime		*Tribune* reports of Chicago crime		*Tribune* reports of all crime	
Murder[a]	627	(0.3%)	26	(30.9%)	12	(4.2%)
Sexual assault[b]	1,907	(0.9%)	10	(11.9%)	74	(25.8%)
Assault	26,451	(12.4%)	12	(14.3%)	34	(11.8%)
Theft/robbery/ burglary/arson[c]	183,920	(86.4%)	36	(42.9%)	167	(58%)
Total	212,905	(100%)	84	(100%)	287	(99.8%)

SOURCE: Compiled from police crime reports and newspaper index.

[a] Murder includes attempted murder and manslaughter.

[b] Sexual assault includes rape.

[c] Theft includes auto thefts.

of personalization, the broader political significance of the story is often lost, and the news becomes trivialized.

Natural or man-made *violence, conflict, disaster,* or *scandal* is the second criterion of newsworthiness. Wars, murders, strikes, earthquakes, accidents, or sex scandals involving prominent people are the kinds of things that excite audiences. In fact, inexpensive mass newspapers became viable business ventures in the United States only when the publishers of the *New York Sun* discovered in 1833 that papers filled with breezy crime and sex stories far outsold their more staid competitors. Mass sales permitted sharp price reductions and led to the birth of the "penny press." People remember dramatic behavior better than they recall the more standard fare. A story of a toddler rescued from a well has become one of the best-remembered events of recent decades. The O. J. Simpson murder trial, the Elian Gonzalez custody case, and the My Lai massacre have become equally memorable.

A third element of newsworthiness is *familiarity.* News is attractive if it pertains to well-known people or involves familiar situations of concern to many. This is why newspeople try to cast unfamiliar situations, such as mass famines in Africa, into more familiar stories of individual babies dying from malnutrition. The public's keen interest in celebrities is demonstrated by the amazing amount of detail that people can retain about the powerful and famous. More than three decades after the assassination of President Kennedy in 1963, many Americans still remember details of the funeral ceremony, as well as where they were when they heard the news of the killing. The sense of personal grief and loss has lingered, bridging the gap between the average person's private and public worlds. People value the feeling of personal intimacy that comes from knowing details of a famous person's life. Somewhat similar feelings are harbored even toward the cast members of soap operas and reality dramas. People whose lives are confined largely to their homes often adopt television stars as part of their families. They avidly follow the trials and tribulations of these people and may even try to model themselves after them.

Proximity is the fourth element of newsworthiness. Strong preference for local news rests on the fact that people are most interested in what happens near them. Next to news about crime and health, people pay most attention to local news, far ahead of news about national and international affairs.[27] Local media flourish because they concentrate on events close to home. Roughly 75 percent of their space is used for local stories. Nonetheless, the public receives so much news from Washington and a few major metropolitan areas that these cities and their newsmakers have become familiar to the nation. This, in a sense, makes such occurrences "local" in what media analyst Marshall McLuhan has called the *global village* created by television.

The fifth element is that news should be *timely* and *novel*. It must be something that has just occurred and is out of the ordinary, either in the sense that it does not happen all the time—such as the regular departure of airplanes or the daily opening of grocery stores—or in the sense that it is not part of the lives of ordinary persons.

Among these five basic criteria, *conflict, proximity,* and *timeliness* are most important, judging from analyses of actual news choices. A story's long-range significance is a lesser concern. It does play a part, however, when major events occur, like national elections, the death of a well-known leader, or a calamitous natural disaster. Nevertheless, most stories are selected and framed primarily to satisfy the five criteria.

Gathering the News

News organizations establish regular listening posts, or "beats," in places where events of interest to the public are most likely to occur. In the United States, beats at the centers of government cover political executives, legislative bodies, court systems, and international organizations. Places in which deviant behaviors are most apt to be reported, such as police stations and hospitals, are monitored. Fluctuations in economic trends are recorded at stock and commodity markets and at institutions designed to check the pulse of the nation's business. Some beats, such as health or education, are functionally defined. Reporters assigned to them generally cover a wider array of institutions on a less regular schedule than is true of the more usual beats.

TABLE 4-5 Frequency of Mention of News Topics: September 1–October 20, 2000 (in percentages)

News topics	Sun Times (3,672)	Chicago Tribune (4,380)	National TV ABC (657)	National TV CBS (558)	National TV NBC (495)	Local TV ABC (690)	Local TV CBS (718)	Local TV NBC (588)
Government/politics								
National government	4.1%	3.1%	6.8%	8.0%	7.2%	6.9%	7.4%	6.7%
Elections	3.8	5.1	5.3	9.0	9.6	4.5	5.1	5.5
State government	1.4	2.3	1.6	1.6	1.8	1.7	1.5	0.9
Local government	2.3	2.4	0.5	0.3	0.2	4.8	3.1	3.6
International news	6.9	4.8	24.2	22.6	18.4	5.9	6.1	6.0
National affairs news	2.0	3.1	5.4	4.8	3.7	1.5	2.3	2.8
Local affairs news	3.9	4.1	0.0	0.0	0.0	10.8	7.5	9.1
Total	24.4	24.9	43.8	46.3	40.9	36.1	33.0	34.6
Economic issues								
Economy	1.8	2.1	2.7	3.2	5.6	0.4	0.5	0.3
Business	9.6	10.0	5.5	6.5	5.5	2.6	1.6	0.8
Labor/unemployment	0.9	1.1	4.1	3.3	3.9	0.6	1.0	1.1
Transportation/energy	1.4	2.5	8.2	8.1	10.9	3.3	2.7	3.4
Health care	1.0	1.4	4.1	3.8	4.2	1.8	2.2	2.3
Total	14.7	17.3	24.6	24.9	30.1	8.7	8.0	7.9
Social issues								
Civil rights/deprived groups	0.5	1.2	0.8	0.6	0.8	0.6	0.7	0.7
Education	1.5	1.8	1.1	1.6	1.2	2.5	1.4	1.2
Media	0.5	2.1	0.7	0.4	0.8	1.2	1.1	0.4
Religion	0.3	0.9	2.5	2.4	3.0	0.3	0.2	0.8
Abortion/contraception	0.4	1.2	1.5	1.4	1.2	0.5	0.7	0.2
Disease	0.1	0.4	2.7	1.6	3.1	0.4	1.8	0.4

Other health issues	0.6	1.8	0.9	1.1	0.7	1.2	2.0	1.5
Disasters/accidents	0.8	0.6	5.5	6.1	4.7	2.2	3.1	2.8
Environment	1.5	0.8	1.3	1.4	1.9	1.1	0.8	1.0
Justice system	1.2	1.0	2.5	2.3	1.1	1.9	2.1	1.4
Individual crime	2.9	3.2	2.2	1.9	1.6	11.2	9.7	9.8
Total	10.7	14.9	21.7	19.8	20.1	23.1	23.6	20.2
Other								
Obituaries	2.2	4.0	0.0	0.0	0.0	0.0	0.0	0.0
Weather	1.6	2.1	3.0	4.5	3.3	6.5	6.9	7.0
Sports	27.3	19.4	6.0	3.5	4.9	20.0	22.4	23.1
Entertainment	19.1	18.4	0.9	1.1	0.7	5.6	6.1	7.2
Total	50.2	43.9	9.9	9.1	8.9	32.1	35.4	37.3

SOURCE: Author's research.

Stories emanating from the traditional beats at the national level, such as the White House, Capitol, or Pentagon, have an excellent chance of publication, either because of their intrinsic significance, the prominence of their sources, or simply because they have been produced by beat reporters on the regular payroll. In the *New York Times* or *Washington Post*, for example, stories from regularly covered beats outnumber other stories two to one and capture the bulk of front-page headlines.[28]

All major media monitor similar beats. Consequently, overall news patterns—the types of stories that are covered and the relative prominence of various topics—are uniform throughout the country and change in tandem when major shifts occur. Shifts include, among others, the trend toward softer news and features.[29] On the nightly national news, the lead story is shared by at least two of the major networks 91 percent of the time. Usually it is featured on the third network in only a slightly less prominent position.[30] As Table 4-5 documents, news media are "rivals in conformity."[31] The table is based on the content analysis of two Chicago newspapers and six nightly television newscasts, half of them local to Chicago, for a randomly selected fifty-day period from September 1 to October 20, 2000. The table presents striking evidence that the same kinds of stories and story types—although not necessarily identical stories—are reported by all news outlets. When the proportions of various types of news are compared, the similarities are greatest among the members of each of the three types of media. National television patterns show heavier proportionate emphases on stories about national affairs and international news and proportionate de-emphases of local news and sports news. Local broadcasters, by definition, pay more attention to local news than do other modalities, and they rank at the bottom for economic news. Thanks to more available space, newspapers carry more nonpolitical news. In fact, it is noteworthy that they devote nearly half of the newshole—the space available for news stories, rather than advertising, legal announcements, circulation information, and the like—to nonpolitical stories. But, though the proportions vary, the array of topics covered is remarkably uniform. This pattern is typical for media systems throughout the United States.[32]

News, as media scholar Leon Sigal has put it, is always "the standardized exceptional."[33] Each day's or week's news is like a familiar play with slight changes in the scenes and dialogue, and with frequent replacements in the cast of minor players (although not of major actors). News is exceptional in the sense that it does not portray ordinary events, such as eating breakfast, washing clothes, or taking the bus to work. It is standardized in the sense that it deals with the same types of topics in familiar ways and produces standardized patterns of news and entertainment throughout the country. Repeated coverage of the same familiar scenes tells the public that all is going according to expectations and that, even when the news is bad, there is little to worry about. It has all happened before, and people have managed to cope.

News organizations, including the giants in the business, cannot afford to have full teams of reporters and camera crews dispersed across the country. In fact, economic declines have forced them to contract their bases. Even in good times, national networks generally station teams in only half a dozen cities where the equipment, support staff, and news personnel are good. Locations are not selected with an eye to covering all parts of the nation equally well or to providing diverse settings. Chance thus determines which locations receive coverage for routine stories and which are neglected.

Table 4-6 shows the percentage of network news stories devoted to individual American states in broadcasts monitored from June 1999 to May 2000. The table also reports the number of electoral votes to which each state was entitled, according to the 1990 census, as a rough measure of that state's population and political significance. Coverage of news about the states is extremely uneven. Twenty-two states were covered by fewer than twenty-five stories annually. Such sparse coverage denies their news and their problems a national audience. Overall, the thirty-three states covered by up to fifty stories annually represent 47 percent of the country in electoral votes but receive only 24 percent of the state news coverage. At the other end of the spectrum, California, New York, and Texas received 40 percent of the national coverage combined, but they represent only 22 percent of the electoral vote.

Much of the picture coverage comes from East Coast cities, such as Washington, D.C., and New York. Others come from Chicago and Los Angeles. Of course, special events will be covered anywhere in the country. Every network reports presidential nominating conventions, wherever they are held, and routinely follows presidential travels, whether the destination is tiny Hope, Arkansas, President Clinton's hometown, or the Great Wall of China. States receive exceptional coverage when major news happens there. In the period covered by Table 4-6, this was the case in Iowa and New Hampshire, sites of key primary elections and caucuses. Colorado suffered from killings at a public school; Washington State experienced mass protests against the World Trade Association; North Carolina was ravaged by weather disasters; and Florida was the scene of the heated contest for custody of Elian Gonzalez. Newsworthy events in remote sites are most likely to be covered if they involve prominent people and are scheduled in advance so that plans can be made to have media crews available.

TABLE 4-6   Network Coverage of State News: June 1999–May 2000

Annual number of stories	States		Percentage of mentions	Percentage of electoral vote
1–24	Alabama Alaska Arkansas Connecticut Delaware Hawaii Idaho Indiana Kansas Kentucky Maine Mississippi	Missouri Montana Nebraska Nevada North Dakota South Dakota Utah West Virginia Wisconsin Wyoming	10.6%	23.2%
25–50	Arizona Illinois Louisiana Minnesota New Jersey North Carolina	Ohio Oklahoma Oregon Tennessee Vermont	13.4	23.8
51–100	Colorado Georgia Iowa Maryland Massachusetts Michigan	New Hampshire New Mexico Pennsylvania South Carolina Virginia Washington	24.6	24.5
101–200	Florida Rhode Island	Washington, D.C.	11.6	5.9
201–474	California New York	Texas	39.6	22.1

SOURCE: Data compiled from the Vanderbilt Television News Archives. Electoral vote totals and percentages for each state and Washington, D.C. were obtained from 1990 census data.
NOTE: N = 3,173.

Prior planning is even important for more accessible events. Time is needed to allocate camera crews, move them into position, and process and edit pictures. The necessity of planning ahead leads to an emphasis on more predictable events, such as formal visits by dignitaries, legislative hearings, or executive press conferences. The news output reflects this preference for formally scheduled events. The development of portable camera equipment to produce videotapes that can be broadcast with little further processing has greatly eased—though not eliminated—this problem. *Spot news* can now be filmed and broadcast rapidly, often via satellite transmission. This is only one example of the profound impact of technological developments on the content of the news.

News Production Constraints

Many news selection criteria reflect the pressure to process and publish news rapidly. That is why pseudo-events—events created for easy reporting by the media or for the media—constitute more than half of all television news stories. For example, politicians frequently plan pictorially attractive happenings, such as bridge dedications or county fair visits, to accommodate newspaper or broadcast deadlines. Presidents routinely provide photo opportunities to allow the press to record the many minor events in their schedules. When newspeople need a quick story about an event, such as a revolution in Central America or youth gang violence, they create it by arranging interviews with familiar leaders, whose remarks, knowledgeable or not, then instantly become *the* Central America or *the* youth gang story.

Once stories reach media news offices, selections must be made extremely rapidly. Ben Bagdikian, a former *Washington Post* editor who studied gatekeeping at eight newspapers, found that stories usually are sifted and chosen on the spot.[34] They are not assembled and carefully balanced with an eye to the overall effects. The typical newspaper gatekeeper is able to scan and discard individual stories in seconds. At such speeds, judgments are almost instantaneous. There is no time to reflect or to weigh the merits of one story over another. Stories are judged more by how they balance previously selected stories than by their intrinsic importance. If the gatekeeper has ideological preferences, these are served instinctively, if at all, rather than deliberately. Stories left over at the end of the day ordinarily will not be used the next day because newer stories will have superseded them. A late-breaking story, therefore, unless it is very unusual or significant, has little chance for publication. Because the network evening news is run on an East Coast schedule, afternoon stories occurring on the West Coast are frequent casualties because they generally happen too late to be used. The growth of round-the-clock news venues, like CNN and MSNBC, has eased this situation.

Fewer than 3 percent of the stories in Bagdikian's study were rejected because the editor did not care for the substance of the story or objected to its ideological slant. Twenty-six percent were rejected because of space shortages. The chief reason for other rejections was lack of newsworthiness. The published newspaper usually contained the same proportions of different types of news as the original pool from which the stories were selected.[35] Rejection rates varied for different types of stories. Overall, nearly all wire service, human-interest, and crime stories were rejected, along with more than two-thirds of farm and science stories. Even though much of the human-interest information was rejected, it still constituted the largest single news category—23 percent of total news. By contrast, science news took 5 percent of total space and farm stories 6 percent.[36] We do not know how variable these rates are over time and how often they are altered to accommodate important breaking news.

Public relations experts and campaign managers know the deadlines of important publications, such as the *New York Times, Wall Street Journal, Time, Newsweek,* and network television news. They schedule events and news releases to arrive in gatekeepers' offices precisely when needed and in easy-to-use formats. Public relations firms distribute thousands of video-taped releases annually. If these releases are attractively presented and meet newsworthiness criteria, journalists find it hard to resist using them. This is especially true for smaller organizations that lack adequate resources to produce their own stories. They relish receiving such information subsidies.[37] Publicists for particular causes thus can influence the news production process. Powerful elites in the public and private sector make ample use of these opportunities. Even though the bulk of public relations releases is discarded, a substantial portion of news stories is based on them, usually without identification of the sources. If publicists want to stifle publicity that is likely to harm their clients, they can announce news just past the deadlines, preferably on weekends when few newscasts are scheduled.

Publications with less frequent deadlines, such as weekly news magazines, have a lot more time to decide which items to publish. That makes it easier to separate the wheat from the chaff. News magazine staffs also have more resources than most daily papers to explore background information and present stories in a context that helps readers to evaluate them. Hence their stories are often far more measured and thought-provoking than corresponding stories in the daily press.

Television news staffs, especially those working for stations that broadcast around the clock, have even less time than newspaper staffs to investigate most stories and far less time to provide background and interpretation. This is why background or investigative stories that appear on television frequently have originated in the print media. The problem of insufficient time pertains not only to preparing stories but also to presenting them. The average news story on television and radio takes about a minute to deliver, just enough time to announce an event and present a fact or two. Complex stories may have to be ignored if they cannot be drastically condensed.

Print media have space problems as well, but these are less severe than the time constraints faced by electronic media. The average newspaper reserves 55 percent of its space for advertising. Straight news stories account for 27 percent of the space, and the remainder is used for features of various types. Some papers reserve a fixed amount of space for news; others expand or contract the newshole depending on the flow of news and advertising. But whether the paper is a slim eight-page version or five to ten times that size, there is rarely enough space to cover stories as fully as reporters and editors would like.[38]

Besides the need to capsulize news stories, television reporters also seek stories with visual appeal. Events that lack good pictures may have to be omitted. Racial violence in South Africa, for example, disappeared worldwide from television news after the government prohibited picture taking. Unfortunately, what is visually appealing may not be important. For instance, during political campaigns the motorcades, rallies, hecklers, and cheering crowds make good pictures while candidates delivering speeches are visually dull. Television cameras therefore concentrate on the colorful scenes rather than on the speeches. If interesting pictures are flashed on the screen in competition with a speech, they often distract attention from it.

Because picture production is expensive for television as well as for print, picture stories selected early are likely to be kept even if more important stories break later. Financial considerations, as well as personnel reasons, also favor information originated by staff members. Stories by employees already on the payroll are preferred to wire service stories by unknown reporters or stories from outside sources for which additional fees must be paid. News executives also have personal relationships with their own staff members and do not want to disappoint them by rejecting their stories.

Effects of Gatekeeping

The gatekeeping influences that have been discussed give a distinctive character to the American news product. There are many exceptions, of course, when one looks at individual programs or stories. There are also noticeable differences in emphases among the conservative rural press, more moderate papers in small- and middle-sized towns, and the liberal press in major metropolitan centers. The unique conditions of Internet journalism have an even more profound impact on news presentation.[39] Unlike journalists in traditional media who must rigorously prune the lush growth of incoming news stories because time or space is scarce, Internet journalists have abundant time and space and must strain to fill it around the clock. Most Internet sites sponsored by traditional newspapers and television operations choose to expand stories that they cover in their traditional media, rather than enhancing the pool of news stories with previously excluded coverage. They update these stories regularly throughout the day and night, often scooping the printed and broadcast stories that they will later feature in their traditional venues. Most news Web sites also provide links to information that broadens and deepens the story by adding new data or refreshing previously published details. The upshot is more in-depth news at a much faster pace. Despite variations in the news story environment, several shared attributes of American news stand out. I will discuss them under four headings: *people in the news, action in the news, info-tainment news,* and *support for the establishment.*[40]

People in the News

The gatekeeping process winnows the group of newsworthy people to a small cadre of familiar and unfamiliar figures. In print and broadcast news, most stories in news magazines and network television news feature familiar people, predominantly entertainers, athletes, and political figures. Fewer than fifty politicians are in the news regularly. The list is headed by the *incumbent president.* Other people may receive coverage primarily for unusual or remarkable activities, but incumbent presidents are covered regardless of what they do. News about *leading presidential candidates* ranks next; in presidential election years it often outnumbers stories about the president.[41]

A third well-covered group consists of *major federal officials,* such as political leaders in the House and Senate, the heads of major congressional committees, and cabinet members in active departments. Major White House staff members are part of the circle. So are former officials such as secretaries of state and secretaries of defense who are asked to comment on the current scene. The Supreme Court is in the news only intermittently, generally when important decisions are announced or during confirmation hearings for Supreme Court justices. Agency heads rarely make the news except when they announce new policies or feud with the president. Some people, however, are regularly in the news regardless of their current political status merely because their names are household words. Members of the Kennedy clan and a host of "experts" such as Federal Reserve chairman Alan Greenspan, consumer activist Ralph Nader, or civil rights activist Jesse Jackson are prime examples.

Below the federal level, the activities of *governors and mayors from large states and cities* are newsworthy if they involve major public policy issues or if the incumbent is unusual because of race, gender, or prior newsworthy activities. *Notorious individuals* also receive frequent attention if their deeds have involved well-known people. Presidential assassins, mass murderers, or terrorists like Timothy McVeigh and Oussama bin Laden fall into this category. Ample coverage also goes to targets of congressional investigations and politicians indicted for wrongdoing in office.

Among the many powerful people rarely covered in the news are economic leaders (such as the heads of large corporations), financiers, and leaders of organized business (such as the National Association of Manufacturers or the U.S. Chamber of Commerce). A few colorful labor leaders, such as George Meany and James Hoffa, have been news figures in the past, but this was probably due more to their personalities than to their jobs. Important military leaders also remain obscure unless they conduct major military operations, such as Gen. Norman Schwarzkopf in the Persian Gulf War or his boss, Gen. Colin Powell. Political party leaders surface during elections but remain in the shadows at other times. Political activists, such as civil rights leaders or the heads of minority parties, or pleaders of special causes, such as right-to-die activist Dr. Jack Kevorkian, come and go from the news scene, depending on the amount of visible conflict they are able to produce. The same holds true for the heads of voluntary associations, such as leaders of antiabortion groups or churches.

Most people never make the news because their activities are not unusual enough to command media attention. Ordinary people have their best chance for publicity if they protest or riot or strike, particularly against the government. The next best chance goes to victims of disasters, personal tragedy, and crime and to the actors who brought about their plight. The grisly nature of crimes, disasters, or other human tragedies, rather than the identity of the people involved, determines their newsworthiness. Ordinary people also make the news if their lifestyles or social activities become highly unusual or if their behavior diverges greatly from the norm for persons of their age, gender, and status. Finally, ordinary people make the news in large numbers as nameless members of groups whose statistical profile is reported or whose opinions have been tapped through polls or elections.

Action in the News

The range of activities reported in the news is quite limited—conflicts and disagreements among government officials (particularly friction between the president and Congress about economic or foreign policies), violent and nonviolent protest (much of it about government activities), crime, scandals and investigations, and impending or actual disasters. When the nation is at war, a large number of war stories are reported.

Government policies involving health care reform, energy, or changes in tax rates also provide frequent story material. These stories generally report the political maneuvers leading to policy decisions rather than the substance of the policy and its likely impact. Government personnel changes, including details about campaigns for office, are another news focus. Finally, two aspects of the ever changing societal scene receive substantial coverage from time to time: major national events such as inaugurations or space adventures, and important social, cultural, or technological developments such as major efforts to raise the quality of public schools, or advances in the fight against killer diseases such as cancer and AIDS.

Info-tainment News

Newsworthiness criteria and news production constraints shape American news and its impact, regardless of a particular subject under discussion. Among these constraints, economic pressures to generate large audiences are often paramount. The pressure leads to an emphasis on soft, shallow news that many critics inside and outside of journalism deplore.

Novelty and Excitement.   Sensational and novel occurrences often drown out news of more lasting significance that lacks excitement. For instance, a fairly typical newspaper such as the *Chicago Sun Times* devotes nearly twenty times more news to sports than to news about the state's government (see Table 4-5). Dramatic events, such as airline hijackings or serial murders, preempt more far-reaching consequential happenings. Preoccupation with a single striking event, such as the Clinton impeachment deliberations in 1999, can shortchange coverage of other news, such as a punitive American airstrike against targets in Iraq. Speculations about a religious broadcaster's chances for success in the 1988 Iowa presidential caucuses drowned out a Soviet leader's announcement of plans to withdraw from the long and bloody war in Afghanistan.

The emphasis on excitement also leads to a stress on the more trivial aspects of serious stories. Inflation becomes a human-interest drama about John and Jane Doe, working-class homeowners who are struggling to pay their mortgage. The larger issues involved in inflation are apt to be ignored, unless emphasis on human-interest aspects of a story is combined with an exploration of its larger societal implications. In such cases, dramatization helps because personalized dramatic stories are far more likely to catch audience attention than dry learned discussions by economic experts.

The search for novelty and entertainment leads to fragmented, discontinuous news that focuses on the present and ignores the past. When breaking news is published in a hurry, it often lacks background that places stories into context. Fragmentation makes it difficult for audiences to piece together a coherent narrative of events. Snippets of news may drive home an easily understandable theme, such as "Washington is in a mess" or "the inner city is decaying," thereby blurring individual news items. A few papers, such as the *Christian Science Monitor,* and a few news programs, such as the *NewsHour with Jim Lehrer,* cover fewer stories so that they can present them in more detail. But that forces them to omit other news for which there is no space.

Familiarity and Similarity. The demand for stories about familiar people and events close to home produces circular effects. When familiar people and situations are covered in minute detail, they become even more familiar and therefore even more worthy of publicity. The reverse is also true. Important people and events are ignored because they involve little-known actors and situations.

Familiar people may become objects of prying curiosity. The details of their private lives may take up an inordinately large amount of time and space in the mass media. The accidental death in a car crash of even distant political figures, such as Princess Diana, ex-wife of the heir to the British throne, may command front-page coverage for extended time periods. Tabloids and serious media alike cover such stories at length. Only rarely do they focus on the potentially significant political consequences that might ensue from such issues, such as their impact on the survival of the monarchy in Britain.

The criteria of newsworthiness used in the United States lead to news that is very parochial compared with news in other countries. Slim coverage of news about foreign people and cultures leaves Americans ignorant about important international affairs, as will be discussed more fully in Chapter 11. The pattern is circular: If events in distant countries are rarely covered, stories about them will require a lot of background if they are to make sense to Americans. This requires more time and space than the media are willing to give to any story, except during a crisis. Therefore, foreign coverage in American media is usually about people from Western cultures whose policies are somewhat familiar, such as the English, the Canadians, and the people of western European countries. Foreign news concentrates on situations that are easy to report, which often means focusing on violent events such as revolutions, major disasters, and the like. This type of coverage conveys the faulty impression that most foreign countries are always in serious disarray.

Conflict and Violence. The heavy news emphasis on conflict and bad news, which is most prevalent in big city media, has three major consequences.[42] The first and perhaps most far reaching is the dangerous distortion of reality that emphasis on negative news events may create. Crime coverage provides examples. Media stories rarely mention that many inner-city neighborhoods are relatively free of crime. Instead, they convey the impres-

Softening Up the News

Wherever one turns in contemporary journalism, the "soft news" trend is inescapable. The major news weeklies, *Time, Newsweek,* and *U.S. News and World Report,* like the major print and broadcast media, are featuring more social and economic news with a human interest flavor at the expense of traditional hard—"give me only the facts"—political news. What is happening and why? Does it matter? The news magazines are an important part of the American cultural scene. They contribute mightily to the public's political education because a slower publication pace allows them to analyze ongoing events in far greater depth than is possible for the daily press. Collectively, the three major news magazines have a circulation of 10 million copies that serves nearly half of all Americans who read their stories more or less regularly.

Three forces are primarily responsible for the growth of soft news. They are the drive toward customer friendliness (coddling the audience to keep it loyal), the proliferation of new media, and budgetary pressures brought on by shrinking income from subscriptions, newsstand sales, and advertising. The traditional news media can no longer compete in the game of covering breaking news faster than anyone else, or at least not much later than anyone else. That game is now controlled by the twenty-four-hour cable news channels and the round-the-clock Web sites that feature periodic news or specialize in reporting it. This is the reason why the traditional media have turned to shedding hard news offerings in favor of soft news stories.

In turn, soft news is turning out to be extraordinarily popular; audiences flock to the news offerings that carry the most soft news. There lies the rub. In an age of sharp competition for the attention of news audiences, all the news media want to be where the largest ones are. Soft news is the name of the game. The staid *New York Times* opens economic news stories with quotations from ordinary folk who express delight or dismay about conditions. Magazine shows, in the image of *Sixty Minutes,* have become regular nightly program features that vie for high ratings with more and more "news you can use" stories. The news weeklies have followed suit. They no longer concentrate on putting the week's hard news events into focus. Their weekly covers herald their changed priorities; hard-news feature story covers are steadily losing out to covers touting soft news topics. In the opening years of the new millennium, *Time,* for example, featured stories on child raising and the science of yoga; *Newsweek* dwelled on brain research and sex on the Internet; and *U.S. News and World Report* had lead stories on adopting a child and the problems of stuttering.

Audiences love soft news because they can understand it more readily and because it tends to cover matters that resonate with their everyday concerns. Today, the public's concerns focus on local affairs and on issues like health, education, and the environment. Much of the hard news of earlier decades has lost its cutting edge. The news from inside the Washington Beltway sounds like constant squabbling over petty political details. The cold war era, with its fears of nuclear holocaust, seems like a dim and distant bad dream. Why worry in prosperous times about Washington peccadilloes or about the disasters that plague much of the world's people when there are still plenty of problems to solve in the neighborhood? Of course, conditions could change rapidly and could once again boost the demand for hard political information.

Meanwhile, those who despair about the soft news trend can take heart in knowing that soft news can be very good news indeed. Unlike hard news, it can move people and inspire them to think and react to important public policy issues that they would ignore except for the sugar coating. Honey still trumps vinegar, as the old saying goes. And that's a major accomplishment.

sion that entire cities are dangerous jungles. This impression may become a self-fulfilling prophecy. In the wake of crime publicity, many people avoid the inner city. They even shun comparatively safe neighborhoods after a single, highly publicized crime. The empty streets then make crime more likely.

Studies of people's perceptions of the incidence of crime and the actual chances that they will be victimized indicate that their fears are geared to media realities. In the world of television drama, the average character has a 30–64 percent chance of being involved in violence; in the real world the average person's chance of becoming a crime victim is a small fraction of that number.[43] In the same way, heavy media emphasis on air crashes and scant coverage of automobile accidents has left the public with distorted notions of the relative dangers of these modes of transportation.

A second consequence is that average people, when presented with clashing claims, often feel confused and find it extremely difficult to determine the truth. They are also left with the disquieting sense that conflict and turmoil reign nearly everywhere. This impression is likely to affect people's feelings toward society in general. They may contract *video-malaise,* characterized by lack of trust, cynicism, and fear.[44] Many social scientists believe that such feelings undermine support for government, destroy faith in leaders, produce political apathy, and generally sap the vigor of the democratic process.

The emphasis on conflict may also cause some people to believe that violence is an acceptable way to settle disputes. Even when exposure of the conflict ultimately promotes its resolution, highlighting a violent process often has adverse side effects. The media usually dramatize and oversimplify conflict, picturing it as a confrontation between two clearly defined sides. It is the hawks against the doves in war, the victors against losers in a legislative battle, the fundamentalists versus the modernizers in a struggle abroad.

Finally, the popularity of violence stories has encouraged groups who seek media coverage to behave violently or sensationally to enhance their chances for publicity. One example comes from a lengthy strike by a union of Chicano workers against a Texas furniture company. To attract media coverage, the leaders decided to stage noisy marches to the capital on the first and second anniversaries of the strike, after peaceful protesting had been ignored by the company and the media. The marches created a confrontation that brought city police to the scene and heightened tensions. Political leaders started to comment about the strike. No longer peaceful, the strike finally received ample publicity. In turn, this created sufficient pressure to bring about a settlement.[45]

A taste for conflict is not the same as a taste for controversy, however. Fear of offending members of the mass audience, or annoying prominent critics and business associates, often keeps stories dealing with controversial subjects such as abortion or distasteful religious rituals out of the media, especially network television. If such stories are reported, the treatment is ordinarily bland, carefully hedged, and rarely provocative. In fact, the world that television presents to the viewer generally lags behind the real world in its recognition of controversial social changes. The civil rights struggle, women's fight for equality, and changing sexual mores were widespread long before they became common issues on the television screen or received serious attention in the print media. Compared with television, newspapers can afford to be more daring because normally there is no other daily paper in the same market. Besides, the nature of the medium makes it easier for the audience to ignore stories its members find offensive or distasteful.

Neglect of Major Societal Problems.　Despite the ascendancy of social responsibility journalism, the constraints of news production still force the media to slight serious persistent societal problems such as alcoholism, truancy, environmental pollution, and the care of elderly and disabled individuals. However, the turn toward softer, human-interest oriented news that began in the 1970s has brought greater attention to such stories. Between 1977 and 1997, coverage of economic and social issues more than doubled in print and broadcast media. The downside of this welcome trend was the fact that much of the gain came from cuts in traditional hard political news.[46] When audience boredom sets in, media coverage evaporates, even for important stories. The same thing happens when trivial sensational happenings blot out matters of long-range significance that have become "old" news while the sensational stories grab the media's and the public's attention.

Inadequate training of media staffs is another reason for unsatisfactory coverage of major stories. Proper appraisal of the merits of health care plans, or prison systems, or pollution control programs requires technical knowledge. As yet, only large news organizations have specialized reporters with expertise in areas such as urban affairs, science, or finance. Moreover, a science reporter can hardly be expected to be an expert in all fields of science. Nor can a reporter skilled in urban problems be expected simultaneously to master all the intricacies of a major city's budget, its transportation system, and its services to juveniles. Because most news organizations throughout the country lack the trained staffs needed to discuss major social and political problems constructively, politicians and all kinds of "experts" can easily challenge the merits of unpalatable media stories.

Support for the Establishment

The gatekeeping process also yields news that supports political and social institutions in America. Although the media regularly expose the misbehavior and inefficiencies of government officials and routinely disparage politicians, they show respect and support for the American political system and its high offices in general. Misconduct and poor policies are treated as deviations that implicitly reaffirm the merit of prevailing norms. News stories routinely embed assumptions that underscore the legitimacy of the current political system. For instance, when police protect a factory from violence by workers, it is assumed that the police are the legitimate guardians of public order engaged in an appropriate government activity. The possibility that workers, rather than capitalists, should own the factories and have a right to wrest them from the control of capitalists is never raised. Similarly, stories discussing the plight of homeless children tacitly assume that these young people ought to be living in conventional family units. The fact that other arrangements might be preferable is rarely considered.[47]

American political symbols and rituals, such as the presidency, the courts, elections, and patriotic celebrations, are treated with a high degree of respect by the media, enhancing their legitimacy. By contrast, news stories cast a negative light on antiestablishment behavior, such as protest demonstrations that disrupt normal activities, inflammatory speeches by militants, or looting during a riot. Obscenity and profanity in public places usually are edited out of news events. When they are included, they generate floods of complaints about disrespect, prying, and poor taste. This puts dampers on such exposés, at least temporarily.

Explicit and implicit support for the established system, as well as sugarcoating of political reality, sometimes helps and sometimes hurts the public interest. It hurts if faults in the established system and prevailing political ideologies are allowed to persist when publicity might lead to correction. The fear of publicity can also have a salutary effect on errant public figures. There are, however, situations in which shielding the shortcomings of the political system and even individual misconduct may be helpful. For instance, at times of national or international crises, when the nation's prestige is an important political asset, detrimental stories can severely weaken the country. Similarly, the ability of elected leaders to govern effectively can be seriously damaged by focusing disproportionately on failures and slighting successes and by dwelling on irrelevant personal issues that diminish a leader's stature.

Generalized support for the establishment and the status quo is not unique to the media, of course.[48] Most institutions within any particular political system go along with it if they wish to prosper. People on government staffs have been socialized to believe in the merits of their political structures. Moreover, financial concerns make it essential for the media to cater to advertisers and audiences who firmly support the American political system. Staff members whose personal ideologies differ usually conform with established norms to avoid conflict with their bosses, advertisers, or affiliated stations. People are socialized throughout their lives to support their country and its policies. They want to believe that the people running their government are competent, honest, and working hard to solve the nation's major problems. They often resent exposés that call into question this comfortable sense of security. Media support for the establishment thus helps to maintain respect for it and to perpetuate it.[49]

Establishment support is further strengthened by the media's heavy reliance on government sources and press releases. Official viewpoints are likely to dominate the news when reporters must preserve access to government beats like the Pentagon or Justice Department, or when story production requires government assistance for the collecting of data. For instance, when correspondents need military personnel to enter war zones, or when reporters need access to local prisons, the stories they write about these ventures are apt to support official views.[50]

Reporters use government officials routinely to verify information, validating stories by attributing them to "official" sources. The higher the official's level and rank, the better. The assumption that government sources such as police departments or Department of Agriculture spokespersons or presidential press aides are reliable information sources is, of course, debatable, especially because the particular thrust given to a story may put agencies into a good or bad light. Many private groups have complained that the nearly exclusive reliance on government sources deprives them of the chance to publicize their own, in their view more accurate, versions of stories and that the result is one-sided reporting tilted toward support of the establishment.

Appraising the News-Making Process

Do newspeople do a good job in selecting the types of news and entertainment categories they cover? Do they allot appropriate amounts of time and space to each of these categories? Do they fill them with good individual stories? The answers depend on the standards that the analyst is applying. If one contends that news can and should be a mirror of society faithfully reproducing a miniature version of life, the news-making process leaves much to be desired. With their emphasis on the exceptional rather than the ordinary, on a few regular beats rather than a wide range of news sources, and on conflict and bad news rather than the ordinariness of daily life, the media picture a world that is far from reality. Reality becomes further distorted because the process of shaping news events into interesting, cohesive stories often gives these events totally new meanings and significance. This is why critics claim that the news creates reality rather than reports it.[51]

If one shares the idealistic belief that the media should serve as the eyes and ears of intelligent citizens who are hungry for news of major social and political significance, one will again find fault with the gatekeeping process. Much space and time are given to trivia, and many interesting developments are ignored or reported so briefly that their meaning is lost. Often the human-interest appeal of a story or its sensational aspects distract the audience from recognizing the story's real significance.[52]

Even if one tests the media by their professed story formulas, appraisal scores are not high. An analysis of 400 randomly selected television news reports that yielded 248 routine average-length stories showed that only one of seven key story elements was nearly always covered. Most stories included major factual elements—*what* actually took place and *where* and *when* it happened (see Table 4-7). Coverage was less regular when it came to stating *who* the important actors were, *why* the reported event took place, *how* it occurred, and in *what* context. The audience received the facts of what occurred but was shortchanged when it came to information that would help it grasp the meaning and implications of these facts.

To find fault is easy; to suggest realistic remedies is far more difficult. Few critics would agree on what is noteworthy enough to deserve publication. Gradations and ranks in significance depend on the observer's world view and political orientation. Much of the published criticism of the media consists of polemical works that take the media to task for omitting the critic's areas of special concern. But one person's intellectual meat is another's poison. Conservatives would like to see more stories about the misdeeds of America's enemies and about waste and abuse in social service programs. Liberals complain that the media legitimize big business and the military and neglect social reforms and radical perspectives.

When the media have featured controversial public policy issues, such as the dangers of nuclear energy generation or the merits of a new health care system, or when they cover political campaigns or demonstrations, each side often charges that political bias dictated the choices made about inclusion and exclusion of media fare and about the story's focus and tone. A number of content analyses of such events definitely refute the charges of pervasive political bias, if bias is defined as deliberately lopsided coverage or intentional slanting of news. These analyses show instead that most newspeople try to cover a balanced array of issues in a neutral manner and do include at least a few contrasting viewpoints. But given the constraints on the numbers of sources that can be used and the desire to produce exciting stories that top the competition, the end product is rarely a balanced reflection of all elite viewpoints and all shades of public opinion.[53] Moreover, as mentioned, the prevailing political culture colors everything because it provides the standards by which events are judged and interpreted.

When coverage is unbalanced, as happens often, the reasons generally spring from the news-making process itself rather than from politically or ideologically motivated slanting. For instance, the media covered famine conditions in Somalia because that country was fairly accessible. They ignored similar conditions in Sudan because travel was too difficult there. Events happening in Chicago are reported more fully nationwide than are similar events in Denver because the networks have a permanently leased

TABLE 4-7 Coverage of News Elements in National and Local Broadcasts (in percentages)

News elements	Who	What	Where	When	Why	How	Context	Total number of stories
Events abroad								
Mideast problems	89%	100%	100%	100%	78%	78%	89%	(9)
Asia politics	100	100	100	100	75	33	50	(12)
Europe politics	83	100	100	100	66	66	83	(6)
Natural events								
Weather/nature	13	100	100	94	33	53	33	(15)
Accidents/safety	27	100	82	82	55	100	55	(11)
Economic issues								
Economic conditions	22	100	56	72	50	50	56	(18)
Fiscal policies	50	100	50	81	56	56	63	(16)
Noneconomic issues								
Local/national government	55	100	68	50	63	26	55	(38)
Public officials	100	100	81	88	81	31	75	(16)
Crime/law enforcement	72	95	77	91	60	70	49	(43)
Other domestic issues	44	100	74	70	96	41	67	(27)
Private-sector news								
Business news	85	100	69	69	100	46	92	(13)
Health/medical news	50	100	13	17	96	67	79	(24)
Average scores	61	99	75	78	70	55	65	(248)

SOURCE: Author's research, based on analysis of 400 randomly selected television news stories from March 7 to April 4, 2001. Feature stories and stories briefer than 20 seconds were omitted.

NOTE: Numbers represent the percentage of stories in each group that covers the question. End column = Ns.

wire from Chicago to New York but not from Denver to New York. The New Hampshire presidential primary receives disproportionately heavy coverage because it happens to be the first one in a presidential election year.

Press output inevitably represents a small, unsystematic sample of the news of the day. In this sense, every issue of a newspaper or every television newscast is a biased sample of current events. Published stories often generate follow-up coverage, heightening the bias effect. Attempts to be evenhanded may lead to similar coverage for events of dissimilar importance, thereby introducing bias.

When news is evaluated from the standpoint of the audience's preference, rather than as a mirror image of society or as a reflection of socially and politically significant events, media gatekeepers appear to be doing well. People like the products of the mass media industry well enough to consume them on a scale unheard of in the past. Three of every four adults say they read newspapers regularly; nearly all homes have radio and television and use them extensively. In the average household, the radio is turned on for three hours a day and television for seven. Millions of viewers, by their own free choice, have switched from other pretelevision sources of diversion to watching shows condemned as trash by social critics and often even by the viewers themselves. These same people ignore shows and newspaper stories with the critics' seal of approval. In a 1998 survey, 85 percent of the respondents expressed high or moderate satisfaction with television news programs—a rate of approval greater than their level of praise for general television programming.[54]

If viewed simultaneously from all three perspectives—mirror of society, recorder of significant political events, and journalistic perfectionist—the media overall have developed a balanced approach. Most newspapers and broadcast enterprises try to mirror at least a portion of the world. Most of the large news organizations also see it as their function to present some serious political and social information and analysis. Of the newspeople polled by Wilhout and Weaver, 90 percent reported thinking that their organizations were doing a good to excellent job in these areas.[55] At the same time, most cater to the audience's appetite for easily digested entertainment and diversion. The end product cannot fully satisfy everyone.

Summary

What is news depends on what a particular society deems socially significant or personally satisfying to media audiences. The prevailing political and social ideology therefore determines what type of information will be gathered and the range of meanings that will be given to it. News collection is structured through the beat system to keep in touch with the most prolific sources of news.

Beyond the larger framework, which is rooted in America's current political ideology, overt political considerations rarely play a major part in news selection. Instead, the profit motive and technical constraints of news production become paramount selection criteria. These criteria impose more stringent constraints on television than on print media because television deals with larger, more heterogeneous audiences and requires pictures to match story texts. Unlike newspapers, which rarely have competition in the local market, television must compete for attention with other electronic outlets.

The end products of these various constraints on news making are news media that generally support the American political system but emphasize its shortcomings and conflicts because journalists see themselves as watchdogs of public honesty. Conflict is also exciting. News is geared primarily to attract and entertain rather than to educate the audience about politically significant events. The pressures to report news rapidly while it is happening often lead to presentation of disjointed fragments and disparate commentary. This leaves the audience with the impossible task of weaving the fragments into a meaningful tapestry of interrelated events.

Judged in terms of the information needs of the ideal citizen in the ideal democracy, the end product of the gatekeeping process is inadequate. This is especially true of television, which provides little more than a headline service for news and which mirrors the world about as much as the curved mirrors at the county fair give a picture of reality. Reality is reflected, but it seems badly out of shape and proportion.

Most of us only faintly resemble the ideal citizen, and most of us look to the media for entertainment rather than for enlightenment. From this perspective, a different appraisal suggests itself. By and large, American mass media serve the general public about as well as that public wants to be served in practice rather than in theory. Entertainment is interspersed with a smattering of serious information. Breadth of coverage is preferred over narrow depth. In times of acute crisis, as we shall see in the next chapter, the media can and do follow a different pattern. Serious news displaces entertainment, and the broad sweep of events turns into a narrow, in-depth focus on the crisis. But short of acute crisis, superficiality prevails most of the time.

Notes

1. The question is explored briefly, but poignantly, by Michael Orestes, Tom Bettag, Mark Jurkowitz, and Rem Rieder in "What's News?" *Harvard International Journal of Press/Politics* 5 (summer 2000): 102–113.

2. G. Cleveland Wilhoit and David H. Weaver, *The American Journalist in the 1990s* (Mahwah, N.J.: Erlbaum, 1996).
3. See chap. 8.
4. C. Richard Hofstetter, *Bias in the News: Network Television Coverage of the 1972 Election Campaign* (Columbus: Ohio State University Press, 1976), 187–207.
5. Wolfram Peiser, "Setting the Journalist Agenda: Influences from Journalists' Individual Characteristics and from Media Factors," *Journalism and Mass Communication Quarterly* 77 (summer 2000): 243–257.
6. Herbert J. Gans, *Deciding What's News: A Study of CBS Evening News, NBC Nightly News, Newsweek, and Time* (New York: Pantheon, 1979), 39–69, 116–145, 182–213; Stanley Rothman, "The Media, the Experts, and Public Opinion," in *The Mass Media in Liberal Democratic Societies,* ed. Stanley Rothman (New York: Paragon House, 1992), chap. 8; Kevin M. Carragee, "News and Ideology: An Analysis of Coverage of the West German Green Party by the *New York Times*," *Journalism Monographs* 128 (August 1991).
7. The survey data are drawn from Pew Research Center for the People and the Press, http://www.people-press.org/press99rpt.htm and Pew Research Center for the People and the Press, http://www.people-press.org/jour00que.htm.
8. Coverage patterns for prominent stories may set the mold for subsequent reporting. This did not happen in the O. J. Simpson murder case. Kimberly A. Maxwell, John Huxford, Catherine Borum, and Robert Hornik, "Covering Domestic Violence: How the O. J. Simpson Case Shaped Reporting of Domestic Violence in the News Media," *Journalism and Mass Communication Quarterly* 77 (summer 2000): 258–272.
9. Thomas E. Patterson, "Political Roles of the Journalist," in Doris Graber, Denis McQuail, and Pippa Norris, *The Politics of News, The News of Politics* (Washington, D.C.: CQ Press, 1998), 17–32. For comparative approaches see Pippa Norris, *A Virtuous Circle: Political Communications in Postindustrial Societies* (Cambridge: Cambridge University Press, 2000); and David Weaver, ed. *The Global Journalist: News People Around the World* (Cresskill, N.J.: Hampton Press, 1998). The unique role of journalists in transitional societies is analyzed in Ellen Mickiewicz, "Transition and Democratization: The Role of Journalists in Eastern Europe and the Former Soviet Union," in *The Politics of News, The News of Politics,* 33–56.
10. Theodore L. Glasser, ed. *The Idea of Public Journalism* (New York: Guilford, 1999); and Arthur Charity, *Doing Public Journalism* (New York: Guilford, 1996). Public journalism has been primarily a print news movement. But there are converts in television news as well, as discussed in David Kurpius, "Public Journalism and Commercial Local Television News: In Search of a Model," *Journalism and Mass Communication Quarterly* 77 (summer 2000): 340–354.
11. Pew Research Center for the People and the Press, http://www.people-press.org/press99rpt.htm.
12. "Mr. President, Ben Bradlee Calling," *Public Opinion* 9 (September–October 1986): 40.
13. See Dominic L. Lasorsa and Stephen D. Reese, "News Source Use in the Crash of 1987: A Study of Four National Media," *Journalism Quarterly* 67 (spring 1990): 60–63, and sources cited therein. Also see Timothy E. Cook, *Governing with the News: The News Media as a Political Institution* (Chicago: University of Chicago Press, 1998), 91–97; Regina Lawrence, "Accidents, Icons, and Indexing: The Dynamics of News Coverage of Police Use of Force," *Political Communication* 13 (1996): 437–454.

14. Jane Delano Brown, Carl R. Bybee, Stanley T. Wearden, and Dulcie Murdock Straughan, "Invisible Power: Newspaper News Sources and the Limits of Diversity," *Journalism Quarterly* 64 (spring 1987): 45–54; and Sharon Dunwoody and Steven Shields, "Accounting for Patterns of Selection of Topics in Statehouse Reporting," *Journalism Quarterly* 63 (autumn 1986): 488–496.

15. W. Lance Bennett, "Toward a Theory of Press-State Relations in the United States," *Journal of Communication* 40 (spring 1990): 103–125.

16. R. Gordon Shepherd, "Selectivity of Sources: Reporting the Marijuana Controversy," *Journal of Communication* 31 (spring 1981): 129–137; Sharon Dunwoody and Michael Ryan, "The Credible Scientific Source," *Journalism Quarterly* 64 (spring 1987): 21–27; Stanley Rothman and S. Robert Lichter, "Elite Ideology and Risk Perception in Nuclear Energy Policy," *American Political Science Review* 81 (June 1987): 383–404; and Susanna Hornig Priest, *A Grain of Truth: The Media, the Public, and Biotechnology* (Lanham, Md.: Rowman and Littlefield, 2001).

17. Lichter et al., *The Media Elite*, 62. The study is reported on pp. 54–71. Also see Hans Mathias Kepplinger, "Artificial Horizons: How the Press Presented and How the Population Received Technology in Germany from 1965–1986," in *The Mass Media in Liberal Democratic Societies*, ed. Rothman, chap. 7.

18. Lasorsa and Reese, "News Source Use in the Crash of 1987."

19. The impact of news stories attributed to highly credible sources is described in Benjamin I. Page, Robert Y. Shapiro, and Glenn R. Dempsey, "What Moves Public Opinion?" *American Journal of Political Science* 81 (March 1987): 23–43. For a negative reaction to the power of anchors, see James Fallows, *Breaking the News: How the Media Undermine American Democracy* (New York: Pantheon, 1996), chap. 1.

20. Peter Braestrup, *Big Story* (Garden City, N.Y.: Anchor Books, 1978).

21. Ibid.

22. Doris Graber, "The New Media," in *Understanding Public Opinion*, ed. Barbara Norrander and Clyde Wilcox (Washington, D.C.: CQ Press, 1996).

23. George Gerbner, "Ideological Perspective and Political Tendencies in News Reporting," *Journalism Quarterly* 41 (August 1964): 495–508.

24. For a discussion of the social systems framework for mass communications analysis, see James S. Ettema, "The Organizational Context of Creativity," in *Individuals in Mass Media Organizations: Creativity and Constraint*, ed. James S. Ettema and D. Charles Whitney (Beverly Hills, Calif.: Sage, 1982), 91–106.

25. Joseph N. Cappella and Kathleen Hall Jamieson, *Spiral of Cynicism: The Press and the Public Good* (New York: Oxford University Press, 1997), 33–34.

26. "1995 Year in Review," *Media Monitor* 10 (January–February 1996): 3. Also see Everett M. Rogers, James W. Dearing, and Soonbum Chang, "AIDS in the 1980s: The Agenda-Setting Process for a Public Issue," *Journalism Monographs* 126 (April 1991).

27. Doris Graber, *Processing Politics: Learning from Television in the Internet Age* (Chicago: University of Chicago Press, 2001), 134–135.

28. Leon V. Sigal, *Reporters and Officials: The Organization and Politics of Newsmaking* (Lexington, Mass.: Heath, 1973), 119–130. Also see Leon V. Sigal, "Sources Make the News," in *Reading the News*, ed. Robert Karl Manoff and Michael Schudson (New York: Pantheon, 1987), 9–37.

29. Graber, *Processing Politics*, 176–180.

30. The leading story is shared by all three major networks 43 percent of the time. Joe S. Foote and Michael E. Steele, "Degree of Conformity in Lead Stories in Early Evening Network TV Newscasts," *Journalism Quarterly* 63 (spring 1986): 19–23.

For comparable data on local news, see William R. Davie and Jung-Sook Lee, "Sex, Violence, and Consonance/Differentiation: An Analysis of Local TV News Values," *Journalism and Mass Communication Quarterly* 72 (spring 1995): 128–138.

31. The phrase is from Stanley K. Bigman, "Rivals in Conformity: A Study of Two Competing Dailies," *Journalism Quarterly* 25 (autumn 1949): 127–131. The figures presented in Table 4-5 should be judged in light of the fact that a presidential election was in progress, as were the Olympic games. Problems with Firestone tires inflated the number of "transportation" stories, and wildfires and earthquakes in California bloated the "disaster" category.

32. Daniel Riffe et al., "Gatekeeping and the Network News Mix," *Journalism Quarterly* 63 (summer 1986): 315–321. For a discussion of variations in individual stories, see Norman R. Luttbeg, "News Consensus: Do U.S. Newspapers Mirror Society's Happenings?" *Journalism Quarterly* 60 (autumn 1983): 484–488.

33. Sigal, *Reporters and Officials,* 66.

34. Ben Bagdikian, *The Information Machines* (New York: Harper and Row, 1971), 99–100.

35. Ibid.; Dunwoody and Shields, "Statehouse Reporting," 488–496.

36. David M. White, "The Gatekeeper," *Journalism Quarterly* 27 (fall 1950): 383–390, replicated by D. Charles Whitney and Lee B. Becker, "'Keeping the Gates' for Gatekeepers: The Effects of Wire News," *Journalism Quarterly* 59 (spring 1982): 60–65. See also Guido H. Stempel III, "Gatekeeping: The Mix of Topics and the Selection of Stories," *Journalism Quarterly* 62 (winter 1985): 791–796.

37. Judy Van Slyke Turk, "Information Subsidies and Media Content: A Study of Public Relations Influence on the News," *Journalism Monographs* 100 (December 1986): 1–29. Also see Jarol B. Manheim, "The News Shapers: Strategic Communication as a Third Force in News Making," in *The Politics of News, The News of Politics,* 94–109.

38. See Leo Bogart, "How U.S. Newspaper Content Is Changing," *Journal of Communication* 35 (spring 1985): 82–91; Richard Campbell, *Media and Culture,* 2d ed. (Boston: Bedford, 2000), 257–259.

39. The content of Web sites sponsored by print and broadcast media is in flux. For one snapshot of Web content on television Web sites, see Sylvia M. Chan-Olmsted and Jung Suk Park, "From On-Air to Online World: Examining the Content and Structures of Broadcast TV Stations' Web Sites," *Journalism and Mass Communication Quarterly,* 77 (summer 2000): 321–339.

40. The first two headings have been adapted from Herbert Gans's study of news magazine and network television news. See Gans, *Deciding What's News,* 8–31. See also Gaye Tuchman, *Making News: A Study in the Construction of Reality* (New York: Free Press, 1978); and W. Lance Bennett, *News: The Politics of Illusion,* 4th ed. (New York: Longman, 2000), chaps. 2 and 4.

41. Karen S. Johnson, "The Portrayal of Lame-Duck Presidents by the National Print Media," *Presidential Studies Quarterly* 16 (winter 1986): 50–65. For a broad discussion of the coverage mix at the federal government level, see Stephen Hess, *The Washington Reporters* (Washington, D.C.: Brookings Institution, 1981), chaps. 3 and 5.

42. Matthew R. Kerbel, *If It Bleeds, It Leads: An Anatomy of Television News* (Boulder: Westview Press, 2001).

43. George Gerbner, Larry Gross, Michael Morgan, and Nancy Signorielli, "Charting the Mainstream: Television's Contributions to Political Orientations," *Jour-*

nal of Communication 32 (spring 1982): 106–107. Small-town newspapers are more apt to highlight the positive, telling what is good rather than what is bad, because conflict is less tolerable in social systems in which most of the leaders constantly rub elbows.

44. The term *videomalaise* is Michael J. Robinson's. See Robinson, "American Political Legitimacy in an Era of Electronic Journalism: Reflections on the Evening News," in *Television as a Social Force: New Approaches to TV Criticism,* ed. Richard Adler (New York: Praeger, 1975), 97–139.

45. Stephen E. Rada, "Manipulating the Media: A Case Study of a Chicano Strike in Texas," *Journalism Quarterly* 54 (spring 1977): 109–113. Also see Gadi Wolfsfeld, "Symbiosis of Press and Protest: An Exchange Analysis," *Journalism Quarterly* 61 (autumn 1984): 550–555.

46. Committee of Concerned Journalists, "Changing Definition of News: Subject of News Stories by Medium," www.journalism.org/lastudy2.htm.

47. Klaus Bruhn Jensen, "News as Ideology: Economics Statistics and Political Ritual in Television Network News," *Journal of Communication* 37 (winter 1987): 8–27; Bennett, *News.*

48. For a strong attack on status quo support, see Edward S. Herman and Noam Chomsky, *Manufacturing Consent: The Political Economy of the Mass Media* (New York: Pantheon, 1988).

49. There is resistance to change, even in entertainment program formats. See Jay G. Blumler and Carolynn Martin Spicer, "Prospects for Creativity in the New Television Marketplace: Evidence from Program-Makers," *Journal of Communication* 40 (autumn 1990): 78–101.

50. A comparison of war movies made with and without Pentagon aid showed that aided movies depicted the military in a more favorable light. Russell E. Shain, "Effects of Pentagon Influence on War Movies, 1948–70," *Public Opinion Quarterly* 38 (fall 1972): 641–647.

51. For a fuller exploration of this issue, see David L. Altheide, *Creating Reality: How T.V. News Distorts Events* (Beverly Hills, Calif.: Sage, 1976); Tuchman, *Making News*; Mark Fishman, Manufacturing the News (Austin: University of Texas Press, 1980); and Bennett, *News,* chaps. 3 and 5.

52. But sensational news often contains a great deal of information. See C. Richard Hofstetter and David M. Dozier, "Useful News, Sensational News: Quality, Sensationalism, and Local TV News," *Journalism Quarterly* 63 (winter 1986): 815–820; and Dan Nimmo and James E. Combs, *Nightly Horrors: Crisis Coverage in Television Network News* (Knoxville: University of Tennessee Press, 1985).

53. Frederick Fico and Stan Soffin, "Fairness and Balance of Selected Newspaper Coverage of Controversial National, State and Local Issues," *Journalism and Mass Communication Quarterly* 72 (autumn 1995): 621–633; Neil J. Kressel, "Biased Judgments of Media Bias: A Case Study of the Arab-Israeli Dispute," *Political Psychology* 8 (June 1987): 211–226; and Lichter et al., *The Media Elite,* 293–301. The difficulties of defining *bias* are explained in Stephen Lacy, Frederick Fico, and Todd F. Simon, "Fairness and Balance in the Prestige Press," *Journalism Quarterly* 68 (fall 1991): 363–370. Also see Todd F. Simon, Frederick Fico, and Stephen Lacy, "Covering Conflict and Controversy: Measuring Balance, Fairness, Defamation," *Journalism Quarterly* 62 (summer 1989): 427–434.

54. Pew Research Center for the People and the Press, "1998 Media Consumption: Section 3: American News Habits," http://www.people-press.org/med98rpt.htm.

55. Wilhoit and Weaver, *The American Journalist,* 11.

Readings

Cook, Timothy E. *Governing with the News: The News Media as a Political Institution.* Chicago: University of Chicago Press, 1998.

Emery, Michael, and Edwin Emery. *The Press and America: An Interpretive History of the Mass Media.* 8th ed. Englewood Cliffs, N.J.: Prentice Hall, 1996.

Glasser, Theodore L., ed. *The Idea of Public Journalism.* New York: Guilford, 1999.

Graber, Doris, Denis McQuail, and Pippa Norris. *The Politics of News, The News of Politics.* Washington, D.C.: CQ Press, 1998.

Hallin, Daniel C. *We Keep America on Top of the World: Television Journalism and the Public Sphere.* New York: Routledge, 1994.

Iyengar, Shanto. *Is Anyone Responsible?: How Television Frames Political Issues.* Chicago: University of Chicago Press, 1991.

Norris, Pippa. *A Virtuous Circle: Political Communications in Postindustrial Societies.* Cambridge: Cambridge University Press, 2000.

Schudson, Michael. *The Power of News.* Cambridge: Harvard University Press, 1995.

Shoemaker, Pamela J., and Stephen D. Reese. *Mediating the Message: Theories of Influences on Mass Media Content.* 2d ed. New York: Longman, 1995.

Wilhoit, G. Cleveland, and David H. Weaver. *The American Journalist in the 1990s: U.S. News People at the End of an Era.* Mahwah, N.J.: Erlbaum, 1996.

c h a p t e r   f i v e

Reporting Extraordinary Events

WHAT COMMON THREAD JOINS the Persian Gulf War, the bombing of a federal building in Oklahoma City, the 1994 earthquake in southern California, and the Los Angeles riots of 1992? The answer is that all were *extraordinary natural or man-made events*. Such events happen rarely. They are dramatic and rich in pictures that tug at human heartstrings. And they seem salient to the lives of media audiences because they threaten their shared values and peace of mind and, for some, their lives and property. Such events receive an extraordinary amount of sustained media coverage and audience attention because people expect to be informed and to be protected by the appropriate agencies.

What politically significant roles do media play when such extraordinary events occur, and how do they go about playing them? To answer these questions, we will take a close look at the four situations just mentioned, along with brief glances at related events. After explaining and illustrating the broad coverage principles, we will turn to a number of pseudo-crises. These are comparatively normal events that crisis-type coverage elevates to the status of being extraordinary.

In times of crisis, the media, particularly radio and television, become vital arms of public and private crisis-control organizations. As with other events, journalists select, shape, and report the news. But in addition, they provide crisis workers quick access to the public by allowing them to use media channels to deliver their messages personally or through media personnel. These messages keep endangered communities in touch with essential information and instructions. They also allow crisis workers, including government authorities, to shape perceptions of the crisis, its causes, and appropriate remedies.

Coverage of extraordinary events highlights major philosophical and policy issues concerning the government–media relationship. In times of crises, citizens pay close attention to the media's messages. The media's responsibility to serve public needs becomes exceptionally acute, as does the government's responsibility to control, direct, and even manipulate the flow of news. The Olympian view of media as distant, neutral observers yields to a vision of journalists forced to cope with disasters at eyeball distance.

Four Crises

We will examine media coverage of four crises that represent typical disasters. They are the war against Iraq in January and February 1991; the riots in Los Angeles that started on April 30, 1992; the earthquake that hit southern California on January 17, 1994; and the bombing of a midtown federal building in Oklahoma City on April 19, 1995.

War Against Iraq

In the summer of 1990, hostilities erupted in the Persian Gulf region when Iraq invaded neighboring Kuwait. After economic sanctions failed to bring about a withdrawal, United Nations members, with the United States in the lead, started military operations. The war lasted forty-four days. It began with bombing attacks on Iraq on January 16, followed by a ground attack on February 23. Half a million American troops were sent to the Gulf, and a similar number were mobilized on the home front. Although most people assumed that Iraq would lose the war, the outcome and the ultimate cost of the war in terms of people and property losses on both sides were uncertain. Scud missile attacks on Israel raised the possibility of large-scale losses by Iraq's enemies.[1]

Los Angeles Riots

On March 3, 1991, after a high-speed chase, several officers of the Los Angeles police stopped an African American motorist for traffic violations. An angry confrontation ensued that ended with the white officers severely beating the motorist. A resident of a nearby apartment building, alerted by the noise, videotaped scenes of the beating. Over the course of the next year, the shocking footage was broadcast thousands of times throughout the nation, creating a widespread consensus among citizens of all races that the police had used excessive force. Police brutality and racism, which had long been simmering public issues, were kept near the boiling point by the repeated airing of the taped scenes.

When news reports informed Americans at the end of April 1992 that an all-white jury had exonerated all but one of the Los Angeles officers on the charges of brutality, protest demonstrations pockmarked the country. In Los Angeles, these demonstrations turned into one of the ugliest urban riots in decades, complete with shootings, beatings, massive arson, and looting. Fifty-three people were killed, and more than two thousand were injured. Property worth millions of dollars was destroyed, leaving sections of the city an economic wasteland that remains to be fully restored. In the wake of the rioting, the focus of the presidential campaign that year turned to the hitherto neglected problems of urban decay, the alienated, impoverished underclass, and deepening tension between races.[2]

Major Earthquake in Southern California

In the predawn hours of January 17, 1994, the strongest earthquake in southern California's history left fifty-five people dead, hundreds injured, and thousands homeless. The main shock lasted for thirty seconds and reached a magnitude of 6.6 on the Richter scale. Numerous severe aftershocks followed. The earthquake and the subsequent aftershocks ignited fires from ruptured gas lines and propane tanks, caused landslides and floods, crumpled highways and overpasses, and toppled buildings, burying victims under tons of debris. Survivors were left without electric power, gas, water, and telephone services and many were isolated for days because of impassable roads. Property damage amounted to billions of dollars.[3]

Oklahoma City Bombing

A car bomb gouged a nine-story hole in a federal office building in downtown Oklahoma City on April 19, 1995. The explosion left 168 people dead, including many young children in a daycare center located in the building. More than 300 people were missing immediately after the blast, though most of them were later found. More than 460 people were injured, many of them critically. The blast was felt as far as fifty miles away, and nearby buildings were destroyed or damaged. Rescue forces had to crawl over debris and corpses for days to try to extricate survivors trapped in the collapsed building. The explosion reminded observers of the terrorist car bombing that killed 6 people and injured 1,000 in 1993 at the World Trade Center in New York City.[4]

Media Responses and Roles

During crises, the public depends almost totally on the media for news and for vital messages from public and private authorities. The mass media are the only institutions equipped to collect substantial amounts of information and disseminate it quickly. Therefore, when people become aware of a crisis, they monitor developments through their radios, television sets, or computer monitors, often round the clock.

Table 5-1 presents data on sources that people used for crisis information in three communities hit by natural disasters. The table demonstrates people's heavy reliance on electronic media, particularly battery-powered radios, and the comparatively small role played by interpersonal communication and direct experience. Community A, located on the Gulf Coast, had experienced numerous hurricanes. Communities B and C in the Midwest had suffered two tornadoes and two major floods, respectively. Community D had no experience with a major natural disaster. A sample of residents in communities A, B, and C was asked, "From what sources have you obtained the greatest amount of information concerning natural disasters?" Several sources could be cited in response.[5] Respondents in the disaster-free control community (D) were asked to speculate about what sources might be most useful were such types of events to occur.

The audience for crisis information is massive and loyal. For example, 58 percent of the American public closely watched news stories about the Oklahoma City bombing. That was more than twice the number that paid close attention to the heated Medicare debate in Congress at the same time.[6] When the Gulf War started, television sets everywhere remained turned on throughout the night and early morning so that people could watch unfolding events. To keep up with CNN's round-the-clock coverage, all the networks sharply increased news coverage of the war. More than one billion people in 108 nations watched CNN's war coverage, making its largely undigested reports of breaking events the leading source of war news. When American audiences were asked in a Gallup poll about their main source of war news, 89 percent mentioned television, 8 percent mentioned radio, and only 2 percent mentioned newspapers.[7]

Besides seeking information, the public looks to the media for interpretations of situations. Media personnel are often the first to try to fit breaking events into a coherent story. Official investigations generally come much later. The media also guide the public's actions during a crisis. They direct people to shelters, announce which areas are unsafe to enter, describe purification processes for polluted food and water, and supply news of missing persons or schedules to be maintained by schools

TABLE 5-1   Principal Sources of Disaster Information
(in percentage of responses)

Sources of information	Site A	Site B	Site C	Site D
Electronic media	66%	59%	75%	75%
Newspapers	24	20	40	64
Magazines	3	7	8	15
Nonfiction books	10	10	11	4
Other persons	17	12	14	9
Direct experience	37	32	20	6
Public education	9	6	5	—

SOURCE: Dennis E. Wenger, "A Few Empirical Observations Concerning the Relationship between the Mass Media and Disaster Knowledge: A Research Report," in *Disasters and the Mass Media: Proceedings of the Committee on Disasters and the Mass Media Workshop* (Washington, D.C.: National Academy Press, 1980), 244. Reprinted by permission.

NOTE: Multiple answers were permitted. *N* = 290 for Site A, hurricane disasters; 281 for Site B, tornado disasters; 209 for Site C, flood disasters; and 341 for Site D, disaster-free control site.

and workplaces. News stories also explain what immediate steps government authorities are taking to cope with the crisis.

Stages and Patterns of Coverage

Observers of crisis coverage have identified three stages that merge almost seamlessly and often overlap.

Stage One. During the first stage, the crisis or disaster is announced as having already struck or impending. Reporters, officials, and onlookers rush to the scene. Radio and television stations interrupt regularly scheduled programs with a flood of uncoordinated bulletins announcing the extraordinary event. The stations may preempt the entire program for reports from the scene.

Minutes after the start of the Los Angeles riots, television and radio reporters broadcast live from the scene. They showed buildings on fire and beating and looting scenes, usually without a single police officer within camera range. Later, these broadcasts were blamed for tipping off rioters about places where they might assault, burn, and loot with impunity. These same stories also helped police find locations where they were sorely needed. Media offices became information collection centers because people phoned them with reports or called them for information. The most important broadcasts at the start of a disaster are messages describing what is happening, directing people to places of safety, summoning police and military units, and coordinating appeals for relief supplies, such as food, blankets, blood donations, and medical equipment.

In the early phase of an event, the number of news broadcasts rises steeply. During the Gulf War and the Los Angeles riots, as well as in the Oklahoma City and southern California disasters, radio and television doubled broadcast time and CNN operated on a twenty-four-hour news schedule. Crisis-related news and interviews replaced many regular programs. News bulletins were issued throughout the day on radio and television. A steady stream of eyewitnesses were interviewed. With little new to report, the same facts were rehashed endlessly. During these types of catastrophes, the initial announcements reach a steadily growing audience by word of mouth, either through face-to-face conversations or by telephone. The news of the attempted assassination of President Ronald Reagan in 1981 illustrates the speed of diffusion of crisis news. The story initially reached a large daytime audience that heard it on radio or television. Then, on average, each person told the news to three other people. More than 90 percent of the American public—over 200 million people— received the news within ninety minutes after the shooting.[8]

Rapidity of communication is the most striking characteristic of initial coverage of extraordinary events. Television, radio, and the Internet, helped by satellite technology, can focus the public's attention almost instantaneously on developing situations throughout the world. In many cases news about the extraordinary event replaces most other stories. On January 18, 1994, following the earthquake in southern California, the *Los Angeles Times* devoted its entire front page, along with many inside pages, to the event. Whatever else happens in the world during crisis periods, regardless of its importance, may be largely blocked out in the affected area or even the entire nation.

During the first stage of crisis, the media are the major sources of information, even for public officials. Media reports serve to coordinate public activities and to calm the audience. For example, the *Los Angeles Times* carried a special report on "Coping with the Quake" right after it struck. The report gave people tips about temporary housing, health care, and ways to cope with damage in their homes.

Next to reaching the disaster site, the chief problem for newspeople during the first stage is getting accurate information. Rumors abound. During the Gulf War, some of the early information, based on raw, unevaluated data, was incorrect. For example, network reporters told about chemical attacks on Israel and Israeli retaliation that had not occurred. The Oklahoma City blast was immediately dubbed a "terrorist" bombing, and false rumors circulated that men of Middle Eastern backgrounds had been sighted near the scene. A connection to Hamas, a Palestinian terrorist organization, was also reported. The number of dead and the extent of injuries are frequently inflated. Newspeople receive so many conflicting reports that they lack enough time to check accuracy. The unrelenting pressure for fresh accounts often tempts media personnel to interview unreliable sources, who may lend a local touch but confuse the situation by reporting unverified or irrelevant information.[9] When reporters focus only on crisis events, as happened during the Los Angeles riots, the audience can be given the wrong impression that, for example, the entire city has been left in ruins.[10]

If highly technical matters, such as explosions, structural failures, and nuclear radiation disasters are involved, it may be impossible to present a coherent story. Government officials, eager to allay the public's fears and prevent panic, usually minimize dangers or hide them by using impenetrable technical jargon. Often lacking the expertise to know when officials are concealing the truth, reporters accept their accounts.

The pressure for news encourages reporters and public officials alike to speculate about the disaster's causes. At times, they spin their own prejudices into a web of scenarios that puts blame for the event or its aftermath on socially outcast groups. Blaming Middle Eastern terrorists for the Oklahoma City bombing was a typical response. In the same way, the Los Angeles riots, which occurred during the 1992 presidential campaign, were blamed by Democrats on Republican inattention to urban blight and by Republicans on the welfare programs that had started during the liberal Democratic administration of Lyndon B. Johnson. "Outsiders" in a community (ethnic minorities or political deviants, for example) often become the hapless scapegoats. The racial riots of the 1960s were routinely attributed to "outside agitators" who were depicted as common criminals, bereft of moral dignity and social consciousness.

Stage Two. During the second stage of a crisis, the media try to correct past errors and put the situation into proper perspective. By that time, the chief dimensions of the crisis have usually emerged. For instance, in the Oklahoma City bombing, the Los Angeles riots, and the earthquake, damage estimates were known and most victims and their injuries were identified. Repairs and reconstruction plans were in place.

In general, the print media are able to do a more thorough job than are radio and television in pulling together the various events and fitting them into a coherent story. Print media have larger staffs for investigation and more room to present background details that make the events understandable. For instance, in the months preceding the outbreak of the Gulf War and in the days following the start of the air war and later the ground war, the *New York Times* and the *Washington Post* probed into the reasons for the hostilities, the cost in human lives and property, and the ecological damage from oil well fires. Web sites with ample links now rival and often surpass newspapers' preeminence in completeness and clarity of coverage.

During this second stage, governments and their critics may try to shape political fallout from the event in ways that support their policy preferences. Gulf War coverage, for example, sanitized the war while appearing to present reality. Television showed precision bombings targeted down chimneys or directly into doors. The U.S. Air Force later admitted that 70 percent of the bombs dropped on Kuwait and Iraq missed their targets. The smart bombs shown on television represented only a tiny fraction of the total. Military censorship prevented featuring casualties or showing the arrival of dead soldiers in body bags at Dover Air Force base. Enemy casualties were rarely shown.[11] During the disasters in California and Oklahoma, political leaders, including the president, earned political plaudits for visiting the afflicted places and expressing sympathy and encouragement as well as announcing emergency aid.

Stage Three. The third stage overlaps with the first two. It involves attempts by media personnel to place the crisis into a larger, long-range perspective and to prepare people to cope with the aftermath. Steps toward restoration of normal conditions may be discussed. Following the Los Angeles riots, presidential candidates Bill Clinton and George Bush toured the damaged neighborhoods and announced plans for rebuilding. The media also reported about clean-up efforts and about restored services, such as mail deliveries and bus transportation. Within days of the southern California earthquake, news stories gave glowing accounts of quick recoveries by California communities struck by previous earthquakes. These stories often described reconstruction efforts in detail. To cope with long-range post-traumatic shock and to sustain morale when crises are prolonged, the media describe how some of the hardest-hit victims are coping and give full coverage to healing ceremonies such as memorial church services.

For instance, during the Three Mile Island incident in 1979, when a nuclear facility near Harrisburg, Pennsylvania, became unsafe, the federal government took unusual public information measures to calm citizens' fears about a potential nuclear disaster. It centralized news releases to halt disquieting conflicting reports and required that all information furnished by government and plant officials about the disaster be cleared through a press center operated by the Nuclear Regulatory Commission near the site of the accident. Although officials of the damaged plant protested the censorship, they complied with the president's order. Later, a formal investigation into how forty-three newspapers and network evening newscasts had reported the accident praised the media for providing balanced treatment during a highly confused and confusing situation.

Positive Effects of Coverage

Information about crises, even if it conveys bad news, relieves disquieting uncertainty and calms people. The mere activity of watching or listening to familiar reporters and commentators reassures people and keeps them occupied. It gives them a sense of vicarious participation, of "doing something." To maintain this quieting effect, media personnel may avoid showing gruesome details of the crisis. Although this was not true of the Los Angeles riots—during which vivid scenes of assaults and looting were filmed by helicopter crews and broadcast immediately—it was true in Chicago a few weeks later. When youths celebrating a sports victory smashed store windows and looted, causing millions of dollars worth of damage, the front-page headline in the *Chicago Tribune* proclaimed "Two for Two: Bulls Still Champs!" Under the banner-size letters, a much smaller headline noted that "Celebration Breaks Out Repeatedly." The story alluded to the disturbances in a single understated sentence: "In a few areas, victory begat broken windows and uninvited shopping." A few short paragraphs on inside pages carried additional news of the looting.[12]

News stories serve to reassure people that their grief and fears are shared. After seeing the same pictures and listening to the same broadcasts, people can discuss a crisis with neighbors, friends, and coworkers and experience feelings of mutual support. Watching military briefings on television during the Gulf War, for example, made Americans feel that they were fully informed about the war's progress and that the authorities were in control of the situation. Similarly, scenes of collapsing buildings or city blocks put to the torch during a riot can seem less frightening if the news shows that police, firefighters, ambulances, and medical personnel are on the scene. Watching the mayor or governor tour a disaster site provides further reassurance. Finally, directions conveyed by the media about appropriate behavior save lives and property and ensure that a stricken community continues to function.

Negative Effects of Coverage

Media coverage also may have adverse effects during a crisis, raising serious questions about the responsibility of media personnel to consider the societal consequences of freedom to publish. The government's duty to prevent harm-producing coverage, possibly by strict censorship, may become a major political issue.

News messages may so disturb people that they cannot act rationally. They may panic, endangering themselves and others. For instance, a precipitous mass exodus of frightened people during an impending flood or storm calamity may clog roads and overcrowd shelters; it may lead to injuries and death for those caught beyond the safety of their homes and workplaces. Pictures of violence may lead to a terrifying multiplication effect. Audiences frequently believe that the violent acts that are shown are merely a tiny sample. One house on fire or the sight of one victim's body may lead to visions of whole neighborhoods on fire and scores of victims killed. Police may be ordered to shoot lawbreakers on sight, and citizens may use excessive violence to protect themselves.

Inflammatory statements are more likely to be publicized in times of crisis because the exceptionally large demand for news and guidance reduces gatekeepers' vigilance. Pack journalism may run rampant when media pool their stories to provide as much coverage as possible. If mistakes are made by news sources or reporters, they are spread by all the media. The rash of erroneous stories linking Middle Eastern terrorists to the Oklahoma City bombing exposed Arab Americans across the United States to hate crimes. After the nuclear mishap at Three Mile Island, workers complained that erroneous media reports about the explosiveness of a hydrogen bubble frightened their families into needless evacuation of the area and threatened the survival of the plant and their job security. Such consequences are commonplace as long as crisis news routinely draws analogies to worst-case scenarios without providing accurate perspectives on their likelihood.[13]

Crisis and disaster news frequently attracts crowds of citizens and reporters to a site, impeding rescue and security operations. News coverage of physical disasters routinely draws looters to the scene. During the Los Angeles riots, police reported that the presence of television cameras seemed to escalate the violence. Rioters actually appeared to perform for the cameras. Sights of looters attracted other looters to the scene, particularly when the pictures revealed that no police officers were present. When violence pits government agents against antigovernment groups, as is often the case in terrorist incidents, ample coverage may incite retaliatory action. Timothy McVeigh, the key terrorist in the Oklahoma City bombing, claimed that he acted to avenge loss of lives during a government attack on an antigovernment group near Waco, Texas, two years to the day earlier.

Extensive media coverage has been called the lifeblood of terrorism because the perpetrators use their assaults to attract attention to their causes and gain sympathy and support. Wide publicity for terrorist acts and heinous crimes (such as airline hijackings, poisoning of food supplies, or serial mass murders) may lead to copycat crimes. The Los Angeles riots, for example, produced copycat violence in Atlanta, Cleveland, Madison, Long Beach, and San Jose. The Oklahoma City bombing encouraged similar threats at many other federal government office buildings. When the media gave extensive coverage in 1999 to the massacre of twelve Colorado high school students and a teacher by two disgruntled fellow students, a rash of school shootings followed.[14]

Economic crises, too, can escalate as a result of media images. When prices on the financial markets plunged precipitously on October 19, 1987, media accounts used highly alarming language. *Panic, carnage,* and *nightmare selling* were common descriptive terms. Moreover, the media frequently compared the crash to the 1929 stock market calamity and discussed the Great Depression that followed. Such gloomy news apparently fanned the growing panic and further weakened the markets.[15]

Planning Crisis Coverage

Because media play such a crucial role in keeping communities going during crises, most media organizations have plans to cope with the problems of crisis coverage. This is particularly true for electronic media. The plans generally are more detailed for natural disasters than for civil disturbances because needs are more predictable, and there is greater consensus about objectives. Nevertheless, much remains to be decided on the spur of the moment.[16] Confusion inevitably reigns at the start of a crisis. Contradictory messages are likely to abound until coordination can be arranged. In addition to media-sponsored plans, most stations are tied into the federal Emergency Broadcast System (EBS), a network for relaying news during emergencies.

Crisis coverage planning has two aspects: preparing for crisis routines and deciding how to present ongoing events. Aside from warning people about impending natural disasters and suggesting preparations, plans to forestall crises are rare, probably because the media focus on short-range happenings and because most crises cannot be accurately predicted. Nonetheless, the media often have been blamed for neglecting preventive coverage. The Public's Right to Information Task Force of the President's Commission on the Accident at Three Mile Island blamed the Commonwealth Edison Company, the Nuclear Regulatory Commission, and the media for ignoring problems at the plant before the accident and for overemphasizing the safety of nuclear power.[17] With regard to race relations, the Kerner commission in 1968 condemned media silence about the plight of African Americans in the United States for allowing frustrations to build up and explode into violence in the mid-1960s. In the same vein, the Los Angeles riots of 1992 were blamed in part on inattention by the media and other institutions to the plight of inner cities and their minority residents.

News coverage designed to prevent the government from involving the nation in war raises several serious issues. For example, media attention to the first Bush administration's support of Iraq's government immediately prior to the Gulf War might have prevented the developments that

Shaping the Story During Crises

When crises strike, blaming becomes big business. Newspeople speculate about who caused the disaster or acted imprudently in forestalling or preventing it and in coping with its aftermath. Their stories frame the public's perceptions of the nature of the crisis, its causes and consequences, and the proficiency of the personnel charged with dealing with crisis damage. When the culprit is a business organization, millions and even billions of dollars of restoration and compensation money may be at stake, as well as the reputation and even the survival of the company. How do companies deal with the news media to influence the framing process?

The flawed press dealings of the Exxon company to cope with oil spill disaster news in Alaska is instructive. When the company's oil tanker *Exxon Valdez* ran aground on a reef in Prince William Sound on March 24, 1989, 11 million gallons of crude oil coated the pristine waters of the Sound. An estimated one million migratory fowl and one-third of the sea otters died, along with seals, sea lions, clams, salmon, and other fish. Alaska's fishery and tourism industries were threatened. Hordes of American and foreign journalists arrived within hours of learning about the environmental tragedy.

Exxon immediately dispatched its Alaska coordinator, who was part of its public affairs team, to the disaster scene to deal with the media. Media relations experts later called this a mistake, pointing out that major disasters require media access to the highest, most authoritative levels of the company. The coordinator set up a media center in Valdez, a small and remote Alaskan town, with limited facilities and accommodations for the large contingent of journalists. That decision also became controversial. Some analysts said that a local office was essential because camera crews had to be near the scene; others argued that the media office should have been in a major city with ample press facilities.

The president of the shipyard from which the tanker hailed served as the official representative of Exxon's management. Unfortunately, he was inexperienced in media relations. When he held a news conference without first consulting public relations personnel, it was a debacle. That demonstrated how essential media savvy has become for business elites who must interact with the media. When Exxon's chief executive officer finally spoke on television, his message was equally ineffective. He calmly discussed the chemicals the company was using to disperse the oil but failed to apologize for the disaster or show emotion about losses. Ten days later, full-page Exxon ads appeared in the press. They expressed the company's concerns about the disaster and vowed to clean up the polluted area of the disaster. Possibly with an eye to discouraging lawsuits, the ads avoided acknowledging responsibility for the spill.

Obviously, Exxon handled its media relations poorly in this case. Conducting media relations was exceptionally difficult because many competing information sources were dispatching conflicting messages. They included the U.S. Coast Guard, the Environmental Protection Agency, Alaska state and local officials, and environmental interest groups like the National Wildlife Federation and Greenpeace. Reporters knew little about oil spills and were trying to simplify a very complex story for a public that knew even less. Blaming all bad happenings on a single villain—Exxon—was the easiest way to go, even though there were many other sinners besides Exxon. With more expertise, Exxon could have shaped media framing to make it more accurate. It should have had well-prepared, top-level personnel available on the scene from the start. It should have issued more-informative, simply written press releases, and it should have soothed the public's anger by acknowledging responsibility for those actions for which it was at fault. A bit more emotion and empathy for others would have evoked more compassion by its critics. As one analyst put it, albeit a bit too simply, "if the media had captured, on video and film, the CEO on the site at Prince William Sound holding an oil-covered bird in his hand and looking as if he were crying, the entire story would be told differently today."[1]

---

1. Kathleen Fearn-Banks, *Crisis Communications: A Casebook Approach* (Mahwah, N.J.: Erlbaum, 1996), 149–150.

led to the war. Would publication have been a patriotic act or undue interference in the nation's foreign policy? The answer is controversial.

In 1980, columnist Jack Anderson reported that an election-minded Carter administration was planning a military invasion of Iran to counteract the humiliation caused by a prolonged hostage crisis in which Iran was holding American citizens captive. The vast majority of papers that normally carried Anderson's column printed it, along with government denials. One paper editorialized, "The recklessness of a politically motivated invasion would be far more dangerous than reckless journalism."[18] No major invasion ever took place. Whether one was planned or whether the column thwarted the plans was never clarified.

Natural Disasters.   Rodney Kueneman and Joseph Wright, who examined plans by seventy-two radio and television stations to cover natural disasters, found that the plans were generally predicated on the assumption that people tend to panic and that coverage must be designed to forestall this. Stories that are graphic enough to arouse a lethargic population to prepare for the disaster unfortunately may cause panic or denial. Such "ostrich" inclinations may explain why some residents of southern California have not taken recommended precautions—such as fortifying buildings and storing emergency supplies—despite frequent warnings about the danger of serious earthquakes.[19]

Widespread warnings about an impending disaster that does not materialize may lead to costly, unnecessary preventive measures. That happened in the winter of 1990, when warnings about a 50 percent chance of an earthquake in the New Madrid earthquake zone in the Midwest prompted residents to flee, public services to be shut down, and numerous business events to be canceled. A controversial climatologist had made the predictions. Despite misgivings voiced by seismologists and geologists, the story was widely believed. Reporters by the hundreds gathered in the "danger zone" ready to report the event, which did not occur.

Civil Disorders.   Most station personnel interviewed for the Kueneman–Wright study assumed that broadcasts about civil disturbances would produce panic and copycat effects among the public. By contrast, social scientists who study disasters deny that panic and contagion occur frequently.[20] Whether or not they are correct, the important fact is that media personnel expect these reactions and act accordingly.

Compared with other types of crises, there has been relatively little advanced planning for coverage of civil disturbances, despite their prevalence. From the riots of the 1960s, media personnel learned that it is wise to de-emphasize media presence when violence occurs because the perpetrators are spurred by the chance to have their actions publicized. Media personnel accordingly try to act unobtrusively. For example, they avoid bringing identified television trucks into areas where disturbances are taking place. For the Chicago riots in the spring of 1992, as mentioned earlier, newspapers kept stories and pictures about the events off their front pages. However, such precautions are largely wasted when, as in the Chicago case, television reporters broadcast live coverage from the scene.

It also helps to avoid inflammatory details or language in news reports. Milder terms can be substituted for words such as *carnage, holocaust, mob action,* or *massacre.* The general rule is "when in doubt, leave it out." Tempers can be soothed by publicizing interviews with public officials and civic leaders who urge calm behavior and who indicate that the situation is under control. During the Los Angeles riots, Mayor Tom Bradley and Gov. Pete Wilson were shown and quoted repeatedly about progress made in quieting the city. Rodney King, the victim of the police beating that sparked the disturbances, also made an impassioned appeal for ending the violence. Following the Oklahoma City bombing, President Clinton, in a speech at Michigan State University, pleaded for replacing hate talk on radio shows with calmer messages. What he failed to note was that the mainstream media's extensive coverage of the activities of extremist groups, in the wake of the bombing, had riveted the nation's attention on such groups and their rhetoric as never before.[21]

The Problem of News Suppression

In natural as well as man-made crises, suppressing news, either temporarily or permanently, raises major policy questions. How much coverage should be presented immediately, at the risk of telling an inaccurate story, spreading panic, and attracting bystanders and destructive participants to the scene? What facts should be withheld initially or permanently? In the Kueneman–Wright study, 80 percent of the newspeople said that they would temporarily withhold information that might provoke troublesome reactions. Some would withhold live coverage entirely, particularly in civil disturbances, believing that it increases the intensity and duration of the crisis. Some news outlets delay live coverage until officials have the situation under control. Others believe that suppression of live coverage will allow the spread of rumors that may be more inciting than judicious reporting of ongoing events. No one knows which of these views is most correct or how different circumstances affect reactions to media coverage of crises.

Deciding whether to suppress coverage becomes particularly difficult when a crisis involves terrorists, prison rioters, assassins of political leaders, or maniacal mass murderers who crave publicity. Live coverage of the crime scene glamorizes their violent acts and may encourage further outrages. "By transforming a killer into a celebrity, the press has not merely encouraged but perhaps driven him to strike again and may have stirred others brooding madly over their grievances to act."[22] As Rep. Edward Feighan, D-Ohio, pointed out after chairing congressional hearings on terrorism and the media, the television age poses new dilemmas for a responsible press. "Terrorism is a new form of symbolic warfare, and the television screen is the battlefield on which these wars will be fought in the future."[23] Even the print media face such dilemmas. The *New York Times* and the *Washington Post* reluctantly agreed in 1995 to publish a lengthy tract by a terrorist. The "Unabomber" had threatened to continue his spree of letter bombings unless his manifesto of complaints against society was published.

Publicity does play into the hands of individuals willing to spread terror through indiscriminate killings and other heinous deeds. However, if the press fails to cover the terrorist acts or subsequent court actions and penalties including death sentences, it can be accused of infringing on the public's right to know, even when some of the information appears on the Internet. The press also forgoes publishing a dramatic event with wide audience appeal and substantial financial rewards. If the press follows the government's official line in describing terrorists and their motives, it may become a government propaganda tool.[24] If it dwells on either the human strengths or the frightful human frailties of the violent actors, it will be accused of making saints out of villains or villains out of hapless victims of society's malfunctions.

The press faces similar difficult decisions about news suppression during international crises and in time of war. During the Gulf War, the military kept tight control over news stories by escorting small groups of reporters to the battlefront and then requiring them to clear their dispatches through military censors. Some reporters resented such constraints and ventured forth on their own in defiance of official rules and at the risk of their personal safety. Although their fellow journalists generally approved, a *Los Angeles Times–Mirror* poll showed that 80 percent of the public felt that news censorship by the military was a good idea. When CNN reporter Peter Arnett broadcast Iraqi president Saddam Hussein's questionable claim that the American air force had bombed an infant formula factory, critics publicly questioned Arnett's patriotism. They felt that in wartime the press ought to avoid publicizing news that might hurt war goals, particularly when the news is broadcast worldwide, as is true of CNN.[25]

Muted coverage is problematic. It generally leads to presentation of the official story only and suppression of unofficial views. The perspectives of civilian and military public security personnel become paramount and accepted by much of the public.[26] As a result, security aspects are stressed, rather than the causes of violent behavior and the political and social changes, including new public policies, that might prevent future violence. Muted coverage of a tense racial incident that involved murder in a New York City neighborhood is a case in point. A review of the incident two years later indicated that the facts had been adequately covered

By permission of Mike Luckovich and Creators Syndicate, Inc.

without further inflaming the tense public. But crucial details about mistakes made by former public officials in handling the crisis had been omitted, largely because these officials had been the main sources of news. These omissions delayed reforms and deepened the community's racial divisions.[27] In terrorist incidents or prison riots, failure to air the grievances of terrorists and prison inmates deprives them of a public forum for voicing their grievances. Their bottled-up anger may lead to more violent explosions. Wartime news suppression may cover up misdeeds and encourage their repetition.

Some observers contend that muted reporting reduces the potential for arousing hatred and creating unbridgeable conflicts. Delayed coverage, these observers argue, can be more analytical and thus more likely to produce reforms. Others contend that the drama of an ongoing crisis raises public consciousness much better and faster than anything else. People will act to remedy injustice only if the situation is acute. If the crisis has already passed, action may seem pointless. A permanent news blackout will make reforms highly unlikely. Those opposed to muted coverage or news suppression are willing to risk paying a high price in lost lives, personal injuries, imprisonment, and property damage in hopes that immediate, complete coverage will shock the community to undertake basic social reforms. Most American political leaders, as well as most newspeople, have hitherto opted for muting violent conflict rather than bringing it to a head.

Finally, there is the unresolved philosophical question about the wisdom and propriety of news suppression in a free society. The true test of genuine press freedom does not come in times of calm. It comes in times of crisis when the costs of freedom may be dear, tempting government and media alike to impose silence. If a free press is a paramount value, then the die must be cast in favor of unrestrained crisis coverage, moderated only by the sense of responsibility of individual journalists.

Covering Pseudo-Crises

Thus far, we have discussed genuinely extraordinary events. But there are many other situations that the press treats like crises because they make interesting news stories. These pseudo-crises become front-page news for days on end, generating many hours of live television and radio coverage. As television critic Rick Kogan put it:

> Real life—not the facsimiles and fantasy versions of it once so persuasively (and successfully) purveyed by entertainment television—gave us the most compelling and, like it or not, engaging TV images of 1991.... The Clarence Thomas hearings, for all their import, also steamed hotter than your favorite soap. The [William Kennedy] Smith rape trial, even with its numbing forensic details, was more arresting than "L.A. Law." Add to that such almost-surreal details as Los Angeles police officers beating a motorist, a failed coup in the Soviet Union, and Henry Kissinger playing weatherman on "CBS this Morning," and you have the making of a TV mega-hit: "The Real World Show."[28]

The various scenarios that make up this "Real World Show" on television, as well as in the print media, cause two serious problems. They exaggerate the significance of events that are not extraordinary, and they crowd out other events that need coverage. Had the media cut back on overblown coverage, as with the events that Kogan cited, their newshole would have been filled by other, possibly more significant stories.

A brief look at these news stories should be instructive. The Clarence Thomas confirmation hearings were important because they involved questions of fitness of a U.S. Supreme Court nominee. Between July 1, 1991, when Thomas was nominated, and October 6, when the hearings took an unexpected turn, the hearings were covered extensively. The networks, for example, ran thirty to forty often lengthy stories each. Collectively, these took up more than four hours of airtime.[29] By comparison, in a three-month span, the networks, on average, devote thirty-six much briefer stories to the Supreme Court's activities, taking up less than one and a half hours of airtime.

The unexpected turn that was played out for nine days starting on October 6 were charges by Oklahoma University law professor Anita Hill that Thomas had sexually harassed her when she had worked in the agency that he headed. Print as well as electronic media featured saturation coverage. The allegations, presented in lurid detail, were the centerpiece of the coverage. The lengthy soap opera undoubtedly deflected attention from more important issues of the candidate's political philosophy and judicial capabilities and displaced other important news in the print and electronic press. However, the coverage was not totally without merit. It called attention to the fact that the Senate Judiciary Committee was composed entirely of white males and that several members seemed unsympathetic to sexual harassment charges. Consequently, the hearings contributed to primary election victories of several women candidates for Congress who had turned the hearings into a campaign issue.

Pseudo-crisis news coverage rarely has the redeeming features witnessed in the Thomas saga. The many hours spent on live coverage of the William Kennedy Smith rape trial were a sorry loss for news coverage, but they pale in comparison with the magnitude of wasted coverage on the sex scandals involving President Clinton.[30] In the case of the Rodney King beating, overly extensive coverage of an important news story contributed to the frustrations that exploded in the Los Angeles riots. The main reason for repeating coverage so frequently was the fact that the pictures were extraordinarily graphic. By contrast, the 1992 trial of mass murderer Jeffrey Dahmer, who told in detail how he drugged, murdered, and cannibalized his young victims, received relatively little coverage, even in the tabloid press, because it offered few good pictures.[31]

Finally, one may take issue with Kogan about whether the failed coup against Soviet president Mikhail Gorbachev received exaggerated, overly dramatic coverage, or whether it was handled properly, considering its political significance. These issues are often controversial. As for the entertainment value of Kissinger reporting the weather, this author offers "no comment."

Summary

In American political culture, the normal feuds of politics are deferred when major emergencies happen. Although this unwritten rule is mentioned most often in connection with foreign policy, where "politics stops at the water's edge," it applies as well to the types of domestic crises discussed in this chapter. When life and property are endangered, when sudden death and terror reign, when well-known leaders are assassinated, or when the nation goes to war, normal media coverage practices are suspended. The media largely abandon their adversarial role and become teammates of officialdom in attempts to restore public order, safety, and tranquility.

The media perform indispensable functions during crises: they diffuse vital information to the public and officials, interpret events, and provide emotional support for troubled communities. Radio is particularly helpful during major disasters because its technical requirements are most adaptable to makeshift arrangements. It can broadcast without regular electric power to isolated people who have only a pocket transistor radio. For similar reasons, cellular telephone technology is emerging as a candidate for disaster messages. Round-the-clock radio, television, and Internet news coverage and satellite transmissions from around the world make it possible to observe extraordinary events wherever and whenever they occur.

Because the media play such a large part in public communication during crises, how they discharge their responsibilities greatly concerns public officials and the community at large. Information gaps, misinformation, and the dissemination of information that worsens the crisis have led to demands for control of the information flow. Many media institutions have formal plans that temporarily set aside the usual criteria for publishing exciting news in the interest of calming the public.

Muted coverage, particularly during civil disturbances and incidents of political terrorism, may be unwise because it may drown out explicit and implicit messages about unmet societal demands. The need to plan for crisis coverage, however, is certain. Modern society faces crises of various sorts so frequently that policy makers in the media and in government would be remiss to make no plans for emergencies. By the same token, they should strive to avoid news distortion and overindulgence in pseudo-crisis coverage when faced with titillating news.

Notes

1. For details of the Gulf War coverage, see William A. Hachten, *The World News Prism: Changing Media of International Communication*, 3d ed. (Ames: Iowa State University Press, 1992), chap. 9.
2. For details of the Los Angeles riots, see "Rage in L.A.," *Chicago Tribune*, May 1, 1992; Erna Smith, *Transmitting Race: The Los Angeles Riot in Television News* (Cambridge: Harvard University Press, 1994).
3. Compiled from miscellaneous reports in the *Los Angeles Times*, Jan. 17–27, 1994.

4. Compiled from miscellaneous contemporaneous television and newspaper reports.
5. Dennis E. Wenger, "A Few Empirical Observations Concerning the Relationship between the Mass Media and Disaster Knowledge: A Research Report," in *Disasters and the Mass Media: Proceedings of the Committee on Disasters and the Mass Media Workshop* (Washington, D.C.: National Academy Press, 1980), 242–244. For a discussion of news gathering techniques during disasters, see Rahul Sood, Geoffrey Stockdale, and Everett M. Rogers, "How the News Media Operate in Natural Disasters," *Journal of Communication* 37 (summer 1987): 27–41.
6. Times Mirror Center for the People and the Press, "The GOP Pays the Price," news release, June 14, 1995.
7. *Gallup Poll Monthly,* January 1991, 21.
8. Walter Gantz, "The Diffusion of News about the Attempted Reagan Assassination," *Journal of Communication* 33 (winter 1983): 56–65.
9. T. Joseph Scanlon, "Media Coverage of Crises: Better than Reported, Worse than Necessary," *Journalism Quarterly* 55 (spring 1978): 68–72. Crisis reporting is especially difficult when competing frames regarding causes of the disaster abound. See Frank D. Durham, "News Frames as Social Narratives: TWA Flight 800," *Journal of Communication* 48 (autumn 1998): 110–114.
10. Wenger, "A Few Empirical Observations," 252–253.
11. Hachten, *World News Prism,* 155–156.
12. Steve Johnson and Susan Kucza, "Two for Two: Bulls Still Champs!" *Chicago Tribune,* June 15, 1992; and Louise Kiernan and John Fountain, "Bulls Fans Stampede over City," *Chicago Tribune,* June 15, 1992.
13. Eleanor Singer and Phyllis Endreny, "Reporting Hazards: Their Benefits and Costs," *Journal of Communication* 37 (summer 1987): 10–26.
14. Marjorie Heins, "Blaming the Media: Would Regulation of Expression Prevent Another Columbine?" *Media Studies Journal* 14 (fall 2000): 14–23.
15. John Corry, "Network News Covers the Stock Market Frenzy," *New York Times,* Oct. 21, 1987; and Alex Jones, "Caution in the Press: Was It Really a 'Crash'?" *New York Times,* Oct. 21, 1987.
16. Private-sector planning for dealing with media in crisis situations is discussed in detail in Kathleen Fearn-Banks, *Crisis Communications: A Casebook Approach,* 2d ed. (Mahwah, N.J.: Erlbaum, 2001).
17. Sharon M. Friedman, "Blueprint for Breakdown: Three Mile Island and the Media before the Accident," *Journal of Communication* 31 (spring 1981): 116–128.
18. Douglas A. Anderson, "Handling of Controversial 'Merry-Go-Round' Columns," *Journalism Quarterly* 59 (summer 1982): 295–298.
19. Rodney M. Kueneman and Joseph E. Wright, "News Policies of Broadcast Stations for Civil Disturbances and Disasters," *Journalism Quarterly* 52 (winter 1975): 671.
20. See the report on the work of the Disaster Research Center at Ohio State University in E. L. Quarantelli and Russell R. Dynes, eds., "Organizational and Group Behavior in Disasters," *American Behavioral Scientist* 13 (January 1970).
21. Robert Reinhold, "Los Angeles Ends Curfew, but Tensions Remain High," *New York Times,* May 5, 1992.
22. *New Yorker,* August 15, 1977, 21.
23. Edward F. Feighan, "After the Hostage Crisis, TV Focuses on Itself," *New York Times,* August 19, 1985.

24. Alex P. Schmid and Janny de Graaf, *Violence as Communication: Insurgent Terrorism and the Western News Media* (Beverly Hills, Calif.: Sage, 1982), 98. For an analysis of the symbiotic relationship of media and sources of crisis news, see Gadi Wolfsfeld, "Symbiosis of Press and Protest: An Exchange Analysis," *Journalism Quarterly* 61 (autumn 1984): 550–555; Regina G. Lawrence, "Icons, Indexing, and Police Brutality: An Exploration of Journalistic Norms" (paper delivered at the annual meeting of the International Communication Association, 1995).

25. Hachten, *World News Prism,* 163.

26. Douglas M. McLeod and Benjamin H. Detenter, "Framing Effects of Television News Coverage of Social Protest," *Journal of Communication* 49 (summer 1999): 3–23.

27. William Glaberson, "Press Has Blind Spots, Too," *New York Times,* July 22, 1993.

28. Rick Kogan, "As the World Churns," *Chicago Tribune,* Dec. 19, 1991.

29. S. Robert Lichter and Linda Lichter, eds., "The Trials of Clarence Thomas: Media Coverage of Judge Thomas' Confirmation Battle," *Media Monitor* 5 (October 1991): 1–6.

30. Larry J. Sabato and S. Robert Lichter, *When Should the Watchdogs Bark? Media Coverage of the Clinton Scandals* (Washington, D.C.: Center for Media and Public Affairs, 1994).

31. James Warren, "Media Gives Dahmer Trial Mild Coverage," *Chicago Tribune,* February 2, 1992.

Readings

Charters, David A., ed. *The Deadly Sin of Terrorism: Its Effect on Democracy and Civil Liberty in Six Countries.* Westport, Conn.: Greenwood, 1994.

Demers, David, and K. Viswanath, eds. *Mass Media, Social Control, and Social Change.* Ames: Iowa State University Press, 1998.

Disasters and the Mass Media: Proceedings of the Committee on Disasters and the Mass Media Workshop. Washington, D.C.: National Academy of Sciences, 1980.

Fearn-Banks, Kathleen. *Crisis Communications: A Casebook Approach.* 2d ed. Mahwah, N.J.: Erlbaum, 2001.

Nimmo, Dan, and James E. Combs. *Nightly Horrors: Crisis Coverage in Television Network News.* Knoxville: University of Tennessee Press, 1985.

Paletz, David, and Alex P. Schmid, eds. *Terrorism and the Media.* Newbury Park, Calif.: Sage, 1992.

Peri, Yoram, ed. *The Rabin Assassination and the Israeli Public.* Stanford: Stanford University Press, 2000.

Singer, Eleanor, and Phyllis M. Endreny. *Reporting on Risk: How the Mass Media Portray Accidents, Diseases, Disasters, and Other Hazards.* New York: Russell Sage Foundation, 1993.

Taylor, Philip M. *War and the Media: Propaganda and Persuasion in the Gulf War.* New York: St. Martin's Press, 1992.

Walters, Lynne Masel, Lee Wilkins, and Tim Walters. *Bad Tidings: Communication and Catastrophe.* Hillsdale, N.J.: Erlbaum, 1989.

c h a p t e r s i x

The Media as Policymakers

In HIS AUTOBIOGRAPHY, LINCOLN STEFFENS, who has been called "America's greatest reporter," tells how a history professor introduced him to an audience as "the first of the muckrakers." Steffens corrected the professor. "I had to answer first that I was not the original muckraker; the prophets of the Old Testament were ahead of me, and to make a big jump in time so were the writers, editors, and reporters (including myself) of the 1890s who were finding fault with 'things as they are' in the pre-muckraking period."[1]

Steffens was right. Public exposés of evil and corruption in high places have been common throughout recorded history. They rest on the assumption that exposure will shame the wrongdoers and lead to public condemnation of their deeds and possibly punishment. Reforms may ultimately ensue.[2] Exposés have always been and always will continue to be an important feature of social responsibility journalism in America. They are a major part of the deliberate manipulation of the political process mentioned in Chapter 1 as one of the media's important functions.

In this chapter, muckraking will be examined to show how it really works, with particular attention paid to the role of public opinion. Agenda building is another media strategy for manipulating politics that merits examination in situations such as leadership crises driven by political scandal, the development of science policy such as regulations affecting global warming, and the support of interest group goals. We will also assess the political impact of nationally broadcast factual and fictional documentaries. The chapter ends with reflections on the responsibility of newspeople to refrain from questionable methods in their zeal to reform society.

The Ethics of Melding Political Activism with Journalism

Like other manifestations of the social responsibility orientation, manipulative journalism raises philosophical, ethical, and news-policy questions. Does muckraking create a witch-hunting climate that intimidates officeholders and deters capable people from careers in politics? Do newspeople lose credibility and jeopardize important professional values, such as objectivity and neutrality, when they try to influence the events that they report? Where can media audiences turn for a reasonably unbiased view of the complexities of political life if the media are partisans? Claims by newspeople that their political activities reflect the wishes of their audiences are questionable as long as the selection and activities of journalists are not subject to control by the publics that they claim to represent. In fact, public opinion polls show mixed rates of approval for many tactics currently used in investigative journalism.[3]

Despite the concerns it raises, the role of the journalist as political actor is currently popular. The rapid spread of civic journalism is one example of journalists trying to influence political activities.[4] Newspapers, television, and radio stations in communities throughout the United States practice civic journalism, in such cities as Chicago, Boston, Miami, Minneapolis, Charlotte, and Wichita. Practitioners of civic journalism explore the political concerns of their audiences by arranging town meetings, focus groups, and interviews. When they have identified community problems, journalists become actively involved in finding solutions.

Journalists thus trade their role as neutral observers and critics for the role of activist citizen eager to find ways to solve problems facing their communities. Journalists also become participants in politics when they write stories that are designed to support a specific politician's policy agenda. Collaboration may begin when politicians leak newsworthy information to journalists. Rather than attempting reforms on their own, these politicians hope to enlist media cooperation to gain their ends. Similarly, citizens routinely contact the media with problems related to public affairs, hoping that media publicity will spur government action. Just as the media have taken over many functions formerly performed by political parties during election times, so too have they assumed many of the ombudsman, reform, and law enforcement functions traditionally performed by other institutions in society. Whether this is the cause or consequence of the weakening of these other institutions is a hotly debated question.

Manipulative Journalism in Perspective

The extent of the efforts of newspeople to participate in policymaking has fluctuated as philosophies of news making have changed. The turmoil of the 1960s, which raised the public's social consciousness; the Watergate scandal, which forced President Richard Nixon to resign in 1974; and the shift toward advocating a social responsibility ethic in journalism schools raised manipulative journalism from a position of disdain in the early 1900s to a position of high esteem in the closing decades of the twentieth century. Approval of these journalistic practices, while not unanimous, has been widespread, especially in elite media circles. Reporters and media institutions whose investigations have led to important social and political reforms frequently win plaudits as well as prestigious prizes for high journalistic achievement.

Independent investigative organizations that collaborate with media sleuths have flourished as well. The nonprofit, foundation-subsidized Center for Investigative Reporting, established in San Francisco in 1977, is an example. The center uses freelance reporters who collectively conduct investigations and who can be hired by various media to undertake projects that cannot readily be handled internally. The Community Information Project in Los Angeles and the Better Government Association in Chicago are other institutions that do investigative work. Investigative Reporters and Editors (IRE), a national organization, has been active in teaching its approaches to mainstream journalists. The Nieman Foundation for Journalism at Harvard University holds annual conferences designed to improve watchdog journalism.[5]

Collaboration between independent watchdog organizations and the media is mutually beneficial. It ensures that the investigations of interest to watchdog institutions will be publicized, thereby increasing chances for corrective action. Tapping into media resources also helps cover the costs of complex investigations that can run into hundreds of thousands of dollars. This added financial support can be crucial. The media, in turn, gain collaborators who are skilled in investigating public issues and who often have excellent connections in government and in the community. The prestige and credibility of watchdog organizations may also enhance the credibility of jointly issued reports.

The substance and style of most investigative stories reflect three major media objectives. The first objective is to produce exciting stories that will appeal to audiences. The second goal is to gain praise from the journalism profession. In addition to these routine journalistic goals, many reporters want a third result, to trigger political action or be part of it. Even when political consequences are not initially envisioned, most reporters feel highly gratified when their stories lead to actions that accord with their political and social preferences.

Sometimes the line between deliberate attempts to produce political changes and incidental sparking of reforms is too fine to distinguish. For example, when the media follow up on a report of a series of deaths in nursing homes and discover and describe deplorable conditions that led to these deaths, is this a case of muckraking designed to manipulate political events and bring about reform? Or does the idea that reform is needed arise naturally and purely incidentally from a routine news story? Was Lincoln Steffens telling the truth when he claimed that he did not intend to be a muckraker?[6] Could he have specialized in writing sensational exposés of corruption in state and local government and in private business for the sheer joy of delving into the muck, with no thought given to major reforms that might follow in the wake of some of his stories?

From the standpoint of the political reformer, it may not matter whether reform was an intended or unintended byproduct of investigative reporting. The distinction matters to newspeople, however, because it raises controversial issues about the proper role of journalism in American society. Journalists, even when they favor social responsibility journalism in the abstract, do not like to admit that they wrote their stories intending to produce social and political reforms. Moreover, they do not call attention to the fact that they often carefully select their sources to support their investigative goals.[7]

Muckraking Models

Investigative journalism leads to political action in three ways. Journalists may write stories about public policies in hopes of engendering a massive public reaction that will lead to widespread demands for political remedies.[8] They may write stories to arouse political elites who are officeholders or who have influence with officeholders. These elites, eager to forestall public criticism, may then attempt to resolve the problems, often even before a media report is actually published. Finally, action may ensue from direct collaboration between investigative journalists and public officeholders who coordinate news stories and supportive political activities.[9]

In each case, muckraking may take the form of one of three models: the simple muckraking model, the leaping impact model, and the truncated muckraking model. Social scientists Harvey Molotch, David Protess, and Margaret Gordon and their coworkers identified and tested these models in typical muckraking situations—sensational exposés of corruption usually involving high-status individuals.[10]

The simple muckraking model begins when journalists decide to investigate a problematic situation and the investigation leads to published news that stirs public opinion. An aroused public then mobilizes policymakers who solve the problem. The process is pictured schematically, although the sequence of the elements in the model may vary:

Journalistic investigation → Publication → Public opinion → Policy initiatives → Policy consequences

When some elements in the model are skipped entirely, it becomes a leaping impact model. For instance, following the investigation and publication of a story, officials may act without pressure from public opinion. Journalistic investigations may have policy consequences even when no reports about the investigation have surfaced because officials often act to forestall adverse publicity.

In the truncated muckraking model, the sequence is aborted at some point so that the investigation fails to lead to corrective policies. This happens when the evidence that journalists discover is insufficient or too risky to publish because it may lead to costly lawsuits or damaging retaliation by compromised individuals or organizations. Such considerations have come into play in investigations of major tobacco companies and racketeering operations. In many instances, published stories do not stir public opinion. An aroused public may not move public officials to act, or policy initiatives may not lead to any symbolic or substantive results.

Several examples of muckraking will illustrate these models. Most of the examples come from intensive studies of muckraking conducted by scholars who had arranged to be alerted to forthcoming media exposés. This enabled them to interview citizens and policymakers concerned with the issues under investigation, both before and after publication of the stories. The impact of the story could then be assessed far more accurately than is usually possible when stories come as a surprise and permit only ex post facto assessment. Actual changes in public policy also were monitored for a period of several months following the exposés.

The journalists' motives and methods in conducting the investigations were judged as well.[11]

Simple Muckraking

A story about shocking conditions at a school for mentally retarded children in Staten Island, New York, illustrates simple muckraking: a seven-minute television report aroused the public to demand action. Some 700 viewers called the broadcast station to express concern. Shocked parents later gathered at the school and solicited promises of help from local public officials. The Staten Island chapter of the Society for the Prevention of Cruelty to Children began hearings and asked the state and federal governments to investigate.[12] But the flurry of activity was short-lived and produced only minor reforms.

Modest outcomes are typical in situations that reflect the simple muckraking model. Media-aroused public opinion rarely is a strong force for change. There are several reasons for this phenomenon. Many Americans are complacent or cynical about the political status quo. It is therefore difficult to spur them to take action on public problems, even those directly affecting them. For example, extensive efforts to arouse public concern about energy shortages and the need for conservation have proved largely futile.[13] Politicians accordingly may feel safe in ignoring swells in public opinion, believing that they involve relatively few people and that the issues will soon subside when new situations capture the public's fancy.

On the other end of the interest spectrum, investigative stories may be about an issue that is already a matter of great concern to the public. Although the investigative story confirms that concern, it does not push the public across the barrier of reluctance to press for political action. For example, a five-part newspaper series in the *Chicago Sun-Times*—"Rape: Every Woman's Nightmare"—dealt with the incidence and consequences of rape in the Chicago area. Interviews conducted prior to the series had shown that the public was already greatly concerned about the problem. The series enhanced that concern but did little to spur new crime-fighting measures. However, the rape series heightened the sensitivity of newspaper staffs to the problem. The number of stories in the *Sun-Times* about rape more than doubled, and coverage became more insightful.[14] Such consequences are unexpected and therefore are rarely recorded as the effects of investigative stories.

Although it is difficult for the media to arouse public opinion, it does happen, as the Long Island school case demonstrates. The elements that aroused the public in that instance included an emotional issue—the treatment of disabled children in the audience's locality; a flamboyant, well-known reporter who dramatized the story; and a local group of citizens directly and profoundly affected by the alleged misbehavior of public officials. When such a story captures people's interest, and they have little prior knowledge about the situation, they may learn much and become highly concerned. Still, major corrective action remains unlikely.[15]

Leaping Impact Muckraking

A media exposé called "Arson for Profit" that ABC aired on its *20/20* program exemplifies the leaping impact model. The investigation indicated that a group of real estate owners had instigated extensive fire damage in Chicago's Uptown neighborhood. The group bought dilapidated buildings, insured them heavily, and then burned them down to collect the insurance. Following the exposé, community leaders voiced concern but failed to act. Nevertheless, the arson stopped because the perpetrators feared further public exposure. Fires declined by 27 percent in the afflicted neighborhood, representing the first decline in five years. Insurance payments for arson also dropped by more than 20 percent in the year following the arson stories. No other metropolitan area showed comparable drops. The Illinois legislature responded belatedly with very minor policy reforms. There were no criminal indictments of the parties implicated in the insurance fraud. This story illustrates the leaping impact model because publication of the story linked directly to correction of the problem, even without elite action and the pressures of public opinion.

Leaping impact is most common when newspeople and public officials openly collaborate. Such *coalition journalism* may be initiated by media or government personnel, or it may arise by chance. Newspeople are eager to involve government officials in investigative stories because the presence of these officials lends credibility and increases the chances of substantial policy consequences. Although it may jeopardize the media's zealous pursuit of the watchdog role, coalition journalism gets results.

The events following an NBC *Newsmagazine* story, "The Home Health Hustle," that exposed fraud and abuse in home health care programs, provide a good example of coalition journalism. Public opinion polls showed that the broadcast aroused the concerns of many viewers who previously had been unaware of problems with these programs. But public opinion apparently was not instrumental in the decision of Congress to introduce appropriate reform legislation. In the fashion of the leaping impact models, legislative results seemed to flow directly from collaboration between investigative reporters and members of the U.S. Senate that preceded airing of the story by several months.

Journalists had met with officials of the Senate's Permanent Sub-committee on Investigations to plan a series of hearings on home health care fraud and to coordinate their broadcasts with the Senate's activities. The hearings were then announced during the broadcast. Senators subsequently credited media personnel with major contributions to the investigation of home health care fraud. However, it is uncertain to what degree the knowledge that television would feature the story spurred the senators to collaborate with the media. The combined investigative activities of the media and the Senate ultimately led to a number of proposals for corrective legislation. Still, in the end, the bills failed to pass. Aside from the effects of increased vigilance by public officials and home health care consumers, no major changes could be directly linked to the investigative stories.[16]

In the same way, when the rape series appeared in the *Chicago Sun-Times,* newspeople had already alerted policymakers about the issue. This permitted the policymakers to time announcements of previously planned measures, such as creation of a rape hotline, to coincide with the investigative series. When a story about unnecessary and illegal abortions in state clinics was about to break in Illinois, the governor immediately associated himself with the media investigators prior to publication. This made it possible to make reform proposals part of the original story. It also enhanced the governor's image as an effective leader.

Truncated Muckraking

The Mirage investigation illustrates the truncated muckraking model. The investigation was conducted jointly by the *Chicago Sun-Times* and CBS's *60 Minutes* program, with the help of Chicago's Better Government Association, a civic watchdog organization. Hoping to demonstrate extensive graft in the city's regulatory agencies, the partners in the investigation opened a bar in Chicago, appropriately named the Mirage. The bar was wired to record transactions between its personnel and city officials. It took little time to gather ample evidence of bribery and fraud.[17]

Public opinion polls recorded that many citizens were outraged when they learned about the illegal transactions. But they did not pressure public officials for reforms to prevent similar graft in the future. The situation ended with the arousal of public opinion, but the elite were not aroused and there were no corrective measures. The failure to produce a correction does not necessarily mean that officials totally ignored the story. Symbolic responses in such circumstances are common. Politicians promise reforms or further studies of the problem, including public hearings, but

Reprinted with permission of Robert Chambers.

no action follows. At other times, policymakers may punish individual offenders but do nothing to correct the underlying situation.[18]

The Minor Role of Public Opinion

These examples of muckraking suggest that the major role attributed to public opinion in producing political action is greatly exaggerated. More often than not, the media fail to arouse the public, even when investigative stories are written to produce public excitement. When stories do agitate the public, little happens, ultimately, as a rule. Politicians and journalists have learned that public anger is short-lived. It can be safely ignored or channeled to support reform movements that are already under way. Corrective action is more likely to come when publicity-shy wrongdoers mend their ways, when the stories arouse elites, or when journalists and political elites have arranged to collaborate. It also helps when follow-ups on the story appear in different media and over a prolonged period of time.

Even though publicity rarely causes a tidal surge of public opinion, fear that it might do so makes the media more successful than other pressure groups in gaining their objectives. Because public opinion is in fact largely irrelevant in generating political reforms, the media's claim that they are handmaidens to the democratic process becomes highly questionable. In fact, the media are using the façade of public opinion support to enhance their already powerful position as political movers and shakers.

The Muddying of Public Figures

Stories about President Bill Clinton's philandering, civil rights leader Jesse Jackson's out-of-wedlock daughter, President George W. Bush's drunken driving conviction, and charges of marijuana possession by Vice President Al Gore's underage son—all of these are part of the epidemic of mudslinging that mars the American political landscape.[19] In each case, incidents in the lives of these individuals were endlessly examined, interpreted, and judged, often regardless of the story's significance, truth, or private nature. It is true that these people are important political figures. Although the American press is entitled to probe the lives and reputations of such public persons, and the American public has a right to know about matters that are politically relevant, there is widespread agreement that the press has become overzealous in such investigations and that it destroys reputations needlessly.

Political scientist Larry Sabato, who refers to mudslinging episodes as "feeding frenzies," puts the blame on the increasingly stiff competition among media for attention and on the need for round-the-clock radio and television enterprises to fill long hours with emotional audience bait.

> In such situations any development is almost inevitably magnified and over-scrutinized; the crush of cameras, microphones, and people combined with the pressure of instant deadlines and live broadcasts hype events and make it difficult to keep them in perspective. When a frenzy begins to gather, the intensity grows exponentially. Major newspapers assign teams of crack reporters and researchers to the frenzy's victims. . . . Television news time is virtually turned over to the subject of the frenzy.[20]

At times newspeople bully politicians and other public figures into action by threatening to publicize stories that these people would prefer to conceal. For example, tennis star Arthur Ashe decided to announce that he had AIDS when he discovered that the media knew his condition and were prepared to publicize it. Overt, implied, or anticipated threats about unfavorable coverage can have major political consequences. Politicians often act or refrain from acting because they know that newspeople might publish damaging information. They especially dread adverse publicity from influential columnists.

Can Watchdog Journalism Survive?

Watchdog journalism is a hallowed tradition in the United States that for decades has contributed mightily to curbing government and business excesses. In the 1990s, for example, it led to scrutiny of the way the Justice Department dealt with defiance by disfavored groups, such as a militant cult that barricaded itself in its compound in Waco, Texas, in 1993. Watchdog journalism stimulated passage of laws to halt invasive strip searches of women by customs officials at Chicago's international airport and called attention to a pattern of brutal rapes of young prison inmates by guards and fellow prisoners. It sparked an investigation of rampant corruption and bribery within the International Olympics Committee and exposed the export to developing nations of dangerous pharmaceuticals that were banned in the United States.

Proliferation of tabloid journalism has brought about abuses of the watchdog role that have undermined the public's high regard for investigative journalism. Media audiences have become disgusted with the never-ending stream of scandals and rumors that mostly concern misbehaviors in the private lives of prominent Americans. The public has tired of innuendo that smears reputations and sleazy stories that dig into events that deserve to remain buried. The costs of watchdog journalism have also grown out of control.

Nonetheless, this major journalistic activity remains so essential to a vigorous democracy. A permanent retreat from serious investigations would be tragic at a time when new worldwide concentrations of power are mushrooming and corruption looms more menacingly than ever.

Why are costs rising and what can journalists do to revive full respect for their investigations?

Turning first to cost factors: Painstaking investigations require countless interviews to elicit and verify facts and make sure that the initial charges that aroused the journalists' interests are meritorious rather than mere grudge fights or ego-trips based on misconstrued, distorted, or false information. Reporters must work hard to become informed about the situations they are investigating and must be psychologically astute in telling truth from falsehood. They must learn how to distinguish stories that potentially jeopardize

(Box continues, next page)

national security from those that high-level officials slyly try to hide under the fig leaf of guarding national security.

Investigative reporters must check with legal counsel to lessen the chances of costly lawsuits for libel or damages caused by misrepresentation. They must also deal with the counterefforts by powerful targets of investigation who hire public relations firms to challenge investigative reports before and after publication. In large bureaucracies, like the Pentagon, journalists must get around the top brass that is backed by public relations staffs and interview the troops in "distant trenches" to get the real story. Besides managing production costs, reporters must sense when a story is likely to appeal to their editors and audiences, and when it is useless to prepare for a crusade for which there are few followers.

To restore the public's faith, watchdog journalists must focus efforts on serious political, economic, or social concerns, preferably matters where public action can repair or forestall major problems that affect a large number of people. Journalists must be willing to take on all types of wrongdoers, even if this requires annoying corporations or alienating advertisers. It should not matter, for instance, that stories about lax security in theme parks or price gouging by pharmaceutical companies involve business giants. Notwithstanding the important objectives of muckraking, journalists must shun illegal investigative means, such as unauthorized wiretaps, spy cameras, ambush interviews, or ruses that constitute entrapments. Anonymous sources should be avoided, although that is often hard to do when people like Kenneth Starr, the independent prosecutor who investigated allegations of serious wrongdoing by the Clinton administration, allowed himself to be quoted, but only without identification. Shrouded sources make it hard for audiences to judge credibility and biases. Investigative stories should always be based on multiple sources because no single source knows everything.

Following such rules does not mean that all watchdog journalism will be well conducted and successful. Even the best watchdog occasionally barks at the wrong time and target. Journalists must understand and accept that; so must their audiences.

SOURCE: The information presented here is based on reports from the Nieman conferences on watchdog journalism held annually since 1998 and on reports published in the *Columbia Journalism Review*. See http://www.nieman.harvard.edu and http://www.cjr.org.

Attack journalism raises a number of important ethical and political issues. From the perspective of the people whose reputations and careers are dragged through the mud and often ruined, attack journalism raises questions about the rights of privacy of public figures and the ethics of journalists who publish such stories even when the subject matter is considered to be politically insignificant. Some journalists justify focusing on such incidents by claiming that they illuminate the individual's character. But many others admit that they are merely jumping on the bandwagon of competition. They argue that if others exploit the story, they must feature it as well. That is hardly the epitome of ethical behavior.

Beyond injury to individual public figures, there are broader consequences. The risk of having long past or more recent indiscretions exposed to public view or having offhand remarks elevated into major pronouncements sharply reduces the pool of people willing to make their careers in politics. Many talented people are likely to prefer the safety of private life over the merciless glare of unstoppable publicity in the public sector. "Gotcha" journalism also contributes to the public's growing cynicism about politics and politicians and erodes its respect for the news profession. Finally, the extraordinary amount of media time and space devoted to mudslinging frenzies comes at the expense of other, more worthwhile news that may never be published. The old Greek admonition "everything in moderation" is relevant. Whenever attack journalism seems appropriate, it should be practiced. But there is never a need for feeding frenzies, joined in by journalists in sorry exhibitions of pack journalism.

Beyond Muckraking: Journalists as Political Actors

Direct media intervention in the government process may take a number of forms other than muckraking. Three types of situations are usually involved: media acting as surrogates for public officials, media acting as mouthpieces for government officials or interest groups, and media deliberately framing stories to slant their interpretation in desired ways.

Acting as Surrogates

News personnel occasionally act as surrogates for public officials by actively participating in an evolving situation, such as a prison riot or a diplomatic impasse. The solution, developed with the assistance of news personnel or at their initiative, may then significantly shape subsequent government action. News anchor Walter Cronkite's impact on relations between Egypt and Israel in 1977, when he served as a go-between to get the parties to the peace table, is a famous example of diplomacy conducted by a journalist. So were the efforts by CNN reporters stationed in Baghdad during the 1991 Persian Gulf War to broker an end to hostilities and the activities of British and Irish media in 1994 to facilitate dialogue between their governments and the Irish Republican movements.[21] More commonly, reporters frequently spark investigations of illegal activities by alerting law enforcement officials. For example, a Chicago television station alerted city officials to the illegal storage of hazardous and flammable chemical waste on the campus of the University of Chicago. Hours later, city fire officials inspected the scene and cited the university for numerous fire code violations.[22]

To prevent impending tragedies and solve existing cases, journalists have also become involved in broadcasts about kidnapped children and in crime-stopper programs that feature reenactments or recountings of unsolved crimes. The programs use media stories, coupled with financial rewards, to elicit information from citizens that may help in solving the crime. They are featured in nearly 500 communities in the United States and Canada and have helped to clear up thousands of felony cases.[23] In fact, the FBI credits such programs with facilitating the capture of up to 30 percent of the criminals on its most wanted list.[24]

Acting as Mouthpieces

A far more common form of interaction occurs when the media become mouthpieces for government officials or interest groups, either because of belief in their causes or in return for attractive stories and other favors. This type of interaction often involves leaks. Government officials who are disgruntled with current policies or practices for personal, professional, or political reasons may leak information to sympathetic journalists to enlist their support. Journalists may cooperate and publish the allegations, or they may investigate the situation, often with the cooperation of the individuals who leaked the information.

When newspeople and officials collaborate, the boundary between ordinary reporting and manipulative journalism can become blurred. It is difficult to tell when one merges into the other because a correct diagnosis of manipulative journalism requires establishing motivations. In many instances, the available evidence strongly suggests that newspeople act as political partisans who use their powers of publicity to foster preferred causes and to suppress others. When the *Philadelphia Inquirer* was tipped off by a congressional committee staff member about shoddy treatment of kidney dialysis patients, the paper rushed to the aid of the patients. It was clear from the start that dialysis providers and a negligent federal government would be the outright villains in the news stories.[25] In other cases, the main objective in publicizing leaked information is mercenary. Newspeople put their services at the command of anyone who promises to be a fertile source for future news or who can provide an attractive story, no matter what the merits of the story may be. Television networks are particularly eager to obtain exciting scoops during *sweeps*. When audience ratings are high during these periods, rates charged for advertising are correspondingly high.

Public officials and political interest groups often exploit the media's access to the public to attain their political objectives. The *New York Times* and the *Washington Post* agreed in 1995 to publish a terrorist's lengthy political ramblings to forestall further lethal bombings. The newspapers acted at the request of Attorney General Janet Reno, who feared another terrorist attack by the crazed "Unabomber." Reno's office also hoped that someone would recognize the writing style or handwriting and thus identify the terrorist.[26] Similarly, the media were accused of playing the game of Miami's Cuban refugee community when they lavished coverage on six-year-old Elian Gonzalez. The Cuban youngster's Miami relatives wanted the boy to remain in the United States, rather than allowing him to return to his father in communist Cuba.

Although the media are often quite willing to publish stories in compliance with government wishes when they believe that the story serves a good purpose, they are loath to become unwitting government tools. In 1986, for example, officials of the Reagan administration were suspected of spreading false information about Libya in an attempt to forestall terrorist attacks. When rumors about the administration's deception surfaced, news executives expressed outrage. The comment of Roone Arledge, president of ABC News, was typical of the general reaction when he called it "despicable to tinker with the credibility of one of our most sacred and basic institutions, the press, for whatever reason."[27]

Acting as Chief Framers

Finally, the media can shape political action by *framing*—reporting the news from a particular perspective so that some aspects of the situation come into close focus and others fade into the background. The degree of controls that journalists exercise over framing varies widely, from merely reporting the frames chosen by regular beat sources or special pleaders to choosing sources who share the frame preferences of journalists, to expressing their own frame choices in editorials and editorialized news. Journalists tend to exercise least control over the framing of uncontroversial news coming from official sources and most control over the framing of news about unexpected events or events unearthed by journalists through their own efforts.

A prominent school violence case is an example of an unplanned event that lent itself to multiple framings, many of them generated by journalists' decisions about how the story should be covered. Content analysis of 607 news stories published in prominent print media in 1999 about two high school students who methodically murdered twelve students and a teacher at Columbine High School in suburban Littleton, Colorado, detected the eighteen framing categories listed in Table 6-1.

High numbers of frames are more common when events are unplanned and unofficial and therefore not limited largely to officially sponsored frames. In most cases, the array of frames that surfaces initially shrinks rapidly. Frames that are repeated more often in news stories than their competing frames seem most reasonable or most authoritative (or may be emphasized for a host of other circumstantial reasons). In the Columbine tragedy, the gun control frame ultimately became dominant. The fact that Congress debated new gun control legislation in response to the shootings was a major factor in propelling the gun frame to the forefront. Additionally, the media's editorial staffs gave priority to the issue of tougher gun control laws in their editorials and op-ed coverage. There was also ample discussion about the glorification of violence in entertainment media, but issues of parenting, teenage mental health, and school counseling services fell by the wayside. Lack of coverage doomed issues other than gun control. Otherwise they might have become major areas of attention and action, especially because parents and educators were very concerned about them.[28] A separate study of gun control frames over a nine-year period revealed that the news media structured the overall tone of the gun control debate and favored frames of their own choosing that differed from the frames offered by politicians and interest groups.[29]

When it comes to influencing debate and action on public policies, journalists' decisions are extraordinarily important if they relate to framing issues either in terms of the substance of the policy or the strategies used in battles about the policy. For example, welfare reform stories in 1996 in the *New York Times,* the *Washington Post,* the *Los Angeles Times, Time, Newsweek,* and *U.S. News and World Report* were focused on the substance of proposed reforms in 47 percent of the stories and on the strategy of passing reform legislation in 41 percent. Both frames were used simultaneously in 12 percent of the stories. Scholars contend that the predominance of the strategy frame in most public policy stories marginalizes the substance of political issues and prevents political leaders from explaining policy substance to the public prior to the adoption of laws. Lack

TABLE 6-1 Framing Categories for Columbine High School Murders

1. Gun control laws are inadequate; too many available guns
2. Television, movies, videogames, pop music feature gun violence
3. Internet encourages antisocial behaviors and fantasies
4. Social norms and civility norms have broken down
5. Religious influence in homes and general society is waning
6. Parents ignore their children, fail to screen activities, disregard trouble signs
7. Social cohesion in community and homes has diminished
8. Schools lack adequate counseling training and services, antiviolence programs
9. Schools lack adequate security measures
10. Criminal justice system copes poorly with youth crime prevention/punishment
11. Mental health system copes poorly with youth depression, mental health
12. Alienation of teenagers from society
13. Teenage culture fads: "trenchcoat mafia," "goth" dress, rap music
14. Teenage social pressures, e.g., exams, grades, teasing, cliques, ostracism
15. Jock culture, overemphasis on sports, athlete popularity
16. Racist ideologies and beliefs, Hitler worship
17. Individual dysfunction: maladjustment, misguidance, lack of moral values
18. Evil: omnipresence of evil in society

SOURCE: Adapted from Regina G. Lawrence, "Defining Events: Problem Definition in the Media Arena," in *Politics, Discourse, and American Society*, ed. Roderick P. Hart and Bartholomew H. Sparrow (Lanham, Md.: Rowman and Littlefield, 2001), 107.

of intelligent public dialogue about public policies is one of the damaging consequences of such framing. Public cynicism is another. [30]

Agenda Building

In many instances, the media create the climate that shapes political action. This makes them major contributors to agenda building. The process goes beyond agenda setting. The media set the public agenda when news stories rivet attention on a problem and make it seem important to many people. The media build the public agenda when they create the political context that shapes public opinions. Agenda building often occurs around a precipitating event; such was the case with the beating of an African American motorist assaulted by police officers in Los Angeles. The incident became a news icon for dwelling at length on the issues of police brutality and racism and turning them into major focuses of public policy.[31]

Constructing Political Climates

The breakup of the Soviet Union is another telling case of agenda building. In 1990, during the annual May Day parade, Soviet television covered the festivities for the nation, as was usual. Camera operators had been told to stop filming if protesters against the government made their appearance. Mikhail Gorbachev, the country's leader, did not wish scenes of unrest to be broadcast. He had given protest groups permission to march to symbolize that he was a more liberal leader than his predecessors. But the television cameras kept filming when protesters came into view carrying banners that asked Gorbachev to resign, condemned the Communist Party and the Secret Service (KGB), proclaimed the end of the Red Empire, praised the secession of Lithuania, and carried images of Christ. The huge, nationwide audience watched—for the first time since the advent of communism—a vivid demonstration of opposition to the government. The broadcast demonstrated that the country was no longer united behind the leadership and that the voices of protest could make themselves heard. In the view of many observers, this televised humiliation built the agenda for the collapse of the Soviet empire.[32]

Newspeople have been criticized for rarely stirring up controversies when established elites agree on matters of public policy.[33] In the absence of conflicting reports, it may seem that no one opposes the policy even when that is not so. When an issue becomes a matter of controversy among political elites, the media frequently zero in on it. Thereby, they "supply the context that . . . gives people reasons for taking sides and converts the problem into a serious political issue. In this sense the public agenda is not so much set by the media as built up through a cycle of media activity that transforms an elite issue into a public controversy."[34] The agenda-building role of the media in policymaking is symbiotic. The media perform essential steps, but ultimate success hinges on major roles played by other political actors as well.

Molotch, Protess, and Gordon make this clear in the conclusion of their study of the role of investigative journalism in the Watergate scandal during the Nixon presidency. The resolution of the issue was not, as popularly believed, a triumph for unaided media power:

> We therefore disagree with those who would assign "credit" for the Nixon exposures to the media just as we would disagree with those who would assign it to the Congress. Nor should the credit go, in some acontextual, additive sense, to both of these sectors. Instead, the Watergate "correction" was the result of the ways in which news of the Nixon scandals fit the goals and strategic needs of important media and policy actors. All of these actors, each with some degree of "relative autonomy" . . . are part of an evolving "ecology of games," . . . part of a "dance" . . . in which actors have, by virtue of their differential skills and status positions, varying access to participate. Because they so continuously antici-

pate each other's moves, their activities are, as a matter of course, mutually constituted.[35]

Sociologists Gladys and Kurt Lang reached similar conclusions. Their study of the role of the media in Watergate traces the precise part played by the media in this "ecology of games" that creates political agendas. A look at the steps makes it clear that there is ample opportunity and often strong temptation for newspeople to guide agenda building deliberately.

Agenda building begins when newspeople decide to publish a particular story. In most instances this is a matter of free choice because few stories are so blatantly significant that omission is unthinkable. The second decision concerns the degree of attention to be given to the story. This is the point where ordinary agenda-setting activities can most readily turn into deliberate agenda building. If newspeople determine that a story should become prominent, they must feature it conspicuously and repeatedly to arouse the attention of the elite media, including national television, and the attention of political elites. The Watergate story, for instance, received extensive and sustained publicity in the *Washington Post* before it finally gained nationwide publicity.

Capturing national attention usually requires several other media-controlled steps. Issues must be put into an interpretive frame that will interest the media's audiences. For instance, as long as the media framed Watergate as an election campaign story, it was discounted by media audiences as just another partisan squabble. Once the media, with the aid of members of Congress, were able to depict it as an issue of pervasive corruption and dishonesty at the highest levels of government, it generated widespread concern. Without this climate of public concern, severe penalties for the Watergate offenders, including President Nixon, would never have been acceptable. In the course of putting issues into a conceptual framework, language becomes an important tool. When newspeople and politicians switched from writing and talking about the Watergate *caper* or the *bugging incident* and began to discuss the Watergate *scandal* and *tragedy,* a seemingly trivial incident became a very serious matter.

The particular sources that journalists choose to cite for their story are important. Skewing inevitably takes place when one human source, rather than another, is tapped for information and interpretation. When major public policy issues are at stake, these sources become symbols that tell media audiences whether a particular position is or is not meritorious. When the media featured prominent Republicans and members of the judiciary who acknowledged the gravity of the issues and the need for an investigation, Watergate became a political crisis justifying drastic action.

Constructing Climates for Science Policies

Agenda building by the media is not limited to political scandals but includes many other types of issues. We will discuss two areas in which agenda building is of vast importance for American political life: science policy and social movements.

Government support and regulation of science operations became highly controversial public policy issues in twentieth-century America.[36] Two environmental issues provide particularly interesting examples. The first one has been called the great greenhouse debate about the threat of global warming.[37] Researchers tracked media coverage of the global warming controversy for an eight-year period from 1985 to 1992 in television network evening newscasts and the *New York Times,* the *Washington Post,* the *Wall Street Journal, Time, Newsweek,* and *U.S. News and World Report.* Coverage was minimal at first, totaling only twenty-five stories from 1985 through 1987 in all the media combined—not enough to arouse government and public concern. Coverage soared in 1989 and 1990, when the first Bush administration sought to defuse growing worldwide pressures for governmental action by expressing doubts about the seriousness of the situation. With the media taking their cues from the science community, the thrust of their coverage indicated otherwise. By a margin of nearly nine to one, news coverage suggested that global warming was indeed a major problem that required preventive government action throughout the world. News stories also focused the public's attention on specific remedies, such as controlling carbon dioxide emissions, halting or reversing deforestation, and conserving energy. In the end, the media's efforts to create a climate favoring stricter control laws faltered because the science community disagreed about the ability to keep global warming in check through various government regulation programs. Coupled with the strongly expressed resistance of the Bush administration to major control measures—which could not be ignored by the media—the earlier climate for controls became far less friendly.

The second tale concerns cancer-causing agents in the environment. Unlike the issue of global warming, it covers a public policy area in which the government was very active in taking preventive measures. The main issues related to identifying which pollutants were most dangerous and therefore required regulation. One would expect that the views of experts in the field of environmentally caused cancers would be the dominant voices that the media would quote, but that has not always been the case.

When journalists select "expert" opinions to quote, they often find that frontline researchers are so deeply involved in their scientific pursuits that they do not wish to talk to the media. When they do, their stories often lack punch because scientists hedge their claims, believing that no truth is absolute. This is why reporters often turn to less well qualified sources who are willing and able to express their views strongly and without caveats. Activists, such as spokespersons for environmental groups, make good storytellers. Reporters may also have their own views about environmental and other dangers and seek out spokespersons who share their views. In the words of David Paletz and Robert Entman, "When values are shared by source and press and probably readers too, there is no felt need on the part of reporters to seek countervailing information elsewhere."[38] Widespread opposition by journalists to the use of nuclear power is an example.[39]

In the case of carcinogens in the environment, ABC, CBS, and NBC television, the three major newsmagazines, and the *New York Times,* the *Washington Post,* and the *Wall Street Journal* paid more attention to man-made chemicals than to any other cancer agent, including tobacco, in the twenty-year period from 1972 to 1992.[40] If judgment is made on the number of stories devoted to each carcinogen, the dangers of tobacco were ranked roughly on a par with those of food additives such as dyes, preservatives, and sweeteners, and reproductive hormones such as birth control pills. By contrast, experts rated smoking, overexposure to sunlight, and diet as prime causes of cancer and downplayed the role of food additives and preservatives.

Figure 6-1 indicates scientists' appraisals of media portrayals of cancer risks. It shows that half or more of the experts in this field believed that the media distorted the dangers of particular carcinogens in nine out of eleven areas. Media coverage got its best ratings—albeit only 60 percent or less approval—in rating the dangers of sunlight and tobacco. It got its worst ratings (less than 39 percent approval) on naturally occurring chemicals in food and food additives, nuclear plants, pollution, pesticides, household chemicals, and dietary choices. Chemicals in the workplace and radon received rankings of "fairly stated" by 42 percent and 50 percent of the scientists, respectively. Given the fact that news stories, particularly in the key media examined for this study, provided the agenda-building context in which government actions and public opinion flourish, it is a worrisome finding that the media may stray widely from scientific opinions in matters of great public concern. The potential for major damage is great because the needed protective measures may be thwarted.

Studies show that media coverage of scientific controversies influences public opinion. For example, when the media cover stories about

FIGURE 6-1   How Scientists Rate Media Portrayals of Cancer Risks

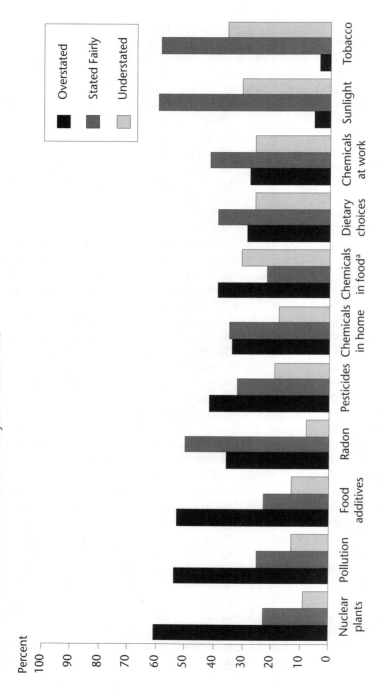

SOURCE: *Media Monitor* 7(8) (November/December 1993): 4.

ª Naturally occurring.

controversial new technologies or medical treatments, public opposition to the highlighted developments is common, even when the coverage is not particularly hostile. When media coverage of the controversy diminishes, opposition diminishes as well. The public, it seems, opts against scientific advances when doubts are raised about their safety. People are especially sensitive to heavily negative safety reports. Political elites, in turn, often are loath to challenge scientific findings that the media have labeled as "expert" opinion or to take actions that may alarm the public.[41]

Similar concerns have arisen about stories in other fields of science. Although some of the coverage is excellent, many stories are flawed. Only a few scientists, distinguished by their controversial positions on public issues, are steady sources for news about new drugs, new medical procedures, and various aspects of genetic engineering. The rest of the scientific community has remained largely excluded, often by its own choice and sometimes because of its disdain for popularized stories. In the same way, only a few potentially risky technologies have been scrutinized by science reporters; choices of which industries will be covered is determined haphazardly or mirrors the interests of effective pressure groups. Many other scientific topics have been ignored and thereby kept off the public agenda, even though they address significant public health and safety issues. This situation is improving with the addition of weekly science sections in many newspapers. However, in the process of popularizing highly technical matters, most media reports contain minor and major errors of omission, emphasis, or fact.[42]

Nourishing Social Movements and Interest Groups

Just as the media regularly boost selected public policy issues, so too can they promote selected groups that are working for specific public causes. Whenever a group needs wide publicity to reach its goals, journalists' decisions to grant or withhold publicity become crucial for the group's success. While most decisions about coverage are made without explicit political motivations to boost a movement or suppress it, there are numerous instances in which the sympathies of newspeople for particular causes guide their choices of news content. This happened in the 1960s with Students for a Democratic Society (SDS), a *New Left* movement. The story is particularly interesting because it demonstrates that attention from sympathetic newspeople may boomerang and produce unintended, highly destructive consequences.

SDS had received little media attention for its activities on American campuses until *New York Times* reporter Fred Powledge wrote a long, supportive story in 1965, some five years after the birth of the movement.[43]

Coverage by a national news medium amounted to symbolic recognition that student radicalism had become an important political issue. When SDS sponsored a march on Washington to protest the Vietnam War in the spring of 1965, the event received nationwide coverage. Although many newspeople sympathized with the left-liberal reforms advocated by SDS, they focused their stories on the movement's most radical leaders and goals, knowing that such publicity might be harmful. The framing produced exciting news, but misled media audiences, including SDS members. The radicals singled out by the media as spokespersons for the organization became celebrities. In turn, this focus attracted new Leninist and Maoist members who expected the organization to perform as pictured in the media. These new members took over the leadership of the organization and turned it away from its long-range reformist goals to short-range and violent antiwar activities.

Sociologist Todd Gitlin contends that the media's decision in 1965 to give wide publicity to SDS ultimately destroyed the movement and with it much of the power of the New Left. In his vivid metaphor, the media spotlight became a magnifying glass that burned everybody to a crisp. Powledge's efforts to bestow legitimacy on the movement through *New York Times* stories had failed totally. As is often true in agenda building, political forces other than the media contributed to the turn of events. Radicalization of the SDS movement was also enhanced by the Johnson administration's escalation of the Vietnam War and by the growing alienation from mainstream society that the involvement produced among many Americans.[44]

Of course, many movements, interest groups, and lobbies have been helped by media coverage, as long as they did not deviate too far from mainstream values. The civil rights movement is a memorable case. The media framed civil rights protesters as victims of racism rather than as troublemakers and lawbreakers, as their opponents would have preferred. Sympathetic nationwide coverage of freedom marches and of battles fought for civil rights in Little Rock, Arkansas; Selma, Alabama; and Oxford, Mississippi helped ready lawmakers and the nation for passage of the Civil Rights Act in 1964.

The benefits of supportive media coverage and the damage done by adverse publicity are well illustrated by two similar rape cases decided in Wisconsin. Citizens' groups had organized to recall a judge who, they believed, had unfairly blamed the victim. They succeeded in the case for which they had media support and failed in the one for which coverage was unfavorable. The media opposed the protesters, ruining their public image and credibility by calling them extremists and lynch mobs.[45]

Media publicity has also legitimized consumer organizations and environmentalist groups in the eyes of the public and the eyes of political elites.[46] Consumer and environmental concerns have become subjects of legislation, implemented by newly created public agencies.

There seems to be a pattern in the role played by media on behalf of successful social movements. That became evident from a fifteen-year study of changed attitudes and laws dealing with conscientious objectors to military service in what was then called West Germany.[47] Most media ignored the movement initially, although a few gave it favorable publicity over a seven-year period. Uncontested favorable coverage legitimized the actions and demands of conscientious objectors and attracted new supporters. The struggle moved to the center of political attention when the establishment press began to criticize the movement in the wake of its protest activities. But it was too late. The movement had become so well accepted that its political demands were unstoppable.

The model illustrated by the case, which is typical for successful social movements, involves four steps. Legitimization of the incipient movement begins with favorable coverage by a few sympathetic journalists. Undisputed media praise then attracts support for the movement among segments of the public. In this favorable climate, the growing movement becomes strong and legitimate enough to make political demands and engage in protest activities. In response, opposing voices are raised in the hitherto silent mainstream media. They come too late, however, to stop the success of the movement in the legislative arena and among important groups within the public.

Protest groups are active partners in the agenda-building game. If they consider publicity essential to the success of their causes, as most of them do, they initiate contacts with potentially sympathetic journalists and create newsworthy events to showcase their objectives. Attracting sustained media attention hinges on the *status* of the group, the perceived *social and political legitimacy* of the group and its goals, the *newsworthiness* of its story, judged by the usual criteria, and the *consonance* of the group's *ideology* with the journalists' inclinations.[48] Journalists prefer to cover high status or otherwise prominent groups that are perceived as legitimate; such groups have interesting stories to tell and pursue worthy goals with which the journalists identify. Exchange theorists point out that a transaction takes place when these requirements are met. The journalists exchange their ability to bestow publicity for the group's ability to supply newsworthy stories.

Low-status organizations whose goals encompass routine human concerns are least likely to attract helpful publicity. Political scientist Edie Goldenberg studied the attempts of four citizens' groups in Massachusetts to attract newspaper coverage to the problems of welfare mothers, senior citizens, low-income tenants, and people treated unfairly by the courts.

She found that these groups had little success and concluded, "There is bias in the system that consistently favors some and neglects others." The favored groups are "haves," those who possess the resources to make and maintain contact with the press and to arrange their operations so that they complement the needs of the press. The unfavored ones are those "most in need of press attention in order to be heard forcefully in the political arena" yet "least able to command attention and . . . least able to use effectively what few resources they do control in seeking and gaining press access." Goldenberg warns, "If intensely felt interests go unarticulated and therefore are unnoticed and unaffected by policymakers, one important aspect of rule of, for, and by the people is weakened."[49] In the eyes of social critics such as Goldenberg, a free press must use its agenda-building powers to benefit all segments of society.

Documentaries and Docudramas

To influence public policy, newspeople are not limited to straight news and feature stories. Fictional productions, such as docudramas shown to millions of viewers on prime-time national television, are used as well. Docudramas are especially compelling because they reconstruct events in highly dramatic, emotional ways. The viewer unfortunately cannot tell what part of the story is real and what part is dramatic frosting.[50]

The political motivations leading to the production and display of many documentaries and docudramas are obvious. As communications scholar Oscar Gandy has pointed out, "Too frequently to be mere coincidence, serial dramas, or the made-for-television movies we describe as docudramas, have been aired simultaneously with the discussion of related issues in Congress."[51] An example of a widely publicized docudrama that coincided with related political events was "The Day After," a two-hour ABC dramatization of a nuclear attack on Kansas City and its aftermath. It was broadcast on Sunday, November 20, 1983, following an extensive pre-broadcast advertising campaign by the network that included an eight-page viewer's guide. The drama was replete with scenes of burned bodies, faces with blinded eyes rotting from radiation sickness, smoldering rubble, and survivors reduced to preying on each other.

At the time of broadcast, nuclear weapons policy was in the limelight. The Reagan administration was attempting to gain support in the United States and in Europe for deploying American missiles in European NATO countries. Antinuclear groups at home and abroad were working feverishly to stop the deployment. The docudrama was aired a few days before the decision to place the missiles was to be approved by the West German legislature. Excerpts of the docudrama were made available to German television.

Supporters of missile deployment feared that the program would lead to massive public demonstrations designed to force a change in nuclear deployment policies. When the Reagan administration was invited to send a representative to participate in a postbroadcast discussion of the lessons of the docudrama, it showed its profound concern by sending Secretary of State George P. Shultz. Throughout the furor raised by the broadcast, ABC denied that the timing had been politically motivated. The November date was chosen, it claimed, to raise ABC's ratings during a sweeps month, when high ratings would boost advertising prices.

What, then, was the political impact of "The Day After," which was viewed by more than 100 million people in homes, schools, churches, and town halls?[52] It appears that the broadcast energized antinuclear groups and aroused fears in pronuclear groups that "The Day After" might generate defeatist attitudes among Americans. Contrary to expectations, public opinion polls after the broadcast did not show massive shifts of public attitudes about nuclear missile policies. In Europe, where immediate drastic political consequences had been expected, the missiles were deployed without major obstacles.

A number of analysts ascribed the lack of impact to flaws in the docudrama, which left the reasons for the nuclear attack uncertain and failed to deal squarely with nuclear policy issues. Others felt that the public had gained knowledge and awareness from the film but had learned to distance itself psychologically from fictional disasters. Therefore, the audience failed to empathize fully with the fictitious stricken residents of Kansas City.

While the apparent consequences of "The Day After" were less than expected, other docudramas as well as full-length motion picture versions of historical events may be more compelling. "J.F.K.," a 1991 movie docudrama, suggested that President Kennedy's assassination sprang from a massive conspiracy that involved the White House, the CIA, and the FBI, among others. Polls subsequently showed that numerous viewers accepted the film's premises.[53] The fictionalized movie reconstruction of President Nixon's life and the false saga of African American soldiers liberating German concentration camps at Dachau and Buchenwald in World War II— broadcast as the PBS documentary "The Liberators" in 1993—found believers who could not tell fact from fiction. Concern or hopes remain high that prime-time broadcasts and the associated media coverage and public discussions may have major political consequences in the long or short run.[54] This potential impact obligates a responsible press to take greater pains to present all sides of an issue and to be more accurate in its depiction, even in fictional programs. Critics of "The Day After" felt that the drama understated the likely consequences of an atomic attack, making it seem less disastrous than the critics' vision. Moreover, the appropriate background for appraising various policy options was lacking. Viewers were not told that the possibility of negotiating a nuclear freeze was severely constricted by the unwillingness of other world powers with nuclear arsenals to reciprocate and to permit verification of compliance.

Methods: Fair and Foul

The fairness and accuracy of news presentations and the appropriateness of news-gathering techniques become important issues when one considers that the media, in combination with other political actors, create the political reality that sets the context for political action.[55] It is a serious matter, therefore, when the media are accused of frequently resorting to improper methods.

Confirming Prejudgments

A famous $120 million libel suit illustrates concerns about the legitimacy of some media tactics. The suit was brought by Gen. William C. Westmoreland against CBS for statements made about him in a ninety-minute documentary on the Vietnam War called "The Uncounted Enemy: A Vietnam Deception." The principal message of the documentary was that the general, while commander of American forces in Vietnam, had deliberately manipulated information about the strength of enemy troops to show the president and Congress that American troops under his command were winning the war. The Viet Cong offensive in the winter of 1968 demonstrated that the enemy's strength and tenacity had been badly underestimated.

The case is ideal for examining questionable media practices because an internal CBS review of production methods was made public. It indicated that the producers of the documentary believed in Westmoreland's guilt from the very start and constructed the story to support their preformed conclusions. The internal report acknowledged that CBS personnel made eleven major errors while putting together the documentary. These included basing charges that a conspiracy was involved on inadequate evidence, interviewing mostly people who supported the producers' overall conclusions, reshooting unsatisfactory testimony after allowing a witness to hear what others had said, and "coddling sympathetic witnesses."[56] The report contained portions of unedited transcripts of interviews in which sources were apparently coached by interviewers. At times interviewers asked loaded questions such as whether the respondent agreed that there had been "a full-fledged conspiracy to fake intelligence reporting." If respondents failed to agree, their remarks were omitted from the final broadcast. Materials that might have undermined the documentary's principal conclusions about General Westmoreland's activities ended up on the cutting room floor.

In the final documentary, eight of the ten persons whose testimony was featured disagreed with Westmoreland. One of the two who did not, Lt. Gen. Daniel Graham, was given a mere twenty-one seconds of airtime, even though he had been the chief of the army's current intelligence and estimates division in Vietnam in the late 1960s. Overall, Westmoreland and his supporters spoke for only five minutes and fifty-nine seconds, whereas his accusers were given nineteen minutes and nineteen seconds, a ratio of better than three to one for the accusers.

Van Gordon Sauter, then-president of CBS News, acknowledged that CBS policies and standards had been violated during the making of the documentary, but argued that these flaws did not impair its editorial integrity. According to him, the presentation gave an accurate account of the distorted estimates of enemy strength by the American military in Vietnam.

After several years of legal sparring, Westmoreland dropped his libel suit, leaving the substantive issues unsettled. The issues of media policy are clearer. As acknowledged in the CBS internal report, there is little disagreement about the standards of fairness and accuracy that should be applied in broadcasts about important public issues. But—and this is the disturbing aspect—these standards continue to be breached all too often. Such breaches raise questions about the sense of responsibility of high-level media personnel. When important public matters are at stake, are the media, especially the influential electronic media, exercising sufficient care to make sure that the preconceptions of media personnel do not taint stories and mislead media audiences?

With investigative journalism growing in popularity, the problem of inaccurate reports has mounted. In 1989, for instance, charges surfaced that a freelance photographer had faked and restaged battle scenes in film used in CBS newscasts and documentaries about the war in Afghanistan. Scenes of sabotaging electric supply lines for Kabul, the capital of Afghanistan, allegedly were reenacted days after the event. The location of refugees was misstated to make the story more dramatic, and a Pakistani jet was misidentified as a Soviet plane.[57] In 1993, NBC's *Dateline* program showed how easily General Motors pickup trucks with sidesaddle gas tanks burst into fire after collision. The problem was that production crews had taped toy rockets to the underside of a truck and had tampered with its gas cap to make sure that the explosion would take place on cue. Caught red-handed in a major deception, NBC quickly settled a suit brought by General Motors.[58]

In many instances, inaccurate reports have permanent economic, professional, and social consequences for the individuals and institutions whose stories are told. In the Westmoreland case, for example, the reputation of a prominent general was at stake. In a case involving the Kaiser Aluminum and Chemical Corporation, business losses could have run into millions of dollars. An investigative report had accused the company of knowingly selling dangerous household electrical wiring under false pretenses. In yet another case, a partially fictionalized documentary about the serial murder of African American youths in Atlanta suggested that the killer might still be at large. It raised doubts about the fairness of the trial of the man convicted as the murderer. The broadcast prompted the mayor of Atlanta and civic leaders to launch a public information campaign to blunt the anticipated ill effects.[59]

The serious injuries inflicted when publicity is careless or biased have become a deep concern for civil libertarians. An executive director of the American Civil Liberties Union has warned, "Justice by press release and summary political punishment are methods we should have by now learned to avoid."[60] The problem is made worse by the fact that rebuttals to misinformation in interpretive stories, if permitted at all by the networks, are subject to their editorial control because they are considered to be opinion pieces, rather than straight news.[61]

Entrapment

Serious ethical issues arise also when newspeople undertake undercover operations or create bogus enterprises to entrap potential and actual wrongdoers. The story told earlier about the Mirage tavern, set up to elicit and record bribery by city officials, illustrates the practice. So does the preparation of NBC's program "Cataract Cowboys" in 1993. NBC's investigative team wanted to tell a story about unnecessary cataract surgeries.[62] When several Florida eye clinics turned down requests by healthy undercover reporters for eye surgery, the producers staged a partly successful entrapment. One "patient," whose requests for surgery had been denied initially, telephoned the clinic to schedule an appointment. The filmed report of her return notes that she "was only a few tests and a half-hour away from surgery." The report neglected to mention that the tests might have forestalled the surgery and therefore did not constitute evidence of malpractice.

Canadian media set a far more massive crime trap to expose organized crime in North America. The investigation resulted in a three-and-a-half hour documentary broadcast by the Canadian Broadcasting Company (CBC) in 1979. CBC reporters and agents who were planted inside organized crime circles used hidden microphones and cameras to obtain dramatic film footage of gangsters discussing their activities. In one instance, a reporter arranged meetings with a woman suspected of helping gangsters to buy real estate in Atlantic City. The reporter pretended to represent a person in Italy who wished to transfer several million dollars from Italy to Canada. The money was then to be funneled into Atlantic City real estate under the guise that the money belonged to legitimate Canadian investors. Through this initial contact, another meeting was set up between a disguised reporter, who had had previous experience as an informant for law enforcement agencies and underworld dealers in illegal real estate. All of these meetings were audiotaped and some parts were filmed.[63]

Sting operations like these raise serious civil liberties issues at best, even when they are conducted by regular law enforcement agencies and are under the watchful eyes of the courts.[64] Concerns about protecting the rights of suspects are even greater when the sleuths are journalists acting without an official mandate and without supervision by a responsible public body. Quite aside from civil liberties issues, sting operations raise fundamental questions about the proper functions of the press. Should its watchdog role be carried to the point where it becomes a quasi-police force, tracking down selected offenders whenever a good story promises to be the likely reward?

Summary

In this chapter we examined direct involvement by journalists in the affairs of government. We began with an analysis of muckraking, comparing reality to a series of models of the process. The media's power to arouse public opinion with exposés of corruption is far less than is popularly believed. Even if the public becomes highly concerned, political action is not guaranteed. It is a mistaken belief that exposés commonly produce reforms because an aroused public then pressures for political action.

The most propitious road to reform is via direct liaisons between newspeople and government officials. When officials provide story leads in areas in which they would like to produce action, or when newspeople can interest officials in taking action on issues that have come to the media's attention, successful political activities are apt to occur. On rare occasions the media are also able to produce action by participating in political negotiations or by using the club of potential unwanted publicity to force officials to act.

The Watergate scandal illustrates how political action can emerge from the interplay of various political institutions. The media, through a series of agenda-building steps, created the climate in which it became possible to force the resignation of a president. Agenda-building examples from science policy and from the realm of interest group politics demonstrate the impact of the media on developments in these fields. The media serve as catalysts that precipitate the actions of other elements within the society. They enhance the influence of some political forces and weaken others, but the ultimate outcome is often beyond their control.

The media's public policymaking roles influence American politics in general as well as the lives of many individuals and institutions. How sensitively and accurately they are performed therefore become matters of grave concern. News gathering and news production frequently are seriously flawed, even when media institutions profess to believe in high standards. How often the ethics and standards of the profession are violated, and what the costs are to people caught in the net of inaccurate publicity, are matters for conjecture.

At the heart of most instances when newspeople become actively involved in politics lies the desire to produce exciting news stories. This is not surprising. Journalism requires telling stories that will attract audiences. That journalists are tempted to be good storytellers above all, even at the expense of other goals, should give pause to those who advocate that those in the media should play the political game actively and regularly. One must ask whether their professional standards equip them to guide politics wisely and well. To put it another way: when issues are put on the crowded political agenda, should their newsworthiness be the controlling factor? If the answer is no, then massive participation by the media in policymaking may be quite troubling.

Notes

1. Lincoln Steffens, *The Autobiography of Lincoln Steffens* (New York: Harcourt Brace, 1931), 357.
2. See Larry J. Sabato, *Feeding Frenzy: How Attack Journalism Has Transformed American Politics* (New York: Free Press, 1991), chap. 2; David L. Protess et al., *The Journalism of Outrage: Investigative Reporting and Agenda Building* (New York: Guilford Press, 1991), chap. 2.
3. David Weaver and LeAnne Daniels, "Public Opinion on Investigative Reporting in the 1980s," *Journalism Quarterly* 69 (spring 1992): 146–155. Ethical reporting guidelines for journalists are laid out in Bruce J. Evenson, *The Responsible Reporter* (Northport, Ala.: Vision Press, 1995).

4. The pros and cons of public journalism as well as the relevant literature are examined in a collection edited by Theodore L. Glasser, *The Idea of Public Journalism* (New York: Guilford Press, 1999).

5. David L. Protess, *Muckraking Matters: The Societal Impact of Investigative Reporting*, Institute for Modern Communications Research Monographs Series (Evanston: Northwestern University, 1987), 13. The public's changing views about investigative journalism are traced in Lars Willnat and David Weaver, "Public Opinion on Investigative Reporting in the 1990s: Has Anything Changed Since the 1980s?" *Journalism and Mass Communication Quarterly*, 75(3): 449–463, 1998. The Nieman Watchdog conference reports are available on the foundation's Web site at http://www.nieman.harvard.edu/.

6. Steffens, *Autobiography*, 357.

7. Protess et al., *Journalism of Outrage*, 214–227.

8. How investigative stories differ from other forms of journalism is described by Matthew C. Ehrlich, "The Journalism of Outrageousness: Tabloid Television News vs. Investigative News," *Journalism and Mass Communication Monographs* 155 (February 1996).

9. Eytan Gilboa, "Media Diplomacy: Conceptual Divergence and Application," *Harvard International Journal of Press/Politics* 3(3) (1998): 56–76, makes a similar distinction.

10. Harvey L. Molotch, David L. Protess, and Margaret T. Gordon, "The Media-Policy Connection: Ecologies of News," in *Political Communication Research: Approaches, Studies, Assessments,* ed. David L. Paletz (Norwood, N.J.: Ablex, 1987), 26–48. Protess et al. model the process somewhat differently in their more recent *Journalism of Outrage*. But the earlier version seems more explicit.

11. Protess et al., *Journalism of Outrage*, chaps. 3–6 detail six investigations.

12. Robert Muccigrosso, "Television and the Urban Crisis," in *Screen and Society,* ed. Frank J. Coppa (Chicago: Nelson-Hall, 1979), 44–45.

13. Chris T. Allen and Judith D. Weber, "How Presidential Media Use Affects Individuals' Beliefs about Conservation," *Journalism Quarterly* 60 (spring 1983): 98–104, 196.

14. Protess et al., *Journalism of Outrage*, chap. 4.

15. Often the chief point of a program is simply to alert the public to a problem; immediate action may not be expected. For example, the PBS documentary "Crisis at General Hospital" was intended to make the public aware of the inequity of a two-tier health system in which people of means are served by excellent private hospitals whereas the remainder of the population receives second-rate care in inferior public hospitals.

16. Protess et al., *Journalism of Outrage*, chap. 3.

17. The full story is told in Zay N. Smith and Pamela Zekman, *The Mirage* (New York: Random House, 1979).

18. Protess et al., *Journalism of Outrage*, 240–244.

19. Larry J. Sabato, Mark Stencel, and S. Robert Lichter, *Peepshow: Media and Politics in an Age of Scandal* (Lanham, Md.: Rowman and Littlefield, 2000), discuss many cases of scandal reporting along with guidelines that media should follow in publishing or ignoring such incidents.

20. Sabato, *Feeding Frenzy*, 53.

21. Philip Seib, *Headline Diplomacy: How News Coverage Affects Foreign Policy* (Westport, Conn.: Praeger, 1997), 108–111; Kirsten Sparre, "Megaphone Diplomacy in the Northern Irish Peace Process," *Press/Politics* 6(1) (2001): 88–104.

22. Protess et al., *Journalism of Outrage*, 134–135.
23. Wayne King, "Houston Finds that Dramatizing Crime Does Pay," *New York Times,* Jan. 23, 1984.
24. Michael Killian, "New FBI TV Series Will Seek Viewer Help in Nabbing Criminals," *Chicago Tribune,* Feb. 5, 1988.
25. Protess et al., *Journalism of Outrage*, 179–180.
26. Tim Jones and Gary Marx, "Unabomber Has Media in a Bind," *Chicago Tribune,* Sept. 20, 1995.
27. Robert D. McFadden, "News Executives Express Outrage," *New York Times,* Oct. 3, 1986.
28. Regina G. Lawrence, "Defining Events: Problem Definition in the Media Arena," in *Politics, Discourse, and American Society,* ed. Roderick P. Hart and Bartholomew H. Sparrow (Lanham, Md.: Rowman and Littlefield, 2001), 107. Also see Regina G. Lawrence, "Game-Framing the Issues: Tracking the Strategy Frame in Public Policy News," *Political Communication* 17(2) (2000): 93–114, for a discussion of the use of framing to influence public policy.
29. Karen Callaghan and Frauke Schnell, "Assessing the Democratic Debate: How the News Media Frame Elite Policy Discourse," *Political Communication* 18(3) (2001): 183–212.
30. Lawrence, "Game-Framing the Issues"; and Joseph N. Cappella and Kathleen Hall Jamieson, *Spiral of Cynicism* (New York: Oxford University Press, 1997), chaps. 3 and 8.
31. Regina Lawrence, *Managing Meaning: Media, Officials, and Police Brutality.* Unpublished Ph.D. dissertation, University of Washington, 1996.
32. Ellen Mickiewicz, *Opening Channels* (New York: Oxford University Press, 1996).
33. W. Lance Bennett, "Toward a Theory of Press-State Relations in the United States," *Journal of Communication* 40 (spring 1990): 103–125; George A. Donahue, Phillip J. Tichenor, and Clarice N. Olien, "A Guard Dog Perspective on the Role of Media," *Journal of Communication* 45(2) (spring 1995): 115–132.
34. Gladys Engel Lang and Kurt Lang, *The Battle for Public Opinion: The President, the Press, and the Polls during Watergate* (New York: Columbia University Press, 1983), 58.
35. Molotch et al., "The Media-Policy Connection," 45, citing Peter Dreier, "The Position of the Press in the U.S. Power Structure," *Social Problems* 29 (February 1982): 298–310; also see Gadi Wolfsfeld, "Media Protest and Political Violence: A Transactional Analysis," *Journalism Monographs* 127 (June 1991); William A. Gamson, *The Strategy of Social Protest,* 2d ed. (Belmont, Calif.: Wadsworth, 1990); and Clarice N. Olien, Phillip J. Tichenor, and George A. Donahue, "Media Coverage and Social Movements," in *Information Campaigns: Balancing Social Values and Social Change,* ed. Charles T. Salmon (Beverly Hills, Calif.: Sage, 1989), 139–163.
36. Oscar H. Gandy, *Beyond Agenda Setting: Information Subsidies and Public Policy* (Norwood, N.J.: Ablex, 1982), 149–162.
37. The title and the information that follows come from "The Great Greenhouse Debate," *Media Monitor* 6(10) (December 1992): 1–6.
38. David L. Paletz and Robert M. Entman, *Media Power Politics* (New York: Free Press, 1981), 144.
39. Stanley Rothman and S. Robert Lichter, "Elite Ideology and Risk Perception in Nuclear Energy Policy," *American Political Science Review* 81 (June 1987): 383–404. For a more general discussion of the problem of sources of science information, see Hans Mathias Kepplinger, "Artificial Horizons: How the Press Presented and How the Population Received Technology in Germany

from 1965–1986," in *The Mass Media in Liberal Democratic Societies*, ed. Stanley Rothman (New York: Paragon House, 1992), 147–176; Kandice L. Salomone, Michael R. Greenberg, Peter M. Sandman, and David B. Sachsman, "A Question of Quality: How Journalists and News Sources Evaluate Coverage of Environmental Risk," *Journal of Communication* 40 (autumn 1990): 117–130.

40. The information about this case comes from "Is Cancer News a Health Hazard? Media Coverage vs. 'Scientific' Opinion on Environmental Cancer," *Media Monitor* 7(8) (November–December 1993): 1–5.

41. Patrick Leahy and Alan Mazur, "The Rise and Fall of Public Opposition in Specific Social Movements," *Social Studies of Science* 10 (1980): 191–205; and Alan Mazur, "Media Coverage and Public Opinion on Scientific Controversies," *Journal of Communication* 31 (spring 1981): 106–115.

42. Renate G. Bader, "How Science News Sections Influence Newspaper Science Coverage: A Case Study," *Journalism Quarterly* 67 (spring 1990): 88–96; Eleanor Singer, "A Question of Accuracy: How Journalists and Scientists Report Research on Hazards," *Journalism Quarterly* 40 (autumn 1990): 102–116.

43. Todd Gitlin, *The Whole World Is Watching: Media in the Making and Unmaking of the New Left* (Berkeley: University of California Press, 1980), 25–26.

44. For models of the roles played by the media in fostering social movements, see Kevin M. Carragee, "News and Ideology," *Journalism Monographs* 128 (August 1991); Wolfsfeld, "Media Protest and Political Violence"; and Gamson, *The Strategy of Social Protest*.

45. Gitlin, *The Whole World*, 284.

46. Laura R. Woliver, *From Outrage to Action: The Politics of Grass-Roots Dissent* (Urbana: University of Illinois Press, 1993).

47. Hans Mathias Kepplinger and Michael Hachenberg, "Media and Conscientious Objection in the Federal Republic of Germany," in *Political Communication Research*, ed. Paletz, 108–128. Also see Fay Lomax Cook and Wesley G. Skogan, "Convergent and Divergent Voice Models of the Rise and Fall of Policy Issues," *Agenda Setting: Readings on Media, Public Opinion, and Policymaking*, ed. David L. Protess and Maxwell McCombs (Hillsdale, N.J.: Erlbaum, 1991), 189–206.

48. Wolfsfeld, "Media Protest and Political Violence," 8–10.

49. Edie Goldenberg, *Making the Papers* (Lexington, Mass.: Heath, 1975), 146–148.

50. The potential impact of docudramas is discussed by William C. Adams et al., "The Power of *The Right Stuff*: A Quasi-Experimental Field Test of the Docudrama Hypothesis," *Public Opinion Quarterly* 49 (fall 1985): 330–339.

51. Gandy, *Beyond Agenda Setting*, 88.

52. Sally Bedell Smith, "Film on a Nuclear War Already Causing Wide Fallout of Partisan Activity," *New York Times*, Nov. 23, 1983.

53. Bernard Weinraub, "Hollywood Wonders if Warner Brothers Let 'J.F.K.' Go Too Far," *New York Times*, Dec. 24, 1991; Jack R. Payton, "'J.F.K.'.'s Premise Is Full of Holes—But So Was Warren Report," *Chicago Tribune*, Dec. 24, 1991.

54. For a discussion of the subtle yet significant consequences that are often missed, see Stanley Feldman and Lee Sigelman, "The Political Impact of Prime-Time Television: 'The Day After,'" *Journal of Politics* 47 (May 1985): 556–578.

55. For a full discussion of the role of the media as political actors, see Timothy E. Cook, *Governing with the News: The News Media as Political Institutions* (Chicago: University of Chicago Press, 1998).

56. Richard Bernstein, "CBS Releases Its Study of Vietnam Documentary," *New York Times*, April 27, 1983.

57. Bill Carter, "The Larger Issues Behind the Dan Rather Case," *New York Times,* Oct. 4, 1989.
58. Pat Widder, "Playing with Fire: Blur of Fact and Fiction Costs NBC," *Chicago Tribune,* Feb. 11, 1993.
59. William E. Schmidt, "TV Movie on Atlanta Child Killings Stirs Debate and Casts Doubt on Guilt," *New York Times,* Jan. 31, 1985.
60. Quoted in Deirdre Carmody, "The Role of the Press in the U.S. Corruption Inquiry," *New York Times,* Feb. 5, 1980.
61. For a typical case involving denial of the right to unedited rebuttal, see Sally Bedell, "ABC Backs Off Charge It Made against Mobil," *New York Times,* June 22, 1982.
62. Walter Goodman, "What's News Worthy Is in the Eye of the Beholder," *New York Times,* Aug. 30, 1993.
63. Andrew H. Malcolm, "TV Film Links to Mob in Toronto," *New York Times,* March 28, 1979.
64. Bennett L. Gershman, "Abscam, the Judiciary, and the Ethics of Government," *Yale Law Journal* 91 (July 1982): 1565–1591.

Readings

Cappella, Joseph N., and Kathleen Hall Jamieson. *Spiral of Cynicism.* New York: Oxford University Press, 1997.

Cook, Timothy E. *Governing with the News: The News Media as Political Institutions.* Chicago: University of Chicago Press, 1998.

Gitlin, Todd. *The Whole World Is Watching: Media in the Making and Unmaking of the New Left.* Berkeley: University of California Press, 1980.

Glasser, Theodore L., ed. *The Idea of Public Journalism.* New York: Guilford Press, 1999.

Graber, Doris, Denis McQuail, and Pippa Norris, eds. *The Politics of News, The News of Politics.* Washington, D.C.: CQ Press, 1998.

Hallin, Daniel C. *We Keep America on Top of the World: Television Journalism and the Public Sphere.* New York: Routledge, 1994.

Lang, Gladys Engel, and Kurt Lang. *The Battle for Public Opinion: The President, the Press, and the Polls during Watergate.* New York: Columbia University Press, 1983.

Popkin, Jeremy D. *Media and Revolution: Comparative Perspectives.* Lexington: University Press of Kentucky, 1995.

Sabato, Larry J., Mark Stencel, and S. Robert Lichter. *Peepshow: Media and Politics in an Age of Scandal.* Lanham, Md.: Rowman and Littlefield, 2000.

Smith, Zay N., and Pamela Zekman. *The Mirage.* New York: Random House, 1979.

Steffens, Lincoln. *The Autobiography of Lincoln Steffens.* New York: Harcourt Brace, 1931.

Media Impact on Attitudes and Behavior

IN ONE EPISODE OF the popular television show *Beverly Hills 90210,* an actor gloated about his flawless tan. But he panicked when his girl-friend noticed a strange mole on the back of his neck that might be cancerous. In a burst of public-mindedness, he then took a megaphone to the beach and reminded sunbathers about the importance of using sunscreen lotions.

What the viewers of this 1999 episode did not know was that officials from the federal Centers for Disease Control (CDC) had suggested the skin cancer warnings to the staff of the television show. As part of its pub-lic health education campaign, the agency had since 1998 asked television producers to include positive health messages in popular shows. *Beverly Hills 90210* seemed especially suitable because it appealed to teenagers and young adults, a group most likely to overdo sun exposure.

The CDC chose this approach to public health education in the wake of studies showing that television dramas are a major source of health information for large numbers of Americans and that health messages transmitted by beloved stars are effective. Entertainment education has been used repeatedly for messages about cancer, childhood immuniza-tion, antibiotic resistance, and sexually transmitted diseases.[1] But how effective are such messages? Do media stories really shape the thinking and behavior patterns of countless Americans? Are people's values and attitudes about social and political issues influenced substantially by what they read and see? Do desirable and undesirable behaviors in television fiction and news programs produce imitations in real life? *How much* do people learn from the media and *what* do they learn?

In this chapter we will examine these questions, beginning with the shaping of attitudes that occurs as an unintended byproduct of media exposure. For the most part, journalists do not try to teach political attitudes and values, nor do people try to learn them. Rather, exposure to individual, dramatic events or to the incremental impact of the total flow of information over prolonged periods of time leads to "incidental" learning about the political world. We also will consider the ways in which people choose the media to which they will pay attention and the sorts of things they will learn. Finally, we will address the question posed at the start: to what degree does exposure to the mass media influence behavior in politically and socially significant ways?

Differential Effects of Print and Broadcast News

Most Americans are exposed to the combined effects of all the media either directly or indirectly through contact with people who tell them what they have heard or seen or read. We may know that the Chinese government detained an American surveillance plane and crew that collided with a Chinese aircraft. We may feel anxiety or anger about the situation and may believe that it is either good or bad foreign policy to consider negotiating to win the release of the crew and plane. But which of these thoughts and feelings come from television, newspapers, conversations, or a combination of media? It is nearly impossible to disentangle such strands of information.[2]

Each medium, however, does make unique contributions to learning. For example, television, because of its visuals, is especially powerful in transmitting realism and emotional appeal. Print media excel in conveying factual details. Because most tests of learning from the media focus on factual learning and rote memory, print media are generally credited with conveying more knowledge than audiovisual media do.[3] Television bashing is popular as social critics search for a scapegoat for the ills of society. They downplay the learning opportunities provided by seeing events unfold on the television screen. Media scholar Neil Postman, for example, warns that massive use of television will turn America into a nation of dilettantes who avoid serious thinking because television trivializes the problems of the world.[4] Rod Hart calls it a "seductive" medium that turns people into passive watchers of the political scene, rather than active participants.

Critics of television claim that audiences who are print—rather than television—reliant gain more knowledge and that this proves the supe-

PSAs

→ *on-line realtime*
not real

riority of print news. That claim is problematic when one puts learning scores into the appropriate context. Demographic differences are crucial. Newspaper-reliant individuals generally enjoy higher socioeconomic status and better formal education. Their status in life, therefore, provides above-average incentives for learning the factual details by which social scientists judge citizens' knowledge.[5] Attitudes toward the media matter as well. Print media are viewed by most people as sources of information, whereas electronic media are viewed as sources of entertainment. These differences, rather than the nature of each medium, may explain some of the differences in the effects of different types of media. Television becomes the most instructive medium if one tests for information that is best conveyed audiovisually, such as impressions of people and the inferences they engender or comprehension and long-term memory for dramatic events.[6]

Television's greatest political impact, compared with that of other media, is derived from its ability to reach millions of people simultaneously with the same images. Despite losing more than half of their nightly news viewers in the closing decade of the twentieth century, the traditional networks remain king of the information market by a wide margin. Televised events still are shared experiences. Millions of Americans were present vicariously to see the aftermath of the 1995 Oklahoma City bombing. They watched the precision aerial attacks during the 1991 Persian Gulf War and the events surrounding the untimely death of British princess Diana. They saw the unfolding of the Clinton impeachment trial in 1998 and 1999 and the counting of disputed ballots in Florida following the 2000 presidential election. America's print media have never equaled the reach of television and the power that flows from it, including the power to shape collective memories.[7] Moreover, 23 million American adults are functionally illiterate and, therefore, are almost entirely beyond the reach of print media. What the poorly educated now learn about politics from television may be fragmentary and hazy, but it represents a quantum leap over their previous levels of exposure and learning.

In short, the research on the differential effects of various types of media reveals that different types present stimuli that vary substantially in nature and content. It would be surprising, therefore, if their impact were identical, even when they deal with the same subjects. However, "there is no evidence of *consistent* significant differences in the ability of different media to persuade, inform, or even to instill an emotional response in audience members."[8] Because current research does not provide adequate answers about the precise effects of these stimulus variations and about the processes by which individuals mesh a variety of media stimuli, we will focus on the end product—the combined impact of all print and electronic media stimuli.

The Role of Media in Political Socialization

Political socialization—the learning about structures and environmental factors and the internalizing of customs and rules governing political life—affects the quality of interactions between citizens and their government. Political systems do not operate smoothly without the support of most of their citizens, who must be willing to abide by the laws and to support government through performing duties such as voting, paying taxes, or serving in the military. Support is most readily obtained if citizens are convinced of the legitimacy and capability of their government and if they feel strong emotional ties to it. If political socialization fails to instill such attitudes, then policies and laws that depend on public support, such as energy conservation or traffic regulations, may become unenforceable. If political socialization fails to provide citizens with sufficient knowledge, elections may become a sham at best; at worst, they may become a mockery in which clever politicians manipulate an ignorant electorate. Likewise, surveillance of government activities is impossible if people lack a grasp of the nature of government and public policies.

Childhood Socialization

Political socialization starts in childhood. Children usually learn basic attitudes toward authority, property, decision making, and veneration for political symbols from their families and other early childhood caretakers. When they enter the more formal school setting, teaching about political values becomes quite systematic. At school, children also learn new factual information about their political and social world, much of it based on information derived from mass media.[9]

Children's direct contacts with the media are equally abundant.[10] Millions of babies watch television. In the winter, young children in the United States spend an average of thirty-one hours a week in front of the television set—more time than in school. Between the ages of twelve and seventeen, the weekly number of hours spent viewing television drops to twenty-four. Eighty percent of the programs children see are intended for adults and show incidents that differ substantially from those in the child's limited personal experiences. Children watch military combat, funerals, rocket launchings, courtships, seductions, and childbirth. If they can understand the message, the impact is likely to be great because, lacking experience, they are apt to take such presentations at face value.

When asked for the sources of information on which they base their attitudes about the economy or race issues, or about war and patriotism, high school students mention the mass media far more often than they mention their families, friends, teachers, or personal experiences.[11] Youngsters who are frequent media users gain substantial information from the media. Compared with infrequent users, they show greater understanding and support for basic American values such as the importance of free speech and the right to equal and fair treatment.[12]

The finding that mass media strongly influence socialization runs counter to earlier socialization studies that showed parents and teachers as the chief socializers. Several reasons account for the change. The first is the increasing pervasiveness of television, which makes it easy for even the youngest children to be exposed to images of the world displayed by the mass media. The second reason involves deficiencies in measurement. Much of the early research discounted all media influence unless it came through direct contact outside the classroom between the child and the media. That excluded indirect media influence, such as contacts with parents and teachers who conveyed media information to the child. These exclusions sharply reduced the findings of media effects. Finally, research designs have become more sophisticated. In the early studies, children were asked to make their own general appraisal of learning sources. A typical question might be, "From whom do you learn the most: your parents, your school, or newspapers and television?" The questions used in recent studies have been more specific, inquiring first what children know about particular subjects, such as immigration or nuclear energy, and then asking about the sources of their information. In nearly every case the mass media were named as the chief sources of information and evaluations.

What children learn from the mass media and how they evaluate it depends heavily on their stage of mental development. According to child psychologist Jean Piaget, children between two and seven years of age do not detect the connections among various phenomena or draw general conclusions from specific instances. Many of the lessons presumably taught by media stories therefore elude young children. Complex reasoning skills develop fully only at the teenage level. Children's interests in certain types of stories also change sharply with age, as do their attention and information-retention spans.[13] Most children strongly support the political system during their early years but often become disillusioned about authority figures during their teenage years. Their skepticism diminishes as education is completed and the young adult enters the workforce. What role the media play in this transformation is unclear.[14] Knowledge is also slim about children's and adolescents' imitation of behavior depicted by media stories, the duration of memories, and the persistence of media effects on learning, behavior, and social relationships.[15]

Adult Socialization

The pattern of heavy media exposure continues into adulthood. The average American adult spends more than four hours a day watching television; well over two hours listening to radio, often while working or traveling by car; eighteen to forty-five minutes reading newspapers; and six to thirty minutes reading a magazine. Time spent with the mass media has jumped 40 percent since the advent of television, mostly at the expense of other leisure activities. Television alone now takes up nearly half the leisure time of most Americans. However, the growth of cable television and the Internet is spreading audiences over a much wider spectrum of stations. On an average day, 80 percent of all Americans are exposed to television and newspapers. On a typical evening, the television audience is close to 100 million people. These numbers can double for extraordinary events.[16]

This massive exposure to information contributes to the lifelong process of political socialization and learning. The mass media form

> the mainstream of the common symbolic environment that cultivates the most widely shared conceptions of reality. We live in terms of the stories we tell, stories about what things exist, stories about how things work, and stories about what to do . . . . Increasingly, media-cultivated facts and values become standards by which we judge.[17]

Once basic attitudes toward the political system have been formed, they usually stabilize so that later learning largely supplements and refines earlier notions. The need to cope with information about new events and shifting cultural orientations force the average person into continuous learning and gradual readjustments, although the basic value structure generally remains intact, even when attitudes are modified.[18] However, major personal or societal upheavals may lead to more or less complete resocialization and revised political ideas.

People learn about political norms, rules, values, events, and behaviors largely from fictional and factual mass media stories. Personal experiences are severely limited compared with the range of experiences offered to us directly or indirectly by the media about the social order and political activities. An accident report, for example, besides telling what happened, may suggest that police and fire forces respond too slowly and that emergency facilities in the local hospital are inadequate. When societal problems such as poverty or pollution are framed as discrete events and reflect just one family's starvation or a particular oil spill, attention is likely to be focused on individual solutions, obscuring the larger societal problems.[19] Soap operas on radio and television may persuade audiences that most politicians are corruptible—after all, the majority of those shown on television are.[20] In fact, fictional stories are the most widely used sources for political information. Surveys show that only one-half to two-thirds of the adult television audience regularly exposes itself to explicit political news.[21]

People's opinions, feelings, and evaluations about the political system may spring from their own thinking about facts supplied by the media; from attitudes, opinions, and feelings explicitly expressed in news or entertainment programming; or from a combination of the two.[22] When audiences have direct or vicarious experiences to guide them, and particularly when they have already formed opinions grounded firmly in their personal values, they are least likely to be swayed by the media.[23] Many people who use the media for information and as a point of departure for formulating their own appraisals nonetheless reject or ignore attitudes and evaluations that are supplied explicitly or implicitly by media stories.[24] For example, the public gave little credence to the widely publicized predictions by media pundits that proof of President Clinton's affair with White House intern Monica Lewinsky would end the Clinton presidency.

People are prone to accept newspeople's views about national and international issues whenever they lack personal experience or guidance from social contacts. Even when people think they are forming their own opinions about familiar issues, they often depend on the media more than they realize. Extensive television exposure has been shown to lead to "mainstreaming," making people's outlook on political life "congruent with television's portrayal of life and society."[25]

The media's persuasiveness does not mean that exposure is tantamount to learning and mind changing. Far from it. Two-thirds of the people generally do not know their newspaper's preferred position on specific economic, social, and foreign policy issues.[26] Most media stories are promptly forgotten. Stories that become part of an individual's fund of knowledge tend to reinforce existing beliefs and feelings. Acquisition of new knowledge or changes in attitude are the exception rather than the rule. Still, they occur often enough to be highly significant.

Patterns in Socialization

Race, ethnicity, gender, age, income, education, region, and city size generate differences in habits of newspaper reading, radio listening, and television viewing. For instance, blacks and Hispanics are more reliant on television than are whites, and women are the primary audience for daytime television. Age has a bearing on newspaper reading, with older people reading more than younger ones. Southerners listen to much less radio than do northerners. Program preferences vary as well. Women ages fifty and older are the heaviest viewers of television news, followed by men fifty and older. Twelve- to seventeen-year-olds are the lightest news watchers. Men far exceed women in following sports coverage, whereas women spend more time watching television drama.

Differences in media-use patterns are particularly pronounced between income levels. High-income families, who usually are better educated than poor families, use print media more and television less than the rest of the population. Upper-income people also use a greater variety of media: 57 percent are multimedia users compared with 27 percent in the lower economic groups. Thus the well-to-do potentially have much more information and a greater variety of information available to them. This helps them to maintain and increase their influence and power in American society.[27] In part, the poor pay less attention to print media because these media cater to upper-income groups rather than the needs and concerns of the poor. Low-income audiences prefer television and radio programs, which are easy to grasp and carry a great deal of light entertainment.

While different media exposure and use patterns offer a partial explanation for knowledge and attitude differences, the notion of vastly different communications environments for various population groups should not be carried too far. The bulk of media entertainment and information is similar throughout the country and is shared by all types of audiences. The same network television and cable programs are broadcast on the East Coast and the West Coast, in big cities and small towns. Differences among individual media enterprises are slight. Hence, television comes close to being a single, nationwide source of news and commentary. Radio is more diverse, but even many radio news programs are little more than national wire service reports. Insofar as newspaper stories are based on wire service information, they too are fairly uniform everywhere.

In Chapter 4 we saw that the news media cover basically the same categories of stories in the same proportions. Specific stories vary, of course, depending on regional and local interests. Newspapers on the West Coast are more likely to devote their foreign affairs coverage to Asian affairs than are newspapers on the East Coast, which concentrate on Europe and the Middle East. Tabloids put more stress on sensational crime and sex stories than do elite papers such as the staid *New York Times*. Nevertheless, news sources everywhere provide a large common core of information and interpretation that imbues their audiences with a shared structure of basic values and information.

Choosing Media Stories

General patterns of media use do not reveal *why* people pay attention to specific stories, but a number of theories have been formulated to help explain how and why such individual choices are made.

Uses and Gratifications Theories

One of the most widely accepted news-choice theories currently is the "uses and gratifications" approach. Put simply, proponents of this approach contend that individuals ignore personally irrelevant and unattractively presented messages and pay attention to the kinds of things that they find useful and intellectually or emotionally gratifying, provided the expenditure of time and effort to digest the material seems reasonable.[28]

Media scholar Lance Bennett groups uses and gratifications into three broad categories: curiosity and surveillance, entertainment and escape, and social and psychological adjustment.[29] For instance, people pay attention to stories that help them in voting or in participating in protest demonstrations. They use the media to gain a sense of security and social adequacy from knowing what is happening in their political environment. People feel gratified if the media reinforce what they already know and believe. Finally, people use the media to while away time, reduce loneliness, participate vicariously in exciting ventures, and escape the frustrations of everyday life.[30] People from all walks of life are most likely to view prime-time programs that are action filled, humorous, and relaxing. They are least likely to choose educational programs, particularly when these presentations involve sophisticated political analysis.[31]

Of course, there is no guarantee that the gratifications that are sought are routinely attained. In fact, media may produce anxieties and fears as well as hatred and alienation. When radio and television were shut down by a long strike in Israel in 1987, the public reacted with relief rather than dismay. Israeli philosopher David Hartman gave this explanation:

> When television and radio become the prisms through which you look at reality, you come away saying, "What an ugly place this is." But when you take away those prisms and people's perceptions of reality are derived exclusively from their own daily experiences, which are for the most part prosaic, they inevitably become more relaxed and stable.[32]

Table 7-1, based on interviews with 6,564 adults in ten small cities throughout the United States, indicates the twenty-five newspaper content areas that are read most widely. People were asked to rate common newspaper topics on a scale of 1 to 5. A score of 1 denoted that they always ignored the topic; a score of 5 denoted that they always read it whenever it appeared. The topics earning the highest scores presumably supply the broadest array of gratifications. Special subcultural needs may lead to significant variations in gratification patterns. For instance, a Jewish person may be particularly eager to receive news from the Middle East and other places that concern Israel. A person of Polish ancestry may look for news about food shortages and political developments in Poland. Women who favor increased job opportunities for women are apt to notice stories about women's expanding presence in the business world. What people actually select depends very much on their lifestyles and the context in which they are exposed to information. What is useful and gratifying in one setting may be less so in another. When people change their lifestyles, such as when they move from full-time employment to retirement or from a desk to a travel job, media patterns may change drastically to bring about closer accord with the people encountered in the new setting.[33]

Table 7-2 shows the kinds of reasons people give when asked why they paid attention or failed to pay attention to particular news stories. Personal, rather than social, gratifications seem most important in choosing stories, whereas lack of interest and casual inattention best explain inattention.

Other Selective Exposure Theories

Although most of the reasons for skipping stories lead to random omissions, systematic omissions occur as well, and various cognitive balance theories try to explain them. According to these theories, people avoid information that disturbs their peace of mind, offends their political and social tastes, or conflicts with information, attitudes, and feelings they already hold. Social scientists explain selective exposure by pointing out that people are uncomfortable when they are exposed to ideas that differ from their own or that question the validity of their ideas. To avoid discomfort, people select information that is congruent with their existing beliefs. Selectivity then lays the groundwork for differential attitudes toward politics. It reduces the already slim chances that an individual's established beliefs, attitudes, and feelings will be altered. Selective exposure therefore helps to explain the considerable stability that exists in cognitions and orientations such as party allegiance or foreign policy preferences.

TABLE 7-1   Rankings of Top Twenty-five Content Categories and
Average Ratings Across Ten Markets

Rank		Rating
1.	Natural disasters and tragedies	3.93
2.	Stories and columns on the national economy (prices, unemployment, inflation)	3.87
3.	News of the local economy	3.82
4.	Column on local people and events	3.72
5.	Stories about national politics and the president	3.72
6.	Service information (TV listings, weather, movie listings, etc.)	3.71
7.	News of international leaders and events	3.70
8.	Stories on energy, conservation, and the environment	3.67
9.	Stories on things to see and do in the area	3.66
10.	Good Samaritan stories (people helping people)	3.60
11.	Humorous stories and features	3.56
12.	Accident and crime news	3.52
13.	Health and medical advice	3.42
14.	How fast the community is growing	3.33
15.	Editorials and letters to the editor	3.32
16.	Schools and education	3.31
17.	City council and local politicians	3.30
18.	News about the governor and state legislature	3.27
19.	Consumer stories and advice	3.27
20.	Stories about human psychology (the way we think and act)	3.22
21.	Nature and outdoor stories	3.19
22.	How-to advice on such things as crafts, auto and home repairs	3.19
23.	News of record (births, deaths, weddings, etc.)	3.10
24.	Space and exploration	3.10
25.	Science and technology	3.08

SOURCE: Judee K. Burgoon, Michael Burgoon, and Miriam Wilkinson, "Dimensions of Content Readership in 10 Newspaper Markets," *Journalism Quarterly* 60 (spring 1983): 79. Reprinted by permission of the Association for Education in Journalism and Mass Communication, publishers of *Journalism Quarterly*.

NOTE: Ratings are based on a 1 to 5 scale. A rating of 1 means "never read"; a rating of 5 means "always read."

Scholars now believe that selective exposure occurs to a lesser extent than was thought initially. Many people find it too bothersome to select news stories carefully, particularly when using electronic media. For instance, when television news programs carry stories that are objectionable to a viewer, there is no easy way to screen out the undesired stories and continue to watch the rest of the broadcast. Many people are actually curious about discrepant information or pride themselves on being open-minded and receptive to all points of view. For instance, Democrats may want to hear what Republicans are saying to find out how the opposition is

TABLE 7-2   Reasons for Attention or Inattention to News Stories

Reasons for attention	Percent	Reasons for inattention	Percent
Personal relevance	26	Missed the story	47
Emotional appeal	20	No interest	28
Societal importance	19	Too remote	10
Interesting story	15	Too busy	6
Job relevance	12	Doubt media	3
Chance reasons	1	Too complex	3
Miscellaneous	7	Redundant/boring	2
		Doubt story	1

SOURCE: Doris A. Graber, *Processing the News: How People Tame the Information Tide*, 2d ed. (New York: Longman, 1988), 102. Copyright © 1988 by Longman Inc. Reprinted by permission of Longman Inc.

NOTE: $N = 453$ for reasons for attention; 1,493 for reasons for inattention.

stating its case. They may also want to determine what counterarguments need to be formulated. Many people actually enjoy hearing news that contradicts their own ideas so that they can refute what they hear. Apparently exposure to discrepant information is not as universally painful as previously thought. News also can be ignored, overlooked, or distorted. The source can be discredited and the message disbelieved.[34]

Much of the evidence for exposure to a highly selective slice of news has come from settings in which available media supported the preferences of the audience. No choice was necessary; selection was de facto rather than deliberate. For example, unionized workers with friends and associates who are also in unions may encounter a lot of prounion information at home and at work. They may not have to make a special effort to seek out only prounion information or reject antiunion opinions. In fact, antiunion information may be unavailable. Genuine rather than de facto selective exposure does occur, of course, but it operates more like a preference than a total exclusion rule. It appears to be most prevalent for those relatively few people who recognize dissonance and find it painful.

Agenda-Setting Theories

If choices of news items were entirely determined by personal needs and pleasures, news selection patterns would show infinite variations. This is not the case. Similarities in the political environment of average Americans and social pressures produce common patterns in the selection of news. As previously mentioned, gatekeeping practices largely account for the similarity in news supply, which is a powerful unifying force. Media also tell people in fairly uniform fashion which individual issues and activities are most significant and deserve to be ranked highly on the public's agenda of concerns.[35] Importance is indicated through cues such as banner headlines, front-page placement in newspapers, or first-story placement on television. Frequent and ample coverage also implies significance.

Many people readily adopt the media's agenda of importance, often without being aware of it, rather than selecting or rejecting news on the basis of what is personally gratifying or displeasing. We look at the front page of the newspaper and expect to find the most important stories there. We may watch the opening minutes of a telecast eagerly and then allow our attention to slacken. As a result, agenda setting by the media leads to uniformities in exposure as well as in significance ratings of news items. When the media make events seem important, average people as well as politicians discuss them and form opinions. This enhances the perceived importance of these events and ensures even more public attention and, possibly, political action.

Numerous studies confirm the agenda-setting influence of the media.[36] When people are asked which issues are most important to them personally or to their communities, their lists tend to correspond to cues in the news sources that they use in their communities. However, agenda setting varies in potency. Audiences follow media guidance but not slavishly. Past and current experiences, conversations with others, and independent reasoning provide alternatives to media guidance.[37] Comparisons of media agendas with public opinion polls and reports about political and social conditions show that media guidance is most important for new issues that have not been widely discussed and for issues beyond the realm of personal experience.[38] Prominent media coverage does ensure that an issue will be noticed, but it does not guarantee that the audience will assign it the same relative rank of importance that media play has indicated. Likewise, information that is useful or gratifying to the audience will be noted, even if it is on the back pages, receives minuscule headlines, or is briefly reported at the tail end of a newscast.[39] The need for raw material for conversation with friends and associates is a particularly strong force in the selection of stories.

Learning Processes

How do audiences process the stories that they have selected? The early models that depicted a straight stimulus–response relationship have been disproven. There is no "hypodermic effect": information presented by the media is not injected unaltered into the minds of audiences.

Rather, the images conveyed by the media stimulate perceptions in audience members that reflect the media stimuli as well as each individual's perceptual state at the time the message was received.

Blending New and Old Information

From childhood on, people develop ideas and feelings about how the world operates. When these ideas relate to politics, they are usually grounded in information drawn from the mass media. Cognitive psychologists call these mental configurations by various names, including *schemas* and *scripts*.[40] As journalist Walter Lippmann explained eighty years ago:

> For the most part we do not first see, and then define, we define first and then see. In the great blooming, buzzing confusion of the outer world, we pick out what our culture has already defined for us, and we tend to perceive that which we have picked out in the form stereotyped for us by our culture.[41]

For instance, most Americans have been conditioned by their environment to consider African Americans as more likely suspects when violent crimes have been committed. Numerous experiments accordingly show that whites often mistakenly identify a black person to be the individual shown wielding a murder weapon even when the pictures in an experiment show a white assailant.[42]

Schemas serve as organizing devices that help people to assimilate new information. If breaking news stories match established schemas, they can be stored easily in memory as another example of a familiar concept. Numerous knowledge-gap studies show that political elites and other well-informed people have developed exceptionally large arrays of schemas allowing them to absorb many stories that are beyond the reach of the poorly informed.[43] They even are more physically stimulated by new information and therefore are more likely to remember it.[44] The knowledge gap between the privileged and underprivileged widens as a result. Those with the least political knowledge are likely to remain politically unsophisticated and impotent. The knowledge gap between the information rich and the information poor also makes mutual understanding of political views more difficult.

Transient Influences

Many transitory factors impinge on news processing. People are intermittently attentive or inattentive and inclined or disinclined to learn. Up to half of television viewers eat dinner, wash dishes, read, or talk on the telephone while watching television. Examination time at school, illness in the family, or the year-end rush at work may preempt the time normally devoted to media. Researchers cannot predict the effect of media messages without knowing the group context in which exposure or conversation took place. For instance, if one watches or talks about a presidential inauguration with friends who are making fun of the way the president talks and acts, the occasion loses its solemnity and becomes banal. How a person interacts with information also depends on the format of that information. If news reports present conflicting facts or opinions, if they are overly long or overly short, if they are repetitious, dull, or offensive, their effect is apt to be diminished. Moreover, the total communications matrix affects the influence of its parts so that the impact of print news may be blunted by prior presentations on television and radio that have removed the edge of novelty.[45]

Source credibility and appeal are other significant factors in news processing. People find television news more believable than comparable print news because viewers tend to trust news anchors; seeing them on their living room television screens makes them familiar and trustworthy. Partisanship, too, may play an important role in source appraisal. It may cast a rosy glow over fellow partisans and a pall over the opposition.

Perceptual and Image Factors

When people receive new information, they combine it with existing beliefs. But does the new reshape the old or the old reshape the new in the final images? Research shows that images of political candidates are largely perceiver determined for those aspects for which the audience already has developed complex schemas. For instance, people assume that Democratic presidential candidates will pursue policies typically associated with Democrats. They read or view the news in that vein, picking up bits of information that fit while rejecting, ignoring, or reinterpreting those that do not fit. The same is likely to hold true for information about big business or big labor, the pope, or England's queen. Average Americans are likely to interpret big business and big labor news negatively. Similarly, if reports about the pope or Queen Elizabeth permit a choice between favorable and unfavorable interpretations, the favorable image is apt to prevail.

Information about aspects of events or people not widely known or stereotyped leads to stimulus-determined images. How the media frame these political issues and depict people largely determines what the audience perceives. The personalities of newcomers to the political scene, assessments of their capabilities, and appraisals of the people with whom they surround themselves, for example, usually are stimulus determined.[46] Likewise, when the media describe present-day China, when they cast doubt on the safety of nuclear energy production, or when they praise the merits of a newly developed drug, they create images that are apt to dominate people's schemas.

The general rule that media are most influential in areas in which the audience knows least does not apply to specialized publications. Professional journals, for instance, often strongly influence their readers' images of professional matters. This happens because the sources are highly credible. The professionals who read these publications willingly subordinate their own views to those of the published experts.

Learning Effects: Knowledge and Attitudes

What kinds of politically relevant knowledge, attitudes, feelings, and actions spring from people's contacts with the media? Because of the limitations of measuring instruments, the answer to this question is difficult. In Chapter 1 we pointed out the impossibility of isolating media influence when it is one of many factors in a complex environment. For example, a sample of citizens who were asked during the Reagan years why their worries about nuclear war had increased cited the following mixture of reasons: increased media coverage (52 percent); Reagan administration policies (19 percent); new weapons/new technology/proliferation (19 percent); unrest in developing countries (13 percent); East–West tensions (11 percent); Soviet belligerence (4 percent); children/grandchildren's lives (4 percent); other reasons (2 percent); don't know/no answer/can't explain (5 percent).[47] Although these answers tell us which factors played a role, they do not indicate the extent of the role. Until researchers can trace an individual's mental processes and isolate and appraise the significance of each of the components that interact and combine to form mental images, the impact of media on knowledge and attitudes cannot be fully assessed. Nor can researchers understand completely just what is learned from media.

Measurement Problems

Research up to now has focused on very small facets of learning such as testing what specific facts individuals learn about political candidates or about a few public policies. Even within such narrow areas, testing has been severely limited. It has zeroed in on the memorization of factual details from stories rather than on total knowledge gains. For instance, election coverage of a presidential candidate teaches more than facts about the candidate. It may also inform the audience about the role played by White House correspondents in campaign coverage and about living conditions in other cities. Such knowledge gains from the story, however important they may be, are usually overlooked. Much learning may even be subconscious. People may be unaware that they have learned something new and may not mention it when asked what they have learned. At times new information may be temporarily forgotten, only to reenter consciousness a short while later.[48]

Although many assumptions about learning that seem intuitively correct remain untested, they are widely accepted as true. The assumption that people deduce important social lessons from specific news stories is one example. For instance, media researcher Joshua Meyrowitz argues that television has radically changed social roles by stripping them of mystery and holding them up to continuous public scrutiny. Women working in the home who were previously isolated have learned about the attractive roles open only to males in American society, and the successes and failures of the women's movement have affected the behavior of these women. Television allows children to experience the adult world long before they are physically and emotionally prepared to cope with these experiences. In the age of television, political heroes have become ordinary mortals, and authority figures are no longer respected because the mystery of social distance has been stripped away.[49]

We believe that adults as well as children often model their behavior after characters they encounter in the media. We assume that unfavorable stereotypes will hurt the self-esteem of the groups so characterized, and so we urge newspeople to present traditionally adversely stereotyped groups—such as those with disabilities, gays and lesbians, or people of color—in a better light. News reports and dramatic shows do teach audiences how lawyers or police officers or hospitals conduct their business. Impressionable people who watch these shows and like what they see presumably will be motivated to aspire to these professions; conversely, distortions in the portrayal of these roles will mislead inexperienced people who regard them as accurate.

Although we assume these effects, and there is every reason to believe that many are quite common, most of them remain unmeasured. An important exception has been the Cultural Indicators project conducted since the mid-1960s at the University of Pennsylvania's Annenberg School of Communications. Using *cultivation analysis,* the investigators have studied trends in the dramatic content of network television and the conceptions of social reality produced in viewers. Their findings confirm that people who watch television drama for more than four hours daily see the world as television paints it and react to that world rather than to reality more than do their demographic counterparts who watch less. For instance, heavy viewers believe that the dangers of becoming a crime victim are far greater than they actually are.[50] They fear crime more and are more distrustful and suspicious than are persons who view television less often. They also are generally more pessimistic and tend to gravitate toward the middle-of-the-road mainstream politics depicted on television.

Like most research on mass media effects, these findings have been challenged on the ground that factors other than mass media exposure account for the results. The characteristics of viewers rather than their exposure to television may be responsible for their images of the world and their addiction to television. The technical aspects of the Cultural Indicators project have also been challenged. Such scientific controversies indicate that research on mass media effects needs a lot more refinement.

This holds true, too, for a number of experimental studies that have found, for example, that television news coverage of specific events "primes" audiences to appraise politicians in light of these events. Consequently, their political perspectives narrow so that single phenomena deflect attention from the broader context.[51] Until such findings have been tested in natural settings to appraise under what conditions and for what length of time they apply, they must be considered incomplete. For example, it is not surprising that experiments indicate that a president's popularity ratings fare better when the audience has been primed with questions about his political successes rather than his failures.[52] But thus far, experiments have failed to tell us how long the priming effects persist in natural situations and their likely political impact.

A neglected research sphere concerns forgetfulness. Much that is learned from the media is evanescent. When Balkan leaders are charged with war crimes or the mayor of New York becomes involved in a nasty divorce battle, the salient names and facts are on many lips, but after the events have passed, this knowledge evaporates rapidly. How rapidly seems to depend on a number of factors, the most important of which is people's ability to store and retrieve information. After three months of inattention, most ordinary stories are hard to recall, even by people with good memories. If stories are periodically revived with follow-ups or with closely related stories, memory becomes deepened and prolonged. In fact, a few crucial incidents have been rehearsed so often that they have become permanent memories. The Great Depression, World War II, and the assassination of President Kennedy are examples.[53]

Factual Learning

Given these limitations on initial learning and on remembering, what can be said about the extent of political learning from the mass media? Average people are aware of an impressive array of politically important topics that have been covered by the media. However, they do not master many details. They recognize information if it is mentioned to them but fail to recall it without such assistance.[54] When John Robinson and Dennis Davis tested recall of the main facts of thirteen television news stories within hours of viewing, scores hovered around 40 percent, with only minor differences among various age groups. Use of additional media boosted fact retention only slightly. Education and prior information levels produced the largest variations in scores, with the best informed scoring 13.8 percentage points higher than the poorly informed; people whose education had terminated in grade school and college graduates' scores were separated by an 11.2 percent gap.

Many people are shocked by low recall scores because they believe that stories cannot be fully understood without memorizing factual details. For example, political scientists Scott Keeter and Cliff Zukin titled their study of voter knowledge gains during the 1976 and 1980 presidential elections *Uninformed Choice* because recall scores were low. Keeter and Zukin argued that most citizens are too uninformed to make intelligent political choices.[55] Such judgments may be unduly harsh because knowledge in these studies is gauged solely by a citizen's ability to recall facts such as the names of prominent officeholders and figures about the length of their terms of office or the growth rate of budget deficits. These factual information tests are inadequate for judging political knowledge and competence. What really matters is that citizens understand what is at stake in major political issues and what policy options are available for coping with various problems. An extensive repertoire of factual detail is not essential for that. As media scholar Michael Schudson puts it: "There's a difference between the 'informational citizen,' saturated with bits and bytes of information, and the informed citizen, the person who has not only information but a point of view and preferences with which to make sense of it."[56]

Are people aware of major political issues and their significance? Are they able to place them in the general context of current politics? When these genuinely important questions are asked, the picture of the public's political competence brightens considerably. People may not remember the content of political speeches very well, but, as mentioned already, they are aware of a wide range of current issues. Moreover, when interviewers probe for understanding, rather than for knowledge of specific facts, they often discover considerable political insight. For instance, people who cannot define either *price deregulation* or *affirmative action* may still have fairly sophisticated notions about these matters. They know about government price controls on some goods and services and fully understand the burdens faced by people hampered in finding a job because of race or gender.[57]

Getting Enough "Spinach" News

Ours is an elitist democracy. The *ideal* citizen is interested in the full panoply of domestic and foreign political, social, and economic problems, and is ever eager to keep fully informed. That vision is a long, long way from reality in nitty-gritty American democracy. Most Americans are deeply concerned about the problems of public life only during times in which the nation is clearly in peril. At other times, average Americans focus on problems of daily life, their families, their jobs, and their neighborhoods. Most are busy, pressured for time, and eager for periodic escapes from the daily rat race. It is no wonder that much of their free time is spent on enjoying light entertainment rather than wrestling with "spinach" news—serious but unattractive political fare.

If one gauges what kinds of offerings media audiences want by the targets of their attention, rather than what they claim to want, the statistics are clear. Soft news and light entertainment—comedy, sex, and violence-oriented soap operas and skits, and sports and beauty contests—are by far the preferred content choices. This also holds true for the newest information provider, the Internet, that attracts the youngest and best-educated audiences overall. Besides being the portal to vast amounts of hitherto inaccessible serious knowledge, it also supplies immense amounts of hitherto elusive pornography. The number of visits recorded by X-rated Web sites in 2001 was close to 30 million, according to Jupiter Media Metrix, even though many such sites charge substantial subscription fees.[1] Statistics covering tabloid news in papers and magazines tell similar stories about audience appeal. Publications featuring more serious approaches to information fare poorly by comparison. "Spinach" television may be good for the public's civic health, but is more often praised than consumed.

Pundits blame media tycoons for filling media channels with soft news and trashy entertainment rather than with the highbrow fare that the visions of an ideal American democracy demand. Free use of the airwaves, the critics charge, carries with it the obligation to serve the public interest, which is not equivalent to what the public finds interesting or what the tycoons find profitable. Such criticism implies that elites, including the media, must offer average Americans the stories that elites think audiences need, and must discourage audiences from tasting the forbidden fruit of low-brow media fare by making less of it available.

That stance raises profound questions. Shouldn't people in a democracy be considered capable of deciding what information best suits their needs and tastes? Shouldn't demand-and-supply forces govern the media market place as long as access to the market is unrestrained? When adults flock to entertainment and soft news and prefer the knowledge they provide to harder, more intellectually demanding offerings, isn't that a prerogative that deserves to be respected? If the answers to these questions are "yes," then it is wrong to quarrel with the public's choices of media fare and with the industry's attempts to satisfy existing demand. The responsibility for the focus of much current programming falls squarely on the shoulders of Jane and John Q Average American, abetted by a willing industry.

The condemnation of mass media enterprises for presenting low-brow fare must be put into the context of what audiences have always wanted, rather than in the context of an idealized vision of a society that has never existed and probably never will. Would-be reformers of the current reality must realize that in the battle for audience attention, informational offerings compete with entertainment. Audiences are attracted to entertainment and soft news stories because they tend to be exciting, emotionally involving, titillating, and—yes—because they often require little mental exertion. To compete effectively requires framing hard news offerings so that they share many of the characteristics of the most appealing entertainment fare. Would-be-reformers should also be comforted by the knowledge that indulgence in light entertainment and shunning of hard news have not prevented average Americans from learning a great deal about politics, the economy, and social issues, especially during times of political turmoil. Most Americans are eager to stay informed, if learning is made easy and the stories are compelling. The audience for serious news triples and quadruples when truly important and novel news stories surface, such as the post-election day battles over the winner of the 2000 presidential contest. The media, despite their focus on soft, flimsy stories, feature an expanding universe of channels that supply unprecedented amounts of serious information. If journalists can make hard news stories as easy to understand and as compelling to watch as the best of the entertainment shows, the future looks promising, indeed, for a better-informed American public.

1. Tim Jones, "Mining the Wasteland," *Chicago Tribune*, May 6, 2001.

Learning General Orientations

Some media stories leave the audience with politically significant feelings that persist long after facts have faded from memory. Although many details of the 1995 Oklahoma City bomb attack have faded in memory, Americans still retain vivid feelings of horror, sympathy, grief, and disappointment. Often news that etches few facts into people's memories may leave them with generalized feelings of trust or distrust. For instance, prominently featured stories of serious corruption in government may lower the public's esteem for the integrity of government. People who read newspapers that are severely critical of various actions taken by the government express significantly less trust in government than do those exposed to favorable views. People who have not gone beyond grade school seem to be particularly susceptible to erosion of trust in the wake of mass media criticism.[58] Cynical people, in turn, tend to participate less than others in civic activities such as voting and lobbying.[59]

As political scientist Murray Edelman has noted, insecurity and security feelings generated by news stories may make people quiescent because they become fearful of interfering with crucial government actions or else complacent about the need for public vigilance. Fear that dissension weakens the government may decrease tolerance for dissidents. Edelman also warns that political quiescence has significant adverse effects. It may lead to acceptance of faulty public policies, poor laws, and ineffective administrative practices.[60]

On a more personal level, millions of people use the media to keep in touch with their communities. Their contacts help to counter feelings of loneliness and alienation because information becomes a bond among individuals who share it.[61] The models of life depicted by the media create wants and expectations as well as dissatisfactions and frustrations. These feelings may become powerful stimulants for social change for the society at large or for selected individuals within it. Alternatively, the feelings may bolster support for the political status quo and generate strong resistance to change. Whether media-induced orientations and actions are considered positive, negative, or a mixture of both depends, of course, on one's sociopolitical preferences.

Deterrents to Learning

Disinterest in politics and distaste for media offerings, as well as deficiencies in the supply of information, deter many people from keeping up with politics. Rather than discussing politics, which they see as a sensitive topic, they prefer to talk about sports, or the weather, or local gossip. In fact, as the level of abstract, issue-oriented content of political news rises, the attentive audience shrivels. People scan the news for major crises without trying to remember specific facts. However, when they sense that events will greatly affect their lives, or when they need information for their jobs or for social or political activities, political interest and learning perk up quickly and often dramatically.[62] For example, media coverage of the post-election day dispute about the outcome of the 2000 presidential election fired up public interest that had smoldered during the campaign. The post-election events received more public attention in five weeks than the entire primary campaign had received during a five-month span.[63]

Serious programs on radio and television often become highly popular, especially when they involve themes of corruption, violence, or other wrongdoing. Examples are *60 Minutes,* which probes a variety of social ills; *The Winds of War,* a made-for-television movie that recounted the history of World War II; and documentaries dealing with rape, child snatching, and prison violence. Broadcasts of congressional hearings on the selection of controversial Supreme Court justices or on the legality of secret activities of the executive branch fall into this category as well.

Widespread public interest in most political crises flares up like a straw fire and then dies quickly. For instance, interest in the Iran-contra scandal involving the Reagan administration ebbed after a few weeks even though it involved highly dramatic events such as espionage, secret weapons deals, and circumvention of congressional mandates. The Republicans' Contract with America in 1994, the debate over the North American Free Trade Agreement (NAFTA) in 1993, and even the impeachment proceedings against President Clinton in 1999 were stale topics within a few months. Attention spans are erratic and brief, even though most Americans believe that, as good citizens, they ought to be well informed about political news and feel guilty, or at least apologetic, if they are not.

Learning is further inhibited by the alienation of many population groups from the media. Many white ethnics, such as Polish Americans or Italian Americans, and police and union members, for instance, consider most mass media hostile. They often believe that the media lie and distort when they cast police as trigger-happy oppressors of the disadvantaged or unions as corrupt and a barrier to economic progress. Public opinion polls in recent decades show considerable erosion of public confidence in the trustworthiness of the media in general. The media now rank near the bottom of trustworthiness, along with Congress and the legal profession.[64]

How media information is presented also affects learning. The public is bombarded daily with more news than it can handle. Most of the news is touted as significant even though much is trivial. The constant crisis atmosphere numbs excitement and produces boredom. Audiences are not likely to try hard to learn a wealth of factual information that does not interest them. Moreover, "happy talk" television news formats and exciting film footage encourage the feeling that news should be viewed as a light-hearted diversion.

The presentation of stories in disconnected snippets complicates the task of making sense out of news stories and integrating them with existing knowledge. This is especially true when stories are complex, as is true of most reports about controversial public policies. People who feel that they cannot understand what is happening are discouraged from spending time reading or listening. Learning also suffers when conflicting stories and interpretations are presented without giving guidance to the audience; guidance is often omitted for fear that it might be considered unacceptable editorializing.[65] If people watch several newscasts, hoping for an enriched news diet, they find that roughly half the material is repetitive. Even within a single newscast a large proportion of every story is rehashed background information that puts the story into perspective for viewers who are seeing it for the first time.

The internal structure of television newscasts also impedes learning. More than 80 percent of all news stories take up fewer than three minutes, yet they are crammed with information that cannot possibly be absorbed in that time. In addition to an abundance of pictures, the average news story contains 3 verbal statements for every 2 pictorial scenes (see Table 7-3). For the fifteen to eighteen stories in a typical newscast, viewers are asked to absorb an average of 18 factual statements and 11 picture scenes per story. That amounts to 324 statements and 198 pictures compressed into twenty-two minutes of news exposure. Furthermore, in most news programs disparate items are tightly packaged without the pauses that are essential to allow viewers to absorb information. Hence, it is not surprising that half the audience after the lapse of a few hours cannot recall a single item from a television newscast. Distracting activities that viewers combine with watching television do not help either.

Despite all of the deterrents to learning, Americans still learn a lot about politics. They also are well socialized into the American system. They may be disappointed and cynical about particular leaders or policies, but relatively few individuals question the legitimacy of the government, object to its basic philosophies, or reject its claims to their support. If one believes in the merits of the system, this finding is, indeed, cause for satisfaction with current political socialization. In this light, the dire predictions about television-induced deterioration of political life and rampant political alienation among citizens have not materialized.[66] If the American population becomes more eager to learn about politics, and if the media improve political reporting, then knowledge levels could rise sharply.

TABLE 7-3   Network Television News Characteristics

Story length (seconds)	Percentage of total stories	Picture exposure (seconds)	Percentage of total stories	Number of pictures	Percentage of total stories
Less than 60	47	1–10	51	1–4	44
60–179	34	11–20	30	5–10	28
180–299	14	21–30	10	11–20	15
300+	5	31+	9	21–54	13

SOURCE: Author's research, based on a sample of 150 news stories from early evening newscasts on ABC, CBS, and NBC, September 1–15, 2000.

However, because television has become the main provider of information, knowledge tests need to be restructured so that they reflect the unique contributions made by audiovisuals to comprehending the world.

Learning Effects: Behavior

Because the media shape people's knowledge, attitudes, and feelings, they obviously can influence behavior. Two areas that have long been of great political concern illustrate the extent of behavioral effects: imitation of crime and violence, particularly among adolescents; and stimulation of economic and political development in underdeveloped regions. In Chapter 8 we will discuss the effects of media coverage on voting behavior and in Chapter 11 the impact of the media on the conduct of foreign affairs.

Crime and Violent Behavior in Children

Many social scientists believe that violence and crime portrayed in the media, particularly on television, lead to imitation, especially by children and young adults. The possible link between television exposure and deviant behavior has been thoroughly investigated. The surgeon general's office has produced a bookshelf full of information on the topic since the 1970s.[67] Congressional committees have spent countless hours listening to conflicting testimony by social scientists about the impact of television violence. Violence in the media has been an issue in campaigns, such as the 2000 presidential contest. Meanwhile, the amount of violent content, particularly in fictional programs, has escalated, though numbers vary widely depending on the definition of *violence*. A 1996 study that defined *violence* broadly as "any overt depiction of the use of physical force or the credible threat of such force intended to physically harm an animate being or group of beings" found most violence on premium cable channels. On HBO and Showtime, 85 percent of programming contained violence. The rate was 59 percent for basic cable channels and 44 percent for broadcast television.[68]

What have studies of the impact of television violence revealed? Despite the strong inclination of many of the researchers to find that crime fiction causes asocial behavior, the evidence is not altogether conclusive. Some children do copy violent behavior, especially when they have watched aggression that was left unpunished or was rewarded and when countervailing influences from parents and teachers are lacking.[69] But, aside from imitating television examples when tempted to do so, children do not ordinarily become violent after exposure to violence in the mass media. It has been estimated that television-inspired violence accounts for a mere 5 percent of the problem.[70] Most children lack the predisposition and usually the opportunity for violence, and most do not live in an environment that encourages asocial behavior. In fact, exposure to crime makes some children more sympathetic toward the suffering of victims of crime and violence.[71] A crude cause-and-effect model is therefore invalid.

Other confounding factors in assessing the impact of television on children are age-linked comprehension differences. Younger children may not be able to comprehend many of the events presented by the media in the same way that adolescents do. The complex social reasoning that adults often ascribe to even young children does not develop until youngsters reach their teenage years. Although young children often imitate what they have seen, they are rarely able to generalize or respond to implied messages. Several studies of children in preschool and early grade school suggest that much of what adults consider to be violent does not seem so to children. Cartoon violence is an example.[72] Therefore, many of the programs that adults consider dangerous may actually be harmless.

The percentage of preadolescents and adolescents in the population who are prone to imitate crime is not known at this time. However, the wide dispersion of television throughout American homes makes it almost certain that the majority of children susceptible to imitating violence will be exposed. Even in the absence of television, many other triggers could arouse these young people to violence. Whatever the source of arousal, even if the actual number of highly susceptible preadolescents and adolescents is tiny and statistically insignificant, the social consequences can be profound. Such considerations prompted Congress to mandate in the Telecommunications Act of 1996 that television sets should include a "V-chip" to enable adults to block violent television programs from transmission to their homes. The device has not been used extensively, and probably least often in the kinds of homes where the most vulnerable youngsters are likely to live, considering the correlation between child delinquency and flawed home environments.

Behavior Change in Adults

What about imitation of socially undesirable behavior by adults? The same broad principles apply. Imitation depends on the setting at the time of media exposure and on the personality and attitudes that viewers bring to a situation. Widespread societal norms seem to be particularly important. For instance, the 1986 report of the Attorney General's Commission on Pornography noted that exposure to aberrant sexual behavior led to comparatively little imitation. In fact, there was some evidence that greater availability of obscene and pornographic materials reduced sex crimes and misdemeanors because vicarious experiences were substituted for actual ones.[73] By comparison, there was a great deal more evidence that exposure to criminal behavior encourages imitation. The difference may be more apparent than real, however, because crime is more likely to be reported, whereas sexual perversions usually remain hidden.

In sum, the precise link between exposure to media images and corresponding behavior remains uncertain. Legislative tampering with media offerings therefore appears premature. It will take a great deal more research and experimentation to determine how media fare can be presented to produce imitation of the many desirable behaviors depicted on television and avoid imitation of undesirable ones. Even assuming that these goals could be reached, it is questionable whether a democratic society should attempt to manipulate the minds of its citizens to protect them from temptations to violate social norms. It may be best to leave control of the content of entertainment programs to widely based informal social pressures. The question of whether social pressures should be allowed to interfere with reporting real-world violence poses even more difficult dilemmas. The possibly adverse effects on behavior must be balanced against the need to keep informed about the real world.

Socioeconomic and Political Modernization

The assumed potential of the media to guide people's behavior has led to great efforts to use the media as tools for social and political development. The results have been mixed; there have been some successes and many failures.

Psychic Mobility. The hope of using the media to bring about industrialization, improved social services, and democratization ran very high in the decades following World War II. A personality characteristic that political scientist Daniel Lerner labeled *empathic capacity* was called the key to human and material development. The idea behind this theory was that when the media present new objects, ideas, and behaviors, audiences presumably empathize with what is happening in the story and try to imitate it. For instance, when the media show how slum dwellers have built new housing, or how flood victims have purified their polluted water supply, audience members apply the information to their own lives.

Before mass media became widely available to average people, direct contact with strangers with different lifestyles and experiences generated what Lerner called "psychic mobility." Because contacts usually were limited to relatively few people, changes spread very slowly. The mass media, however, made it possible for the first time in human history to reach millions of people with comparative ease and to expose them to developmental stimuli, either directly or through contact with others reached by the media. Transistor radios and satellite television and, potentially, the Internet, have opened even remote and inaccessible regions to modern communication and have brought news of current lifestyles to isolated communities.

Crediting the media with a major role in modernization and democratization rests on three assumptions. First, the mass media can create interest and empathy for unfamiliar experiences. Second, the mass media provide graphic audiovisual examples of new practices, which audiences can readily understand and copy. Third, development, once started, encourages people to increase their knowledge and skills. Where formal education is not readily available, the media provide information and enhance the capacity to learn. Progress in urbanization, industrialization, living standards, and political advancement that has followed the spread of media to many formerly information-deficient regions is cited as proof that the assumptions are correct.[74]

Psychological Barriers to Modernization. Although many technologically and politically underdeveloped regions have shown measurable progress, with the media apparently serving as catalysts, social and political change has been far slower and more sporadic than development theorists expected. A number of psychological and physical obstacles have kept therapists' dreams from coming true. Impediments have included outright hostility by individuals or communities to change and unwillingness to alter long-established patterns. Mass media may actually become a negative reference point when people condemn the lifestyles depicted by the media. The various fundamentalist groups around the world—such as Ayatollah Khomeini's followers in the Middle East or ultra-Orthodox Jews in Israel—that have mobilized to censor mass media offerings and stop social and political changes provide examples.

People who are not overtly hostile to change still may be totally uninterested in altering their lifestyles. They may doubt their ability to cope with new challenges and be reluctant to add more complications to a difficult life. People exhibiting such attitudes cannot be persuaded by the mass media without the intervention of a trusted person, such as a priest, a health care provider, or a family member. The influence of the mass media then becomes a "two-step flow" that moves from the media to opinion leaders and then to their followers.

Putting unaccustomed behaviors and skills into words and concepts that people with little formal education can understand has also turned out to be exceedingly difficult. For instance, teaching new ways to keep food pure, to apply for aid from a government agency, or to mark a ballot in a multicandidate election involves concepts that may require formal schooling to grasp. The disparity in social backgrounds between journalists and their audiences may further confound communication problems.

Changes that require adopting new social values or abandoning old habits are the most difficult of all and the least likely to occur. For example, people who were taught to abhor capitalism find it difficult to become entrepreneurs even when the media praise new forms of economic enterprise. Ingrained habits, such as driving without seat belts or engaging in unsafe sexual behaviors, are difficult to break despite extensive mass-mediated public education campaigns. Even after people have become aware of the dangers inherent in their behavior, and even when they concede that behavioral change is in their best interests, most still forgo voluntary change.

Adoption of Changes.   Despite the difficulties, many mass media campaigns do succeed in bringing about socially desirable changes. How do they do it? We will outline five steps involved in change and indicate how the mass media fit into the picture. First people must become *aware of the possibility for change.* Here the media are especially helpful. Radio can inform people about new energy-saving devices or new child-rearing methods. Television and movies can show new technologies and new styles of political participation. Second is *understanding how to accomplish the suggested changes.* For example, people may be aware that public assistance is available, but they may not know how to apply for it. Mass media usually fail to supply detailed information. On the average, only one-third of all stories that might inspire action of various types, such as environmental protection or energy conservation, contain information about implementation.[75] Unless this gap is filled, the chain leading to the adoption of innovations is broken.

Third is evaluation. People *assess the merits of the innovation* and decide whether they want to adopt it. Innovations often fail to take root because

prospective users reject them as bad, inappropriate, too risky, or too difficult. Media messages alone may not be persuasive enough. It may also be
crucial to have a trusted person urge or demonstrate adoption of the
innovation. Fourth is trial. The effect of the media in *getting people to try*
innovations is limited. Factors beyond media control are more important,
such as social and financial costs of the change as well as the audience's
willingness to change. In general, young men are most receptive to innovations; older people are most skeptical and cautious. Fifth is adoption.
The media contribute most to this phase by *encouraging people to stick with*
the changes that they have made part of their life and work styles. For
example, adoption of birth control is useless unless its use is continuous.
The same holds true for many health and sanitation measures or improved
work habits. To ensure continuity, mass media must cover a topic regularly, stressing long-range goals and reporting progress.

Predicting which media campaigns designed to change behavior will
succeed and which will fail has proven difficult.[76] Douglas S. Solomon,
who studied health campaigns conducted by private and public institutions, believes that four factors account for success or failure. To succeed,
campaigns must *set well-specified, realistic goals* that are tailored to the
needs of various target groups. They must *carefully select appropriate media*
and media formats and present them at key times and intervals. *Messages*
must be properly *designed for greatest persuasiveness*. There also must be
continuous evaluation and appropriate readjustments.[77]

In some instances, the media's efforts to mobilize people have produced unanticipated attitudes and changes in behavior. For instance, when
television was introduced in several Canadian Eskimo communities in the
1970s, programs were designed to show the viewers how to modernize their
living conditions and to acquaint them with Canadian affairs in general.
Rather than aspiring to modernize their lifestyles, however, Eskimo adults in
the communities with televisions turned their eyes to the past. They wanted
to return to traditional ways. This attitude was not apparent in localities
without television. Whether it sprang from nostalgia for the past or aversion
to the lifestyle changes foreshadowed by television is unclear. It is interesting that after the introduction of television the adults wanted the old life for
themselves but aspired to a modern lifestyle for their children.[78]

Above all, the success of the mass media in bringing about change
hinges on the receptivity for change. Ongoing efforts to use the media to
modernize developing areas, to turn former communists into democratic
citizens, or to bring socially helpful information to individuals who are
poor, elderly, and handicapped must concentrate on identifying the specific circumstances most likely to bring success. Responding to requests
initiated locally rather than designing information campaigns from the

" I AM NOW AVAILABLE BY PHONE, FAX, E:MAIL, SNAIL MAIL, VOICE MAIL, OVERNIGHT DELIVERY, CAR PHONE, CELL PHONE AND PAGER............HIDE ME. "

Reprinted with special permission of King Features Syndicate.

outside, and integrating local traditions into new approaches, seem to hold the most promise.[79]

Summary

The mass media play a major role in political socialization and in the learning and accepting of norms and rules, structures, and environmental factors that govern political life. Contrary to earlier findings that indicated limited impact, the media are very influential and consequently represent a tremendously powerful political force.

However, the impact of the media on political socialization and other aspects of political learning is not uniform for all members of the media audience. The media affect individuals in different ways, depending on lifestyles and circumstances. Psychological, demographic, and situational factors influence perceptions and the ensuing political consequences. So do the manner of news presentation and the perspectives from which news is presented. Although many factors contribute to diversity in socialization and learning, there are powerful unifying forces as well. Most Americans are exposed to similar information and develop roughly similar outlooks on what it means (and ought to mean) to be an American both politically and socially.

Various theories explain why and how individuals select particular information to remember. The learning of specific facts presented by the media is quite sparse. Nonetheless, people become aware of many political problems and appreciate their basic significance, even without remembering details about them. Equally important, exposure to the media can produce apathy, cynicism, fear, trust, acquiescence, or support—moods that condition participation in the political process, which may range from total abstinence to efforts to overthrow the government by force.

The media may also produce or retard behavior that affects the quality of public life. In this chapter we assessed the role of the media in fostering socially undesirable behaviors, especially crime and violence. We also explored the ways in which the media influence the political and social development of various population groups. The media are most successful in informing people and creating initial attitudes that are least effective in changing established attitudes and ingrained behaviors.

Given the many largely uncontrollable variables that determine media influence, concerted efforts to manipulate media content to foster societal goals are risky at best. They could set dangerous precedents for inhibiting the free flow of controversial ideas or for using the media as channels for government propaganda.

Notes

1. Sheryl Gay Stolberg, "C.D.C. Plays Script Doctor to Spread Its Message," *New York Times*, June 26, 2001. The story refers to a 1999 survey finding that 48 percent of the people who watched soap operas at least twice a week learn something about disease prevention. A Kaiser Family Foundation study of audiences viewing the emergency room drama *E.R.* reported that one-third of the audience was helped by the show in making their own health decisions.
2. Impact differences between print and electronic media are discussed in W. Russell Neuman, Marion R. Just, and Ann N. Crigler, *Common Knowledge: News and the Construction of Political Meaning* (Chicago: University of Chicago Press, 1992); Marion Just and Ann Crigler, "Learning from the News: Experiments in Media, Modality, and Reporting about Star Wars," *Political Communication and Persuasion* 6 (1989): 109–127. For the view that differences in media modality are very important, see Patricia Moy and Michael Pfau, *With Malice Toward All? The Media and Public Confidence in Democratic Institutions* (Westport, Conn.: Praeger, 2000).
3. Michael X. Delli Carpini and Scott Keeter, *What Americans Know about Politics and Why It Matters* (New Haven: Yale University Press, 1996).
4. Neil Postman, *Amusing Ourselves to Death: Public Discourse in the Age of Show Business* (New York: Viking Penguin, 1985). For a good discussion of the dif-

ferences between the effects of print and television news on people's behavior, see Joshua Meyrowitz, *No Sense of Place: The Impact of Electronic Media on Social Behavior* (New York: Oxford University Press, 1985), 94–106.

5. The advantages of learning from audiovisuals are detailed in Doris A. Graber, *Processing Politics: Learning from Television in the Internet Age* (Chicago: University of Chicago Press, 2001).

6. Ibid., chap. 3.

7. The importance of collective memories is spelled out in Yoram Peri, "The Media and Collective Memory of Yitzhak Rabin's Remembrance," *Journal of Communication* 49 (3) (summer 1999): 106–124.

8. W. Russell Neuman, *The Future of the Mass Audience* (New York: Cambridge University Press, 1991), 99 (emphasis added). Zhongdang Pan, Ronald E. Ostman, Patricia Moy, and Paula Reynolds, "News Media Exposure and Its Learning Effects during the Persian Gulf War," *Journalism Quarterly* 71 (1) (spring 1994): 7–19.

9. John E. Chubb and Terry M. Moe, "Politics, Markets, and the Organization of Schools," *American Political Science Review* 82 (1988): 1065–1088.

10. Bruce Watkins, "Television Viewing as a Dominant Activity of Childhood: A Developmental Theory of Television Effects," *Critical Studies in Mass Communication* 2 (1985): 323–337. Average high school graduates have spent 15,000 hours watching television and 11,000 hours in the classroom. They have seen 350,000 commercials.

11. M. Margaret Conway, Mikel L. Wyckoff, Eleanor Feldbaum, and David Ahern, "The News Media in Children's Political Socialization," *Public Opinion Quarterly* 45 (summer 1981): 164–178; and Gina M. Garramone and Charles K. Atkin, "Mass Communication and Political Socialization: Specifying the Effects," *Public Opinion Quarterly* 50 (spring 1986): 76–86.

12. Suzanne Pingree, "Children's Cognitive Processes in Constructing Social Reality," *Journalism Quarterly* 60 (fall 1983): 415–422. Also see Judith Torney-Purta, John Schwille, and Jo-Ann Amadeo, eds., *Civic Education Across Countries: Twenty-Four National Case Studies from the IEA Civic Education Project* (Amsterdam: International Association for the Evaluation of Educational Achievement, 1999).

13. Jean Piaget, *The Language and Thought of the Child*, 3d ed. (New York: Harcourt Brace, 1962). See also Pamela Johnston Conover, "Political Socialization: Where's the Politics?" in *Political Science: Looking to the Future; Political Behavior*, vol. 3, ed. William Crotty (Evanston: Northwestern University Press, 1991), 125–152.

14. A study of prime-time values on television showed that fewer than 4 percent concerned citizenship values such as patriotism or citizen duties. Gary W. Selnow, "Values in Prime-Time Television," *Journal of Communication* 40 (summer 1990): 69.

15. Robert Kubey, "Media Implications for the Quality of Family Life," in *Media, Children, and the Family*, ed. Dolf Zillmann, Jennings Bryant, and Aletha C. Huston (Hillsdale, N.J.: Erlbaum, 1994), 61–70.

16. Neuman, *Future of the Mass Audience*, 89–91. See also Pew Research Center for the People and the Press, 2000, "The Questionnaire and Overall Breakdown," http://www.people-press.org/med00sec5.htm.

17. George Gerbner, Larry Gross, Marilyn Jackson Beeck, Suzanne Jeffries Fox, and Nancy Signorielli, "Cultural Indicators: Violence Profile No. 9," *Journal of Communication* 28 (summer 1978): 178, 193. See also George Gerbner, Larry Gross, Michael Morgan, and Nancy Signorielli, "Political Correlates of Television Viewing," *Public Opinion Quarterly* 48 (summer 1984): 283–300. The media's role in shaping social attitudes is discussed in Benjamin I. Page and Robert Y. Shapiro, *The Rational Public* (Chicago: University of Chicago Press, 1992), 35.

18. The importance of preadult political learning for subsequent political orientations is discussed in Paul Allen Beck and M. Kent Jennings, "Pathways to Participation," *American Political Science Review* 76 (1982): 103–110. Also see Doris A. Graber, *Processing the News: How People Tame the Information Tide,* 2d ed. (Lanham, Md.: University Press of America, 1993), 184–188, 210–213; and Graber, *Processing Politics,* chap. 2.

19. Shanto Iyengar, *Is Anyone Responsible? How Television Frames Political Issues* (Chicago: University of Chicago Press, 1991), 136–143.

20. Stanley Rothman, S. Robert Lichter, and Linda Lichter, "Television's America," in *The Mass Media in Liberal Democratic Societies,* ed. Stanley Rothman (New York: Paragon House, 1992), 221–266.

21. Paula M. Poindexter, "Non-News Viewers," *Journal of Communication* 30 (autumn 1980): 58–65; and Michael X. Delli Carpini and Bruce A. Williams, "Constructing Public Opinion: The Uses of Fictional and Nonfictional Television in Conversations about the Environment," in *The Psychology of Political Communication,* ed. Ann N. Crigler (Ann Arbor: University of Michigan Press, 1996), 149–175.

22. For examples of various types of general and specific information supplied by entertainment programming, see Gary W. Selnow, "Solving Problems on Prime-Time Television," *Journal of Communication* 36 (spring 1986): 63–72; Selnow, "Values in Prime-Time Television"; G. Ray Funkhouser and Eugene F. Shaw, "How Synthetic Experience Shapes Social Reality," *Journal of Communication* 40 (summer 1990): 75–87; W. James Potter and William Ware, "The Frequency and Context of Prosocial Acts on Primetime TV," *Journalism Quarterly* 66 (summer 1989): 359–366, 529.

23. Stephen D. Reese and M. Mark Miller, "Political Attitude Holding and Structure: The Effects of Newspaper and Television News," *Communication Research* 8 (April 1981): 182.

24. Graber, *Processing the News,* 90–93.

25. Gerbner et al., "Political Correlates," 286.

26. Reese and Miller, "Political Attitude Holding," 182. For a different perspective, see Donald L. Jordan, "Newspaper Effects on Policy Preferences," *Public Opinion Quarterly* 57 (1993): 191–204; and William Schneider and A. I. Lewis, "Views on the News," *Public Opinion* 8 (August–September 1985): 5–11, 58–59.

27. However, the benefits derived from the use of a particular medium vary for demographic groups. For example, while use of local news media coincides with civic participation for most audiences, this does not hold true for African Americans. Their civic participation is encouraged more by interpersonal networks.

Teresa Mastin, "Media Use and Civic Participation in the African-American Population: Exploring Participation Among Professionals and Nonprofessionals," *Journalism and Mass Communication Quarterly* 77(1)(2000): 115–127.

28. Karl Erik Rosengren, Lawrence A. Wenner, and Philip Palmgreen, eds., *Media Gratifications Research: Current Perspectives* (Beverly Hills, Calif.: Sage, 1985). Also see Gina M. Garramone, "Motivation and Political Information Processing: Extending the Gratifications Approach," in *Mass Media and Political Thought*, ed. Sidney Kraus and Richard Perloff (Beverly Hills, Calif.: Sage, 1985), 201–222; David L. Swanson, "Gratification Seeking, Media Exposure, and Audience Interpretations: Some Directions for Research," *Journal of Broadcasting and Electronic Media* 31 (1987): 237–254.

29. W. Lance Bennett, *News: The Politics of Illusion*, 4th ed. (New York: Longman, 2001), chap. 6; and Charles Atkin, "Information Utility and Selective Exposure to Entertainment Media," in *Selective Exposure to Communication*, ed. Dolf Zillman and Jennings Bryant (Hillsdale, N.J.: Erlbaum, 1985), 63–92.

30. Michael Morgan, "Heavy Television Viewing and Perceived Quality of Life," *Journalism Quarterly* 61 (autumn 1984): 499–504; Philip Palmgreen, Lawrence A. Wenner, and J. D. Rayburn II, "Relations between Gratifications Sought and Obtained: A Study of Television News," *Communication Research* 7 (April 1980): 161–192; Robert W. Kubey, "Television Use in Everyday Life: Coping with Unstructured Time," *Journal of Communication* 36 (summer 1986): 108–123.

31. Neuman, *Future of the Mass Audience*, 122.

32. In Thomas L. Friedman, "No TV? Israel Is Savoring the Silence," *New York Times*, Nov. 6, 1987.

33. Graber, *Processing the News*, 133–136. See also Stuart H. Schwartz, "A General Psychographic Analysis of Newspaper Use and Life Style," *Journalism Quarterly* 57 (autumn 1980): 392–401; also see William D. Wells, *Life Style and Psychographics* (Chicago: American Marketing Association, 1974).

34. The literature is reviewed in Zillman and Bryant, *Selective Exposure to Communication*, passim.

35. Roy L. Behr and Shanto Iyengar, "Television News, Real-World Cues, and Changes in the Public Agenda," *Public Opinion Quarterly* 49 (spring 1985): 38–57. For a discussion of replacement of older issues by newer ones, see Hans-Bernd Brosius and Hans Mathias Kepplinger, "Killer and Victim Issues: Issue Competition in the Agenda-Setting Process of German Television," *International Journal of Public Opinion Research* 7(3) (1995): 211–231.

36. Maxwell E. McCombs, "The Agenda-Setting Approach," in *Handbook of Political Communication*, ed. Dan D. Nimmo and Keith Sanders (Beverly Hills, Calif.: Sage, 1981), 121–140; Shanto Iyengar and Donald R. Kinder, *News that Matters: TV and American Opinion* (Chicago: University of Chicago Press, 1987); Benjamin I. Page, Robert Y. Shapiro, and Glenn R. Dempsey, "What Moves Public Opinion?" *American Political Science Review* 81 (March 1987): 23–43; Benjamin I. Page and Robert Y. Shapiro, *The Rational Public: Fifty Years of Trends in Americans' Policy Preferences* (Chicago: University of Chicago Press, 1991); Donald L. Shaw and Shannon E. Martin, "The Function of Mass Media

Agenda Setting," *Journalism Quarterly* 69(4) (1992): 902–920; and Wayne Wanta, *The Public and the National Agenda* (Mahwah, N.J.: Erlbaum, 1997).

37. Diana Mutz, *Impersonal Influence: How Perceptions of Mass Collectives Affect Political Attitudes* (Cambridge: Cambridge University Press, 1998); Robert Huckfeldt and John Sprague, *Citizens, Politics, and Social Communication: Information and Influence in an Election Campaign* (Cambridge: Cambridge University Press, 1995).

38. Christine R. Ader, "A Longitudinal Study of Agenda Setting for the Issue of Environmental Pollution," *Journalism and Mass Communication Quarterly* 72(2) (summer 1995): 300–311; Behr and Iyengar, "Television News"; and Michael B. MacKuen and Steven L. Coombs, *More than News: Media Power in Public Affairs* (Beverly Hills, Calif.: Sage, 1981).

39. The importance of personal and contextual factors in news selection and evaluation is discussed in Lutz Erbring, Edie Goldenberg, and Arthur Miller, "Front-Page News and Real World Cues: Another Look at Agenda-Setting by the Media," *American Journal of Political Science* 24 (February 1980): 16–49; and David B. Hill, "Viewer Characteristics and Agenda Setting by Television News," *Public Opinion Quarterly* 49 (fall 1985): 340–350.

40. Graber, *Processing the News*, 27–31, and for details on learning processes, chaps. 7–9. Also see Robert H. Wicks, "Schema Theory and Measurement in Mass Communication Research: Theoretical and Methodological Issues in News Information Processing," *Communication Yearbook* 15 (Newbury Park, Calif.: Sage, 1991), 115–154. An excellent discussion of processing of audiovisual information research, including a lengthy bibliography, is presented by Annie Lang, "The Limited Capacity Model of Mediated Message Processing," *Journal of Communication* 50(1)(2000): 46–70. How learning goals affect processing is reported by Li-Ning Huang, "Examining Candidate Information Search Processes: The Impact of Processing Goals and Sophistication," *Journal of Communication* 50(1) (2000): 93–114.

41. Walter Lippmann, *Public Opinion* (New York: Harcourt Brace, 1922), 31.

42. See, for example, Mary Beth Oliver, "Caucasian Viewers' Memory of Black and White Criminal Suspects in the News," *Journal of Communication* 49(3) (1997):46–60, and references cited there; and Robert M. Entman and Andrew Rojecki, *The Black Image in the White Mind: Media and Race in America* (Chicago: University of Chicago Press, 2001).

43. Vincent Price and John Zaller, "Who Gets the News? Alternative Measures of News Reception and Their Implications for Research," *Public Opinion Quarterly* 57(1) (1993): 133–164; and Cecilie Gaziano, "Forecast 2000: Widening Knowledge Gaps," *Journalism and Mass Communication Quarterly* 74(2) (1997): 237–264. For evidence of shared reactions to television programs, irrespective of educational level, see W. Russell Neuman, "Television and American Culture: The Mass Medium and the Pluralist Audience," *Public Opinion Quarterly* 46 (winter 1982): 471–487.

44. Maria Elizabeth Grabe, Annie Lang, Shuhua Zhou, and Paul David Bolls, "Cognitive Access to Negatively Arousing News: An Experimental Investigation of the Knowledge Gap," *Communication Research* 27(1)(2000):3–26.

45. Larry L. Burriss, "How Anchors, Reporters and Newsmakers Affect Recall and Evaluation of Stories," *Journalism Quarterly* 64 (summer/autumn 1987): 514–519. The impact of framing on the perception of the legitimacy of social protest is discussed in Douglas M. McLeod and Benjamin H. Detenber, "Framing Effects of Television News Coverage of Social Protest," *Journal of Communication* 49(3) (1999): 3–23; also see Annie Lang, "The Limited Capacity Model of Mediated Message Processing," *Journal of Communication* 50(1) (2000): 46–70; William L. Buscemi, "Numbers? Borrinnnggg!!! *PS: Political Science & Politics* 30(4) (1997): 737–742; and Patti M. Valkenburg, Holli Semetko, and Claes H. de Vreese, "The Effects of News Frames on Readers' Thoughts and Recall," *Communication Research* 26(5) (1999): 550–569.

46. Shanto Iyengar, "Television News and Citizens' Explanations of National Affairs," *American Political Science Review* 81 (September 1987): 815–831. The impact of stereotyped beliefs on public policy is discussed in detail in Gilens, *Why Americans Hate Welfare,* passim.

47. Michael A. Milburn, Paul Y. Watanabe, and Bernard M. Kramer, "The Nature and Sources of Attitudes toward a Nuclear Freeze," *Political Psychology* 7 (December 1986): 672.

48. An overview of hypermnesia research is presented in Robert H. Wicks, "Remembering the News: Effects and Message Discrepancy on News Recall over Time," *Journalism and Mass Communication Quarterly* 72(3) (autumn 1995): 666–682.

49. Meyrowitz, *No Sense of Place.*

50. The chances of becoming a crime victim are small in real life, but in television life they are 30 percent to 64 percent. See Gerbner et al., "Cultural Indicators," 106–107. For a critique of the work of Gerbner and his associates, see W. James Potter, "Cultivation Theory and Research: A Methodological Critique," *Journalism Monograph* 147 (October 1994). James Shanahan and Michael Morgan, *Television and Its Viewers: Cultivation Theory and Research* (Cambridge: Cambridge University Press, 1999), lays out the pro and con arguments of the cultivation research program. Exposure to news about actual crime predicts salience of crime better than does personal exposure to crime. Edna F. Einsiedel, Kandice L. Salomone, and Frederick P. Schneider, "Crime: Effects of Media Exposure and Personal Experience on Issue Salience," *Journalism Quarterly* 61 (spring 1984): 131–136.

51. Iyengar, *Is Anyone Responsible?*; Iyengar and Kinder, *News That Matters.*

52. An example of corroborative research is Jon A. Krosnick and Donald R. Kinder, "Altering the Foundations of Support for the President through Priming," *American Political Science Review* 84 (June 1990): 497–512.

53. John Stauffer, Richard Frost, and William Rybolt, "The Attention Factor in Recalling Network Television News," *Journal of Communication* 33 (winter 1983): 29–37. Also see Graber, *Processing Politics,* 25–30.

54. Graber, *Processing the News,* chap. 2; Teun A. Van Dijk, *News as Discourse* (Hillsdale, N.J.: Erlbaum, 1988), 139–174; and John P. Robinson and Mark R. Levy, *The Main Source: Learning from Television News* (Beverly Hills, Calif.: Sage, 1986), 57–175. Also see Samuel Popkin and Michael A. Dimock, "Political

Knowledge and Citizen Competence," in *Citizen Competence and Democratic Institutions,* Stephen L. Elkin and Karol Edward Soltan, eds. (University Park: Pennsylvania State University Press, 1999), 117–146.

55. Scott Keeter and Cliff Zukin, *Uninformed Choice: The Failure of the New Presidential Nominating System* (New York: Praeger, 1983). But see Arthur Lupia and Mathew D. McCubbins, *The Democratic Dilemma: Can Citizens Learn What They Need to Know?* New York: Cambridge University Press, 1998. Also see Delli Carpini and Keeter, *What Americans Know about Politics and Why It Matters.*

56. Michael Schudson, *The Power of News* (Cambridge: Harvard University Press, 1995), 27.

57. V. O. Key, with the assistance of Milton C. Cummings, Jr., *The Responsible Electorate* (Cambridge: Harvard University Press, 1965), 7, reached the same conclusion. Also see Page and Shapiro, *The Rational Public,* 383–390, regarding the wisdom inherent in public opinion and Daniel R. Anderson, "Educational Television Is Not an Oxymoron," *Annals of the American Academy of Political and Social Science* 557 (May 1998): 24–38.

58. Arthur H. Miller, Edie N. Goldenberg, and Lutz Erbring, "Type-Set Politics: Impact of Newspapers on Public Confidence," *American Political Science Review* 73 (March 1979): 67–84.

59. Joseph N. Cappella, and Kathleen Hall Jamieson, *The Spiral of Cynicism: The Press and the Public Good* (New York: Oxford University Press, 1997).

60. Murray Edelman, *Politics as Symbolic Action* (New York: Academic Press, 1976), and Murray Edelman, *Constructing the Political Spectacle* (Chicago: University of Chicago Press, 1988).

61. Susan Hearold, "A Synthesis of 1043 Effects of Television on Social Behavior," in *Public Communication and Behavior,* vol. 1, George A. Comstock, ed. (New York: Academic Press, 1986), 66–133. Also see George E. Marcus, W. Russell Neuman, and Michael MacKuen, *Affective Intelligence and Political Judgment* (Chicago: University of Chicago Press, 2000), and Antonio R. Damasio, *Descartes' Error: Emotion, Reason, and the Human Brain* (New York: Grosset/Putnam, 1994).

62. The desire to be politically informed varies widely. News selection criteria are discussed in Graber, *Processing the News,* chap. 4.

63. Center for Media and Public Affairs, "Florida Trouble Triples TV Attention," http://www.cmpa.com/pressrel/electpr13.htm.

64. Harold W. Stanley and Richard G. Niemi, *Vital Statistics on American Politics, 1997–1998* (Washington, D.C.: CQ Press, 1998). Published every two years. Also see Pew Research Center for the People and the Press, 2000. "The Questionnaire and Overall Breakdown," http://www.people-press.org/med00sec5.htm.

65. Cappella and Jamieson, passim.

66. For dire predictions see Jarol B. Manheim, *All of the People All the Time: Strategic Communication and American Politics* (Armonk, N.Y.: M. E. Sharpe, 1991), 204–209; Robert Entman, *Democracy without Citizens: Media and the Decay of American Politics* (New York: Oxford University Press, 1990), chap. 7. For a more positive view see Graber, *Processing the News,* 251–258; and Page and Shapiro, *Rational Public,* 383–390.

67. None of these studies focuses on the effects of exposure to nonfictional vio-
    lence in the media because the First Amendment would be a strong bar to
    censorship of news. Surgeon General's Scientific Advisory Committee on
    Television and Social Behavior, *Television and Growing Up: The Impact of Tele-
    vised Violence* (Washington, D.C.: U.S. Government Printing Office, 1971). For
    a critical review of the follow-up report, see Thomas D. Cook, Deborah A.
    Kendzierski, and Stephen V. Thomas, "The Implicit Assumptions of Television
    Research: An Analysis of the 1982 NIMH Report on 'Television and Behav-
    ior,'" *Public Opinion Quarterly* 47 (spring 1983): 161–201.
68. "Violence Dominates on TV, Study Says," *Chicago Tribune,* Feb. 7, 1996.
69. Russell G. Geen, "Television and Aggression: Recent Developments and Theory,"
    in *Media, Children and the Family,* ed. Zillmann et al., 151–162; Jerome L. Singer,
    Dorothy G. Singer, and Wanda S. Rapaczynski, "Family Patterns and Television
    Viewing as Predictors of Children's Beliefs and Aggression," *Journal of Communi-
    cation* 34 (summer 1984): 73–89. The politics of research on the effects of televi-
    sion violence are discussed by Willard D. Rowland, Jr., *The Politics of TV Violence:
    Policy Uses of Communication Research* (Beverly Hills, Calif.: Sage, 1983).
70. Elizabeth Kolbert, "Television Gets Closer Look as a Factor in Real Violence,"
    New York Times, Dec. 14, 1994.
71. James M. Carlson, *Prime Time Law Enforcement: Crime Show Viewing and Atti-
    tudes toward the Criminal Justice System* (New York: Praeger, 1985); Marjorie
    Heins, "Blaming the Media: Would Regulation of Expression Prevent Another
    Columbine?" *Media Studies Journal* 14(3)(2000): 14–23; Marjorie Heins, *Not
    in Front of the Children: Indecency, Censorship and the Innocence of Youth* (New
    York: Hill and Wang, 2001).
72. Robert P. Snow, "How Children Interpret TV Violence in Play Context," *Jour-
    nalism Quarterly* 51 (spring 1974): 13–21.
73. *Attorney General's Commission on Pornography: Final Report,* published in 1986;
    see also Richard A. Dienstbier, "Sex and Violence: Can Research Have It Both
    Ways?" *Journal of Communication* 27 (summer 1977): 176–188; Presidential
    Commission on Obscenity and Pornography, Report of the Commission on
    Obscenity and Pornography (New York: Bantam Books, 1970).
74. David O. Edeani, "Critical Predictors of Orientation to Change in a Devel-
    oped Society," *Journalism Quarterly* 58 (spring 1981): 56–64. The carefully
    measured impact of the introduction of television into a Canadian community
    is presented in Tannis MacBeth Williams, ed., *The Impact of Television: A Nat-
    ural Experiment in Three Communities* (Orlando: Academic Press, 1985).
75. James B. Lemert, Barry N. Mitzman, Michael A. Seither, Roxana H. Cook, and
    Regina Hackett, "Journalists and Mobilizing Information," *Journalism Quarterly*
    54 (winter 1977): 721–726.
76. Ronald E. Rice and Charles K. Atkin, eds., *Public Communication Campaigns,*
    2d ed. (Newbury Park, Calif.: Sage, 1989).
77. Douglas S. Solomon, "Health Campaigns on Television," in *Television and
    Human Behavior,* ed. George Comstock, Steven Chaffee, Natan Katzman,
    Maxwell McCombs, and Donald Roberts (New York: Columbia University
    Press, 1978), 316–319.

78. Sheldon O'Connell, "Television and the Canadian Eskimo: The Human Perspective," *Journal of Communication* 27 (autumn 1977): 140–144; and Gary O. Coldevin, "Anik I and Isolation: Television in the Lives of Canadian Eskimos," *Journal of Communication* 27 (autumn 1977): 145–153.

79. John L. Crompton and Charles W. Lamb Jr., *Marketing Government and Social Services* (New York: Wiley, 1986); Marc L. Lame, "Communicating in the Innovation Process: Issues and Guidelines," in *Handbook of Administrative Communication,* James L. Garnett and Alexander Kouzmin, eds. (New York: Marcel Dekker, 1997), 187–201.

Readings

Gamson, William A. *Talking Politics.* New York: Cambridge University Press, 1992.

Graber, Doris A. *Processing Politics: Learning from Television in the Internet Age.* Chicago: University of Chicago Press, 2001.

Kubey, Robert, and Mihaly Csikszentmihalyi. *Television and the Quality of Life: How Viewing Shapes Everyday Experience.* Hillsdale, N.J.: Erlbaum, 1990.

Lupia, Arthur, and Mathew D. McCubbins. *The Democratic Dilemma: Can Citizens Learn What They Need to Know?* New York: Cambridge University Press, 1998.

Marcus, George E., W. Russell Neuman, and Michael MacKuen. *Affective Intelligence and Political Judgment.* Chicago: University of Chicago Press, 2000.

Neuman, W. Russell, Marion R. Just, and Ann N. Crigler. *Common Knowledge: News and the Construction of Political Meaning.* Chicago: University of Chicago Press, 1992.

Schudson, Michael. *The Power of News.* Cambridge: Harvard University Press, 1995.

Shanahan, James, and Michael Morgan. *Television and Its Viewers: Cultivation Theory and Research.* Cambridge: Cambridge University Press, 1999.

Zillmann, Dolf, Jennings Bryant, and Aletha Huston. *Media, Children, and the Family: Social Scientific, Psychodynamic, and Clinical Perspectives.* Hillsdale, N.J.: Erlbaum, 1994.

Elections in the Internet Age

THE PRESIDENTIAL ELECTION OF 2000 was one of the closest in American history. Polls throughout the final months of the campaign showed Republican governor George W. Bush and Democratic vice president Albert Gore in a deadheat race that pollsters said was too close to call. The closeness of the race gave special excitement to election night broadcasts that were recording actual votes.

On election day, about eight o'clock in the evening eastern time, the Associated Press and the major networks announced that Gore had won Florida's electoral votes. Earlier reports had declared him the winner in other states essential for amassing a majority of the electoral college votes. The Florida win made it almost certain that Gore would be the next president.

The problem was that the announcements were premature. They were made when a small number of polling stations in counties favoring Bush were still open in Florida. To avoid influencing the decisions of voters, news venues had agreed to delay predictions until all polls were closed in a state. Even worse, the Voter News Service exit poll data, on which the predictions were based, were flawed because of data processing and sampling errors.[1] When the errors were discovered roughly two hours later, the networks negated their earlier announcements and put Florida back into the "undecided" category at a time when voting was still continuing in many western states. In the wee hours of the day following the election — almost eight hours later — the media finally called Bush the winner of the Florida contest. But even that was not the last word. A recount battle to determine the correct winner of the state's electoral votes dragged on for

five more weeks and was finally settled in favor of Bush by a highly controversial U.S. Supreme Court decision.

In the wake of the flawed election day announcements, long-standing
arguments reemerged about the impact of releasing election results before
voting has ended in a particular state—or even in any state in the nation.
Do voters fail to cast their ballots when they hear that the die is already cast?
The political consequences of media interference can be major. Contenders in close elections may lose the critical votes that might have spelled
victory for them. Winners may show smaller margins of victory and thereby
encourage future opponents. Candidates for low-level offices may lose crucial votes when voters do not show up to vote for high-level officials. The key
question underlying all of these concerns is the extent of the power of the
media to affect various aspects of elections. Although the link between the
media and election outcomes has been studied more thoroughly than other
media–politics links, the dynamics remain unclear. Definitive answers are
lacking for most cause-and-effect questions in this area.

The State of Research

Understanding the role of the mass media in elections is hampered
by imbalances in research. Presidential elections have been most extensively studied, and congressional elections draw increasing attention. Far
less is known about the media's role in gubernatorial elections and about
their impact in various types of local elections. The limited evidence available suggests that the role of the media varies substantially, depending on
the particular office at stake and the news appeal of a campaign. In congressional elections, for example, exciting campaigns are covered while routine ones are ignored.

Even at the presidential level little genuinely comparative research
has been done to explore the differences in the role of the media from
one election to the next. Before the 2000 presidential campaign, high costs
discouraged most researchers from studying media influences throughout
entire campaigns from the preprimary period, when candidate selection
takes place, to the general election. Generous funding by several foundations alleviated that problem and created a massive data pool for the
presidential contest in 2000, but it is too early to know how researchers will
exploit these new databases.[2] The influence of factors such as incum-
bency, three-way competition, or major national crises has not been thoroughly investigated either. It stands to reason that the effect of the media
will vary depending on the changing political scene, the type of coverage
chosen by newspeople, and the fluctuating interests of voters.

Another serious obstacle to understanding is the dearth of media content analyses. Election news content, including commercials, and the context of general news in which it is embedded have been examined in detail only rarely, making it impossible to test what impact, if any, diverse messages have on viewers' perceptions. Another problem is researchers' failure to ascertain media exposure accurately. Investigators frequently assume that people have been exposed to all election stories in a particular news source without checking precisely which stories have come to the attention of various individuals and what these individuals learned from these stories.

A shortage of good data also prevented researchers prior to the Reagan era from ascertaining the effects of political advertising on political campaigns. Candidates and their supporters spend a large share of their campaign budgets on political advertising that is displayed on bumper stickers and billboards, printed in newspapers, disseminated through videotapes, or broadcast with clockwork regularity on radio and television. Researchers who study television commercials now know that these messages are major factors in campaigns. But the role commercials play when they are carried by other media remains largely unexplored. In addition, Internet messages of all types are new territory waiting for thorough analysis.

The Consequences of Media Politics

The advent of television and its ready availability in nearly every home, the spread and improvement of public opinion polling, the use of computers in election data analysis, and the emergence of election-related sites on the Internet have vastly enhanced the role of the mass media in elections. In this era of media politics, what major changes have been wrought by these technologies? We will consider four major consequences: a sharp decline in party influence, an increase in the power of journalists to influence the selection of candidates, the requirement for candidates to "televise well," and the emergence of made-for-media campaigns.

Decline in Party Influence

Foremost among the changes aided and abetted by the Internet age is the declining influence of political parties, particularly in presidential elections. During the 1940s, party allegiance was the most important determinant of the vote. Next in rank were voters' feelings of allegiance to a social group, assessment of the candidate's personality, and consideration of issues, in that order. This ranking has been reversed. The candidate's character has become the prime consideration at the presidential level. Issues associated with the candidate have become intertwined with considerations of character because issues are used to infer character traits.[3] Party affiliation and group membership now rank last. When voters base their decisions on a candidate's personality and stand on issues, the media become more important because the images they publicize are the chief sources of information about these matters.

Correspondingly, political parties have become less important. Voters who can see and hear candidates with their own eyes and ears can make choices that differ from those made by their party. Split-ticket voting has become common. Rather than voting only for candidates of one party, many voters now use radio and television to choose individuals from various parties. Candidates can reach voters without the assistance of parties, thereby weakening party control. They can raise their own money and build their own organizations. With the aid of the media new candidates can gain a wide following rapidly. This new independence of voters and candidates makes primary and general election races more crowded and less predictable. Party regulars who have groomed themselves for years to attain positions of power may find themselves bypassed.

Party affiliation remains more important at the state and local levels where average voters learn little about most candidates. Media information in these areas is scant, particularly on television. This is not true, however, in many local elections when candidates run without overt or covert party designation and endorsement or when candidates of the same party compete against each other in primary elections. When criteria for making choices by party are lacking, and when personal experience or advice from opinion leaders is unavailable, voters turn to whatever guidance the media may offer. Some will follow expressed or implied media endorsements; others will take these endorsements as cues to vote the opposite way. In either case, what the media say about the candidates influences voting decisions.

Media as King Makers

More than ever before, journalists can influence the selection of candidates and issues.[4] Candidates, like actors, depend for their success as much on the roles into which they are cast as on their acting ability. In the television age, media people usually do the casting for presidential hopefuls, whose performance is then judged according to the assigned role. Strenuous efforts by campaign directors and public relations experts to dominate this aspect of the campaign have been only moderately fruitful.

Casting occurs early in the primaries when newspeople, on the basis of as yet slender evidence, predict winners and losers in order to narrow the field of eligibles who must be covered. Concentrating on the front-runners in public opinion polls makes newspeople's tasks more manageable, but it often forces trailing candidates out of the race prematurely. Early highly speculative calculations become self-fulfilling prophecies because designated "winners" attract supporters whereas "losers" are abandoned.

For example, in 1999—the "preseason" year for the 2000 presidential race—only candidates from the major parties who scored well in public opinion polls received more than scattered attention from television news. On the Democratic side, Vice President Al Gore received the lion's share of coverage. Among Gore's competitors, the networks considered only former senator Bill Bradley seriously. On the Republican side, Texas governor George W. Bush received one-third more coverage than all his competitors combined. These imbalances persisted throughout the primary season, seriously handicapping the campaigns that remained in the shadows.[5]

Candidates who exceed expectations in garnering votes are declared winners; candidates who fall short are losers.[6] When journalist Pat Buchanan finished sixteen points behind George Bush in the 1992 New Hampshire Republican presidential primary, the media declared him the winner because he had exceeded their expectations. They did the same for Bill Clinton, who had trailed former senator Paul Tsongas in the Democratic primary in New Hampshire in 1992. The candidacy of Republican senator Bob Dole during the 1996 primaries was prematurely declared dead when he finished behind his competitors in a few early and insignificant contests.

Media coverage and public opinion polls tend to move in tandem in the early months of a campaign. Candidates who receive ample media coverage usually do well in the polls. Good poll ratings then bring more media coverage. Once the caucus and primary season has started in the spring of the presidential election year, the outcomes of these contests become more important predictors of media attention. The winners and candidates whose scores seem surprisingly good receive heavy media coverage; the media neglect the losers. One other pattern is common, though not universal. The substance of stories tends to be favorable for trailing candidates in the race and unfavorable for front-runners. Between January and March 2000, for example, more than 60 percent of the television comments about Sens. John McCain and Bill Bradley were favorable. That compared to 40 percent favorable for Vice President Gore and 22 percent for Governor Bush.[7]

The media's role as kingmaker or killer of the dreams of would-be kings is often played over a long span of time. Image making for presidential elections now begins on a massive scale more than a year before the first primary. The "pre-precampaign," on a more limited scale, begins shortly after the previous election with newspaper and magazine stories about potential presidential candidates. Senators and governors who have received favorable publicity over many years may gradually come to be thought of as likely presidential nominees.

In the past, captains of the media industry often used their personal influence and the power of the media under their control to support nominations for their favorites and to harm opponents. That practice has become less overt and may even be vanishing. Examples include the efforts of publisher Henry Luce to entice popular war hero Dwight Eisenhower to run for the presidency in 1952. Luce put his publications, including *Time* and *Life,* at Eisenhower's service. Kyle Palmer and the Chandler family, through their control of the *Los Angeles Times,* were instrumental in getting Richard Nixon a seat in the U.S. House of Representatives in 1946 and a U.S. Senate seat in 1950. Col. Robert McCormick used the powerful *Chicago Tribune* to defeat policies of Presidents Franklin D. Roosevelt and Harry S. Truman and to put Republican politicians into office in Illinois.[8]

The power of the media has also been wielded to destroy candidacies. This happened to two Democratic candidates for the presidency in 1988, Sen. Joseph Biden of Delaware and Sen. Gary Hart of Colorado. Biden was forced out of the campaign by widely publicized charges that his speeches contained plagiarized quotations from other political leaders; Hart withdrew after charges of philandering. Recurrent media references to the Chappaquidick incident, which mentioned Sen. Edward Kennedy, D-Mass., in conjunction with the drowning of a young woman on his staff, also have dampened efforts by his supporters to draft him as a presidential contender. However, adverse publicity can be overcome. In the 1992 campaign, Bill Clinton was accused of adultery and draft dodging, charges that caused his poll ratings and positive media appraisals to plummet. Despite the bad publicity, Clinton managed to win major primaries and the presidency.

Media images, especially those conveyed audiovisually, can be vastly important during general election campaigns. For instance, the Kennedy–Nixon television debates of 1960, the Reagan–Mondale debates of 1984, and the Bush–Gore debates of 2000 helped to soften the public's impressions that John F. Kennedy, Ronald Reagan, and George W. Bush were unsuited for the presidency.[9] Kennedy was able to demonstrate that he was capable of coping with the presidency despite his youth and relative inexperience, and Reagan in 1984 conveyed the impression that despite advanced age he remained mentally fit for a second term. Bush's performance in the second debate served to counteract charges that he lacked sufficient intellect and debating skills to become an effective president.

Adverse media coverage of policy issues sharply diminished the chances of Presidents Lyndon Johnson, Jimmy Carter, and George Bush to be elected for a second term. When the major media extracted only unflattering statements from the full record of Johnson's public justifications of his Vietnam policies, they gutted the case that the president needed to make in order to become a strong second-term candidate in 1968. Johnson subsequently decided not to seek another term. In Carter's case, the media chose to commemorate the anniversary of a major foreign policy failure—the prolonged captivity of American hostages in Iran—just before the 1980 presidential election. Disapproval of Bush in the 1992 election was directed mainly at his failure to solve major problems in the domestic economy during the last year of his term.

Media-operated public opinion polls are yet another weapon in the arsenal for kingmaking. The CBS/*New York Times* poll, the NBC/Associated Press poll, the ABC/*Washington Post* poll, and the CNN/*USA Today* poll all conduct popularity ratings and issue polls throughout presidential elections. The results are publicized extensively and then become benchmarks for voters, telling them who the winners and losers are and what issues should be deemed crucial to the campaign. Depending on the nature and format of the questions asked by the pollsters and the political context in which the story becomes embedded, the responses spell fortune or misfortune for the candidates. Polls may determine which candidates enter the fray and which keep out. In the 1992 presidential campaign, major Democratic politicians chose to keep out of the race because they believed that President Bush's high approval ratings following the Persian Gulf War doomed their candidacies. That provided an opening for a little-known governor from Arkansas named Bill Clinton to propel himself into a two-term presidency.

Television-Age Recruits

A third important consequence of the new politics is the change it has wrought in the types of candidates likely to be politically successful. Because television can bring the image of candidates for high national and state office directly into the homes of millions of voters, political recruiters have become extremely conscious of a candidate's ability to look impressive and to perform well before the cameras. Candidates require the flair to act self-confidently and seemingly naturally in front of a bevy of photographers. People who are not telegenic have been eliminated from the pool of available recruits. Abraham Lincoln's rugged face probably would not have passed muster in the television age. President Truman's "Give 'em hell, Harry" homespun style would have backfired had it been presented nationwide rather than to small gatherings. Franklin D. Roosevelt's wheelchair appearances would have spelled damaging weakness. Roosevelt, in fact, was keenly aware of the likely harmful effects of a picture of him in a wheelchair and never allowed photographs to be taken while he was being lifted to the speaker's rostrum.

Actors and celebrities from other walks of life who are adept at performing before the public now have a much better chance than ever before to be recruited for political office. Ronald Reagan, a former actor; Pat Buchanan, a television news commentator; and Jesse Jackson, a charismatic preacher, are examples of typical television-age recruits whose chances for public office would have been much slighter in an earlier era. As columnist Marquis Child has put it, candidates no longer "run" for office; they "pose" for office.[10]

In fact, good pictures can counterbalance the effects of unfavorable verbal comments. During the 1984 presidential campaign, favorable pictures fostered favorable poll results despite predominantly negative verbal commentary. When CBS reporter Leslie Stahl verbally attacked President Reagan for falsely posturing as a man of peace and compassion, a Reagan assistant promptly thanked her for showing four-and-a-half minutes of great pictures of the president. He was not in the least concerned about the scathing remarks. The pictures had shown the president

> basking in a sea of flag-waving supporters . . . sharing concerns with farmers in a field, picnicking with Mid-Americans, pumping iron . . . getting the Olympic torch from a runner . . . greeting senior citizens at their housing project, honoring veterans who landed on Normandy, honoring youths just back from Grenada, countering a heckler . . . wooing black inner-city kids . . . .[11]

During the 1996 campaign, President Clinton and his staff members staged an endless series of events designed to capture favorable television coverage, ranging from lengthy Oval Office sessions with teenagers who resisted pressures to smoke to White House meetings with auto industry representatives who were celebrating increased car exports to Japan.[12] Former Senate leader Bob Dole, an experienced politician, by contrast, was rated as a poor television performer during the 1996 presidential campaign and was vastly inferior, on that score, to his rival President Clinton.

Candidates who perform poorly on television now spend considerable time and money on professional coaching. The results have been mixed. During the 2000 campaign, Vice President Gore strove mightily to overcome the image that he was pedantic, boring, and wooden. Television advisers have become year-round regular members of presidential and gubernatorial staffs, and their names have become almost as well known as the names of the political bosses of yesteryear. These experts create commercials for the candidates and generate and handle general news coverage of the campaign. Roughly two-thirds of the budgets of presidential contenders are expended on their television contests. The cost of 1.2 million spot advertisements for the 2000 presidential campaign was estimated as close to $800 million if one counts only the 75 largest television markets. If one includes advertising expenditures for the 800 stations in the nation's 135 smaller markets, overall costs for advertisements commissioned by candidates and advocacy groups were estimated at $1 billion.[13]

Given the high cost of television commercials and of gaining news exposure, a candidate's personal wealth or ability to raise money remains an important consideration, even when federal funding is available. Activities, statements, and policy proposals that are likely to alienate donors are shunned. Although there is evidence that the best-financed candidates do not always win, folklore says they do. Hence, falling behind in the race for money to finance media exposure is a sharp brake on political aspirations. The political consequences in recruitment and postelection commitments that spring from such financial considerations are enormous.

Campaigning for the Media

A fourth major aspect of the new politics is the fact that mass media coverage has become a pivotal campaign function. Campaigns are structured to garner the best media exposure before the largest suitable audience and, if possible, with the greatest degree of candidate control over the message. To attract media coverage, candidates concentrate on photo opportunities, talk show appearances, or trips to interesting events and locations. Even when candidates meet voters personally in rallies, parades, or visits to shopping centers, they generally time and orchestrate these events to attract favorable media coverage.

The New Media. Appearances on various entertainment shows, once considered "unpresidential," have become routine. Maverick candidate Ross Perot started the pattern during the 1992 presidential race by announcing his presidential aspirations on CNN's *Larry King Live* call-in television show. The other candidates followed the talk show trek, preferring the lighter banter and the respectful questions of callers to the pointed inquisition in interviews by the national press. Adorned with shades, Governor Clinton played the saxophone on the hip *Arsenio Hall Show;* he even bought television time to stage his own call-in show. By 2000, it seemed almost obligatory for presidential contenders to appear on talk shows hosted by television personalities Larry King, Oprah Winfrey, Jay Leno, and David Letterman.

Candidates' control over messages has also increased through satellite interviews in which contenders chat directly with local correspondents, most of whom are unlikely to ask hostile questions or limit the candidate's speech to sound bites of less than ten seconds. Even network morning news shows now devote entire hours to conversations with the candidates and accept telephoned questions from viewers during the show. All in all, the trend seems to be toward more direct contact by candidates with voters and increased candidate control over campaign messages, all at the expense of message control by the major media.

Candidate-sponsored Web sites, like the Nader site shown on the next page, are the newest addition to the venues that campaigners have used since 1996 to offer voters a carefully selected information diet. Major as well as minor parties used these relatively inexpensive venues to tell their stories to the voters in the 2000 elections. Governor Bush's Web site, for example, showed videos about Bush's issue positions and other topics and allowed live, interactive chats with campaign personnel. It allowed visitors to register to vote, to donate money to the campaign or volunteer to work for it, and to check campaign sites in their states. Vice President Gore's site was similar, but visitors to it were also able to download fliers for distribution in the community. Some pages were designed for various groups, like nurses, law enforcement personnel, or Native Americans. Pages for children allowed youngsters to search for the Gores' pet dog, whose picture was hidden in several spots on the site. Unfortunately, computer glitches were still common on these sites in 2000 and many computer users lacked the high-speed Internet connections to download technologically sophisticated offerings.

By the time of their conventions, the major campaigns had developed e-mail lists through which they kept in touch with their supporters. Potential voters kept abreast of new features on candidates' Web sites. The e-mail lists proved exceedingly useful as a get-out-the-vote device during the final days of the campaign.[14] On the negative side, campaigns had to worry about unwary viewers who would stray into Web sites hostile to the candidate but parading under official-sounding Web addresses (URLs). In fact, it became a political game in 2000 and earlier to pre-empt likely Web addresses for campaign sites so that these addresses could be sold later at a high price to the campaign or to parties intending mischief.[15]

The political consequences of using these more candidate-centered approaches to campaigning are not entirely clear. Several studies indicate that audiences who watch talk shows and use political Web sites score higher on scales of political interest and knowledge than audiences who do not use these media.[16] They also show that these viewers are also the most faithful users of traditional media; so the "new" media largely supplement an already rich information diet. The traditional print and elec-

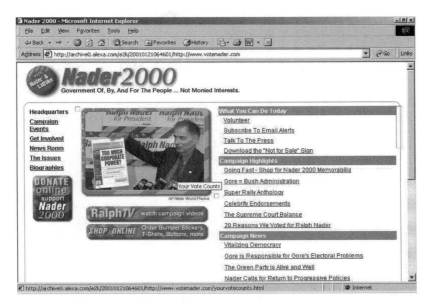

Green Party candidate Ralph Nader's Web site (partial view).

tronic media, including cable television, remain for now the staple for campaign information, even though network news and newspaper audiences have declined sharply (see Table 8-1).

Events that are poorly covered by traditional media, such as the Republican and Democratic conventions in 2000, are notable exceptions to the predominance of traditional media. The major television networks largely ignored the conventions, estimating correctly that most of their audiences would prefer regular programming instead. They knew that cable television stations would offer full coverage. Those eager to watch the conventions could do so on cable stations and Internet sites that presented minute-by-minute accounts of happenings inside and outside the convention halls.

The chief contributions of the Internet to campaigning thus far consist of the use of e-mail as a Pied Piper to lure voters to the polls and to recruit their services and money; the Internet also supplements the information presented—or ignored—by traditional media with a huge amount of diverse campaign-related information that is accessible around the clock. The contents of Internet campaign information and the manner in which it is framed follow familiar journalistic patterns even for stories produced by amateurs. Quality typically ranges from excellent to vile. Lacking shared ethics or other controls, campaigning on the Internet is a free-for-all, used wisely as well as irresponsibly.

TABLE 8-1   Voters' Main Sources of Campaign News: 1992, 1996, and 2000 (in percentages)

News sources	1992	1996	2000
Television	82%	72%	70%
Cable	29	21	36
Network	55	36	22
Local	29	23	21
Newspapers	57	60	39
Radio	12	19	15
Internet	—	3	11
Magazines	9	11	4

SOURCE: Pew Research Center for the People and the Press data from a telephone survey of 1,113 voters, November 10–12, 2000, http://www.people-press.org/post00que.htm.

NOTE: Respondents were asked, "How did you get most of your news about the presidential election campaign? From television, from newspapers, from radio, from magazines or from the Internet?" Television users were then asked, "Did you get most of your news about the presidential campaign from network TV news, from local TV news, or from cable news networks such as CNN or MSNBC?" Respondents could name two sources.

Despite the boost in available campaign information and the easier and cheaper access to (and by) voters, most scholars believe that the influence of the Internet on election outcomes has been small.[17] They point to the fact that only 11 percent of the respondents to polls cited Web sites as their main Campaign 2000 information source (although another 19 percent claimed that they got at least some information from the Internet).[18] However, sheer numbers may not tell the full story. Visitors to Web sites, including visiting journalists, diffuse the information that they gather to their personal and professional networks, making it available even to people who do not use the Internet. Moreover, the Internet audience is younger than population averages and is drawn from segments of the population that constitute the most promising pool for future leaders. The most politically pregnant question may thus be "Who draws information from the Web?"

Campaign Tactics. Irrespective of the nature of each medium, candidates must plan their schedules to dovetail with its coverage habits. Contenders spend disproportionate amounts of time during the primary season campaigning in Iowa and New Hampshire, where media coverage of the earliest contests is usually heavy. In 1988, for example, when the outcome of the Iowa race was less certain, Iowa and New Hampshire, which have less than 3 percent of the U.S. population, received more coverage during the primaries than all the other primaries combined.[19] In 1996, primary coverage for each of these states dwarfed television news coverage of later primaries by more than a four-to-one ratio.[20] Ample media coverage does not guarantee benefits at the polls, however. In 1988, Gov. Pete DuPont spent ninety-one days and $560,000 in Iowa, but he won only 7 percent of the Republican vote.

To keep a favorable image of their candidates in front of the public, campaign managers arrange newsworthy events to familiarize potential voters with their candidates' best aspects. Because most television producers do not like "talking heads"—shots of the faces of speakers— candidates may engage in staged activities merely to provide attractive, action-oriented, and symbol-laden pictures. Reporter Leslie Stahl describes how Carter courted the voters in 1980:

> What did President Carter do today in Philadelphia? He posed, with as many different types of symbols as he could possibly find.
>
> There was a picture at the day care center. And one during the game of bocce ball with the senior citizens. Click, another picture with a group of teenagers. And then he performed the ultimate media event—a walk through the Italian market.
>
> The point of all this, obviously, to get on the local news broadcasts and in the morning newspapers. It appeared that the President's intention was not to say anything controversial. . . . Simply the intention was to be seen.[21]

Incumbents have a distinct advantage over challengers. Although they may attract about the same number of campaign stories, incumbents receive additional attention through coverage of their official duties. Incumbents may also be able to dictate time and place for media encounters. When a president schedules a meeting for reporters in the White House Rose Garden, ample coverage is ensured. There even is a quasi-incumbency status for promising challengers. Once they have attained wide recognition as front-runners, newspeople compete for their attention. Their power to grant or withhold attention can be translated into influence over the quality and quantity of coverage.

The newsworthiness of campaign stories is judged by general news criteria. Therefore, minor candidates and newcomers whose chances for success are questionable do not get much coverage. Their efforts to attract the media are apt to fail because their names simply are not big news. Lack of coverage, in turn, makes it extremely difficult for them to become well known and increase their chances of winning elections. This is one of many examples of unintentional media bias that redounds to the benefit of established politicians.

Many campaign events are now staged as prime-time television spectacles with live coverage. Aside from presidential debates, the party conventions used to be the biggest single media events of presidential campaigns. Both major parties still select their convention cities with an eye to effective television coverage. Convention managers try to keep a tight rein on speakers and demonstrations to ensure that "good" messages appear in prime time and "bad" ones are banished to off hours. They want to make certain that desirable images are conveyed and that important speeches are made when the television audience is likely to be at peak numbers. For their part, journalists who cover conventions try to structure the flow of words and pictures to cover unfolding events and still tell a coherent, dramatic story. The difficulty of sustaining interest in nominating conventions when the identity of the nominee has already been firmly established has sharply reduced live prime-time coverage by the major television networks. The gap has been more than filled by gavel-to-gavel coverage by C-SPAN, and extended broadcasts on CNN and PBS and by assorted daytime and nighttime cable programs.

Structuring and staging campaign activities to make them newsworthy has enhanced showmanship at the expense of substance. Because conflict is deemed attractive and memorable, journalists often goad campaigners into confrontations by asking questions that point up existing conflicts or that spur new battles. When journalists have selected the battlegrounds for presidential contests, they have shaped the political agenda during the campaign as well as afterward. Campaign statements coaxed from unwilling candidates may be subsequently construed as commitments to act.

Media Content

What kinds of newspaper and television coverage have recent elections received? Did the media sufficiently cover the issues that would be likely to require attention from the new president? Were adequate criteria supplied to enable voters to decide which of several policy options would best suit their priorities? Were voters informed about each viable candidate's positions on the issues? Did they receive enough information about each candidate's personality, experience, and ability to evaluate the candidate's likely performance as president? Following some general comments about the media mix, we will address these questions and assess the adequacy of the information supply for making rational voting choices.

Unscrambling the Message Omelet

When Humpty-Dumpty, the egg, fell off the wall in the nursery rhyme, all the king's horses and all the king's men couldn't put him together again. The various components of the media message omelet have had a similar fate. Campaign commercials, for instance, have become a major ingredient of contemporary campaigns and often bestow a distinctive flavor to them. But it is well-nigh impossible to isolate their contribution because all of the ingredients—print and electronic news stories, editorials, talk-show banter and punditry, Internet messages, advertisements, even political jokes and skits on entertainment shows—mix inextricably with each other and become transformed in the process. Ads generate and influence news stories and news stories induce and influence ads that, in turn, lead to other ads and news stories and editorials. And so it goes.

This is why I discuss campaign information as a whole without, in most instances, making distinctions among the unique contributions made by various types of media. Distinctions exist, of course, and become apparent in experimental studies when research participants are exposed to single-format messages so that the impact of various types of formats can be compared. Such studies show, for instance, that television and news magazine formats are superior to newspapers for conveying particular messages to various population groups and that the contents of advertising messages are often discounted because they are regarded as self-serving propaganda.[22]

If we single out television commercials for a closer look, what are some of their distinctive features, aside from the fact that their message transmission labors under a cloud of suspicion?

First of all, ads capture the attention of voters. Uncommitted voters, highly interested voters, and partisans of the advertised candidate are most likely to be influenced by the content of television commercials. On the whole, people see in commercials pretty much what they want to see—attractive images for their favorite candidates and unattractive ones for the opponent. Attempts to glamorize political actors and hide their weaknesses may succeed for a while, but the effects last for only a short time. Commercials of opposing candidates, media exposés of deceptive messages, and people's cynicism about campaign propaganda see to that. Even when commercials do not alter ultimate voting choices and voters discount their messages, they do make significant contributions to voters' images of candidates and policies. Like other persuasive influences, the impact of commercials tends to be greatest during early primaries when voters form initial opinions about unknown contenders.[23] The claims that television commercials can manufacture fairyland candidates and make them believable to credulous audiences apparently are vastly exaggerated whenever voters have alternative means to learn about the candidates.[24] Major campaign issues are often covered as extensively in the lengthier television commercials as in network newscasts. Most viewers—particularly those who do not read newspapers and are poorly informed—remember more from commercials than from television news. Simplicity of content, expert eye-ear appeal, and repetition of the message produce this result. Most ads carry messages about candidates' personal qualities, but specific policies also receive substantial attention. In 2000, for example, policy content ran high at 43 percent, rising from 28 percent in 1996.

Whether commercials can inject crucial issues into a campaign remains a debated subject. In the heat of campaigns, wins and losses are often attributed by the candidates to particular commercials or to the ability of the candidates to buy ample television time. George Bush's 1988 victory, for example, has been attributed to advertisements attacking the environmental and criminal justice policies of Massachusetts governor Michael Dukakis, Bush's opponent. "Boston Harbor," a code word for Dukakis's failure to rid Boston Harbor of pollution, and "Willie Horton," a symbol for coddling of criminals, became famous election battle cries. Scholarly corroborations are lacking for most of the claims that Bush's supposed memorable ads produced election victories and defeats.[25] Most wins and losses spring from a combination of factors. Nevertheless, the battle of the airwaves has become fiercer in recent campaigns, especially during primary contests. It has also begun to branch out from over-the-air television to cable outlets and, since the 1996 presidential campaign, the Internet. Advertising rates are cheaper on cable television—an attractive medium because messages can be more readily tailored to the needs of the smaller cable audiences.

Television commercials often provide the only chance to gain attention for the many candidates who are ignored by the media. That includes the vast majority of also-rans for national office who seem unelectable to the major media as well as most candidates competing for local and even state offices. At the local level, the impact of commercials can be decisive. Indeed, wisely spent advertising funds can buy elections, even for congressional candidates who receive news story coverage.[26] To quote political scientist Michael Robinson, commercials for congressional candidates "can work relative wonders," especially when they are not challenged by the other side. "A well-crafted, heavily financed, and uncontested ad campaign does influence congressional elections."[27] This fact raises the chilling specter that wealthy candidates may be able to buy major public offices by investing their fortunes in expensive advertising campaigns. That fear has escalated with the entry of multimillionaires such as Ross Perot and Steve Forbes into the presidential sweepstakes. Perot bought large blocks of television time for info-mercials—data-packed commercials—in the 1992 presidential campaign. Forbes used personal funds to finance an expensive advertising blitz in the 1996 Republican primaries.

Patterns of Coverage

Any evaluation of how the media perform their tasks must also take *their* concerns into consideration. It is extremely difficult for the media to mesh the public's preference for simple, dramatic stories with the need to present sufficient information for issue-based election choices. Information that may be crucial for voting decisions often is too complex and technical to appeal to much of the audience. Hence newspeople feel compelled to feature exciting, human aspects of the election, even when the issues are trivial, without totally neglecting essential, unglamorous information useful for more reasoned decision making.

Prominence of Election Stories. In a presidential election year, election stories constitute roughly 13 percent of all newspaper political coverage and 15 percent of television political news. That puts these stories on a par with foreign affairs news or coverage of crime. Election news receives average attention in terms of headline size, front-page or first-story placement, and inclusion of pictures, but stories are slightly longer than average. Although election stories are quite prominent when primaries, conventions, and significant debates are held, they do not dominate the news. Normally, it is quite possible to read the daily paper without noticing election news and to come away from a telecast with the impression that election stories are just a minor part of the day's political developments. Election news competes for audience attention with many other types of stories; this accounts, in part, for its limited impact on news audiences.

Uniformity of Coverage Patterns. Patterns of presidential election coverage are remarkably uniform, regardless of a newspaper's partisan orientation. Media personnel at highly regarded papers everywhere select the same kinds of stories and emphasize the same types of facts, despite the wealth of diverse materials available to them. The major difference generally is that small newspapers carry fewer election stories and that news stories vary in their evaluation of candidates, issues, and campaign events.[28] Television news patterns are also uniform.

Content analysis studies during congressional, state, and local campaigns show similar patterns. The political portraits that various media paint of each candidate match well in basic outlines and in most details. But the time and space allotted to various aspects and the tone of evaluations can vary significantly (see Table 8-2). Campaign news on public television, for example, covered the 2000 election in far greater depth and in a far more positive tone, stressing strengths as well as weaknesses, than ABC, CBS, and NBC, collectively, despite slightly less available broadcast time.

Election news patterns are quite stable in successive elections and are uniform for all media covering a particular election. Thus Americans receive similar types of information on which to base their political decisions. Similarity in coverage of election campaigns has benefits as well as drawbacks. The large degree of homogeneity introduced into the electoral process is an advantage in a heterogeneous country such as the United States, where it can be difficult to develop political consensus. But it also means uniform neglect of many topics and criteria for judging candidates. Shared knowledge is marred by shared ignorance. A uniform information base obviously

TABLE 8-2   Campaign Coverage on Public and Network Television: Labor Day to Election Day 2000

	PBS	Network
Amount of coverage		
Minutes per day	16.5 minutes	12.5 minutes
Candidate airtime	3:40 hours	1:42 hours
Candidate sound bites	~57 seconds	~8 seconds
Who speaks?		
Journalists	24% airtime	74% airtime
Candidates	21	12
Others	55	14
Story content[a]		
Horse race	32	71
Policy issues	67	40
Positive comments		
About Bush	59	37
About Gore	60	40

SOURCE: Adapted from S. Robert Lichter, "A Plague on Both Parties: Substance and Fairness in TV Election News," *Press/Politics* 6(3)(2001): 8–30.

[a] Stories covering both categories are counted twice.

has not produced totally uniform political views throughout the country. Differences in political evaluations, even among audiences that share the same news, must be attributed to news commentators' varying interpretations of the same facts and to the different outlooks that audiences bring to the news. As pointed out in the previous chapter, the impact of news frequently is perceiver determined rather than stimulus determined.

Of the factors that encourage uniform coverage, journalists' professional socialization appears to be the most important. Newspeople share a sense of what is newsworthy and how it should be presented. Reporters cover identical beats in fashions that have become routine for election coverage. That means keeping score about who is winning and losing and reporting dramatic incidents and juicy personal gossip. It means avoiding dull facts as much as possible without totally ignoring essential information.

Coverage does not follow the *campaign model* of reporting.[29] In this model—the utopia of campaign managers—the rhythm of the campaign as produced by the candidates and their staffs determines what is covered. Reporters dutifully take their cues from the candidates. Press coverage conforms instead to an *incentive model*. Whenever exciting stories provide an incentive for coverage, they are published in a rhythm dictated by the needs of the media and the tastes of their audiences. For instance, papers geared to ethnic audiences or to business and labor groups focus on aspects of the campaign that are of primary concern to those audiences and slight the rest. The needs and tastes of the candidates may be ignored unless they manage to generate the kinds of stories and pictures that journalists find irresistible. This is why most candidates now employ professionals who know how to get good media coverage for their clients.

Political and Structural Bias. Does election coverage give a fair and equal chance for all viewpoints to be expressed so that media audiences can make informed decisions? Are the perennial charges of bias leveled by disappointed candidates evidence that newspeople always show favoritism? Or are they merely reactions to coverage that did not advance the candidates' causes? Media people in general try to produce balanced coverage for all major candidates for the same office. This holds true for print journalists, who have no legal obligation to keep coverage balanced, as well as for broadcasters, who are obliged to give equal coverage for special election programs but who are free to indulge in unequal exposure in regular news programs. However, there are no universally accepted standards of fairness and balance.

Newspeople traditionally aim for rough parity in the number of stories about each candidate and rough parity in the balance of overtly favorable and unfavorable stories. Nonetheless, imbalanced coverage occurs frequently because of *structural bias,* caused by the circumstances of news production. Completely fair and balanced reporting may be impossible because candidates' newsworthiness and willingness to talk to reporters vary. Incumbent president Reagan, dubbed "the Great Communicator," was far more newsworthy throughout 1984 because he was the president than was his challenger, Sen. Walter Mondale. Structural bias differs from *political bias,* which involves slanting the news for partisan reasons. Nonetheless, structural bias, even though it lacks partisan motivations, may profoundly affect people's perceptions about campaigns.[30]

When several scholars reviewed the major studies of bias in presidential campaigns from 1948 to 1996, they found no evidence of significant political bias in newspapers, news magazines, and television.[31] The research encompassed bias in gatekeeping that might affect story selection, bias in coverage that might give some candidates short shrift, and bias in the amounts of positive and negative coverage.

At times it is difficult to identify the nature of bias. For example, in 1992 was it because of structural or political bias that the media stressed the economy, which put incumbent president Bush in a bad light, rather than foreign policy, which would have given him a favorable image? It is also difficult to put balance into an appropriate context. Is it fair, for example, to attempt to balance coverage when the situations surrounding candidates are not comparable? Reducing an incumbent's coverage to that accorded to a challenger seems inappropriate because the public needs to know what officeholders are doing. It would be equally inappropriate to automatically expand a challenger's coverage to match the coverage of an incumbent.

Unbiased coverage does not mean discussing the candidates from the same perspectives, quoting their friends and enemies in equal proportions, or giving their stories similar time, space, or placement. Accordingly, was it or wasn't it political bias during the 1992 campaign, when sound bites on ABC, CBS, CNN, and NBC used quotations from sources hostile to the Bush–Quayle ticket far more often than quotations from enemies of candidates Clinton and Gore?[32]

Editorials, of course, are intrinsically biased because their primary purpose is to express opinions. As part of the editorial function, many news media endorse candidates. Republican candidates have received the bulk of endorsements for the presidency in the past hundred years; nonetheless, twelve Democrats have succeeded in the twenty-six presidential elections during this period. Endorsements for less exalted offices have been more influential, particularly in elections in which voters had little information to make their own decisions.[33] Influential papers, such as the *Los Angeles Times,* the *Washington Post,* and the small but influential *Manchester Union Leader,* can be extraordinarily successful in promoting the election of candidates they have endorsed and in defeating unacceptable contenders. At the presidential level news coverage tends to be essentially evenhanded, regardless of the candidate who has been endorsed. Below the presidential level, the media tend to give more coverage to their endorsed candidates than to those they have not endorsed.

The effort to keep coverage balanced does not extend to third-party candidates. Anyone who runs for the presidency who is not a Republican or Democrat is out of the mainstream of newsworthiness and is slighted or even ignored by the news profession. Especially newsworthy third-party candidates, such as Robert La Follette of the Progressive Party in 1924, George Wallace of the American Independent Party in 1968, John Anderson of the National Unity Campaign in 1980, independent Ross Perot in 1992, and the Green Party's Ralph Nader in 2000, were notable exceptions. Newsworthiness considerations also account for the sparse coverage of vice presidential candidates despite the importance of the office. Vice presidents sometimes replace a deceased incumbent, but that possibility always seems remote until it happens. A total of 95 percent of the coverage in a typical presidential election goes to the presidential contenders and only 5 percent to their running mates.

Substance of Coverage: Candidates, Issues, and Events

The candidate qualifications highlighted by the media fall into two broad groups: those that are generally important in judging a person's

By permission of Mike Luckovich and Creators Syndicate, Inc.

character and those specifically related to the tasks of the office. Included in the first group are personality traits (such as integrity, reliability, and compassion), style characteristics (such as forthrightness or folksiness), and image characteristics (such as the ability to appear productive and levelheaded). Professional qualifications at the presidential level include the capacity to conduct foreign and domestic affairs, the ability to mobilize public support, and a flair for administration. The candidate's political philosophy is also a professional criterion. Presidential candidates over the years have been most frequently assessed in terms of their trustworthiness, strength of character, leadership capabilities, and compassion. Professional capacities—the very qualities that deserve the fullest discussion and analysis—have been covered scantily and often vaguely even when an incumbent is running.[34] Only a handful of professional qualifications have been mentioned with any frequency. These include general appraisals of the capacity to handle foreign affairs, which was deemed crucial throughout the twentieth century, and the capacity to sustain an acceptable quality of life for all citizens by maintaining the economy on an even keel and by controlling crime and internal disorder. The same types of qualities reappear from election to election. Treatment of individual candidates is usually dissimilar. Such disparate coverage makes it very difficult for the electorate to compare and evaluate the candidates on important dimensions. Effective comparisons are also hindered by contradictions in remarks reported about the candidates. Bound by current codes of objective reporting and neutrality in electoral contests, the media rarely give guidance to the audience for judging conflicting claims.

In 2000, as in most recent elections, verbal news commentary about the political candidates was quite negative, especially for the incumbent. Gore's evaluations were 60 percent negative and Bush's 63 percent on network television. Journalists criticized the candidates' policy agendas, their political skills and, most of all, their campaign tactics. Again, as is typical in campaigns, heavy adverse criticism tends to come in waves. Bush benefited from a let-up of attacks during the final campaign weeks. The typical downbeat mood of election coverage is epitomized by the lead paragraph in a *Time* magazine story at the end of the 1980 race between Reagan and Carter: "For more than a year, two flawed candidates have been floundering toward the final showdown, each unable to give any but his most unquestioning supporters much reason to vote for him except dislike of his opponent."[35] Such negative characterizations, which have plagued all recent presidential elections, are hardly fair to capable candidates who often possess great personal strengths and skills that should be praised rather than debased.

On the whole, newspaper and television coverage are quite similar except that the features are starker on television. The usual one- or two-minute television story gives little chance for in-depth reporting and analysis. To conserve their limited time, television newscasters create stereotypes of the various candidates early in the campaign and then build their stories around these stereotypes by merely adding new details to the established image. Once established, stereotypes stubbornly resist change. There is a feeling that leopards do not change their spots. During the 1980 presidential campaign, Reagan was typecast as an amiable dunce stumbling into the presidency almost by mistake.[36] During the 1992 campaign, Clinton became "Slick Willy" and President Bush an aimless drifter incapable of guiding the ship of state. Dole's political longevity was satirized by comedian David Letterman, who joked in 1996 that Dole's earliest campaigns had been easy because "there were only thirteen colonies."[37] Gore was painted as an overbearing, fudging smart aleck in 2000, while Bush was stereotyped as a grammar-garbling, dimwitted Texas bumpkin.

Journalists' overriding consideration in choosing issues, as in other political coverage, is newsworthiness rather than intrinsic importance. This is why the changing record of happenings on the campaign trail, however trivial, receives extended coverage. Rather than exploring policy issues in depth, news stories emphasize brief, rapidly paced, freshly breaking events. In fact, the amount of coverage for particular issues often seems to be in inverse proportion to their significance. For instance, during the 1992 primaries, one of every six campaign stories on the television networks referred to Governor Clinton's personal life. Sexual foibles, reputed drug use during college days, slips of the tongue, bad jokes, all made headlines and were repeated endlessly on various entertainment programs. The pattern persisted during the 1996 campaign. In the 2000 campaign, a story about Bush's arrest on drunken driving charges twenty-four years earlier received more coverage during the last three days of the campaign than all foreign policy issues had received since Labor Day.[38]

Three major features stand out in coverage of issues and events. First and most significantly, the media devote a large amount of attention to "horserace" aspects of campaigns—the so-called game frame that dwells on each candidate's odds for winning or losing. By comparison, they slight political, social, and economic problems facing the country and say little about the merits of the solutions proposed, unless these issues can be made exciting and visually dramatic. Second, information about issues is patchy because the candidates and their surrogates try to concentrate on issues that help their campaigns and try to avoid issues likely to alienate any portion of the huge and disparate electorate from which all are seeking support. During the 1992 presidential election, for example, news stories concentrated on the economy. Other issues were slighted unless there was a triggering crisis. Third, there is more issue coverage, albeit unsystematic, than scholars have acknowledged in the past because commentary about issues is embedded in many horserace stories and discussions of candidates' qualifications. For example, the claim that a candidate is compassionate may be linked to his or her concern about health care laws. When content analysis designs focus narrowly on recording only one issue per news story, multifaceted stories are forced into a single category and important facets become obscured.

Media issue coverage is much narrower than issue coverage of party platforms. In recent elections, some twenty-five issues, like taxes or social security or education, have usually surfaced intermittently in the press and some twenty on television. Typically, only half of these receive extensive and intensive attention. Many important policy questions likely to arise during a forthcoming presidential term are totally ignored. Although candidates like to talk about broad policy issues, such as war and peace or the health of the economy, newspeople prefer to concentrate on narrower, specific policy positions on which the candidates disagree sharply.

As is the case for coverage of presidential qualifications, issues discussed in connection with individual candidates vary. Voters thus receive little aid from the media in appraising and comparing the candidates on the issues.

Compared with print media, television news usually displays more uniform patterns of issue coverage for all the candidates and involves a more limited range of issues. Television stories are briefer, touch on fewer aspects of each issue, and contribute to the stereotypic images developed for particular candidates. Events are often fragmented and barren of context, but what is left is dramatized to appeal to the audience. No wonder that most people turn to television for news about the candidates and their campaigns.

Media coverage should be assessed not only in terms of the numbers of stories devoted to various topics but also in terms of political impact. There are times when election politics is particularly volatile and a few stories may carry extraordinary weight. Rapid diffusion of these stories throughout the major media enhances their impact. Michael Robinson calls such featured events *medialities*—"events, developments, or situations to which the media have given importance by emphasizing, expanding, or featuring them in such a way that their real significance has been modified, distorted, or obscured."[39] Medialities usually involve policy scandals, economic disasters, and personal foibles. Such key stories can have a far more profound impact on the campaign than thousands of routine stories and should be appraised accordingly.

Adequacy of Coverage

How adequate is current election coverage? Do the media help voters sufficiently to make decisions according to commonly accepted democratic criteria? As discussed, appraisal of candidates and issues is not made easy for voters. In presidential contests information is ample about the major, mainstream candidates and about day-to-day campaign events. It is sketchy and often confusing about the candidates' professional qualifications and about many important policy issues. Most primary contenders, candidates of minor parties, and vice presidential candidates are largely ignored. This is not surprising because the field of candidates is usually much larger than most Americans realize. Usually several hundred individuals register as formal candidates for the presidency. The prevalence of negative information makes it seem that all of the candidates are mediocre or even poor choices. This negative cast appears to be a major factor in many voters' decisions to stay home on election day. It also undermines the ability of newly elected officials to command essential support after the election, especially from members of the opposing party.

Nonetheless, voters are generally satisfied with the amount of election information they receive (see Table 8-3). In the 1992, 1996, and 2000 presidential campaigns, only one in five voters felt inadequately informed. Their satisfaction does not extend to the content of political ads, however.

TABLE 8-3   Adequacy of Campaign Coverage: 1992, 1996, and 2000

Adequacy of coverage	Campaign 1992	Campaign 1996	Campaign 2000
Learned enough	77%	75%	83%
Did not learn enough	20	23	15
Don't know	3	2	2

SOURCE: Pew Research Center for the People and the Press data from a telephone survey of 1,113 voters, November 10–12, 2000, http://www.people-press.org/post00que.htm.

NOTE: Respondents were asked, "During this campaign, did you feel you learned enough about the candidates and the issues to make an informed choice between Gore, Bush, Nader, and Buchanan, or did you find it difficult to choose because you felt you did not learn enough from the campaign?"

After the 2000 presidential election, for instance, only 29 percent of the voters said that commercials had helped them to make voting choices. These percentages compare to 25 percent in 1996 and a high of 38 percent in 1992, when the names on the ticket were unfamiliar to many voters.[40] Contrary to earlier studies that claimed that advertisements were a major source of campaign information, the modern thirty-second clip apparently adds little to the audience's fund of knowledge.

In presidential contests the deficiencies of media coverage are most noticeable during the period of primaries, when a large slate of same-party candidates is competing in each primary. The media meet this challenge by giving uniformly skimpy treatment to all candidates except those designated as front-runners. It is not uncommon for two or three front-runners to attract 75 percent or more of the coverage, leaving a pack of trailing contenders with hardly any attention at all. As political scientist Thomas Patterson has noted, "Issue material is but a rivulet in the news flow during the primaries, and what is there is almost completely diluted by information about the race."[41] While the quality of coverage during the primaries may be thin, the quantity is substantial, although it is unequally distributed so that the races in well-covered states become disproportionately influential. By the middle of the primary season, interest in these contests dwindles. Coverage shrivels. It perks up slightly during the conventions and when the final campaign starts following the Labor Day holiday in September.

Media Effects

What do people learn from campaign coverage? The answer varies, of course, depending on their interest in the campaign, prior political knowledge, desire for certain information, and political sophistication. But several general trends emerge from national surveys, such as those conducted biannually by the Survey Research Center at the University of Michigan, and from intensive interviews of smaller panels of voters, such as those that I have conducted.

Learning about Candidates and Issues

The foremost impression from interviews with voters is that they can recall very little specific campaign information. That does not necessarily mean that they have not learned anything. As discussed in Chapter 7, when people are confronted with factual information, such as news about a particular presidential candidate, they assess how it fits into their established view of that candidate. If it is consonant, the information strengthens that view and their feelings about the candidate. If it is dissonant, it is likely to be rejected outright or noted as a reasonable exception to their established schema. The least likely result is a major revision of their established beliefs about the candidate. Once people have processed the news, they forget most of the details and store only their summary impression in memory. When they are later quizzed about details, they are likely to recall only what was frequently repeated in recent news stories. Online processing thus creates the false impression that the average person has formed opinions about the candidate without having learned the appropriate facts.[42]

What kinds of information are people likely to select for attention and processing from the vast amounts of presidential campaign information available to most Americans who pay attention to mass media messages? The answer is "not very much at any one time," except possibly from the debates, which serve as a last-minute cram session for preparing the voting public. In 2000, for instance, two-thirds of the voters who watched the debates called them very helpful or somewhat helpful in selecting candidates.[43] Average citizens manage to gather quite substantial amounts of information about the candidates and the issues during the lengthy campaign, especially because many stories are covered repeatedly and often resurface from one election to the next.[44]

Unlike campaigns at state and local levels, which rarely draw a great deal of attention, most citizens are interested in presidential campaigns. Still, interest in the presidential campaign competes with interests in many other events and issues in their public and private lives. This explains why one panel of voters who kept diaries on the important news stories that came to their attention throughout a presidential election year devoted only 11 percent of their entries to election stories. When asked to name "major current events or issues," 38 percent of the panelists never named the election in four interviews conducted during the primary season.[45] Likewise, during the early months of the 1988 campaign, 69 percent of the respondents to a national Gallup poll said that they had closely watched news accounts about Jessica McClure, a Texas toddler who was trapped in an abandoned well for several days. Some 40 percent of the respondents said that they had followed the news of the 1987 stock market plunge avidly, as had 37 percent for accounts about the U.S. Navy's escort of Kuwaiti tankers through the Persian Gulf. The presidential campaign ranked lowest in mention among the prominent news events about which the respondents were questioned. Only 15 percent claimed to have paid close attention to the Democratic race, and only 13 percent claimed close interest in the Republican contest.[46]

In the past, comparisons of election information supplied by respondents' newspapers with information mentioned by them revealed roughly similar patterns. As Table 8-4 shows, that was not true in 2000, possibly because newspaper use for campaign information had plunged dramatically along with confidence in the media. A nationwide sample of people was asked to mention good and bad points about 1996 presidential nominees, Bill Clinton and Bob Dole, that might affect their voting choices. Overall, news stories emphasized personality traits more in judging the candidates' fitness for office, while the citizens who were polled gave more weight to each candidate's "presidential" qualities. The elements considered essential for professional competence were also weighted differently, with news stories stressing philosophy, capacities, and relations with the public having somewhat less value. Media and public images differ most in emphases and richness of detail. The public mentions fewer issues and qualities and describes them less precisely.

Overall, the majority of the answers people give when asked what they have learned about candidates and issues or why they would vote or refrain from voting for a certain candidate concern personality traits. People are interested in the human qualities of their elected leaders, particularly their trustworthiness, principled character, strength, and compassion. Their judgments about the extent to which a leader embodies these traits are often based on issue stands. For instance, a presidential candidate who pledges to increase aid for the poor is apt to be characterized as compassionate. The dividing line between knowledge about qualities and knowledge about issues thus is fuzzy.

The issues people typically mention as important in the campaign represent a much abbreviated and imprecise version of media issue coverage. As Table 8-5 indicates, people express much more concern about economic and social issues than do the media. This is not surprising; these

TABLE 8-4   Presidential Qualities Mentioned by Individuals and by Their Newspapers (in percentages)

Qualities	Likes		Dislikes		Newspapers
	Clinton	Dole	Clinton	Dole	
Personal suitability					
Personality traits	13%	13%	44%	9%	40%
Presidential traits	45	28	37	29	20
Style	1	2	2	1	5
Total	59	43	83	39	65
Professional competence					
Capacities	8%	23%	6%	31%	16%
Relations with public	16	3	2	5	1
Philosophy	17	31	9	25	18
Total	41	57	17	61	35

SOURCE: Survey data from the 1996 Election Survey, Center for Political Studies, Survey Research Center, University of Michigan; newspaper data from author's matching research, Sept. 1– Oct. 15, 2000.

NOTE: The percentages are based on responses to the question, "Is there any quality in particular about Mr. Clinton/Mr. Dole that might make you want to vote for/against him?" N = 140 for Clinton likes, 644 for Dole likes, 930 for Clinton dislikes, 884 for Dole dislikes. N = 2,434 mentions of qualities by newspapers. Newspaper research: Lexis-Nexis search of the *Boston Globe, Chicago Sun-Times, New York Daily News, Minneapolis Star Tribune, Christian Science Monitor, Los Angeles Times, New York Times,* and *Washington Post.*

issues are personal. People do not need media coverage to know that inflation, unemployment, poverty, crime, race relations, and environmental pollution are serious problems requiring attention from presidents. Nor is it surprising that people put much less emphasis on campaign hoopla, covered so plentifully by the media. Although they find these fleeting events entertaining, people make little effort to remember them.

Knowledge Base for Voting

Many social scientists accuse the media of providing the public with a flimsy diet of election information, particularly when it comes to policy issues. But the worry and blame are largely misplaced. Although election news definitely stresses personality traits over issues and dwells heavily on day-to-day campaign events and trivia, it does supply plentiful issue coverage in old and "new" media. Links on Internet election sites are a uniquely rich source for facts and interpretations that facilitate in-depth analyses. Voters who want to know the candidates' stands on specific issues can find that information. When voters are poorly informed about issues,

TABLE 8-5   Comparison of Mention of Issues and Events
by Newspapers, Television, and Survey Responses (in percentages)

Issues and events	Newspapers	Television	Survey responses
Campaign events	47%	61%	0%
Domestic politics	21	15	16
Foreign affairs	16	7	11
Economic policy	10	11	60
Social problems	6	6	14

SOURCE: Survey data come from the 1996 Election Survey, Center for Political Studies, Survey Research Center, University of Michigan; media data come from author's research.

NOTE: Survey responses specify the most important national problem. $N = 4,726$ for newspapers, 985 for television, and 1,714 for survey responses. Media survey periods (newspapers and television) = Sept. 1–Oct. 15, 2000. The newspaper survey material was gathered from a Lexis-Nexis search of the *Boston Globe, Chicago Sun-Times, Daily News, Star Tribune, Los Angeles Times, New York Times, Christian Science Monitor,* and *Washington Post.* The television survey material was gathered from ABC, CBS, and NBC. The question asked of survey respondents was, "What does Respondent think is the most pressing problem facing the country?"

it is chiefly because they do not consider elections important enough to take the time to learn about them. Forming opinions about complex issues such as arms limitation or monetary policies is extraordinarily difficult, particularly when experts' policy recommendations conflict. This is why voters ignore most issues and pay attention to only a few that are of major interest generally or personally.

Although the media furnish most people with more information than they are willing or able to use, the media fall short of supplying the needs of political elites. Opinion leaders and the mass public that often relies on their guidance would benefit from more complete coverage of the candidates' stands on major and minor issues, more point-by-point comparisons of candidates and policies, and more ample evaluations of the political significance of differences in candidates and their programs. Where resources permit, journalists should research important topics neglected by the candidates and make this information available. More coverage should also be given to third-party candidates and vice presidential contenders and less coverage to often meaningless polls.

Voting Behavior

Does campaigning through the media change votes? The answer to this perennial question so dear to the hearts of campaign managers, public relations experts, and social scientists hinges on the interaction between audiences and messages. Crucial variables include the voter's receptivity to a message urging change, the potency of the message, the appropriateness of its form, and the setting in which it occurs. A vote change is most likely when voters pay fairly close attention to the media and are ambivalent in their attitudes toward the candidates. Messages are most potent if they concern a major and unpredicted event, such as a successful or disastrous foreign policy venture or corruption in high places, and when individuals find themselves in social settings where a change of attitude will not constitute deviant behavior. This combination of circumstances is fairly rare, which explains why changes of voting intentions are comparatively uncommon. Fears that televised campaigns can easily sway voters and amount to "electronic ballot box stuffing" are therefore unrealistic.

However, even small numbers of media-induced vote changes may be important. Many elections at all levels are decided by tiny percentages of votes, often less than 1 percent, as was demonstrated dramatically in the 2000 election, which was ultimately decided by fewer than a thousand votes. The media may also have a crucial impact on election outcomes whenever they can stimulate or depress voter turnout. This is a more likely consequence of media publicity than of changes in voting choices. It has led to concern about the changes in turnout that may be produced by broadcasts that predict election results before voting has ended. Despite several investigations of the problem, the precise impact of early forecasts of election outcomes remains disputed. Current evidence indicates that the effects, if they do occur, have rarely been substantial.[47]

Attempts to stop immediate dissemination of projections of winners and losers have run afoul of First Amendment free speech guarantees. This may explain why the laws passed in more than half of the states to restrain exit polling are seldom enforced.[48] Congress has tried since 1986 to pass a Uniform Poll Closing Act. Although the measure has thus far failed to pass, prospects for ultimate success are good, especially after the presidential election of 2000 in which the issue of broadcasting election results while polls remained open in parts of the United States became a huge political controversy. The major television networks have pledged to refrain from projecting the outcome of a presidential election until the polls have closed. The concern about the impact of exit polls and early forecasts may be overdrawn. Voters are bombarded throughout the election year with information likely to determine their vote and turnout. Why should there be squeamishness on the very last day of the campaign?

The most important influence of the media on the voter does not lie in changing votes, once predispositions have been formed, but in shaping and reinforcing predispositions and influencing the initial selection of candidates. When newspeople sketched out the Clinton image and held him up as a potential winner during the 1992 primaries, ignoring most of his rivals, they made the obscure governor of a small southern state into a viable candidate. Millions of voters would never have cast their ballot for the unknown Arkansas politician had not the media thrust him into the limelight as a likely winner.

By focusing the voters' attention on selected individuals, their characteristics, and issue stands, the media also determine to a large extent the crucial issues by which the competence of the candidates will be gauged. Very early in the campaign, often long before formal campaigning starts, media interpretations of the significance of issues can shape the political and emotional context of the election.

Newspeople shape election outcomes by molding the images of political reality that lead to voting decisions rather than by suggesting voting choices to an electorate that prefers to make up its own mind. As Leon Sigal noted many years ago, they

> play less of an independent part in creating issues, sketching imagery, and coloring perceptions of the candidates than in getting attention for their candidacies. Newsmen do not write the score or play an instrument; they amplify the sounds of the music makers.[49]

Although voters pay most concentrated attention to media coverage just before elections, the crucial attitudes that determine voting choices may already be so firm that the final vote is a foregone conclusion.

Summary

The role played by the media, especially television, in recent campaigns is powerful and pervasive. It has transformed election politics for high offices. Major changes are weakening the influence of political parties and other political actors, dominating the campaign strategies and schedules, and placing the media in the role of kingmakers in political recruiting and in the promoting of candidates, particularly at the presidential level.

In this chapter we have scrutinized newspaper, television, and Internet election coverage. General coverage patterns, the substance and slant of coverage, and the manner of presentation were considered. The media have placed more emphasis on the candidates' personal qualifications for the office and on the ups and downs of the race than on substantive issues. Stories are chosen for their newsworthiness, not their educational value. Structural biases abound and have important political consequences, but outright political bias is rare.

We also have examined the effects of media output on the people who are exposed to it. Although the public claims, off and on, to be very interested in learning about the election, it absorbs only a small portion of the considerable amount of available information. Nonetheless, the bits of information that people absorb create sufficient political understanding to permit sound voting choices based on appraisal of a chosen candidate's character. Minute changes brought about by the media in final voting decisions or voter turnout may alter the outcome of a close election and the course of political life.

Claims that the media have minimal impact on elections rest on obsolete election studies from the 1940s and 1950s. This early research preceded the age of television dominance and was concerned primarily with massive changes in individual voting decisions. More recent research has cast the net much wider to include the media's effects on all phases of the election campaign, from the recruitment and nomination stages to the strategies that produce the final outcome. In addition to studying the media's impact on the final voting choice, social scientists now look at political learning during campaigns and at the information base that supports the voting decision. Television news stories and commercials, in particular, have changed the election game rules, especially at the presidential level. The Internet and its ramifications may bring even greater modifications, though the precise nature of future changes is still speculative. One thing is certain: candidates and media have become inextricably intertwined. Those who aspire to elective office must play by the evolving rules of media politics.

Notes

1. Pippa Norris, "Too Close to Call: Opinion Polls in Campaign 2000," *Press/Politics* 6(1) (2001): 3–10.
2. The most extensive data archives were created at the Annenberg School for Communication in Philadelphia and the Shorenstein Center at Harvard University's Kennedy School. For one of the first major attempts to study the full campaign cycle, covering multiple phases of the 1992 presidential campaign, see Marion R. Just et al., *Crosstalk: Citizens, Candidates, and the Media in a Presidential Campaign* (Chicago: University of Chicago Press, 1996).
3. Just et al., *Crosstalk*, 151–176.
4. For a well-reasoned argument questioning television influence, see Michael J. Robinson, "News Media Myths and Realities: What the Networks Did and Didn't Do in the 1984 General Campaign," in *Elections in America*, ed. Kay Lehman Schlozman (Boston: Allen and Unwin, 1987), 143–170. An equally well-reasoned argument supporting television influence is presented in Dean Alger, "Television, Perceptions of Reality and the Presidential Election of '84," *PS* 20 (winter 1987): 49–57.
5. "Campaign 2000—The Primaries," *Media Monitor* 14 (March–April 2000): 1–5.

6. Larry M. Bartels, "Expectations and Preferences in Presidential Nominating Campaigns," *American Political Science Review* 79 (September 1985): 804–815. The importance of the winner image is discussed in Henry E. Brady and Richard Johnston, "What's the Primary Message: Horse Race or Issue Journalism?" in *Media and Momentum: The New Hampshire Primary and Nomination Politics,* ed. Gary R. Orren and Nelson W. Polsby (Chatham, N.J.: Chatham House, 1987), 127–186.

7. "Campaign 2000—The Primaries," 1–5.

8. Richard Rubin, *Press, Party, and Presidency* (New York: Norton, 1981), 129, 138.

9. For analysis of the impact of debates, see David J. Lanoue and Peter Schrott, *The Joint Press Conference: The History, Impact, and Prospects of American Presidential Debates* (Westport, Conn.: Greenwood, 1991). Also see Judith S. Trent and Robert V. Friedenberg, *Political Campaign Communication: Principles and Practices,* 4th ed. (Westport, Conn.: Praeger, 2000), chap. 8; and Sidney Kraus, *Televised Presidential Debates and Public Policy,* 2d ed. (Mahwah, N.J.: Erlbaum, 2000).

10. Quoted in Edwin Diamond, *Sign-off: The Last Days of Television* (Cambridge: MIT Press, 1982), 175.

11. Martin Schram, *The Great American Video Game: Presidential Politics in the Television Age* (New York: Morrow, 1987), 26.

12. William Neikirk, "Clinton Keeping Image Bright," *Chicago Tribune,* April 13, 1996.

13. Katharine Q. Seelye, "Report Focuses on Price of Political Ads," *New York Times,* March 6, 2001.

14. Leslie Wayne, "E-Mail Part of the Effort to Turn Out the Voters," *New York Times,* Nov. 6, 2000.

15. Marjorie Randon Hershey, "The Campaign and the Media," in *The Election of 2000,* ed. Gerald M. Pomper (New York: Chatham House, 2001).

16. Eric P. Bucy, Paul D'Angelo, and John E. Newhagen, "The Engaged Electorate: New Media Use as Political Participation," in *The Electronic Election: Perspectives on the 1996 Campaign Communication,* ed. Lynda Lee Kaid and Dianne G. Bystrom (Mahwah, N.J.: Erlbaum, 1999). Also see Bruce Bimber, *Information and American Democracy: From* The Federalist *to the Internet* (Cambridge: Cambridge University Press, forthcoming), chap. 5.

17. Richard Davis and Diana Owen, *New Media and American Politics* (New York: Oxford University Press), 1998; Gary W. Selnow, *Electronic Whistle-Stops: The Impact of the Internet on American Politics* (Westport, Conn.: Praeger, 1998); Michael Margolis and David Resnick, *Politics as Usual: The Cyberspace "Revolution"* (Thousand Oaks, Calif.: Sage, 2000).

18. Pew Research Center for the People and the Press data from a telephone survey of 1,113 voters on November 10–12, 2000, http://www.people-press.org/post00que.htm.

19. Emmett H. Buell Jr., "'Locals' and 'Cosmopolitans': National, Regional, and State Newspaper Coverage of the New Hampshire Primary," in *Media and Momentum: The New Hampshire Primary and Nomination Politics,* ed. Gary R. Orren and Nelson W. Polsby (Chatham, N.J.: Chatham House, 1987), 66.

20. *Media Monitor* (March–April 1996): 2.

21. Michael J. Robinson and Margaret Sheehan, "Traditional Ink vs. Modern Video Versions of Campaign '80," in *Television Coverage of the 1980 Presidential*

Campaign, ed. William C. Adams (Norwood, N.J.: Ablex, 1983), 18; Pew Research Center for the People and the Press, survey, Nov. 10–12, 2000, http://www.people-press.org/post00que.htm.

22. W. Russell Neuman, Marion Just, and Ann Crigler, *Common Knowledge: News and the Construction of Political Meaning* (Chicago: University of Chicago Press, 1992), 39–59; Just et al., *Crosstalk,* 62–66; Darrell M. West, *Air Wars: Television Advertising in Election Campaigns, 1952–2000,* 3d ed. (Washington, D.C.: CQ Press, 2001), 13–19.

23. Michael Pfau et al., "Influence of Communication Modalities on Voters' Perception of Candidates during Presidential Primary Campaigns," *Journal of Communication* 45 (winter 1995): 122–133; Trent and Friedenberg, chap. 10.

24. Owen, *Media Messages,* 25–60. Also see Stephen Ansolabehere and Shanto Iyengar, "The Craft of Political Advertising: A Progress Report," in *Political Persuasion and Attitude Change,* ed. Diana C. Mutz, Paul M. Sniderman, and Richard Brody (Ann Arbor: University of Michigan Press, 1996).

25. West, *Air Wars,* chap. 5.

26. Bruce E. Gronbeck, "Mythic Portraiture in the 1988 Iowa Presidential Caucus Bio-Ads," *American Behavioral Scientist* 33 (1989): 351–364; J. Gregory Payne, John Marlier, and Robert A. Baucus, "Polispots in the 1988 Presidential Primaries," *American Behavioral Scientist* 33 (1989): 365–381.

27. Michael J. Robinson, "The Media in 1980: Was the Message the Message?" in *The American Elections of 1980,* ed. Austin Ranney (Washington, D.C.: American Enterprise Institute, 1981), 186.

28. For comparisons of coverage in Boston, Los Angeles, Fargo–Moorhead, N.D., and Winston-Salem, N.C., see Just et al., *Crosstalk,* 92–96.

29. C. Richard Hofstetter, *Bias in the News: Network Television Coverage of the 1972 Election Campaign* (Columbus: Ohio State University Press, 1976), 39–41; Paul S. Herrnson, "The Congressional Elections," in *The Election of 2000,* ed. Pomper. For a comparison of campaigns in Senate and House elections, see Paul Gronke, *The Electorate, the Campaign, and the Office: A Unified Approach to Senate and House Elections* (Ann Arbor: University of Michigan Press, 2000), chaps. 4 and 5.

30. Hofstetter, *Bias in the News,* 32–36. For an interesting discussion of the special concerns involved in covering African American candidates, see Jannette Lake Dates and Oscar H. Gandy Jr., "How Ideological Constraints Affected Coverage of the Jesse Jackson Campaign," *Journalism Quarterly* 62 (autumn 1985): 595–600.

31. Dave D'Alessio and Mike Allen, "Media Bias in Presidential Elections: A Meta-Analysis," *Journal of Communication* 50(4) (2000): 133–156. The reasons behind unwarranted bias claims are discussed in David Domke et al., "The Politics of Conservative Elites and the 'Liberal Media' Argument," *Journal of Communication* 49(4) (1999): 35–58.

32. Dennis T. Lowry and Jon A. Shidler, "The Sound Bites, the Biters, and the Bitten: An Analysis of Network TV News Bias in Campaign '92," *Journalism and Mass Communication Quarterly* 72 (spring 1995): 33–44.

33. Byron St. Dizier, "The Effect of Newspaper Endorsements and Party Identification on Voting Choice," *Journalism Quarterly* 62 (autumn 1985): 589–594.

34. Doris A. Graber and David Weaver, "Presidential Performance Criteria: The Missing Element in Election Coverage," *Harvard International Journal of Press/Politics* 1 (winter 1996): 7–32. A companion analysis of the 2000 election yielded similar findings.

35. Quoted in Anthony King, "How Not to Select Presidential Candidates: A View from Europe," in *The American Elections of 1980,* ed. Ranney, 305.

36. Typecasts have been extracted from Michael Robinson, "A Statesman Is a Dead Politician, Candidate Images on Network News," in *What's News: The Media in American Society,* ed. Elie Abel (San Francisco: Institute for Contemporary Studies, 1981), 178–182.

37. Quoted in *Media Monitor* (March–April 1996): 6.

38. S. Robert Lichter, "A Plague on Both Parties: Substance and Fairness in TV Election News," *Press/Politics* 6(3) (2001): 12.

39. Robinson, "The Media in 1980," 191.

40. Pew Research Center for the People and the Press, survey, Nov. 10–12, 2000, http://www.people-press.org/post00que.htm.

41. Thomas Patterson, *The Mass Media Election: How Americans Choose Their President,* 3d ed. (New York: Praeger, 1988), 250. Also see Eric R. A. N. Smith, *The Unchanging American Voter* (Berkeley: University of California Press, 1989).

42. Milton Lodge and Patrick Stroh, "Inside the Mental Voting Booth: An Impression-Driven Process Model of Candidate Evaluation," in *Explorations in Political Psychology,* ed. Shanto Iyengar and William J. McGuire (Durham: Duke University Press, 1993).

43. Pew Research Center for the People and the Press, survey, Nov. 10–12, 2000, http://www.people-press.org/post00que.htm.

44. Michael X. Delli Carpini and Scott Keeter, *What Americans Know about Politics and Why It Matters* (New Haven: Yale University Press, 1996), 4.

45. Doris A. Graber, *Processing the News: How People Tame the Information Tide,* 3d ed. (Lanham, Md.: University Press of America, 1993), 140.

46. "The Girl in the Well Outpolls the Men in the Race," *New York Times,* Nov. 19, 1987.

47. Paul Wilson, "Election Night 1980 and the Controversy over Early Projections," in *Television Coverage,* ed. Adams, 152–153; Percy H. Tannenbaum and Leslie J. Kostrich, *Turned-On TV/Turned-Off Voters: Policy Options for Election Projections* (Beverly Hills, Calif.: Sage, 1983); and Paul J. Lavrakas and Jack K. Holley, eds., *Polls and Presidential Election Campaign News Coverage: 1988* (Evanston: Northwestern University Press, 1988).

48. For a discussion of how state laws have fared in the courts, see Stephen Bates, "Lawful Exits: The Court Considers Election Day Polls," *Public Opinion* 8 (summer 1986): 53–54.

49. Leon V. Sigal, "Newsmen and Campaigners: Organization Men Make the News," *Political Science Quarterly* 93 (fall 1978): 465–470.

Readings

Bimber, Bruce. *Information and American Democracy: From* The Federalist *to the Internet.* Cambridge: Cambridge University Press, forthcoming.

Davis, Richard. *The Web of Politics: The Internet's Impact on the American Political System.* New York: Oxford University Press, 1999.

Just, Marion R., Ann N. Crigler, Dean E. Alger, Timothy E. Cook, Montague Kern, and Darrell M. West. *Crosstalk: Citizens, Candidates, and the Media in a Presidential Campaign.* Chicago: University of Chicago Press, 1996.

Kaid, Lynda Lee, and Dianne G. Bystrom, eds. *The Electronic Election: Perspectives on the 1996 Campaign Communication.* Mahwah, N.J.: Erlbaum, 1999.

Kaid, Lynda Lee, and Anne Johnston. *Videostyle in Presidential Campaigns: Style and Content of Televised Political Advertising.* Westport, Conn.: Praeger, 2001.

Margolis, Michael, and David Resnick. *Politics as Usual: The Cyberspace "Revolution."* Thousand Oaks, Calif.: Sage, 2000.

Patterson, Thomas. *Out of Order.* New York: Knopf, 1993.

Selnow, Gary W. *Electronic Whistle-Stops: The Impact of the Internet on American Politics.* Westport, Conn.: Praeger, 1998.

Semetko, Holli A., et al. *The Formation of Campaign Agendas: A Comparative Analysis of Party and Media Roles in Recent American and British Elections.* Hillsdale, N.J.: Erlbaum, 1991.

West, Darrell M. *Air Wars: Television Advertising in Election Campaigns, 1952–2000.* 3d ed. Washington, D.C.: CQ Press, 2001.

The Struggle for Control:
News from the Presidency
and Congress

"CLINTON REWROTE THE PRESIDENCY, probably forever, by making use of dramatic changes in the news media to talk directly to the public in a casual, intimate style. He seized on the phenomenon of 24-hour television and the advent of news on the Internet to adopt an empathetic air, looking and sounding like everyone's neighbor or friend." This is how Naftali Bendavid, a Washington-based reporter for the *Chicago Tribune*, described political communication over the eight-year Clinton presidency. There is abundant evidence to support this characterization.[1]

Unlike many of his predecessors, Clinton did not use the presidency as a bully pulpit for summoning the nation in ringing phrases to battle against foreign enemies or even domestic plagues. He talked instead—in "kitchen-table" style, friend to friend—about middle-class concerns, involving issues such as college costs and health care and teen pregnancy. And he talked often! Clinton averaged 550 public talks annually, compared to 320 for the "Great Communicator" Ronald Reagan and a meager 88 for President Harry Truman. Thanks to television, much of the world knew Clinton's expressive face, his thrust of jaw while he bit his lower lip, and his engaging speaking style. Millions loved it.

Clinton's ability to communicate with people high and low won him the friendship of much of the nation. Supporters were willing to put up with perennial soap opera scandals in return for a friend in the White House who cared, especially as long as the economy kept purring along at a steady high pace. But, as has been said about other leaders, those who live by the tube are also at risk of dying from it. Constant media scrutiny led to publicity about personal misbehavior and ultimately to impeachment proceedings that weakened the president and the presidency itself. Having to admit to a nationwide television audience that his televised plea of innocence in an affair with White House intern Monica Lewinsky was a lie was bound to diminish Clinton's stature. The scandals, which would have remained hidden in a less intrusive media environment, took their toll in the 2000 election. The Democrats, who were expected to win by large numbers thanks to the good economic news, lost because scandal news had created "Clinton fatigue." Their small edge in the popular vote reflected that fatigue and denied them a winning margin in the electoral college. The winner was another folksy, comparatively telegenic candidate—George W. Bush.

Why do top-level political leaders throughout the world put so much energy into their media strategies when, in the end, the media may be their undoing? Why do they expose themselves to frequently hostile interrogations by journalists who routinely write stories attacking them and their policies? The answer is that politicians desperately need the media to achieve their goals. They know that the media need them as much as or more than the politicians need the media to get information for important stories. They both hope that their interdependence will temper their love-hate relationship. Because the two institutions have conflicting goals and missions and operate under different constraints, they cannot live comfortably with each other. Yet they dare not part company.[2]

The Adversarial Relationship

To gain and retain public support and maintain their power, executives and legislators want to influence the information that is passed on to the public and to other officials. They want to define situations and project images in their own way to further their objectives. Newspeople, however, have different goals. They feel bound by the economics of the news business to present exciting stories that will attract large audiences. This often means prying into conflict, controversy, or ordinary wheeling and dealing—matters that government officials would like to keep quiet. Government wants its portrait taken from the most flattering angle; at the least it wants to avoid an unflattering picture. The media, eager to maximize audience size, prefer candid shots that show government at its worst.

In this chapter we will take a closer look at the interrelationship of the media and the executive and legislative branches of government at the national level. The interface of the media and the court system and subnational levels of government are targeted in the next chapter. Casual as well as systematic observations readily establish that the media devote a

TABLE 9-1   Evening Network News Coverage of the Three Branches of
             Government: July 1999–June 2000 (comparison data
             for August 1994–July 1995)

Month	President		Congress		Supreme Court	
	N	Time	N	Time	N	Time
1999						
July	29	1:00	50	1:21	0	0:00
August	38	1:10	17	0:31	1	0:05
September	54	2:02	21	0:31	6	0:07
October	42	1:18	49	1:35	9	0:11
November	36	0:57	17	0:28	5	0:05
December	29	1:02	10	0:15	3	0:03
2000						
January	37	1:09	12	0:20	14	0:21
February	30	1:01	9	0:21	3	0:04
March	73	2:32	20	0:49	9	0:11
April	37	1:14	8	0:22	6	0:12
May	44	1:29	29	1:07	7	0:05
June	43	1:17	32	1:12	32	0:55
Total	492	16:11	274	8:52	95	2:18
Monthly average	41	1:21	23	0:44	8	0:11
Comparison data	107	4:22	24	0:56	5	0:08

SOURCE: Compiled by the author from the Vanderbilt Television News Archives Indexes.

NOTE: Three major networks (ABC, NBC, and CBS) have been combined; time is listed in hours and minutes.

great deal of attention to the affairs of the national government, particularly the presidency. As Table 9-1 shows, during the twelve-month span from July 1999 to June 2000, the early evening news broadcasts of ABC, CBS, and NBC ran an average of forty-one network television stories per month about some aspect of the presidency. It was the most common story topic by far. The numbers for Congress and the Supreme Court were considerably lower, with a monthly average of twenty-three congressional stories and just eight stories about the Supreme Court. However, the number of congressional stories would nearly double if stories devoted to individual members were added. The Clinton scores would easily have equaled the three-digit average scored five years earlier, except for the media's concentration on the Lewinsky sex scandal and the subsequent impeachment procedures. These stories diverted press attention from the usual heavy focus on presidential business.

TABLE 9-2   Changing News Story Emphasis (in percentages)

News sources	Traditional political		Economic and social		Entertainment /weather	
	1977	1997	1977	1997	1977	1997
ABC	71.6%	44.9%	15.0%	33.6%	13.4%	21.5%
CBS	67.8	40.3	17.3	41.7	14.5	18.3
NBC	54.6	38.8	21.8	36.7	24.7	24.7
L.A. Times	74.8	62.0	11.7	25.9	13.5	12.4
N.Y. Times	63.8	69.3	29.7	23.2	5.2	7.5
Time	48.1	19.2	30.7	44.3	21.1	36.6
Newsweek	46.1	25.0	21.0	48.1	32.7	26.9
20/20	—	10.0	—	70.1	—	19.9
48 Hours	—	10.0	—	35.0	—	55.0
60 Minutes	—	22.3	—	50.3	—	27.8
Prime Time	—	13.3	—	46.7	—	40.0
Dateline	—	13.7	—	48.0	—	38.4

SOURCE: Condensed from Committee of Concerned Journalists, "Changing Definitions of News: Subject of News Stories by Medium" (1998). http://www.journalism.org/ccj/resources/chdefonews4.html

NOTE: The "traditional political" category combines the original categories of government, military, domestic affairs, and foreign affairs. The "economic and social" category combines the original categories of business/commerce, science, technology, arts, religion, personal health, and crime. The "entertainment/weather" category combines entertainment/celebrities, lifestyle, celebrity crime, sports, and weather/disaster. Front pages of newspapers and network broadcasts were coded for March 1997; magazine cover stories were coded for the entire year; prime time news magazine stories were coded during the fall season in 1997.

Table 9-1 indicates that coverage was unevenly distributed with several peaks and valleys for each branch of the government. Compared to Clinton's first-term coverage, the second-term figures represent a sharp drop in attention to the presidency, a light drop in attention to Congress, and a boost in stories about the Supreme Court. These figures herald a steady decline of attention to the presidency and Congress and, to a lesser degree, the Supreme Court. Compared to 1990–1991, the average monthly number of network stories has dropped 69 percent for the presidency, 75 percent for Congress, and 33 percent for the Court. The length of time allotted to such stories has dropped even more sharply—a decline of 83 percent for the presidency, 76 percent for Congress, and 59 percent for the Court. As Table 9-2 shows, this phenomenon is part of an overall trend away from covering traditional news to placing more emphasis on social and economic issues. It affects television news and news magazines as well as print news and news magazines, although the change is somewhat less apparent in the print media.

TABLE 9-3   Evening Network News Coverage of the Three Branches of Government in Percentage of Network Time: July 1999 – June 2000

Network	President	Congress	Supreme Court
ABC	57.7%	32.2%	10.1%
CBS	62.0	29.7	8.3
NBC	61.4	31.4	7.2
Average	60.4	31.1	8.5

SOURCE: Compiled by the author from Vanderbilt Television News Archives Indexes.

NOTE: *N* for ABC = 456 minutes (7 hours, 36 minutes); *N* for CBS = 581 minutes (9 hours, 41 minutes); *N* for NBC = 567 minutes (9 hours, 27 minutes).

Differences among the three networks in number of stories and time allotments were small, as Table 9-3 indicates. Interestingly, the most popular network, ABC, spent the least amount of time on stories about the three branches of government. It used seven hours and thirty-six minutes compared to nine hours and forty-one minutes for CBS and nine hours and twenty-seven minutes for NBC. The president's share of this television time amounted to roughly 60 percent, compared to 31 percent for Congress and 9 percent for the Supreme Court.

The similarities between print and broadcast media in their patterns of coverage do not mean that various media organizations project identical images of public officials. For example, when a local newspaper, an elite newspaper, and network television covered two items—a proposal by President Ronald Reagan to cut taxes and the president's 1984 trip to Europe—three different sets of images emerged from the stories.[3] The *Durham Morning Herald,* a local paper from North Carolina with limited resources for independent news analysis, presented accounts drawn largely from the wire services. These stories featured the themes, ideas, and perspectives provided by the White House and cast the president and the events into a favorable light. The elite *New York Times* also reported the White House version of events, but subjected the White House reports to critical analysis. This created a much less rosy impression of the state of affairs. The "CBS Evening News" presented a more mixed picture. Verbal images were predominantly negative, but visual images, based on presidentially controlled photo opportunities, were highly favorable. Audiences for these three news sources thus were informed about the same events, but the tint of the interpretive lenses varied.

The Media and the Executive Branch

Four Major Functions

The media perform four major functions for government executives.[4] First, they *inform them about current events,* including developments in other parts of the government. This information sets the scene for policies. When the media highlight problems such as environmental hazards or growing homelessness, major or minor executive action often follows. Not infrequently, the media furnish daily news more quickly than bureaucratic channels. Stories about foreign affairs often reach presidents faster through the *New York Times* on the Web or CNN than through State Department bulletins that first must be coded and then decoded.

Second, the media *keep executive branch officials attuned to the public's major concerns.* They do this directly by reporting on public opinion and indirectly by featuring the stories likely to shape public opinion. Public officials assume that newspeople keep in touch with popular concerns, which are then reflected in their stories. Readers and viewers, in turn, take their cues about what is important from the media.

Third, the media *enable executives to convey their messages to the general public as well as to political elites* within and outside of government. These channels of communication, to which presidents have fairly ready access, provide unparalleled opportunities to explain the administrations' policies. Political elites need them as much as the public does because there is no effective communication system that directly links government officials who are dispersed throughout the country. As one pundit noted:

> Nearly all of our political comment originates in Washington. Washington politicians, after talking things over with each other, relay misinformation to Washington journalists who, after further intramural discussion, print it where it is thoughtfully read by the same politicians. It is the only completely successful system for the recycling of garbage that has yet been devised.[5]

Political elites also use media channels to publicly attack opponents' positions, forcing opponents to take stands they may wish to avoid.

Fourth, the media *allow chief executives to remain in full public view on the political stage,* keeping their human qualities and professional skills on almost constant display. Newspapers, television, and radio supply a steady stream of commentary about a president's daily routines. Coverage of personal life may be extensive, even for the vice president. For instance, when Vice President Dick Cheney underwent minor heart surgeries in 2001, extensive daily medical news briefings kept the public apprised of his progress. The media reported intimate details of the vice president's condition, including his energy level, his tolerance of various medical procedures, and his daily diet. Beyond providing human-interest tidbits, such coverage reassures the public that it is fully informed about the disability and the patient's fitness to continue official functions. Human-interest stories help to forge close personal ties between people and their leaders. They make it easier for them to trust the leader and therefore support policies, as happened with President Clinton. But they may also diminish the stature of presidents by making it obvious that they are quite ordinary human beings, despite the majesty of the office. That, too, was part of the Clinton experience.

Media Impact

The political significance of the relationship between the media and the executive branch is much greater than the few functions just described. Media coverage is the very lifeblood of politics because it shapes the perceptions that form the reality on which political action is based. Media do more than depict the political environment; they *are* the political environment. Because direct contact with political actors and situations is limited, media images define people and situations for nearly all participants in the political process. The quantity of such images is rising thanks to new technologies.

As we saw in previous chapters, the age of television politics that began in the 1950s has vastly enhanced the impact and, hence, the power of the media. In the past a story might have caused ripples on the political seas when thousands of people in one corner of the country read it in the paper or heard it on the radio. Today that same story can cause political tidal waves when millions worldwide see and hear it simultaneously on television and computer screens. Politicians feel compelled to react. They now can visit with millions of potential followers in their living rooms, creating the kinds of emotional ties that hitherto came only from personal contact. Electronic contacts may affect the political future of a member of Congress more than service on an important congressional committee.

Television has tipped the political scales of power among the three branches of government in favor of the presidency, but increased coverage of Congress has begun to reverse the imbalance. We have already described how strongly the news media influence who becomes eligible for presidential office and how profoundly they affect the conduct and outcome of elections. After elections, the success of presidential policies; the length, vigor, and effectiveness of a president's political life; and the general level of support for the political system depend heavily on images that the media convey. Making sure that these images are favorable therefore becomes a prime concern. Staffs of various presidents concur that "the national media play a very significant role in the White House decision-making process . . . in White House meetings, on the whole, more time is spent discussing the media than any other institution, including Congress . . . all policies are developed and presented with media reaction in mind."[6]

The media frequently raise issues that presidents and other public officials would prefer to keep out of the limelight. Budget deficits, crumbling highways and bridges, and inefficient veterans' hospitals are just a few examples. The Whitewater real estate scandal that harmed the Clintons throughout their White House years demonstrates how constant media prodding can keep a damaging issue at the top of the public agenda despite massive presidential efforts to downplay it. The list of major and minor scandals that the media have highlighted to the government's dismay is seemingly endless. Media coverage can also increase public support for a president's policies and raise approval ratings. This is particularly important in national emergencies when backing by Congress and the public is vital. Thanks to war news that highlighted military successes and ignored failures, President George Bush's approval ratings during the Persian Gulf War in the spring of 1991 reached nearly 90 percent. Such steep gains may be short-lived because memories fade quickly and more careful media reviews of the war record reveal its flaws. Nine months after his high approval scores, Bush's ratings were below 50 percent and still dropping. Premature predictions that wartime success would sustain his popularity throughout the 1992 election campaign proved incorrect.

Sensational adverse publicity can kill programs and new technologies. For instance, alarmist publicity following a contained accident at the Three Mile Island nuclear plant in Pennsylvania in 1979 resulted in sharp curbs in the production of nuclear energy and restrained the commercial use of nuclear energy ever since. Welfare programs, such as Head Start's pre-kindergarten training for underprivileged children or financial aid for minority businesses, were sharply cut in the wake of news about inefficient management and corrupt handling of money in these programs. Media publicity can also be crucial in determining whether a presidential appointee will be confirmed by the Senate. During the Clinton administration, highly unfavorable media publicity was instrumental in killing the nominations of Zoë Baird and Kimba Wood for attorney general. Media stories about womanizing, heavy drinking, and other personal excesses by former senator John Tower were blamed in his failure to gain Senate approval as Secretary of Defense during the first Bush administration. As television critic Tom Shales said about the failed Supreme Court nomination of Judge Robert Bork in 1987, "Television may not have cooked 'his goose' but it certainly did some gourmet basting."[7]

Direct and Mediated Transmission

News about the government is conveyed either directly or indirectly. Direct transmission allows government officials to convey their messages with a minimum of shaping by the media. President Harry S. Truman was the first to use the direct mode by broadcasting his entire State of the Union message in 1947 to a nationwide audience. In January 1961 President John Kennedy further expanded direct coverage by allowing news conferences to be broadcast live. Among public officials, presidents enjoy the greatest opportunities for uncontrolled access to the American people, although C-SPAN's gavel-to-gavel coverage of Congress has leveled the playing field. Other political leaders who are competing with the president for power and public support have tried for matching privileges with only moderate success.

Of course, even live television and radio broadcasts are not totally devoid of media influence because camera angles and other photographic techniques slant all presentations somewhat. For example, in 1985, when President Reagan visited a military cemetery in Bitburg, Germany, to honor the war dead, CBS filmed the president against the backdrop of Nazi storm troopers' graves to suggest that the ceremony could be interpreted as support for the Hitler movement. The White House, disclaiming any intent to honor fallen Nazi soldiers, tried but failed to persuade the network to film the scene from a different angle.[8]

Instant commentary following presidential speeches has often blunted their impact. This happens, for instance, when the State of the Union message is instantly rebutted by a leader from the opposing party. Likewise, print news stories describing a presidential news conference, even when such stories are followed by the full transcript, involve shaping by media personnel. However, compared with the great leeway that newspeople usually have in choosing and interpreting information about the presidency, this type of control remains minimal.

Indirect or mediated transmission—the shaping of news presentations by media personnel—lies at the heart of the tensions between media and government because it bestows more power on the media than governments like to surrender. Mediated transmission permits journalists to pick and choose among the facts given to them. They routinely chop lengthy official statements into brief one- or two-sentence quotations and then weave them into an account often supplemented with information

TABLE 9-4　How Network Sources Rated President Clinton's Policies:
January 20, 1993–June 20, 1994 (in percentages)

Policies	Positive	Negative	Number of sources
Foreign policies			
NAFTA	49%	51%	380
Russia	43	57	81
Korea	31	69	90
Bosnia	26	74	380
Somalia	24	76	98
Haiti	17	83	126
Total foreign policies	31	68	1,155
Domestic policies			
Ethics in government	46%	54%	147
Economy	43	57	222
Crime	35	65	97
Budget	34	66	313
Health care	33	67	623
Gays in the military	26	74	189
Taxes	18	82	146
Total domestic policies	34	66	1,737

SOURCE: *Media Monitor* 8(4) (July/August 1994): 5.

NOTE: Figures combine ABC, CBS, and NBC nightly news broadcasts.

gathered from hostile sources. Television sound bites, which used to average forty-five seconds in earlier decades, now average under nine seconds. They rarely exceed twenty seconds. Thus the story is presented in a framework chosen and controlled by the media.

By judiciously selecting spokespeople for specific points of view, and by structuring questions to elicit answers that fit neatly into the desired scripts, newspeople can control the evaluations of public officials and policies. These appraisals are frequently negative, especially when the popularity of an administration is already falling. Newspeople are often accused of using mediated coverage deliberately, or at the least carelessly, to hurt public officials and their policies. Table 9-4 shows how various news sources quoted on the three major networks appraised President Clinton's foreign and domestic policies during the initial seventeen months of his term. Unlike most of his predecessors, the president received higher marks, albeit still predominantly negative ones, for domestic than for foreign policies. Predictably, Democratic sources were twice as favorable (35 percent) as Republican sources (17 percent).[9]

Media Goals and Tactics

Media personnel refute the charge that they go out of their way to show incumbent administrations in a bad light. They contend that they are looking for lively, significant stories that will earn them the respect of their colleagues and the acclaim of their readers and viewers. They see themselves instead as guardians of the public interest who help to make government more honest and efficient, and they believe that they have a duty to report the government's problems and wrongdoings. The politicians who produced the problematic situation, not the newspeople who reported it, should be blamed, they argue. Politicians who attack the media for focusing on bad news are accused of resembling the ancient Greeks who often killed bearers of bad tidings. This is what reporter William J. Small had in mind when he entitled his book about government and the media *To Kill a Messenger.*[10]

Because news focuses on nonroutine aspects of political life, journalists cover many stories that deal with isolated instances of socially undesirable behavior that reflect badly on government. Media personnel assigned to the presidential beat regularly feature harsh criticism of presidential programs, particularly if the attacks are voiced by politically influential opponents. Minor sins are often blown up as if they were major transgressions. For example, a trivial story about drunk driving charges leveled against candidate George W. Bush twenty-four years earlier created a major stir in the 2000 election. Some commentators thought the revelation might derail the Bush candidacy because it would sully his image as Mr. Clean fighting against a Clinton–Gore team stained by charges of multiple lies and unethical campaigning.

Managing a Rocky Marriage

All presidents profess to believe in a free press and to run an open government, but they rapidly develop a distaste for many of the reports about their administration. As President Kennedy told a news conference midway into his term in 1962, "[I am] reading more and enjoying it less."[11]

Presidents' displeasure with media coverage is readily understandable. Media coverage not only embarrasses them regularly and deprives them, to varying degrees, of control over the definition of political situations; it also forces them to talk in sound bites that reporters find attractive and, in the process, to put themselves on record in ways that may narrow their options for future action. Media disclosures of secret activities, such as an impending military intervention or a planned price freeze, may actually force the president's hand. Bargaining advantages may be lost through premature publication of news; trivia, conflict, and public wrong-doing may receive undue emphasis.

In the rocky marriage between the press and the president, open battles are comparatively rare. Despite traded accusations that the government manipulates and lies and that the press distorts and entraps, each side is fully aware that it depends on the other. If presidents refuse to talk to reporters, as happened often during the Nixon and Reagan years, or if they instruct their staffs, major departments, and agencies to refuse interviews, important stories cannot be covered firsthand. Alienating the prime news maker and source of government news is a major catastrophe for any news organization. Reporters' eagerness to get the news firsthand gives the president a tremendous advantage in influencing the substance and spin of news stories.

The media, for their part, can withhold publicity that the president needs or can force unwanted publicity. They can stress the positive or accent the negative. They can give instantaneous live coverage or delay broadcasts until a time of their choosing. In 1993, for example, NBC broadcast only thirty minutes of President Clinton's first evening news conference. ABC and CBS, despite presidential pleading, refused to carry the event. All of the networks refused to broadcast President Bush's last prime-time news conference in June 1992.[12] In 2000, network news slighted the presidential election debates as well as the nominating conventions.

The upshot of interdependence between the press and the government is a good deal of fraternizing and cronyism between these two "enemies," often to the dismay of those who favor an adversarial relationship. Each side works hard to cultivate the other's friendship. They often collaborate in examining political issues and problems. At national party conventions, the leaders regularly provide the networks with live television feeds from different camera angles. Such coziness may reduce journalists' zeal to investigate government's misdeeds. Indeed, charges of collusion have been made particularly when media suppress news at the request of government departments or the White House. Many of these instances have concerned questions of national security. In 1980, for example, the press delayed publicizing plans for a U.S. invasion of Iran to rescue American hostages. In 1987 it suppressed technical data about eavesdropping devices designed to intercept information from Soviet marine cables. Similarly, the press failed to disclose in 1995 that U.S. contingents within NATO had used potentially cancer-causing depleted uranium shells while bombing Bosnia in 1995 and Kosovo in 1999.[13]

The relationship between the media and the chief executive often displays three distinct phases.[14] Initially, there used to be a honeymoon period, a time of cooperation when the media conveyed the president's messages

Reprinted by permission of Sam Rawls.

about organization of the new administration, appointment of new officials, and plans and proposals for new policies. At this early stage few policies and proposals traditionally are implemented, so there is little opportunity for adverse criticism. Presidents and their advisers, eager to get their stories across, make themselves readily available to the media and supply them with ample information. The incoming Bush administration in 2001 illustrates the shriveling of the honeymoon period. Bush received far less attention from newspapers, news magazines, and network television news than either Clinton or the elder Bush had garnered. George W. Bush, as well as Clinton, had their honeymoon spoiled by predominantly negative comments about their initial legislative programs.[15]

Once the administration embarks on controversial programs and becomes vulnerable to criticism of its record, the honeymoon ends. As indicated, this is happening earlier and more abruptly now than in the past.[16] Controversies are attractive to the Washington press corps when they involve dramatic conflicts at the highest levels of government. They can be easily covered through interviews with Washington-based sources. The White House may retaliate by withholding news, by restricting presidential contacts with the press, and by increasing public relations activities.

If the rifts between media and the executive branch become exceptionally wide, there may be a third period in which both sides retreat from their mutually hostile behavior to take a more moderate stance. This phase frequently coincides with a reelection campaign, when newspeople try harder to provide impartial coverage, and presidents are more eager to keep newspeople happy. The president may also be able to arrange numerous trips abroad so that the focus of coverage switches to foreign affairs. That ordinarily is the area least likely to generate hostile coverage. There is political magic in scenes of American presidents meeting with world leaders in foreign capitals. While presidents are abroad, domestic criticism abates because the president's foes do not want to be accused of undermining U.S. foreign policy.

The ability of various administrations to get along with the media differs considerably. The president's interpersonal skills as well as the nature of the political problems faced by an administration account for much of the variation. In recent history the Kennedy and Reagan administrations have been particularly good at press relations, whereas the Nixon administration was especially bad. Nixon's Watergate problems might never have developed into a major scandal had he been able to charm the press. The Clinton years featured a mercurial relationship, fluctuating between passionate love and passionate hate on both sides.

The relationship between the chief executive and the media varies not only from one administration to the next but also from one part of the country to another. Frictions are greatest between the White House and the Washington press corps because they are most interdependent. Familiarity breeds a certain amount of contempt and dependence breeds resentment. The northeastern seaboard press has a reputation of being more critical than the press in the rest of the country. This is why recent presidents often try to circumvent the Eastern press by scheduling news conferences in other parts of the country and making major policy announcements away from the East Coast. They may also make concerted efforts to schedule media interviews for cabinet members and other high-level officials away from the Washington area.

In the same way, Presidents Ronald Reagan, George Bush, Bill Clinton, and George W. Bush arranged to visit small communities throughout the country to bask in the adulation of local audiences and local media for the benefit of nationwide television viewers. Taking advantage of new satellite technology, presidents can now be interviewed from the White House television studio by local television and radio stations throughout the country. They can tailor unedited, unfiltered messages for specific demographic groups and transmit them to local anchors in selected locations pleading for their support. All recent presidents have broadcast weekly radio addresses, hoping to bring their unfiltered messages to the attention of the public.

Presidential Communication Strategies

Besides circumventing the Eastern press, presidents use an array of strategies to control the substance and tenor of news. Four approaches are particularly common. First and most important, presidents try to win reporters' favor. This is not difficult because presidents are constantly surrounded by people who must have fresh news to earn their pay. Second, presidents try to shape the flow of news to make good publicity more likely and bad publicity less likely. Third, they pace and arrange their work schedules to produce opportunities for favorable media coverage. Fourth—and this is a most recent trend—they try to evade news media gatekeeping hurdles by publishing their news on government Web sites. Each of these strategies will be discussed in turn.

Winning Favor. To woo reporters, presidents offer good story material as well as occasional scoops that may bring distinction to individual reporters. They cultivate reporters' friendships by being accessible, treating them with respect, and arranging for their creature comforts. To keep reporters in line, presidents may threaten them directly or obliquely with a withdrawal of privileges. Privileges include accommodations on the presidential plane, special interviews, or answers to their specific questions during news conferences. Presidents may also publicly condemn individual reporters or their organizations for undesirable reporting.

Shaping the News Flow. Presidents try to guide the flow of news by the thrust of their commentary and by their control of contacts with the press. For example, when publicity about illegal transfers of arms to Nicaragua had damaged President Reagan's administration, he managed to divert media attention from the affair by sponsoring a popular Economic Bill of Rights, which included a balanced budget and line-item veto. A monthly economic bulletin was distributed nationwide simultaneously. It contained camera-ready copy praising the economic successes of the Reagan administration, including his records on job growth and lowered inflation. When President Clinton retaliated with extraordinary speed to a terrorist bombing of U.S. embassies in Kenya and Tanzania in 1998, observers wondered about the link to Clinton's domestic troubles. Was the retaliatory strike a diversionary move to shift attention away from the Lewinsky investigation?

To avoid questions about embarrassing failures, presidents periodically restrict their contacts with the media largely to picture sessions. Presidents also may space out news releases so that there is a steady, manageable flow of news. If they want emphasis on a particular story, they may withhold competing news that breaks simultaneously. Sometimes a barrage of news is released or even created to distract attention from sensitive developments. Criticism by the Eastern press has been averted by the withholding of advance copies of speeches or by timing them late enough in the evening to preclude adequate coverage in the morning papers in the East.

To control news flow and assure that the administration speaks with a single voice, presidents may prohibit their staffs, on pain of dismissal, from publicly disagreeing with their policies. In addition, they may require administrative departments to clear interviews through the White House to avoid conflicting pronouncements on public policies. Some recent administrations have insisted that officials who are privy to sensitive information receive approval of their superiors prior to granting interviews to the press.

Orchestrating Coverage. Ways of arranging activities to create favorable publicity are numerous. They include creating newsworthy events, heightening suspense through news blackouts prior to major pronouncements, and staging public ceremonies as media spectacles at times when there are few competing events. Political successes may be coupled with political failures in hopes that publicity for the success will draw attention away from the failure. The Carter administration reportedly timed its announcement of the opening of formal relations with the People's Republic of China late in 1978 to buffer negative publicity in case its attempts to clinch a peace settlement between Israel and Egypt failed. In the same way, the Reagan administration hoped that pictures of the American marines' successful military takeover of the tiny island of Grenada would counteract the images of the 1983 bombing of American marines in Lebanon.

Occasionally news management may even intentionally deceive the press so that it will convey a smokescreen message to the public. For instance, in 1961, the Kennedy administration told Miami reporters that five thousand U.S. troops had invaded Cuba's Bay of Pigs. This news was intended to encourage Cubans to rise up in support of a large invasion force. In truth, only one thousand troops had been sent. After the troops ran into trouble, officials admitted that only a few hundred American troops had actually been involved and that their chief mission had been to deliver supplies for anti-Castro guerrillas in Cuba rather than to invade the country. When reporters discovered that they had been used to spread false stories, they were furious. The credibility of the executive branch plummeted.

Presidential Web Sites

The White House maintains its own Web site at http://www.whitehouse.gov/. It is an electronic portal to the president, his family, the official mansion, and to a variety of messages prepared for public display by the incumbent and the presidential staff. It is also the gateway to http://www.firstgov.gov/, which contains electronic links to the entire national government. From there, visitors have access to the Web sites of all three branches of the national government as well as state government, local government, and international sites. Visitors can search for specific agencies or for policy areas such as consumer services, education, or veterans' benefits. Many sites are interactive so that people can ask questions as well as request forms that can then be submitted electronically. The main sites, their links, and links to the links form a fantastic treasure trove of information.

What sorts of information do these links contain? Most important, one must keep in mind that the sites are completely controlled by the government and its agencies. Therefore, they contain only what these site owners wish to include in the manner in which they wish to frame it. Aside from that important shared characteristic, sites vary tremendously in their completeness and timeliness of their offerings. Some are little more than public relations portals, while others genuinely try to cater to citizens' needs and to be transparent about their activities.

A great deal of research is still needed if we are to assess how useful these sites are for the president's communication within the executive branch, with Congress, with various interest groups, and with the citizenry at large. By and large we do not know who visits and for what purposes. We do know that these sites are widely used, and this suggests that they may be quite influential. We also know that service-oriented sites have more visits than policy-oriented sites.[17] Finally, we do know that the executive branch considers these sites important enough to allocate ample resources to them. This translates into attractive, user-friendly sites that present the government's story in words and pictures that reflect official, rather than journalistic, preferences.

Institutional Settings

Relations between the president and the media are so important and so complex that they require involvement by established as well as specially created institutions.

On the President's Side. A president can shape the news indirectly through appointments to the Federal Communications Commission (FCC) and other public agencies concerned with the media and through informal contacts with personnel in these agencies. Financial lifelines can be controlled through the Office of Management and Budget (OMB), which screens the budgetary requests of all federal agencies, including those dealing with the mass media. Control can also be wielded through the Justice Department. For instance, the Antitrust Division can challenge the FCC's approval of mergers and can carry appeals through the courts and ultimately to the Supreme Court.

Presidents involve themselves directly in media policymaking through various White House organizations, study commissions, and task forces. In

1970 President Nixon created the Office of Telecommunications Policy—the first permanent agency within the White House to plan communications policy. The Carter administration replaced this office with a less powerful organization within the Commerce Department, the National Telecommunications and Information Administration. By downgrading the agency, Carter gave the impression that the White House had distanced itself from communications policy questions and would leave the FCC free from White House pressure. However, a small policy planning staff remained in the White House to advise the president. This divorce of planning from operations still characterizes federal communications policymaking and has impeded strong executive leadership.

The Office of the White House Press Secretary and the Office of Communications. The Office of the White House Press Secretary supplies Washington-based reporters with news about the White House. By custom, the press secretary meets almost daily with the White House press corps to make announcements and take questions. These briefings supply reporters with the president's interpretation of events, which reporters then cast into perspectives of their own choice.

The Office of Communications, which has existed in various incarnations since the Nixon years, is concerned with long-range public relations management of the presidency. In consultation with the president, it determines the images that the administration needs to convey to gain and retain the approval of important constituencies in the public and private sectors and to win support for desired policies. The office also coordinates the public relations activities of executive branch departments and agencies.

In recent administrations, the work of the Office of Communications has been subdivided in various ways. The first Bush administration, for instance, organized five distinct sections. Media Relations dealt directly with media for matters such as scheduling public officials for talk show appearances. Public Affairs coordinated public relations activities throughout the executive branch. Public Liaison set up bimonthly meetings between the president and groups of editors, publishers, and reporters outside Washington. Two other divisions dealt with Speechwriting and Research. In the Clinton administration, the administrative setup was enlarged to include a Foreign Affairs and a News Analysis office as well as sections devoted to planning and policy coordination. The goal was to control, as much as possible, news reports about the administration and its policies.[18] If the president's approval ratings plunge, the communications director is likely to get the axe. As George Stephanopoulos, a victim of the communications wars during the Clinton administration, explained, "By definition, if the President isn't doing well, it's a communication problem. That's always going to be a natural place to make a change."[19]

Modern public relations activities employ many different techniques. "Focus groups and polling data are used to fashion presidential messages; sound-bites are written into the public pronouncements of the president and his underlings to articulate those messages; public appearances are choreographed so that the messages are reinforced by visual images; and the daily line is enforced to prevent the articulation of conflicting messages."[20] To spread messages throughout the country, the administration sends cabinet officers and others on speaking tours and arranges satellite interviews in local markets.

It is, of course, essential for presidents to "sell" their policies by soliciting wide support for them and by presenting a united front within their administration. However, in the process democracy may be imperiled because "Style is substituted for substance. Complicated issues are transformed into simple slogans and slick sound-bites . . . timid, self-interested policymakers . . . shy away from responsibility for their actions and delude themselves and their constituents with their own symbolic spectacle."[21]

On the Media's Side. The White House press corps consists of fewer than seventy newspeople who cover the president regularly. Many have considerable experience and notable reputations. As a group, they are older and better educated and trained than the average American journalist.[22] The *New York Times, Washington Post, Los Angeles Times, Chicago Tribune, Philadelphia Inquirer,* and other major newspapers have full-time reporters exclusively assigned to the president. So do a number of newspaper chains, such as the Scripps-Howard papers, the Hearst press, and the Newhouse papers. Smaller papers may send their Washington bureau chiefs to the White House whenever there is news of special interest to their region.

Each of the major broadcast networks, as well as CNN, has several reporters at the White House on a regular basis; smaller networks have one. C-SPAN provides twenty-four-hour White House cable coverage as well as gavel-to-gavel coverage of the House of Representatives. The White House is covered by several all-news cable services, Internet news operations, weekly news magazines, and periodicals, as well as photographers and their supporting staffs. Hard economic times in the early 1990s forced cutbacks in personnel and increased pooling of resources among media organizations. Even major events, such as presidential trips abroad or the national party conventions, are now covered by a smaller corps of journalists. Many reporters now work for several major news organizations simultaneously.

Most of the country's dailies do not have a regular Washington correspondent or part-time "stringer" to cover the White House. The same still holds true for most of the country's television and radio stations. Inexpensive satellite time, however, has lowered news transmission costs and boosted the numbers of stations that can afford direct coverage of the Washington scene. Satellites have enabled many small stations to view the activities of the national government through the prism of local interests. News organizations without staffs in Washington rely heavily on wire service news. Major domestic and foreign wire services have full-time reporters accredited to the White House; they cover the beat continuously, including presidential trips.

Forms of Contact

Press Releases and News Briefings. The release of news by chief executives or their aides takes a number of routinized forms. Most of these represent a concerted effort to control the news output. The most common is the *press release,* a story prepared by government officials and handed to members of the press, usually without an opportunity for questions. Officials hope that the text will be used verbatim. To make sure that the release appears at the most opportune time, it often has a dateline that stipulates the earliest time when it may be published. In a *news briefing,* reporters have an opportunity to ask the press secretary about the news releases. But because executive officials furnish the news for the briefing, they control the substance and tone of the discussion. Although most press secretaries, as well as members of the press, believe that daily news briefings are unnecessary and could be covered just as well by press releases, the briefings have become traditional.

News Conferences. Although a *news conference* may appear to be a wide-open question period, the official being questioned usually tries to control it tightly. Seemingly spontaneous answers usually have been carefully prepared by experts on the executive's staff and rehearsed during extensive briefings. Theodore Roosevelt was the first president to summon reporters to the White House regularly. Before Kennedy's presidency, press conferences were not covered live, permitting the White House to make corrections before conference records were published. Kennedy, who was a gifted extemporaneous speaker, stripped away this cloak of protection by allowing live filming of the conference. At the time, press critics called it "goofy" and likened it to "making love in Carnegie Hall."[23]

The live format remains controversial because it leads to posturing by the president as well as by members of the press. It also causes embarrassment for presidents who misspeak or suffer memory lapses. The senior George Bush lowered the risk by mostly holding informal news conferences on short notice, which made it difficult to broadcast the live event without costly interruptions of scheduled programs. The multiplication of media channels has sharply reduced the potential audience for news conferences because the president must compete with popular entertainment shows. There were fewer news conferences during the Clinton presidency as a result.

News conferences, as well as press briefings by press secretaries, often begin with a lengthy statement that is designed to set the tone. There may be advance notice to selected journalists that certain types of queries will receive very interesting answers. Presidents can often control the subject and tone of a news conference by recognizing friendly reporters for questions and avoiding follow-up questions. But no president has been able to squelch embarrassing questions entirely or to deny reporters the chance to use their questions as opportunities to express their own views about controversial issues.[24] Reporters revel in acting like prosecutors trying to extract a confession of major crimes from a hapless subject. Through posing leading questions, they try to force the president or press secretary to comment on matters that they may not wish to discuss. The questions listed in the box, which follows, give a taste of the sorts of interrogations that presidents face.

Backgrounders.   Some news conferences are off-the-record *backgrounders.* They are called by high officials to give newspeople important background information that they are honor bound to keep entirely secret or to publish only without revealing the source. Various forms of vague attribution are usually permitted, such as "government sources say," "it has been reported by reliable sources," or even more specifically, "the White House discloses" or the "Defense Department indicates."

Government officials like backgrounders because they are a relatively safe way to "test the waters." They permit officials to bring a variety of policy ideas before their colleagues and the public without openly identifying with them. In the Nixon administration, Secretary of State Henry Kissinger used backgrounders to submit foreign policy options for public debate and to warn foreign countries that their behavior was unacceptable to the United States. To discourage the Soviet Union's support of India in a war with Pakistan, Kissinger told reporters in a backgrounder that Soviet policy might lead President Nixon to cancel a planned trip to Moscow. If the statement had been officially attributed to Kissinger, the words would have constituted a threat that might have undermined détente with the Soviet Union. Similarly, Secretary of Defense Caspar Weinberger provided reporters in 1982 with background data on Soviet military capacity to substantiate the administration's claim that the Soviet Union posed a grave military threat to the United States and Europe. Weinberger hoped that the backgrounder would deter reporters from publicly questioning the administration's claims of danger. Public support for the government's defense policies might then have increased.

Unlike government officials, reporters are ambivalent about backgrounders. They like having access to news that might otherwise be unavailable, but they dislike being prevented from publishing all aspects of the story or from giving the source of the information so that the story can be placed in its proper perspective. At times reporters have evaded the prohibition on source disclosure by refusing to attend a background briefing and then reporting the story as told to them by reporters who actually had been present. To prevent such leaks, government officials have occasionally solicited

Questioning a New President

On March 30, 2001, ten weeks into his presidency, President George W. Bush held his second press conference. As is customary, the press largely ignored his brief opening statement that was intended to guide reporters to issues that Mr. Bush wished to discuss—U.S. efforts to cool the conflict between Israel and the Palestinians. Here, slightly abbreviated and without follow-ups, are the reporters' often irreverent questions from first to last.

1. Mr. President, the Senate, as you know, is finishing up legislation to ban all soft money. What do you think of the bill, particularly the ban on individual contributions that you forcefully opposed in the campaign? . . . would you sign it?

2. Mr. President, is your administration reviewing U.S. aid to Russia to stop the spread of nuclear, biological and chemical weapons? Are you considering reducing that aid? And if so, why?

3. Mr. President, in the last few weeks, you have rolled back health and safety and environmental measures proposed by the last administration . . . This has been widely interpreted as payback time to your corporate donors. Are they more important than the American people's health and safety? And what else do you plan to repeal?

4. . . . what are you prepared to do immediately to stimulate the economy, because it would appear that your long-term tax package does not do it, yet you dismiss, out-of-hand, attempts from the Hill to give back a rebate of some $60 billion this year unless it's tied to longer-term tax relief? Why can you not sign a short-term package and then pursue your long-term package separate to that?

5. . . . you and officials in your administration have indicated that you wanted to step back from constant involvement . . . in the conflict [in the Middle East] and in the peace process. Was that a mistake, given the escalation of both violence and the rhetoric over there? And is what you are doing today perhaps an admission that the involvement of the United States and the president of the United States publicly and personally is necessary for the parties?

6. Mr. President, . . . there is an energy crisis. And yet the budget resolutions do not include any revenue from the drilling in the Arctic National Wildlife Refuge. I've talked to the people who've made that decision, and they said . . . [t]hat you could not, nor could they, create the majorities in either the House or the Senate to bring

about drilling in A.N.W.R. . . . Does this not represent a rejection from your own party of dealing with the energy situation?

7. Mr. President . . . there are stories consistently about tensions, persistent tensions, between you and Senator John McCain . . . I wonder if you could address that, not just on the campaign finance reform bill but also on the Patients' Bill of Rights which—McCain supporters believe you don't want to sign . . . with McCain's name on it.

8. Sir, why is it that you have not decided to invite Yasir Arafat here? Have you concluded that he's part of the problem, not part of the solution?

9. Mr. President, allies of the United States have complained that you haven't consulted them sufficiently on your stance with negotiations with North Korea, Kyoto Treaty, your deteriorating relations elsewhere. If you read the international press, it looks like everyone's mad at us. Mr. President, how do you think that came to be? And what, if anything, do you plan to do about it?

10. . . . You will be meeting tomorrow with the president of Brazil, Fernando Henrique Cardoso . . . who is not in a rush to come to a free-trade agreement . . . Is your administration interested in getting the free-trade agreement by the 2003 year instead of the 2005 year, as has been agreed? And how do you expect to convince Mr. Cardoso tomorrow to follow that?

SOURCE: Excerpts from President Bush's news conference as transcribed by the Federal News Service, *New York Times*, March 30, 2001.

written pledges from reporters that they would keep information released during briefings secret. Usually reporters refuse to sign.

Ad Hoc Encounters

In addition to formal encounters, reporters and the president or White House staff meet informally in work or social settings. The most probing stories about White House activities often come from reporters who are not ordinarily assigned to cover the president. The regulars would be too vulnerable to retaliation by the White House. Top government officials, and occasionally the president, may agree to be interviewed on programs such as *Nightline, Good Morning America,* the *Today* show, *Meet the Press,* or *Face the Nation.* Questioning on these shows can resemble a no-holds-barred cross-examination. Executive branch officials participate in this ordeal because these programs provide excellent opportunities to present the administration's position to an interested nationwide audience. Besides, if questioning becomes excessively harsh, the audience often feels sorry for the targets and sides with them.

Leaks. An even less formal release of news occurs through *leaks,* the surreptitious release of information by high- and low-level government sources who wish to remain anonymous or who do not want to release the information formally. Many leaks are sanctioned at the highest levels. But some officials may also leak information that they are not authorized to release. Sometimes low-level officials leak information to gain attention from top officials.

Leaks are mixed blessings. They can destroy the timing of negotiations, alienate the parties whose secrets have been betrayed, and cause great harm by disclosing politically sensitive matters. They also may bring important suppressed issues to needed public attention, serve as trial balloons, and permit government officials to release information anonymously. Although presidents frequently leak confidential stories, they passionately hate news leaked by others. As long as the source remains hidden, personal confrontation and punishment are impossible. All recent presidents have therefore used federal investigative agencies such as the Federal Bureau of Investigation (FBI) and the Central Intelligence Agency (CIA) to find the sources of news leaks.

A typical leak occurred in 1991 during the Senate confirmation battle over the nomination of Judge Clarence Thomas to the U.S. Supreme Court. Confidential allegations about sexual harassment by the nominee that had been presented to the Senate Judiciary Committee were leaked to the press. The leaks led to a second round of lengthy, acrimonious hearings before the nominee was confirmed. The episode did serious harm to Judge Thomas's reputation and undermined faith in the integrity of the confirmation process.

The harm that leaks cause must be weighed against their benefits. In a system in which the executive maintains tight control over the formal channels of news, leaks provide a valuable counterbalance. President Reagan's controversial budget proposals in 1983 are a case in point. Administration insiders, eager to bring their concerns to the public and to Congress, resorted to almost daily leaks of economic appraisals that contradicted the president's views. An irate Reagan proclaimed, "I've had it up to my keister with these leaks," but he modified his budget plans nonetheless.[25]

The Media and Congress

According to political folklore, the television age has permanently altered the balance of political power. The presidency basks in the limelight of publicity at all times while Congress waits in the shadows, making the president dominant and the legislature inferior. As Sen. J. William Fulbright, D-Ark., told Congress in 1970, "Television has done as much to expand the powers of the President as would a constitutional amendment formally abolishing the co-equality of the three branches of government."[26]

Image Versus Reality

/   If one probes beyond these impressions to the underlying facts, the situation appears less clear. When coverage of areas of legislative concerns is added to coverage that mentions Congress explicitly, Congress and the presidency receive roughly the same amount of national news attention. Moreover, it must be remembered that the bulk of coverage of Congress comes through stories about individual members that are published in their home states. Although local coverage does not generally attract national attention, it is politically crucial for each member.

Table 9-5 presents a comparison of ten issues that emerged in television coverage of the president and Congress from August 1994 to July 1995. The scores represent a combination of offerings by ABC, CBS, and NBC. Besides showing the number of stories in each category and the length of broadcast time devoted to them, the table also records whether the story appeared in the first, second, or last ten-minute segment of the broadcast. It also identifies the six issues covered prominently for both institutions and the four issues unique to each. The three networks chose almost identical types of issues for stories about the presidency and Congress and placed them in similar positions within broadcast segments. However, they differed in the total amounts of time allotted to particular stories. Stories about Congress generally were fewer, shorter, and less prominently placed than news linked to the presidency, confirming that "435 members of the House and 100 members of the Senate compete for the crumbs of network time left after the president has got his share."[27]

Why does Congress fare worse than the presidency? There are several reasons. Most importantly, the presidency makes a better media target because it is a single-headed institution readily personified and filmed in the visible person of the chief executive. This gives media audiences a familiar, easily dramatized focus of attention. A president is like a superstar surrounded by a cast of supporting actors. Even stories originating from congressional sources frequently feature the president as the main actor. As the personification of the nation, the president can usually command national television or radio time, often at prime time and simultaneously on all major networks. During a recent ten-year period, forty-four out of forty-five presidential requests for coverage were granted compared to three out of eleven congressional requests.[28]

TABLE 9-5   Top Ten Issues on Network Evening News about the President and
Congress: August 1994–July 1995

Issue	Story rank[a] 1	2	3	Time	N	% of N
President						
Bosnia[b]	60	32	8	7:13	142	11.0
Health care	63	22	5	4:20	95	7.4
Crime bill	79	16	6	3:18	77	6.0
Budget	67	16	16	2:47	61	4.9
Russia[b]	44	46	10	2:10	45	3.5
Oklahoma City bombing	76	11	13	2:03	42	3.3
Economy[b]	58	24	18	1:56	41	3.2
Haiti	80	5	15	1:40	36	2.8
U.S. elections	69	28	4	1:39	35	2.7
Welfare reform[b]	64	18	18	0:58	22	1.7
Average (total)	66	22	11	(26:04)	(596)	(46.5)
Congress						
U.S. elections	47	32	21	1:53	34	12.1
Budget	42	46	13	1:04	24	8.5
Crime bill	88	12	0	0:51	17	6.0
Health care	38	31	31	0:44	16	5.7
Oklahoma City bombing	78	14	7	0:40	14	5.0
Contract with America[b]	39	39	22	0:36	13	4.6
Balanced Budget Amendment[b]	50	30	20	0:21	10	3.5
Whitewater scandal[b]	88	11	0	0:20	9	3.2
Haiti	57	29	14	0:17	7	2.5
Unfunded mandates law[b]	33	67	0	0:13	6	2.1
Average (total)	56	31	13	(0.50)	(150)	(53.2)

SOURCE: Compiled by the author from the Vanderbilt Television News Archives.

NOTE: *N* for president = 1,288; *N* for Congress = 282. The numbers are combined monthly
scores for ABC, CBS, and NBC early evening newscasts. Stories are rank ordered by time.
Time is in hours and minutes. Some percentages have been rounded.

[a] Position of story in first, second, or third ten-minute segment of broadcast; expressed in
percentage of number of stories on particular issue.
[b] Top-ranked issues not shared by Congress and the president.

In contrast to the presidency, Congress is a many-headed Hydra with
no single widely familiar personal focus. Its activities are conducted simultaneously in more than one hundred locations on Capitol Hill. No individual member can command nationwide media coverage at will. Even well-
known senators and representatives are viewed as spokespersons for their
own or their party's views or as potential presidential candidates, not as
spokespersons for Congress as an institution. Their celebrity status often

has little to do with their legislative activity in Congress. In fact, there has never been a single spokesperson for Congress in general, or even for the Senate or House, because senators and representatives are loath to designate one of their number as *primus inter pares* (first among equals). Consequently, most stories about Congress deal with individual members or legislative activity on specific issues rather than with the body as a whole.

Another reason why stories about Congress escape wide attention lies in the nature of its work. The legislative branch drafts laws, makes compromises among conflicting interests, forges shifting coalitions, and works out legal details. Stories about the executive branch that describe *what* is actually done are far more memorable than reports about *how* the laborious process of hammering out legislation works. Besides, the most interesting aspect of the legislative process, the shaping of broad guidelines for policy, is usually reported by the media as part of the work of the executive branch.

Congressional coverage is frequently not as useful to the public as it could be. In the early stages of the legislative process, when there is still time for citizens to influence a bill, congressional coverage tends to be sparse despite the fact that members of Congress try hardest at that time to get media attention for their version of legislative proposals. Coverage usually focuses on final action after the shape of the legislation is already firm.[29] Citizens then learn what the new policies are without being exposed to the pros and cons and the political interplay that led to the ultimate compromise.[30] Live television coverage of congressional sessions is changing this tradition and is making Congress more vulnerable to pressures from constituents and interest groups.

Fearing that legislative floor sessions would present an unedifying, boring spectacle, Congress resisted live radio and television coverage of most sessions until the late 1970s. Prior to 1979 only selected committee hearings were televised, primarily those involving spicy topics such as labor racketeering, communists in government, or high-level corruption. In 1979 the House of Representatives lifted the prohibition on televising its floor sessions. The action was prompted in part by the desire to counterbalance the political advantages reaped by the executive branch from heavy media attention. The rules for coverage by the House-run closed circuit system are strict: only the member speaking may be filmed, *not* the listeners, unless the Speaker decrees otherwise. This stipulation bars the public from seeing the typically near-empty House chamber and inattentive members. Commercial, cable, and public television systems have access to House broadcasts but rarely cover them, except for live gavel-to-gavel coverage by C-SPAN. In 1986 the Senate finally followed suit and permitted live coverage of its proceedings. It was prodded by Sen. Robert Byrd's (D-W. Va.) concern that the

Senate was "fast becoming the invisible half of Congress," compared to the White House and the House of Representatives.[31]

Unlike the presidency, Congress has rarely become a first-rate "show" for the American public, although its media coverage is vital for inside-the-Beltway Washington politics. Representatives themselves are among the most avid watchers of House coverage because the television cameras permit them to monitor sessions that they would otherwise miss. Now they can keep up on floor action and issues reported by committees other than their own. Members of Congress use their appearances to create favorable images for themselves and their pet political projects among congressional and executive branch constituencies and the elite media.

Brief, quotable statements made by members in time to appear on the evening news have multiplied. Some members have claimed that recent sharp increases in the time spent to pass legislation are largely due to television coverage. More members want to be heard and they are likely to take more extreme positions because the media tend to focus on such confrontations.[32] The added publicity also may make incumbent representatives even more unbeatable at the polls than they are now. Broadcasting may make it more difficult for congressional leaders to keep the voices of dissident members muffled or to hide pork barrel legislation and other congressional mischief. It may be harder to reach legislative compromises once representatives have publicly committed themselves to definite positions. However, there is little solid proof thus far that television coverage has harmed consensus-building in the chamber.

Congress on the Web

Congress entered the Internet scene in earnest in 1995 with a formal Web site that features all texts of bills, resolutions, and amendments introduced on the House floor, along with brief, nontechnical descriptions of the contents of these documents.[33] The Web site also provides a minute-by-minute summary of floor action. The actual contents of debates can be monitored on an on-line version of the *Congressional Record*. The Senate now has a similar Web site. In addition, the majority of the members of Congress have their own Web sites that vary greatly in comprehensiveness, quality, and timeliness. Besides featuring the member's vital statistics and major accomplishments—but not failures—most sites also link to the Web sites of committees on which the member serves and describe committee actions and the current status of specific bills. This type of ongoing coverage is extremely useful for lobby groups and other Congress-watchers. It has enhanced their ability to make themselves heard at key junctures in the legislative process. The Web site and its links are also a gold mine of information for reporters who want to incorporate detailed current information into their stories. However, a few sites, such as the Legislative Information System, which offers research material on legislation, and sites operated by each party and its subdivisions, are purely for internal use by members of Congress.

E-mail has become the most prolific Internet message system linking Congress with its various publics. But, like the multiplying buckets in Paul Dukat's "Sorcerer's Apprentice," the floodtide of e-mails threatens to overwhelm congressional navigation resources. Given their limited staffs, members of Congress find it impossible to cope promptly and adequately with e-mail from constituents, not to mention e-mailings from outsiders, including spammers, and from computer hackers who generate mail intended to clog communication arteries. Efficient electronic sorting and automatic response protocols ameliorate the problem but do not resolve it.

Writing Congress Stories

Newspeople from the general press who are assigned to the congressional beat use their normal criteria of newsworthiness and gatekeeping to decide who and what will be covered and who and what will be ignored. Exciting, novel, or controversial topics that can be made personally relevant to the public and be simply presented have precedence over recurrent complex and mundane problems, such as congressional reorganizations or the annual farm bill. Orderly, dispassionate debate usually is passed over in favor of purple rhetoric and wild accusations that can produce catchy headlines. Heated confrontations are more likely to occur in the more intimate committee hearings than in full sessions. Accordingly, committee hearings attract most extensive coverage, particularly on television.

Because congressional coverage is a regular beat, daily press briefings are conducted by the leaders of each chamber. Major media organizations such as the *Washington Post* and the *New York Times,* major newspaper chains such as Gannett, Hearst, and Knight, and the television networks and wire services have full-time reporters covering Congress. Some of these reporters are specialists in various areas of policy. Some wire service reporters, for example, concentrate on news of interest to specific regions such as the West or South. There are also Washington "stringer" bureaus whose reporters serve assorted subscriber news services throughout the country. Specialized news services such as Congressional Quarterly and two highly competitive newspapers—*Roll Call* and *The Hill*—cover the congressional beat in detail for particular audiences. The beat is also covered by faxed newsletters and several on-line publications. Among these, *Thomas,* the Web site of the Library of Congress, is most comprehensive;

most congressional Web sites link to it. *Thomas* (http://thomas.loc.gov/) provides much information that is sparse on the Web sites of individual representatives. For example, it contains information about bill sponsorship and the texts of otherwise unrecorded speeches. In all, more than seven thousand correspondents are accredited to the press galleries in the House and Senate. The ratio of journalists to senators thus is seventy-one to one; for representatives it is sixteen to one.[34]

Congressional press releases and written reports provide news to media sources that lack regular reporters on Capitol Hill. These documents are prepared and distributed by congressional press secretaries because wire service reporters are unable to attend the many hearings occurring simultaneously. Press releases enable members of Congress to tell their stories in their own words. They often use this opportunity to highlight problem areas, hoping that news media publicity will shame Congress into action.[35] Although all representatives now assign staff to serve the needs of the press, fewer than ten percent of House members receive weekly coverage on national television. The rest appear rarely or not at all.[36]

Senators generally receive considerably more press coverage than do representatives, even though an equal number of reporters cover both houses. On network television, stories about senators outnumber those about representatives almost seven to one, probably because senators have greater prominence, prestige, and publicity resources; their larger constituencies also make them of interest to a wider audience. In general, high media visibility for senators as well as representatives hinges on serving in important leadership positions and being a congressional veteran. By contrast, sponsoring legislation or service on important committees matters little. *Who* one is obviously counts more than *what* one does. In practice, this means that more than half of the congressional membership receives no national television exposure at all. A mere twenty members of the Senate garner the lion's share of attention.[37]

Unlike the president, neither senators nor representatives enjoy automatic coverage of whatever they say and do, even though they issue frequent press releases and call occasional news conferences. However, on certain topics, such as tax policy or investigation of executive activities, congressional spokespersons, rather than the president, are routinely sought out. In addition, many members of Congress receive regular local coverage through their own news columns or radio or television programs. They usually find their relations with the local media far more congenial than relations with a national press corps, which cares little about focusing on the problems of particular congressional districts. Local media depend on senators and representatives for local angles to national stories because local slants make these stories more attractive to the target audiences.

Because their Washington-based senators and representatives are ideal sources, local newspeople are loath to criticize them. The Washington press corps lacks such qualms. During the first year and a half of the 103rd Congress, during the Clinton presidency, 64 percent of all congressional stories broadcast on national news were negative, with the Senate earning a 64 percent negative rating and the House a 61 percent negative rating. Congress as an institution received the most hostile coverage (68 percent), whereas 61 percent of the stories about members were negative. Overall, Congress's press was a shade worse than the president's press during this time period.[38]

Functions of Media

The functions performed by the *national* media for Congress and by Congress for the national media parallel press–presidency relations. However, there are major qualitative differences in the relationship. Neither Congress nor the media need the services of the other as much as the presidency needs the press. The national media can afford to alienate some legislators without losing direct access to congressional news. Similarly, except when the passage of major controversial laws is involved, legislators can ignore national publicity and rely instead on publicity in their own districts. News items about national events and national public opinion are also somewhat less important to most members of Congress than to the president. The home media, rather than national news providers, are particularly important to legislators as sources of news relevant for their own constituents and as channels for transmitting messages to the home district while they are in Washington.

National as well as local media provide senators and representatives with forums to express their views on political issues and to attract public support for themselves and their causes. Publicity is especially important for minority party leaders, who may need the media to pressure an unresponsive majority to accede to their concerns. However, most members cannot use "outsider strategies" as publicity effects of the out-of-power party are called, because they rarely receive enough coverage to greatly enhance their legislative effectiveness or chances at reelection. Once members achieve visibility, their fame often grows by its own momentum. They become regulars on interview shows, and their opinions are solicited when national issues are debated. For most members, however, media attention carries few benefits and has several drawbacks; for example, elected officials become more visible targets for lobby groups and their exposure provides ammunition for rival candidates during the next election campaign. For members of Congress who do not need nationwide attention to achieve their legislative goals, favorable media coverage in their districts is the key objective. Local coverage lets their constituents know what they are doing and paves their way for reelection. Many members also communicate through newsletters and individual correspondence sent to selected constituents. Some prepare cable television programs for their district or transmit carefully chosen video excerpts from committee meetings to the media in their home districts. Still others, eager to push their legislative agendas, write op-ed pieces for the local and national media.

A Cautious Relationship

Just as the functions that media perform are similar for the executive and legislative branches, so is the love-hate relationship. But it, too, is less ardent for Congress, even though mutual recriminations are plentiful. Senators and representatives compete with peers for media attention and bemoan the lack of coverage for their pet projects and pronouncements. They complain that reporters treat them as if they are scoundrels conspiring to defraud the public and resent the cross-examinations that reporters love to conduct with an air of infallibility. They charge and can prove that the media emphasize trivia, scandals, internal dissent, and official misconduct, but often ignore congressional consensus and the passage of significant legislation. They blame the media for the declining prestige of Congress. Still, despite ample negative coverage, the media generally treat congressional leaders and Congress with a fair amount of deference and respect. Individual presidents have been more bloodied by adverse publicity than have individual members of the House. As Michael Robinson concluded from a detailed analysis of the impact of media coverage on Congress, the media have fostered a stronger presidency but weaker presidents, and a weaker Congress but more durable representatives.[39]

Journalists, in turn, complain with justification about legislators' efforts to manage the news through their professional publicity staffs. They point to members' lack of candor and to their exclusion of media personnel from many congressional meetings and executive sessions. Broadcasters also resent the strict controls placed on their coverage of congressional sessions. They are barred from taping their own stories and are limited in the subjects they can photograph.

But senators and representatives realize that they need the media for information and for the publicity that is crucial to passing or defeating legislation. They know that the media will discreetly ignore their personal foibles so long as no official wrongdoing is involved. Newspeople, in turn, realize that they need individual legislators for information about congressional activities and as a counterfoil and source of leaks to check the executive branch. Members are valuable for inside comments that can personalize otherwise dull stories. Congress often creates story topics for the media by investigating dramatic ongoing problems like auto or aircraft safety. A congressional inquiry may be the catalyst that turns an everyday event into a newsworthy item. The story then may ride the crest of publicity for quite some time, creating its own fresh and reportable events until it recedes into limbo once more. Newspeople do not want to dry up these sources; nor do media enterprises want to forgo the financial rewards generated by paid campaign commercials.

Congress and Communications Policy

The media, particularly radio and television, are aware of the power Congress has over regulatory legislation. In the past Congress made little use of its power to legislate communications policy, viewing it as a hornet's nest of political conflict best left alone. The major exception was passage of the Communications Act of 1934 and its 1996 sequel and of supplementary laws dealing with technical innovations and other changes in the mass communication scene. Whenever strong, unified pressures from industry or consumer groups develop and overcome the strong resistance to change in this controversial policy field with multiple major stake holders, Congress's powers to legislate communications policy become extremely important. As the sixty-two-year time gap between major communications laws demonstrates, there usually is a vacuum in both policy formulation and oversight of administration that neither the president nor the FCC has attempted to fill.[40] Communications industry representatives occasionally jump into the breach. They are in a strong position to push their ideas because they enjoy a near monopoly over the basic information needed for making policy.

The communications subcommittees of the Commerce, Science, and Transportation Committee in the Senate and of the Energy and Commerce Committee in the House also influence communications policy largely through the power of investigation. The FCC has been investigated more frequently than most regulatory bodies. In fact since 1970 more than fifty different congressional committees and subcommittees have reviewed various FCC activities, but there have been few dramatic results. Investigations have included reviews of specific FCC actions, studies of FCC operations and structures, examinations of broad policy issues such as the impact of television's portrayal of the aged or of alcohol and drug abuse, and studies of corruption in television game shows. The appropriations committees have wielded their power over the FCC's purse in a desultory way. They occasionally have denied funds for the commission or explicitly directed which particular programs should be funded.[41] However, monetary control became stricter when Congress changed the FCC in 1982 from the status of a permanently authorized agency to one requiring biennial renewal.

Although the Senate has seldom used confirmation hearings to impress its views on new FCC commissioners, this does not mean that the views of powerful senators have been ignored. Prospective commissioners are likely to study past confirmation hearings carefully and take their cues from them. Most presidential nominees have been confirmed. Appointments are usually made to reward the politically faithful. Although congressional control over the FCC has generally been light, there is always the possibility of stricter control. All the parties interested in communications policy, including the White House and the courts, pay deference to that possibility.

Congressional control over the media also includes matters such as postal rates and subsidies, legislation on permissible mergers and chain control of papers, and laws designed to keep failing newspapers alive. Copyright laws, which affect print and electronic media productions, are involved, too. So are policies and regulations about telecommunication satellites, broadcast spectrum allocations, and cable television. The vast, congressionally guided changes in the telephone industry are yet another area of major concern to media interests.

Laws regulating media procedures occasionally have a strong impact on media content and policies. For instance, FCC encouragement of the diversification of radio programs was largely responsible for the development of a sizable number of FM rock music stations that provide alternatives to more conventional programs. Congressional scrutiny of documentaries may chill investigative reporting. Congress probed the circumstances surrounding a documentary on drug use at a major university because the events were allegedly staged. It also looked into the accuracy of charges of illicit public relations activity by the Pentagon. Congressional failure to act may also have far-reaching consequences for the mass media. For instance, as long as Congress did not regulate cable television, this medium was left under control of the FCC, the courts, and various state and local governments. Congress has passed some laws—for the rest, the FCC, courts, and states take over.

Summary

In this chapter we have examined the relationship between the media and the presidency and Congress. Coverage is ample, but the goals of the media differ from those of government officials. Officials want stories that report about them and their work accurately and favorably. They also want to dominate the news-sifting process so that published news mirrors their sense of what is important and unimportant. Newspeople, however, want stories that are newsworthy, judged by the usual criteria. They believe that their publics are more interested in exciting events and human-interest tales than in academic discussions of public policies, their historical antecedents, and their projected impact expressed in statistics. Newspeople also feel a special mission, like Shakespeare's Mark Antony, "to bury Caesar, not to praise him." And, like Brutus, they claim that their criticism is not disloyalty. They do not love the government less; they only love the nation more.

Each side in this tug of war uses wiles and ruses as well as clout to have its own way. The outcome is a see-saw contest in which both sides score victories and suffer defeats, but each is most attuned to its own failures rather than to its victories. The public interest is served in equally uneven fashion. If we equate the public interest with a maximum of intelligible information about important issues and events, media presentations fall short. But coverage is good in that it is continuous, often well informed, with sufficient attention to audience appeal to make dry information palatable. Investigative reporting has brought to light many shortcomings and scandals that otherwise might have remained hidden. The fear of exposure by the media has undoubtedly kept government officials from straying into many questionable ventures, although this effect is hard to document. On the negative side, fear of media coverage and publicity has probably inhibited desirable actions.

Because the contacts between officials of the national government and the media are so constant, a formal institutional structure has been established to handle these interactions. The fairly elaborate setup at the presidential level and the simpler arrangements for Congress have been described. We also have indicated some of the problems that newspeople face in covering a flood tide of complex news expeditiously, accurately, and with a modicum of critical detachment and analysis.

Problems in communications policymaking remain. All three branches of government shape communications policy, but there is little coordination among them. Even within the executive and legislative branches, control is dispersed among so many different committees and agencies that drift rather than direction has resulted. Few major policy decisions have been made except in times of crisis, and even then the weaknesses of government structures have made it easy for industry spokespersons to dominate decision making.

The government's weakness in this area may be a blessing in disguise and in the spirit of the First Amendment. Because the Constitution commands that Congress shall make no law abridging the freedom of the press, it may be well to keep all communications policymaking to the barest minimum. As Chief Justice John Marshall warned early in the nation's history, the power to regulate is the power to destroy.[42] Policymaking and regulation overlap. A uniform, well-articulated communications policy, however beneficial it may seem to many people, still puts the government imprint indelibly on the flow of information.

Notes

1. Naftali Bendavid, "Clinton's Legacy: The Personal Presidency," *Chicago Tribune,* January 14, 2001.
2. Joe S. Foote, *Television Access and Political Power: The Networks, the Presidency, and the "Loyal Opposition"* (New York: Praeger, 1990), 135, reports that just before President Carter publicly announced that he would recognize the People's Republic of China, he invited the anchors of the three major networks to Washington to break the news to them first. "This incident was tacit recognition that network anchors had assumed a status comparable to congressional leaders for whom this special type of briefing was usually reserved. The media stars had become a powerful force who deserved special handling."
3. David L. Paletz and K. Kendall Guthrie, "The Three Faces of Ronald Reagan," *Journal of Communication* 37 (autumn 1987): 7–23.
4. Presidential communication in general is discussed by John Tebbel and Sarah Miles Watts, *The Press and the Presidency* (New York: Oxford University Press, 1985); and Barbara Hinckley, *The Symbolic Presidency: How Presidents Portray Themselves* (New York: Routledge, 1990). Also see Samuel Kernell, *Going Public: New Strategies of Presidential Leadership,* 3d ed. (Washington, D.C.: CQ Press, 1997). Books about the relations of individual presidents with the press include Frederic T. Smoller, *The Six O'Clock Presidency: A Theory of Presidential Press Relations in the Age of Television* (New York: Praeger, 1990); and Carolyn Smith, *Presidential Press Conferences: A Critical Approach* (New York: Praeger, 1990). Also see Mark J. Rozell, *The Press and the Ford Presidency* (Ann Arbor: University of Michigan Press, 1992).
5. John Kenneth Galbraith, famed economist, quoted in William L. Rivers, *The Other Government: Power and the Washington Media* (New York: University Books, 1982), 19.
6. Quoted in Timothy E. Cook, *Governing with the News: The News Media as a Political Institution* (Chicago: University of Chicago Press, 1998), 131.
7. Quoted in S. Robert Lichter and Linda S. Lichter, eds., "Bork: Decline and Fall," *Media Monitor* 1 (October 1987): 5.
8. Martin Linsky, *Impact: How the Press Affects Federal Policymaking* (New York: Norton, 1986), 37–38.
9. *Media Monitor* 8(4) (July/August 1994): 3; also Cook, *Governing with the News,* chap. 6.

10. William J. Small, *To Kill a Messenger* (New York: Hastings House, 1970).
11. *Kennedy and the Press: The News Conferences* (New York: Crowell, 1965), 239.
12. Refusal problems are discussed in Matthew A. Baum and Samuel Kernell, "Has Cable Ended the Golden Age of Presidential Television?" *American Political Science Review* 93(1) (1999): 99–114.
13. Tom Hundley, "Uranium Hysteria Sweeps Europe," *Chicago Tribune,* January 28, 2001.
14. Michael Baruch Grossman and Martha Joynt Kumar, *Portraying the President: The White House and the News Media* (Baltimore: Johns Hopkins University Press, 1980); and Martha Joynt Kumar, *Wired for Sound and Pictures: The President and White House Communications Policies* (Baltimore: Johns Hopkins University Press, forthcoming).
15. "The Disappearing Honeymoon: TV News Coverage of President George W. Bush's First 100 Days," *Media Monitor* 15(3) (May/June 2001): 1–5; Committee of Concerned Journalists, "The First 100 Days: How Bush Versus Clinton Fared in the Press," http://www.journalism.org/publ_research/100days1.html (May 2001).
16. Smoller, *The Six O'Clock Presidency,* 61–77.
17. Michael Margolis and David Resnick, *Politics as Usual: The Cyberspace "Revolution"* (Thousand Oaks, Calif.: Sage, 2000), 79–93.
18. John Anthony Maltese, *Spin Control: The White House Office of Communications and the Management of Presidential News,* 2d ed. (Chapel Hill: University of North Carolina Press, 1994), chap. 8; also see Martha Joynt Kumar, "The Office of the Press Secretary," Report No. 31 and "The Office of Communications," Report No. 33 in the White House 2001 Project White House Interview Program (Washington, D.C., January 2001) at http://whitehouse2001.org.
19. Martha Joynt Kumar, "The Office of Communications," Report No. 33 in the White House 2001 Project White House Interview Program (Washington, D.C., January 2001), 5, at http://whitehouse2001.org.
20. Maltese, *Spin Control,* p. 253.
21. Ibid., p. 6.
22. Stephen Hess, "A New Survey of the White House Press Corps," *Presidential Studies Quarterly* 22(2) (spring 1992): 311–321.
23. Smith, *Presidential Press Conferences,* 41.
24. For a thorough analysis of presidential press conferences, see Smith, *Presidential Press Conferences;* Blaire Atherton French, *The Presidential Press Conference: Its History and Role in the American Political System* (Washington, D.C.: University Press of America, 1982); and Frank Cormier, James Deakin, and Helen Thomas, *The White House Press on the Presidency: News Management and Co-Option* (Lanham, Md.: University Press of America, 1983).
25. Steven R. Weisman, "Reagan, Annoyed by News Leaks, Tells Staff To Limit Press Relations," *New York Times,* January 11, 1983. For a list of measures taken by the Reagan administration to stop leaks, see Ronald Berkman and Laura W. Kitch, *Politics in the Media Age* (New York: McGraw-Hill, 1986), 195–197. The Bush administration tried equally unsuccessfully to stop further leaks following the Thomas affair.

26. Robert O. Blanchard, ed., *Congress and the News Media* (New York: Hastings House, 1974), 105.

27. Kathleen Hall Jamieson, *Eloquence in an Electronic Age: The Transformation of Political Speechmaking* (New York: Oxford University Press, 1988), 14.

28. Stephen Hess, *The Washington Reporters* (Washington, D.C.: Brookings Institution, 1981), 99. The figures are based on 921 newspaper and 87 television stories.

29. Ronald D. Elving, "Making News, Making Law," *Media Studies Journal* 10 (winter 1996): 50.

30. Hess, *The Washington Reporters*, 104–105; and Karen M. Kedrowski, *Media Entrepreneurs and the Media Enterprise in the U.S. Congress* (Cresskill, N.J.: Hampton Press, 1996), chap. 5.

31. Quoted in Steven V. Roberts, "Senators Squint into a Future under TV's Gaze," *New York Times,* February 4, 1986.

32. Timothy E. Cook, *Making Laws and Making News: Media Strategies in the U.S. House of Representatives* (Washington, D.C.: Brookings Institution, 1989), and Kedrowski, *Media Entrepreneurs,* provide the most complete analysis of congressional newsmaking.

33. Diana Owen, Richard Davis, and Vincent James Strickler, "Congress and the Internet," *Press/Politics* 4(2) (1999): 10–29.

34. "Media and Congress," *Media Studies Journal* 10(1) (winter 1996): 12; and Stephen Hess, *Live from Capitol Hill: Studies of Congress and the Media* (Washington, D.C.: Brookings Institution, 1991), 117. On pages 33–61, Hess presents a content analysis of media coverage of Congress; also see Cook, *Making Laws and Making News,* 57–70; and Michael J. Robinson and Kevin R. Appel, "Network News Coverage of Congress," *Political Science Quarterly* 94 (Fall 1979): 407–418. For an excellent discussion of congressional press galleries, see Melissa Merson, "Big Picture and Local Angle," *Media Studies Journal* 10(1) (winter 1996): 55–66.

35. Patrick J. Sellers, "Congress and the News Media: Manipulating the Message in the U.S. Congress," *Press/Politics* 5(1) (2000): 22–31.

36. *Media Monitor* 8(5) (September/October 1994): 2.

37. Ibid.; Timothy E. Cook, "House Members as National Newsmakers: The Effects of Televising Congress," *Legislative Studies Quarterly* 11 (summer 1986): 203–226; and Stephen Hess, *The Ultimate Insiders: U.S. Senators and the National Media* (Washington, D.C.: Brookings Institution, 1986). Also see Hess, *Live from Capitol Hill,* 55–58, and Kedrowski, *Media Entrepreneurs,* chaps. 5, 8.

38. *Media Monitor* 8(5) (September/October 1994): 2.

39. Michael J. Robinson, "Three Faces of Congressional Media," in *The New Congress,* Thomas E. Mann and Norman J. Ornstein, eds. (Washington, D.C.: American Enterprise Institute, 1981).

40. For a history on the politics of communications policy formulation, see Erwin G. Krasnow, Lawrence D. Longley, and Herbert A. Terry, *The Politics of Broadcast Regulation,* 3d ed. (New York: St. Martin's, 1982), 87–132; and Robert Britt, *The Irony of Regulatory Reform: The Deregulation of American Telecommunications* (New York: Oxford University Press, 1989), chap. 6; also Patricia Aufderheide, *Communications Policy and the Public Interest* (New York: Guilford Press, 1999), chaps. 1, 5.

41. Krasnow, Longley, and Terry, *The Politics of Broadcast Regulation*, 99.
42. *McCulloch v. Maryland*, 17 U.S. (4 Wheat.) 316 (1819).

Readings

Cook, Timothy E. *Governing with the News: The News Media as a Political Institution.* Chicago: University of Chicago Press, 1998.

————. *Making Laws and Making News: Media Strategies in the U.S. House of Representatives.* Washington, D.C.: Brookings Institution, 1989.

Hess, Stephen. *Live from Capitol Hill: Studies of Congress and the Media.* Washington, D.C.: Brookings Institution, 1991.

————. *The Ultimate Insiders: U.S. Senators and the National Media.* Washington, D.C.: Brookings Institution, 1986.

Kedrowski, Karen M. *Media Entrepreneurs and the Media Enterprise in the U.S. Congress.* Cresskill, N.J.: Hampton Press, 1996.

Kernell, Samuel. *Going Public: New Strategies of Presidential Leadership,* 3d ed. Washington, D.C.: CQ Press, 1997.

Kumar, Martha Joynt. *Wired for Sound and Pictures: The President and White House Communications Policies.* Baltimore: Johns Hopkins University Press, forthcoming.

Maltese, John Anthony. *Spin Control: The White House Office of Communications and the Management of Presidential News,* 2d ed. Chapel Hill: University of North Carolina Press, 1994.

Smith, Carolyn. *Presidential Press Conferences: A Critical Approach.* New York: Praeger, 1990.

Covering the Justice System and State and Local News

IN HIS CLASSIC STUDY OF MEDIA AND PUBLIC OPINION, the renowned American journalist Walter Lippmann likened the performance of the media to "the beam of a searchlight that moves restlessly about, bringing one episode and then another out of darkness into vision." The media were not a "mirror on the world," as others had claimed. Lippmann concluded, "Men cannot do the work of the world by this light alone. They cannot govern society by episodes, incidents, and eruptions."[1]

What Lippmann observed and concluded in 1922 is as true today as it was then. The media provide spotty coverage, leaving much of the political landscape obscured. The political life of the institutions that will be covered in this chapter—the courts, state governments, and local governments—have been in the shadows of media coverage. We know too little about them, and so it is difficult for us to become informed citizens. Just like journalists, social scientists have largely ignored these less glamorous areas of politics. Fortunately, that is beginning to change.

The Media and the Courts

Of the three branches of the national government, only the judiciary has been sparsely covered. As Table 9-1 showed, this is the case even for the highest court in the nation. The pattern of sparse coverage is evident when one looks at individual networks, as Table 9-3 suggests, as well as when one scans major newspapers. For example, between July 1999 and June 2000, ABC devoted 4 hours and 39 minutes to presidential stories,

2 hours and 45 minutes to congressional stories, and 46 minutes to stories about the Supreme Court.

Federal-level judges are rarely in the limelight. They infrequently grant interviews, almost never hold news conferences, and generally do not seek or welcome media attention, primarily because they fear that their impartiality and mystique might be compromised. Remoteness enhances the impression that judges are a breed apart, doling out justice to lesser mortals. At the state and local levels, where many judges are elected rather than appointed to office, media coverage is somewhat more common, and the aura of judicial majesty recedes accordingly.

The immunity from personal media scrutiny that U.S. Supreme Court justices enjoy does not extend to the hearings conducted prior to their appointment to the Court. These hearings, and the public debate they engender, can be highly acrimonious. Examples include the 1987 political battle that scuttled the nomination of conservative judge Robert Bork and the soap opera hearings about alleged sexual improprieties committed by judge Clarence Thomas, whose appointment was ultimately approved in 1991. Because dramatic hearings have great audience appeal, they are now often broadcast live by Court TV, a cable channel that specializes in reporting dramatic judicial proceedings, along with commentary by selected pundits.

Hearings also demonstrate how pressure groups use the media to influence judicial politics. For instance, during the confirmation hearings for Bork and Thomas, liberal as well as conservative groups mounted a massive media campaign to gain publicity for their perceptions of the merits of these appointments. Spokespersons for groups such as the American Civil Liberties Union (ACLU), the National Association for the Advancement of Colored People (NAACP), the National Organization for Women (NOW), and the American Federation of Labor and Congress of Industrial Organizations (AFL-CIO) spoke for the liberal camp, and conservatives lobbied through Pat Robertson's Christian Coalition and the Conservative Victory Committee. Tactics included television and radio advertisements, talk-show appearances, essays appearing in the editorial opinion sections of newspapers, the wining and dining of media personnel, and careful research and coordination work.

The institutional aspects of the federal courts also receive comparatively little coverage. There are exceptions, of course. The courts' difficulties in coping with the flood of legal actions, the problems of disparate sentencing policies, and the flaws in the correction system have all been the subject of sporadic media investigations. Speeches by Supreme Court justices to public bodies such as the American Bar Association have been telecast and reported nationwide. Chief Justice Warren E. Burger even consented to regular questioning about his annual State of the Judiciary speech. The news conference before the speech remained off the record, however, and the chief justice could not be quoted directly.

Although judges and court systems at the federal level are not very newsworthy because they generally do not become embroiled in open battles about policies, their work—judicial decisions—does make the news. This is particularly true of U.S. Supreme Court decisions, which frequently have major consequences for the political system. For example, *Brown v. Board of Education* (1954) was widely publicized because it declared unconstitutional the separate schooling of children of different races, and *Roe v. Wade* (1973) and *Planned Parenthood v. Casey* (1992) received ample media attention because they involved the emotional issue of a woman's right to have an abortion.[2] The Court continues to be in the news whenever it rules on issues that are likely to have an immediate pronounced impact on the lives of average Americans. But the focus of news stories is limited to the formal decision. The decision-making process remains largely shrouded in secrecy.[3]

Impact of Coverage

Publicity about Supreme Court decisions is very important because it informs public officials at all government levels, as well as the general public, about the substance of selected decisions. A small corps of reporters is responsible for choosing the decisions to be covered. At the Supreme Court, full- and part-time reporters combined number about fifty people. Of these only a dozen correspondents for major wire services and for major newspapers are full-time.[4]

Supreme Court coverage is difficult. The justices usually announce multiple decisions on a single day, forcing reporters to digest voluminous and often contradictory opinions rapidly. This must be done without help from the justices who authored the opinions. Reporters' deadlines may be only minutes away and the news may be stale after more than twenty-four hours have elapsed. Advice from outside commentators, including legal experts, is usually unavailable initially because such experts are not allowed to preview the opinions. Leaks of advance information are rare. The Supreme Court does have a press office, which provides some reference materials and bare-bones records of the Court's activities. But it refuses to provide interpretations of the justices' decisions in laypersons' terms, fearing entanglement in legal controversies. However, brief analyses of important pending cases are available to the media through publications sponsored by the legal profession.[5]

Because of the shortage of skilled legal reporters, much reporting on the courts—even at the Supreme Court level—is imprecise and sometimes even wrong. Justice Felix Frankfurter once complained that editors who would never consider covering a baseball game through a reporter unfamiliar with the sport regularly assigned reporters unfamiliar with the law to cover the Supreme Court. This situation has improved considerably in recent years, but it is far from cured. Many editors do not want to assign reporters whose knowledge of fine points of the law might make their stories too technical and dull.

Two landmark decisions—*Engel v. Vitale,* which outlawed school prayer, and *Baker v. Carr,* which invalidated many electoral district boundaries— provide examples of faulty reporting.[6] Stories about these two decisions in sixty-three metropolitan daily papers featured misleading headlines and sketchy and uninformative coverage.[7] Ill-informed statements by well-known people opposing the Court's decisions made up the major part of the stories. Several stories contained serious errors. For instance, the wrong clause of the Constitution was cited as the basis for the decision outlawing classroom prayer in public schools. Arguments made in lower courts were erroneously attributed to Supreme Court justices. Moreover, the media covered the prayer decision more heavily because it was relatively easy to grasp and presented an emotionally stirring story, although the duller reapportionment decision was of far greater political significance.

The media completely ignore many important decisions. They privilege social policy issues, like civil rights, school prayer, and abortion, and little else.[8] During one typical Supreme Court term even the *New York Times* failed to mention one-quarter of all written opinions. In the stories about the remaining 112 opinions, 49 lacked essential information. The *Detroit News* failed to mention 70 percent of the written opinions.[9] However, when the print media decide to focus on a case, coverage can be excellent, including commentary on legal issues and the long-range implications of the case.[10] A study of network coverage of the 1978 *Bakke* racial discrimination case and the 1989 *Webster* abortion rights case showed that three out of four news stories about these prominent cases featured interpretations along with the factual account.[11]

The thrust of judicial complaints about sketchy, inaccurate, out-of-context reporting is the same as for coverage of the presidency and Congress. However, reporting of Court activities seems to be more superficial and flawed than its presidential and congressional counterparts.[12] The reasons are not difficult to understand. The volume of decisions is large, frequently clustering near the end of the annual term. The subject matter is often highly technical, and is hard for reporters to understand and make understandable. With notable exceptions, stories about judicial decisions lack the potential to become exciting, front-page news. They are hard to boil down into catchy phrases and clichés. They rarely lend themselves to exciting visual coverage. The Supreme Court beat tends to be understaffed. All of these factors make it difficult for the assigned reporters to prepare interesting, well-researched accounts.

The information supplied to the public, though inadequate for providing important insights into the law and the judicial process, usually sustains respect for the judiciary and compliance with its rulings. This is crucial because the Court lacks the power and institutional structure to enforce its decisions. Most people are poorly informed about the Supreme Court, but they still hold its work in high esteem.[13] Occasionally Court publicity has the opposite effect, however. For instance, Justice Tom Clark, one of the participants in the 1962 prayer decision, complained that misunderstanding of *Engel v. Vitale* made this ruling unpopular. He blamed inadequate reporting for confusing the public, failures to comply with the decision, and an abortive movement to nullify it through a constitutional amendment.

Public reactions to Supreme Court decisions may affect future decisions of the Court because justices are influenced in their work by what they read and hear from the media. Media reports of crime waves, or price gouging by business, or public opposition to aid for parochial schools are likely to set boundaries to judicial policy making.[14] This makes it tragic that much of the reporting leaves the public unprepared to make sound assessments of the Court's rulings. Recent research provides evidence that news stories can influence court personnel. For example, the amount of publicity given to a crime influences prosecutors. When there is little publicity, prosecutors are less likely to press for a trial of the case and more likely to agree to a plea-bargain settlement. In federal murder trials, more pretrial publicity for defendants tends to be followed by longer sentences.[15] The effects of media coverage tend to persist for subsequent similar cases.

News about Crime and the Justice System

Publications of decisions by the Supreme Court and lower courts are by no means the only significant news generated about the judiciary. General news about crime and the work of the justice system are also important in creating images of the quality of public justice. Here a plentiful media diet is available, especially on local television news where nearly 16 percent of the coverage is devoted to the topic. Business and consumer news issues receive less than one-third as much attention.[16] Like stories about other government activities, crime and justice system stories tend to focus on sensational events, often at the expense of significant trends and problems in the legal system that might benefit from greater public attention.[17]

The nature of crime news coverage and its prevalence in the media, particularly television, has long been a matter of concern to public officials and

**"In lieu of a trial jury, my client has elected
to plea bargain with the media."**

the public. It is widely believed that current coverage practices deflect attention from the social causes of crime and the policies needed to curb it. Sensational stories lead to exaggerated fear of crime because the focus is on the most violent incidents, which in real life constitute only a tiny portion of crime. As Table 4-4 shows, nearly 43 percent of the crime stories in the *Chicago Tribune* in 2000 dealt with murder or sexual assaults in a year when these crimes constituted just slightly over 1 percent of the actual crimes in the city. By contrast, white-collar crime, which is widely prevalent and often threatens public health and safety, received little coverage, which concealed its seriousness as a social problem. Many experts on criminal behavior contend that extensive graphic coverage of crime can glamorize it and thereby encourage imitation by would-be offenders. News stories that focus selectively on sensational aspects of the case can also mislead the public—and possibly jurors—about who is guilty and who is innocent. When that happens, guilty defendants may escape justice and innocent ones may be convicted.

Probably the most graphic aspect of the "tabloidization" of crime news is overemphasis on crimes involving celebrities or crimes that seem particularly heinous. The total amount of coverage is disproportionate, especially since much of it is little more than a repeated spinning out of insignificant, often irrelevant details. Coverage is also disproportionate compared to other important stories that need attention. For example, a Lexis-Nexis search of sixty-five major newspapers showed that there were 22,610 stories about the murder case involving football legend O.J. Simpson between 1994 and 1997,[18] including 1,471 front-page stories. During the same period, the three national networks aired 1,225 Simpson stories, roughly four times the number of stories given to Medicare and welfare policies combined. The Simpson celebrity crime story was topped only by reports about the investigation of President Clinton's relations with intern Monica Lewinsky that totaled 25,975 stories in the sixty-five papers in just one year (1998), including 1,959 front page stories.

Such stories are bonanzas for media enterprises because they sharply increase audience size and with it rates that can be charged for advertising. CNN, for example, more than tripled its average ratings at the height of the Simpson trial and more than quadrupled them during the peak phases of the Lewinsky affair.[19] A Web browser search in November 1998 found 498,932 Web pages on Netscape mentioning the Simpson trial and 622,079 mentioning either Monica Lewinsky or Paula Jones, two principals in the Clinton saga. No wonder, then, that 97 percent of the public were familiar with these cases, compared with 12 percent who could identify William Rehnquist as the Chief Justice of the U.S. Supreme Court.

If there is widespread agreement that current patterns of crime news coverage are excessive and undesirable, why do they continue in daily newspapers and on national and local television throughout the country? There are several reasons. Most importantly, despite their complaints, audiences flock to crime news, partly because it involves personal security but mostly to satisfy a hunger for excitement. This has been the case since the birth of tabloid newspapers more than 150 years ago. When crime news makes huge front-page headlines, paper sales rise sharply and audience ratings for television news channels skyrocket. The local television news, with its heavy crime component, has eclipsed national news, which carries more serious political stories and less crime, in the battle for high audience ratings. In the entertainment world, crime shows are highly popular. Besides audience appeal, crime news has the advantage of ease of coverage. The police beat can supply a steady diet of new crimes for hungry reporters who prefer to mine a news-rich source rather than working leaner beats.

Publicizing Justice

Statues of the Goddess of Justice show a blindfolded woman holding scales. For Americans, blind justice suggests that some things, like the race or gender of an accused person, should remain out of the picture in legal situations. But should blindness shroud executions in death penalty cases?

That age-old question was raised again when Timothy McVeigh faced execution in 2001. He had confessed to a politically motivated bombing attack in Oklahoma City in 1995 that killed 168 people and injured 500 more. In the eighteenth century, American executions were routinely performed in public. They were considered important civic rituals that would bring the community together to share in watching justice done and to learn collectively that the wages of serious crime are death.

But things have changed. Americans have become squeamish about watching people being put to death, partly because of scruples about killing a human being, no matter how heinous the crime, and partly because it seems ghoulish to want to see a human being die.

Still, when a date had been set for the McVeigh execution, 1,400 reporters, editors, and technicians from the various news media notified the Bureau of Prisons that they planned to be in Terre Haute, a small Indiana town of 60,000 people, for the event. They asked for space outside the prison for portable buildings, trailers, and staging platforms so that the event could be televised. More than 100 television journalists, including top names in the field, requested interviews.

The condemned man was not shy about publicity; in fact, he asked for nationwide television coverage of his execution by lethal injection. He gave interviews to the press, including one to *60 Minutes*, and worked with two reporters from the *Buffalo News* who wrote a book about him. Nonetheless, U.S. Attorney General John D. Ashcroft denied the request for national coverage, allowing only closed-circuit television viewing by 250 family members of the victims and by official witnesses, including ten reporters selected by lot. Ashcroft also ruled that during the days preceding the execution, McVeigh could speak with reporters for no more

(Box continues, next page)

than fifteen minutes a day for a total of five hours; none of the interviews could be recorded.

The decision to refuse open television coverage and to place restraints on publicity are controversial. Some critics see these as denial of the public's right to know and to watch the ultimate reality programming. Others revert to the earlier arguments that open executions rally the public around the justice system and deter criminals. Opponents of capital punishment urge publicity to impress the public with the barbarism of executions. But it didn't happen. The event remained concealed from most Americans.

That leaves key questions unanswered. Should a public act be hidden from the public in whose name it was decreed? Weren't all Americans victims of the terrorist act, not just the immediate families of the victims? Is it convincing to say that showing the execution would coarsen American culture and turn McVeigh into a martyr, who would inspire right-wing fringe groups? Among American institutions of government, the justice system is unique in subordinating First Amendment free press rights to other hallowed principles, such as the right to a fair trial and the right to privacy. But should it be that way? What do *you* think?

SOURCE: The account is based on Reuven Frank, "Death as Entertainment," *The New Leader* 84(4) (May/June 2001): 54–56; and Mike Dorning, "McVeigh Execution: A Conflicted Culture Awaits Retribution," *Chicago Tribune*, April 22, 2001.

Judicial Censorship

Although news covering all aspects of the U.S. crime and justice system is amply covered by the media, there are important omissions. The Supreme Court bars reporters from all of its deliberations prior to the announcement of decisions. On the few occasions when information about a forthcoming decision has been leaked ahead of time, justices have reacted with great anger and have curtailed contacts between newspeople and Court personnel. Television cameras are barred most of the time from federal courts, and their proceedings may not be broadcast directly. Federal district and appellate courts allowed cameras in the courtroom as a three-year experiment in 1991. They ended coverage in 1994 on the grounds that the cameras were distracting to the jurors and witnesses even though appraisals of the experiment had found little or no impact on the administration of justice.

For years many state courts prohibited radio and television reporters from covering trials and other proceedings. This restriction was grounded in fears, spawned by the sensational 1935 Lindbergh baby kidnapping trial, that recording devices might produce a carnival atmosphere that would intimidate participants, endanger witnesses, and harm the fairness of the proceedings. To allow citizens to watch how their courts operate, most states have now opened their courts to electronic coverage. Rules about coverage try to protect many of the actors in the judicial drama from undue invasion of their privacy.[20] However, the debate about the wisdom of televising court proceedings reemerged in the wake of the massive media attention to the O. J. Simpson murder trial, which drowned out much other news for nearly a year. Critics of electronic coverage claimed that showboating by the judge and lawyers distorted and delayed the verdict and diminished the public's regard for the legal system. Others disagreed, arguing that the public is entitled to monitor the courts' performance in a public trial.[21]

Restraints on live audio- and videotape coverage are not the only limitations on judicial publicity. In the interest of ensuring fair trials, courts also limit the information that may be printed while court proceedings are in progress. These types of restrictions were discussed in Chapter 3.

Communications Law

Judges' views on communications law also interest newspeople. The judges interpret the First Amendment's free press provisions, the legality of federal statutes dealing with media enterprises, such as the 1996 Telecommunications Act, and the legality of rulings made by the FCC. In an average year, fifteen to twenty appeals involving FCC decisions about various aspects of communications policy are brought to the courts. Appeals are easy because the law permits any person who is "aggrieved" or whose interests are "adversely affected" by the orders of the FCC to seek a court review. But the courts, including the U.S. Supreme Court, have been sympathetic to the FCC, upholding most of its rulings. In general, the federal judiciary, including the Supreme Court, rules in favor of protecting press freedom when it clashes with other rights.

Although the influence of Congress and the executive branch over communications policy seems greater than the role played by the courts, it is difficult to gauge how much impact the prospect of judicial review has on legislative and executive branch activities. Agencies frequently modify their behavior to avoid reversals by the judiciary. The government bodies that deal with mass media laws and rules at the national and state level are no exception.

Covering State and Local Affairs

It is an axiom of American politics that "all politics is local." Decentralized politics is essential and invigorating in a nation that spans a continent and embodies diverse political cultures and contexts. Because politics at the national level is glamorous and important, it is easy to ignore the grassroots that nourish and shape it. It is therefore not surprising that most research attention has focused on the national level, despite the importance of coverage of local politics and local perspectives on national politics.

The Changing Media Grid

Mirroring the nation's political geography and culture, American newspapers and radio and television stations have been primarily structured to serve a multitude of local markets. At the start of the twentieth century, every large and medium-sized city and even many small towns had at least one newspaper and often more, geared to local political needs. When electronic media made their appearance they, too, were situated in nearly every city to serve local audiences. Technological changes and large-scale migration of former inner-city dwellers to the suburbs have taken their toll on the local focus of many American media enterprises. The numbers of newspapers have shrunk so that most cities are now served by a single newspaper, and many communities no longer have a paper of their own. Electronic media are serving ever larger regions. It is not uncommon for television stations and metropolitan dailies to reach people in fifty counties. Typically their domain then includes some 1,300 governmental units, whose policies should be reported because they involve important public issues, including the power to tax. Numerous state legislators, as well as several national legislators, are elected within these counties. Given the many active political units that require media attention, reporting, of necessity, is highly selective and superficial. As media critic Ben Bagdikian has stated:

> News distribution is no longer designed for individual towns and cities. American politics is organized on the basis of the 20,000 urban and rural places in the country, which is the way citizens vote. But the media have organized on the basis of 210 television "markets," which is the way mer-

chandisers and media corporations sell ads. As a result, the fit between the country's information needs and its information media has become disastrously disjointed.[22]

The Vanishing Metropolitan Focus. Because market areas and political communities no longer coincide, reporting has turned away from strictly local problems to more generalized topics of interest to the entire market area. That has meant more focus on soft news like sports and human interest stories. It has also meant less information about important local problems that face citizens as well as more cynical coverage about the human motivations that drive politics.[23] This is happening despite the fact that nationwide polls show that more Americans are most interested in local news. In 1998, 61 percent of the adults interviewed in a nationwide poll said that they watched local news routinely, rather than only if events seemed particularly interesting or important. Only 52 percent expressed similar interest in national news and even fewer (34 percent) in international news.[24]

Ironically, Internet news, despite its unique global reach, may ease the problem. A comparison of print and Internet versions of six Colorado newspapers found more local content in the Internet version.[25] The newspapers vary in circulation from below 50,000 to over 250,000 subscribers. Local stories constituted 22–38 percent of the coverage in 3,403 print stories and 24–68 percent of the coverage in 1,383 on-line stories. Another boost for access to local news comes from community access cable channels that allow constituents to watch local government in action. City council meetings, committee hearings, and court procedures have become directly accessible to the public without the intervention of journalists. The suburbs, where such channels have been scarce in the past, are joining the parade, thereby providing more competition for suburban newspapers. However, audiences for broadcasts of local government activities are generally quite small.

Umbrella Competition Patterns. In response to major population shifts from inner cities to sprawling suburbs, print media have developed a structure of "umbrella competition" in which smaller units operate within the area covered simultaneously by the larger units.[26] Suburban newspapers have been thriving, and metropolitan newspapers have developed special sections targeted to different communities in the metropolitan area and suburbs.[27] Nonetheless, metropolitan newspapers have shrunk in circulation, often drastically. In 1970, roughly 78 percent of American adults read the daily papers; by 1999 the numbers had shrunk to 57 percent.[28]

The umbrella pattern consists of four layers. In the first layer, large metropolitan dailies provide substantial amounts of international, national, and regional coverage. In the second layer, smaller satellite dailies resemble their larger cousins but carry more local news. The third layer contains suburban dailies. They emphasize local news, much of it nonpolitical, and are a rapidly growing sector. Though still below the metropolitan circulation figures, suburban papers are profitable because they offer an attractive advertising opportunity to the many businesses whose customers now cluster in suburban areas. The fourth layer consists of weekly newspapers and "shoppers" that are distributed free of charge because they contain mostly advertising and only a sprinkling of news and feature stories.

The emphasis on local news increases as one moves through these layers. This has happened because newspapers with a narrower reach try to distinguish themselves from the metropolitan papers and thereby make themselves more attractive to their clientele. But because of the lack of fit between media markets and political units, most of the local news avoids discussion and analysis of localized public issues, leaving these issues bereft of essential coverage. The fact that metropolitan papers now must share the advertising pie with suburban papers, as well as with "shoppers"—the advertising-dominated newspapers delivered free of charge to local households—has been a major factor in the death of dailies in multipaper cities, leaving most of them without the kind of competition that invigorates political dialogue.

Television stations in smaller markets also tend to feature more local and less national and international news than their larger cousins.[29] Citizens rely heavily on these broadcasts, especially when print sources fail to cover the local scene.[30] Most radio news stations, which feature only news or a large amount of news, likewise devote more than half of their airtime to local news. However, stations in smaller radio markets tend to present fewer stories simply because there is less local news available.[31]

The Alternative Press. In addition to the four layers discussed, there is also an alternative press at both the national and local levels. It tends to focus narrowly on issues of interest to people representing minority political cultures or people with distinctive lifestyles and cultural tastes. For example, many specialized media are targeted to various ethnic, racial, and religious groups, as well as to groups with unorthodox lifestyles. Some specialized media are published in foreign languages to meet the needs of immigrants. Although they provide in-depth coverage of local, national, and international news of interest to their clientele, they omit news covering broader concerns. Their readers may therefore live in a narrow communications ghetto that keeps them from fully understanding their surroundings.

Specialized media also often try to generate support for issues favored by their audiences and may play a role in influencing local elections. Media serving African American and Hispanic communities are good examples.

Besides having their own print media, large subcultural groups in the United States are also served by electronic news media tailored to their special concerns. Over-the-air and cable television and radio stations geared to the needs of various subcultures are multiplying and flourishing throughout the country.

Government/Press Relations at Subnational Levels

Subnational news is important for state and local politics for the same reasons that make the media important on the national scene. Subnational news plays a significant role in setting the agenda for public policies. It helps or hinders politicians in achieving their goals. It influences the election and appointment of public officials. It informs the public and officialdom about political affairs and politicians' wrongdoings. However, there are differences in emphasis between national and subnational political coverage, largely because subnational politics operates on a much smaller scale and often performs different functions. Unfortunately, scholars have largely neglected the study of the subnational media, despite unmistakable signs of their importance. For instance, the political fate of members of Congress cannot be explored effectively without analysis of the local press in their district.[32]

How Officials Use the Press. At the subnational level, public officials find it much easier to stay in touch with each other about their work without relying on news stories. They also remain in closer direct contact with a comparatively tiny corps of reporters so that formal press conferences are less necessary. Moreover, their news is rarely so exciting that they can count on decent attendance if they do schedule a news conference.

Fewer officials at the subnational level are experts in gaining publicity and using it to advantage. In fact, the public information and public relations materials they present to the media are often so poorly done that they do more harm than good. Often their jobs are highly technical and difficult to explain to the lay public in brief news stories. When officials do make the effort to tell their stories, reporters generally lack technical expertise to judge the accuracy of the account. Consequently, when the story relates to a policy decision involving major technical issues—for example, whether to start, continue, or stop a project, how to finance it, and similar matters—the official views are likely to define the situation with little media scrutiny.

Media scholar Phyllis Kaniss has identified six media styles that are especially common at the subnational level.[33] The *paranoid media-avoider* fears the press and tries to avoid it as much as possible. Information-hungry journalists are likely to retaliate with unfavorable publicity whenever an opportunity to do so presents itself. The *naive professional* supplies the media with information and talks freely with journalists without realizing that uncontrolled release of information empowers reporters to determine what will be published and the perspectives that will be reflected. The *ribbon cutter* is a media junkie who is heavily concerned with initiating events, however trivial, that are likely to attract journalists. The ensuing publicity may have few political payoffs. *Dancing marionettes* take their cues from media editorials and report and take action in areas suggested by newspeople, rather than initiating policies independently. The reward is likely to be favorable coverage, although the policy agenda favored by newspeople may be undesirable from the official's perspective. *Colorful quotables* excel in creating attractive sound bites and making sure that these come to the attention of reporters. Like ribbon cutters, their political rewards are apt to be small. Finally, *liars* conceal or slant information or distort it outright to put themselves in a favorable light.

In place of such unproductive strategies, Kaniss recommends that state and local officials, like their national counterparts, learn to understand the needs of local media so that they can structure the information they supply accordingly. That requires judicious choices of information for release and careful attention to the framing of stories.[34] For example, Chicago's Mayor Richard Daley's press secretary Avis LaVelle always tried to provide reporters with story materials selected and written from a reporter's perspective. In that way, she managed to control news flow in line with the mayor's goals while still pleasing the press.

The era of informal, inexpert handling of the press by subnational officials may be ending. Currently, all governors and most big-city mayors have press secretaries or public information offices. Like their counterparts at the national level, they try to use these offices to push executive programs through recalcitrant legislatures and to disseminate news about their activities to various political elites and interested citizens. However, as on the national level, such efforts often fail. Fearing to be hoodwinked by clever professionals, the media may turn out to be suspicious, cynical commentators, rather than trusting friends.

Eagerness for good media coverage is not limited to elected officials. Appointed officials, too, need good images to help them in their battles for funding and for support of the policies that their agencies try to pursue. A poll of high-level federal officials showed that 79 percent thought that positive coverage increased their chances of achieving major policy goals.[35] Legislatures rarely deny support to seemingly popular agencies. By the same token, bad publicity can hurt. When media frame stories in ways that suit media, rather than official goals, public officials may be forced to recast their own focus of attention. For example, city sanitation departments have been forced to concentrate on cleaning up lesser problems and neglecting more serious ones when publicity has highlighted a particular situation.

As on the national level, strategies designed to win media attention include press conferences, press releases, staging events that media are likely to cover, writing op-ed pieces, and writing letters to the editor. Press releases, the most common form of public relations, are also the least productive because they tend to be sparsely used by media. Rates of use may be as low as 5 percent, unless the releases have interesting local angles.[36] Contacting media personnel directly seems to be the best approach, and apparently it is quite successful. Estimates are that more than half of the content of the print and electronic media originates with news sources, rather than springing from questions asked first by journalists. Government officials at all levels provide a large share of these so-called news subsidies.[37]

In the past, most efforts to gain media coverage at the subnational level were directed at the print media, which generally were deemed by governors, lieutenant governors, attorneys general, secretaries of state, and various legislative leaders to be the most effective transmitters of state and local political news.[38] That is changing, however. More and more local officials realize that television and the Web are most important for mobilizing public opinion. They therefore watch closely how activities of interest to them are covered on local news to infer from the coverage what public reaction is likely to be. They have also increased their efforts to get television and Web site coverage for themselves and the agencies they represent.[39]

How Reporters Operate at Subnational Levels. Reporters are also somewhat different at the subnational than the national level. Taken as a group, they have less formal education and considerably less job experience. In fact, the officials' level of education may rank considerably above that of reporters and the "locals" may be more informed overall. Turnover rates are high among reporters. They are often forced to move to a different market when they switch jobs because clauses in their contracts forbid them to work for a competitor in the same area. Unfamiliarity with local politics in their new surroundings may strain relations between reporters and officials when they disagree in their analyses of political events. However, most of the time, personal relations between reporters and officials tend to be more cordial at the subnational level because they interact more. In fact, ties of friendship have been blamed for the dearth of press criticism of officials and local businesses at subnational levels.[40]

Aside from metropolitan newspapers, news organizations at the subnational level are usually considerably smaller than their national counterparts. Consequently, reporters have to cover many beats rather than becoming specialists. Roving reporters must depend more heavily on routine sources, such as daily inquiries at the police and fire departments, local newspapers, assorted press releases, tips from viewers, wire service stories, and the wire service "day books" that list major local events.[41] Stories with the best pictures and best sound bites tend to become leads, even when they are not necessarily the most important stories.

Because many state and local stories are technical and undramatic, journalists strive mightily to make them entertaining. That means featuring colorful, charismatic politicians who speak well in ten-second sound bites or well-known key officials in major cities. Reporters may haunt victims of various tragedies and their families by intruding into their homes and hospital rooms to get stories. It means bypassing opportunities for detailed exposition of problems because that might bore the audience. In the process of tabloidizing news, the importance of events and their broader and long-term consequences may be lost.

Because most government business stops in the early evening hours, late evening local news broadcasts depend heavily on the staples supplied by police and fire department records.[42] Serious political news featured on early evening national newscasts is deemed "stale" by nine or ten at night.[43]

Journalists who work in large metropolitan areas tend to pay more attention to inner-city affairs than to the politics of outlying areas. For Philadelphia, Kaniss reported the ratio as roughly 2 to 1 for newspapers. On local television, nearly all of the political stories covered inner-city politics, ignoring the suburbs.[44] Unfortunately, suburban reporters did not pick up the slack. A look at the contents of suburban news showed that 73 percent of the stories dealt with crime, accidents, disasters, and the like, slighting stories about other suburban concerns.

There are several reasons for "city myopia" by metropolitan media.[45] Among them is the fact that metropolitan newspaper offices usually are closer to the central city hall than to the suburbs. That makes inner-city officials and other news sources located in the inner city easier to reach. City officials are also more willing to make the trip to newspaper offices and radio and television studios that are located nearby than are their geographically distant suburban colleagues. Inner cities are also more likely to generate the kind of news that political reporters ordinarily cover, such as political wheeling and dealing, ample doses of corruption, and heavy slices of crime. Stories of spectacular fires are more common in inner-city neighborhoods, as are stories about ethnic and racial strife and protest demonstrations.[46] Most journalists find the city more exciting and relate its problems to events in the suburbs rather than the other way around. When reporters are assigned to suburban stories on a regular basis, they view it as akin to exile in Siberia. The smaller size of the press corps also accounts for the lack of coverage for many important subnational stories and for more pack

TABLE 10-1   Government/Politics News Distribution (in percentages)

Level of news	*Sun Times*	*Chicago Tribune*	National ABC	National CBS	National NBC	Local ABC	Local CBS	Local NBC
National	36%	45%	40%	47%	50%	36%	45%	43%
International	31	19	55	49	45	16	18	17
State	6	9	4	3	4	5	5	3
Local	27	26	1	1	1	43	32	37
N	226	249	438	463	409	361	330	346

SOURCE: Author's research.

NOTE: Based on stories recorded September 1–October 20, 2000 from the *Chicago Sun Times,* the *Chicago Tribune,* and the national and local networks in Chicago. Election news has been excluded.

journalism, generated by the close contacts that often characterize smaller groups.

The Contents of Subnational News

All of the news media—print, radio, and audiovisual—slight news about state politics. News media situated in state capitals are the only exception. Among stories about government and politics, the share of state news is less than 10 percent in all the media. As Table 10-1 shows, the share allotted to local news garners one-quarter to close to half of the stories in newspapers and on local newscasts.

State News: A Neglected Stepchild

Why does state news receive the least attention when states play such important roles in politics? As we have seen, some media specialize in national news, like the national television networks, and other media specialize in local news, like many network affiliates. But few daily publications specialize in state news.

The Local Emphasis. Within states, the major media enterprises that have enough resources to cover more than local news are usually located in the state's most populous cities where local news abounds, rather than in state capitals.

Moreover, most state coverage has traditionally focused on the legislature rather than the governor. Because state legislatures have relatively brief sessions, the flow of news from the capital is intermittent. Many daily papers therefore do not make the state capital a regular full-time beat. In

TABLE 10-2   Regional Focus of Network News Coverage: June 1999–
May 2000

Regions	Percentage of mentions	Percentage of electoral vote	Discrepancy
Northeast			
(D.C., Del., Md., N.J., N.Y., Pa.)	22.9%	15.6%	+7.3
Pacific			
(Alaska, Calif., Hawaii, Ore., Wash.)	19.3	14.7	+4.6
Southwest			
(Ark., La., Okla., Texas)	14.2	10.6	+3.6
New England			
(Conn., Maine, Mass., N.H., R.I., Vt.)	9.9	6.5	+3.4
Mountains			
(Ariz., Colo., Idaho, Mont., Nev., N.M., Utah, Wyo.)	6.7	7.4	−0.7
Plains			
(Kan., Neb., N. D., S. D.)	2.0	3.2	−1.2
Middle Atlantic			
(N.C., S.C., Va., W. Va.)	5.7	7.4	−1.7
South			
(Ala., Fla., Ga., Ky., Miss., Tenn.)	9.0	13.6	-4.6
Middle West			
(Ill., Ind., Iowa, Mich., Minn., Mo., Ohio, Wis.)	10.1	20.9	−10.8

SOURCE: Author's research based on the Vanderbilt Television News Archives.

NOTE: $N = 3,173$ mentions in news stories. Figures for the three networks (ABC, NBC, and CBS) have been combined. The distribution of 538 electoral votes is based on 1990 census figures. Regions have been ranked from most advantaged to least advantaged by network news coverage. Figures are rounded.

some cases—New Hampshire is an example—the state's media markets overlap state boundaries so that news must appeal to residents of more than one state. That also puts a damper on state news.[47]

The National Emphasis. State news is a double loser. Besides being extremely sparse on national television, it is also extremely spotty. National television highlights a small number of states and neglects the rest. As Table 10-2 shows, some regions of the country receive more ample coverage than one might expect, judged by the size of their populations (as reflected in their electoral votes), whereas others receive considerably less. The concerns of people in the Middle West rate the least attention relative to their electoral votes, whereas people in the Northeast and Pacific regions dominate. The degree of discrepancy in regional coverage, favorable and unfavorable, is shown in the last column of the table.

TABLE 10-3   State Distribution of Network News Attention, Ten Leaders and
Trailers: June 1999–May 2000

| State | Region | Overcovered States | | |
		Percentage of mentions	Percentage of electoral vote	Discrepancy
New York	Northeast	13.6%	6.1%	+7.5
Texas	Southwest	11.3	6.1	+5.2
California	Pacific	14.9	10.1	+4.8
Rhode Island	New England	3.8	0.7	+3.1
New Hampshire	New England	2.5	0.7	+1.8
New Mexico	Mountains	1.7	0.9	+0.8
Iowa	Middle West	2.0	1.3	+0.7
Colorado	Mountains	2.1	1.5	+0.6
Washington	Pacific	2.5	2.1	+0.4
Maryland	Northeast	2.2	1.9	+0.3
Vermont	New England	0.9	0.6	+0.3

| State | Region | Undercovered States | | |
		Percentage of mentions	Percentage of electoral vote	Discrepancy
Ohio	Middle West	0.9%	3.9%	-3.0
Illinois	Middle West	1.5	4.1	-2.6
Pennsylvania	Northeast	1.7	4.3	-2.6
Indiana	Middle West	0.5	2.2	-1.7
Missouri	Middle West	0.6	2.1	-1.5
New Jersey	Northeast	1.5	2.8	-1.3
Alabama	South	0.5	1.7	-1.2
Tennessee	South	0.9	2.1	-1.2
Michigan	Middle West	2.4	3.4	-1.0
Connecticut	New England	0.6	1.5	-0.9

SOURCE: Author's research based on the Vanderbilt Television News Archives.

NOTE: $N = 3,173$ mentions in news stories. Figures for the three networks (ABC, NBC, and CBS) have been combined. The distribution of the 535 electoral votes (Washington, D.C., was excluded) is based on the 1990 census figures.

Table 10-3 provides a closer look at individual states. It shows the ten most covered and the ten least covered states and the degree of favorable and unfavorable imbalance.

From a political perspective, it is impossible to make sense out of the findings. Some comparatively insignificant states, such as Rhode Island and New Hampshire, bask in excess coverage whereas economically more important states, such as Ohio, Illinois, and Pennsylvania, are undercovered. The explanation lies in journalistic criteria. The states with the most ample coverage provided the best story materials at a place and time that was most convenient for the media. New Hampshire, for example, played a key role in the presidential primary elections in spring 2000. Rhode Island was mourning the death of its senator (John Chafee), the crash of EgyptAir Flight 990, and a series of weather disasters. States lacking in such unusually stirring events suffered from neglect, which could be costly to the state's economic and political welfare. Compounding such problems, state news coverage on the national networks also lacked political substance, focusing primarily on disaster, crime, and trivia stories. State economic, political, and social conditions and policies were ignored even when they had major national ramifications. Print media coverage of state news tends to be more ample and considerably better.[48] That suggests that the networks could report more state news if they choose to do so.

Complaints about inadequate coverage must always be tempered by the realization that media space and time are limited. What kinds of stories should the networks have omitted to make room for more news about the states? The answer is painful, given the fact that audiences love the entertainment and trivia stories that should be cut to make room for more politically meaty content. Nonetheless, the growing importance of state politics has made it essential to provide more adequate coverage for the benefit of interested publics, as well as political leaders.

When pollsters asked people in a 1987 survey to rate the importance of various types of news, 75 percent rated general state news as "important" or "very important" and 65 percent said the same about state legislative news. Unfortunately, appraisals of the appeal of state news are rare and are excluded from most major surveys. For instance, a nationwide telephone survey of 3,142 adults conducted in spring 2000 asked respondents only about their attention to local, national, and international news. In that survey, 73 percent of the respondents said that they followed print and electronic news about "people and events in your community" closely or very closely. Sixty-three percent claimed that they were following news about "local government" closely or very closely. The figures were 60 percent and 59 percent, respectively, for news about "political figures and events in Washington" and "international affairs."[49] Where state news would rate in such a survey remains a mystery.

Local News Characteristics

Local television news has become the biggest game in town. Fifty-six percent of the adult population watches it regularly, compared to 30 percent who watch news on the national networks.[50] Local stations first started to emphasize local news heavily in the 1970s because they could keep the advertising income. For broadcasts of national news, most advertising revenue is remitted to the national networks.[51] Production of local news is also attractive because it is popular and far cheaper than most nationally produced entertainment shows. Hence, news programs multiplied in numbers as well as length, with some local news programs running as long as ninety minutes.

Primary Concerns. As part of its mandate to ensure that the electronic media serve the public interest, the FCC has urged local television and radio stations to gear their programming to local needs, including coverage of local politics. That mandate has been honored more by lip service than by actual performance. Local stations do carry some local political news, and more than three quarters of their stories originate locally. But the primary emphasis is on local crime and disasters and on entertainment, weather, and sports. This is hardly what the FCC had in mind when it called for "local" programming.

When images of young Americans on national television are compared with their images on local television, it is readily apparent that the national media take a much more serious approach. A study, completed in winter 1999, analyzed a sample of 9,678 stories broadcast on ABC, CBS, NBC, and CNN national news as well as local news from Los Angeles, Chicago, Boston, Seattle, and Columbia, South Carolina. The national media highlighted education issues like student achievement and general policies. The local media highlighted youths as crime victims or perpetrators or involved in accidents. Fifty-two percent of the national stories were thematic, linking a particular story to a broader social context. By contrast, 94 percent of the local stories were purely episodic, reporting details about an event without drawing any lessons from it. In part, but only in part, the contrast relates to the different mission of national and local news. National media cover broad trends that apply everywhere, while local media tell a specific story to the people most likely to care about the details of events in their neighborhood. The end result is essentially positive coverage of young people in the national media compared to the "if it bleeds, it leads" negative coverage on local television.

Although these figures show that local news is far fluffier than national news, one must keep in mind that there are generally more local newscasts. With more news time to fill, there is bound to be more filler material. Conversely, although the proportion of serious news may be smaller, the total amount of news may still be greater. But there is another caveat—there may be more stories, but many of them are likely to be updates or outright repetition of earlier news. Moreover, despite the fact that there may be more news available, the majority of viewers are not glued to their television sets, eager to watch successive newscasts as the day develops.

Diversity. Just as one cannot lump all national media together for purposes of analysis, so one must differentiate local media along a number of dimensions. Size is one of them. Stations in the largest markets offer considerably more political news than stations in smaller markets.[52] Likewise, larger television stations devote a slightly smaller percentage of news space to local news and pay somewhat more attention to national and world events.[53] Stations in larger markets seem to be moving away from emphasizing local news as urged by the FCC's "localism doctrine."

National News on Local Media

One reason for growing attention to national and world news by local stations is greater ease of access. New satellite and microwave technology permits local stations to tap into the pool of national news at will and report it from a local angle. In addition, local stations are increasingly entering into cooperative news-gathering systems, such as Conus and Newsfeed, that allow member stations to send their stories to other members in the system via satellite. Local stations consequently have become less dependent on network coverage for national and world events.

As we saw in Chapter 9, national newsmakers are eager to reach the hinterlands, where coverage tends to be gentler and more in tune with the newsmakers' agendas. Members of Congress rely heavily on publicity in their home states and make extensive efforts to supply local media with stories and videotapes. Washington also abounds with news bureaus that transmit national news, often presented from local angles, to member organizations or independent local clients. Washington news gathered by the Washington press corps but presented locally has a distinctive flavor. It is more upbeat and less critical. Lacking insider knowledge, local reporters are less likely to subject national political leaders to tough questioning. They tend to pay more attention—and more favorably—to their senators and representatives than the national media.[54]

Election Coverage at the Local Level

The entire American electoral system is organized to reflect local and statewide politics. All national officials—the president, senators, and representatives—are selected from state-based electoral districts, as are state officials and the half million local officials who occupy legislative, executive, judicial, and administrative positions throughout the states. Candidates for most of these offices, including scores of positions on local government boards and committees, are of prime interest to geographically limited constituencies. They rarely attract the attention of nationwide broadcasts or the few newspapers that have a nationwide circulation. Their political fate—and that of the areas that they serve—therefore depends largely on the kind of coverage provided by local media.

News about the Candidates. The role of the local media in promoting candidates in state and local campaigns is similar to what was described in Chapter 8 for national campaigns. It is a growing role because state officials are spending more money on their media campaigns now than in earlier years. A large share of campaign spending goes toward efforts to obtain general media coverage rather than relying only on advertisements. In the past, subnational officials relied heavily on radio advertisements because of the high costs of television. Cable channels have changed that situation because their advertising rates are much cheaper.

Although comparative data remain scarce, some evidence suggests that the quality of local election coverage may be on a par with national coverage. In the 1989 Virginia gubernatorial campaign, local coverage was superior to national news media stories. The national media focused on the historic nature of the campaign, which pitted a white and black gubernatorial candidate against each other in a southern state, and on the candidates' diverging stands on abortion. Most of the national coverage related to the black Democrat; the white Republican received little attention. The local papers excelled in providing profiles of both candidates and highlighting an array of issues facing the state.[55] Both national and local media painted a highly favorable picture of the Democrat and an unfavorable one of his Republican opponent. Similarly, a study of a race for chair of the Fairfax County (Virginia) Board of Supervisors concluded: "It appears that a different kind of press coverage occurs at the 'lower levels' of government—one in which more serious, substantive reporting is taking place."[56] Other studies have concluded that coverage characteristics and quality are similar for state and national coverage of gubernatorial races.[57]

Newspaper endorsements are also more important below the national level. Most candidates for state and local offices are less familiar to the voters, who therefore turn more to the news media for guidance.[58] When viewers were asked to compare debates among presidential contenders at the national level with debates among candidates for state and local offices, they reported that they found the presidential debates more important and interesting, but learned more and were influenced more by the debates at state and local levels.[59] Before watching the debates, 70 percent of the viewers in the local debate were undecided about their voting choices, compared to 40 percent of viewers in the presidential debate. If lack of information is a disease that plagues national elections, it apparently occurs in a far more virulent strain at the subnational level.

The fact that news media are now organized to serve larger markets often makes it difficult for candidates whose districts overlap several markets, or just a small slice of a large media market, to gain coverage. The media will not report about them as part of regular news coverage because limited time for news is reserved for stories of wider interest. Paid advertising coverage may be too expensive because rates are based on the numbers of people within the market, not on the much smaller numbers that are constituents of the candidate. A state representative who serves a district of 50,000 voters rarely can afford to pay for access to many times that number just because the advertising "Area of Dominant Influence" in which her or his district is located covers a multitude of urban, suburban, and rural counties.

News about Referenda. Elections involving local politics often are completely issue-centered. Referenda on prospective policies are examples. Although these political contests have low visibility, their impact on the average citizen can dwarf that of the more publicized contests. After studying seventy-two referenda in Massachusetts, Michigan, Oregon, and California between 1976 and 1982, political scientist Betty Zisk concluded that they were impartially covered. Despite the liberal stance of the papers under investigation (the *Boston Globe,* the *Detroit Free Press,* the *Portland Oregonian,* the *Los Angeles Times,* and the *San Francisco Chronicle*), issues were amply discussed from a variety of perspectives.[60] However, Zisk faults newspeople for merely reporting charges and countercharges rather than analyzing the merits of proposals and unmasking misleading rhetoric and advertisements.[61] When ballots were tallied, voters had agreed with newspaper recommendations about 68 percent of the time.[62] It is impossible to know with certainty whether this indicates media influence or merely an independently occurring concurrence of views. The side spending the most money, much of it to gain media coverage, won in three out of four cases (fifty-six of the seventy-two campaigns—78 percent). Zisk argues that money purchased victory, rather than good causes attracted the most money.

Radio and television, the main sources of political information for average voters, carried little news and few editorials about the referenda. Thirty- and sixty-second television spot advertisements were totally inadequate to cover the important points of most of these complex issues. However, some radio talk shows gave extensive coverage to referenda, albeit often generating more heat than light.[63] Unlike television, major regional newspapers provided comprehensive coverage of referendum issues. They carried extensive background features, pro and con articles and editorials, and news about campaign activities in the major urban centers, though not elsewhere in the jurisdiction covered by the referenda.

The Quality of Local News

Maintaining high-quality coverage is often more difficult for local than for national media. As mentioned, compared to most national television networks, local television has a far greater appetite for news because it usually has three or more daily newscasts. That puts a premium on broadcasting the latest news, rather than repeating more important stories that were featured earlier in the day. To maintain profitability through a wide audience reach, local television usually pitches its programs to a moderately educated middle-income audience that, presumably, is uninterested in sophisticated political analysis.

It is also more difficult for local newscasters to get high-quality news commentary for local political stories. Many local officials lack the skills and experience required to be good media information sources. Because their jobs are often technical—fire chiefs or health commissioners, for example—they are chosen for their technical abilities and managerial skills, with no regard for public relations expertise. The end result is a dearth of political commentary on local stations. One content analysis of fourteen television stations of assorted sizes from five different markets found that only 43 (1.4 percent) of 3,037 stories that were examined included commentary.[64]

Lack of economic resources is also a problem for local stations and for local newspapers. It may force them to go after the cheapest stories rather than originating stories on their own and investigating them. Usually, it is cheapest to base news on handouts by various public relations practitioners or on rehashed reports by metropolitan newspapers—facetiously dubbed "plagiarism news."[65] In a study of three network affiliates in the western United States, 75 percent of the news at the small, economically weak stations came from handouts, 20 percent started with tips that were investigated, and 5 percent originated with reporters. For the largest, economically soundest station the figures were 50 percent from handouts, 36 percent from tips, and 13 percent originated by their own staffs. As Ben Bagdikian has put it in his inimitable style, journalism is "a daily battle between God and Mammon. Too much of the time, it's Mammon 100 and God 5."[66] Larger local stations and newspapers with greater financial resources do somewhat better in seeking out important news, providing context for their stories, and resisting pressures from advertisers.[67] Smaller news outlets cannot afford to antagonize the advertising hand that feeds them.

The difficulties in maintaining high-quality news have serious consequences at the local level because there are few competing information sources for local politics. National problems and national politicians are widely scrutinized by a multitude of media, governmental investigating bodies, interest groups, and academicians. That rarely happens at the local level. Reporting by the local media may be the sole source of information available to interested citizens as well as government officials.

Critics of local news have often charged that it does not perform the important watchdog functions of the press. They complain that reporters are soft on local politicians because they are not comfortable stirring up conflict with people whom they know personally. They are also soft when it comes to local projects and policies out of a sense of local boosterism. Reporters rarely question estimates of costs and benefits of local development projects. They tend to be upbeat in reporting about local business leaders and economic trends. They may examine local problems and report about sad consequences, but they rarely turn to genuine investigative reporting. As Kaniss has noted, "While there is much in the news and editorial columns that is critical of local officials, this criticism is limited when compared with the amount of information that is taken directly, and almost unquestioningly, from official bureaucratic sources."[68] There are, of course, major exceptions to these criticisms, particularly in large cities with well-staffed news media. But even there, whenever budgets get tight, investigative reporting is among the first casualties of malnourishment.

Summary

The media spotlight falls unevenly on various features of the body politic. In this chapter, we examined institutions that do not receive sufficient light so that the American public and political leaders can adequately assess these institutions and the roles they play in America's political life. At the national level, the judicial branch suffers from inadequate news coverage. We have explained the reasons for this problem and some of the political consequences, given the federal courts' importance in shaping American political life. We have also noted problems that arise when the crime and justice system is in the news and the focus turns to sensational matters, rather than political substance. The controversy about the appropriateness of allowing cameras in courtrooms during various judicial proceedings highlights many of these issues.

The discussion then turned to media coverage of subnational news. Here we noted that state news is neglected nearly everywhere in the United States. Hence, most citizens remain uninformed about state politics in their own as well as sister states. However, coverage seems to be adequate for the needs of state-level politicians, who find it easy to work with the local press when needed. We also noted that governmental publicity efforts are becoming more professionalized at the subnational level.

There is far more ample coverage of local than state news. Many regions within metropolitan areas, as well as suburbs and outlying communities, have local newspapers. But the quality of coverage of politics has deteriorated since the beginning of the twentieth century. Markets reflect technological and merchandising conditions rather than political needs. News media design their offerings accordingly. Fewer cities now have their own daily newspapers, and intracity competition among major dailies has almost vanished. The political dialogue has suffered. However, it seems too early to mourn the death of solid local politics coverage. The new technologies that make it feasible to tailor broadcasts to the needs of small audiences may restore the vigorous publicity that is essential in a democracy.

Notes

1. Walter Lippmann, *Public Opinion* (New York: Free Press, 1965; reissue of 1922 text), 229.
2. 347 U.S. 483 (1954); 410 U.S. 113 (1973); 112 S. Ct. 2791 (1992).
3. Richard Davis, "Lifting the Shroud: News Media Portrayal of the U.S. Supreme Court," *Communications and the Law* 9 (October 1987): 46; and Bob Woodward and Scott Armstrong, *The Brethren* (New York: Simon and Schuster, 1979), claim to present an insider's view of Court proceedings.
4. Richard Davis, *Decisions and Images: The Supreme Court and the Press* (Englewood Cliffs, N.J.: Prentice Hall, 1994), chap. 4.
5. Ibid., chap. 3.
6. *Engel v. Vitale*, 370 U.S. 421 (1962); *Baker v. Carr*, 369 U.S. 186 (1962).
7. Chester A. Newland, "Press Coverage of the United States Supreme Court," *Western Political Quarterly* 17 (1964): 15–36. Also see Kenneth S. Devol, *Mass Media and the Supreme Court*, 2d ed. (New York: Hastings House, 1976).
8. Jerome O'Callaghan and James O. Dukes, "Media Coverage of the Supreme Court's Caseload," *Journalism Quarterly* 69 (spring 1992): 195–203.
9. David Ericson, "Newspaper Coverage of the Supreme Court: A Case Study," *Journalism Quarterly* 54 (autumn 1977): 605–607. See also Michael E. Solimine, "Newsmagazine Coverage of the Supreme Court," *Journalism Quarterly* 57 (winter 1980): 661–664; and Ethan Katsh, "The Supreme Court Beat: How Television Covers the Supreme Court," *Judicature* 67 (1983): 6–12. Also see Elliot E. Slotnick and Jennifer A. Segal, *Television News and the Supreme Court* (New York: Cambridge University Press, 1998).
10. Stephanie Greco Larson, "How the *New York Times* Covered Discrimination Cases," *Journalism Quarterly* 62 (winter 1985): 894–896; also see Stephanie Greco Larson, "Supreme Court Coverage and Consequences" (Paper presented at the annual meeting of the Midwest Political Science Association, Chicago, April 1989).

11. *Regents of the University of California v. Bakke,* 438 U.S. 265 (1978) and *Webster v. Reproductive Health Services,* 109 S. Ct. 3040 (1989); Slotnick and Segal, *Television News and the Supreme Court.*

12. Davis, *Decisions and Images,* chaps. 4–6; also see Frank J. Sorauf, "Campaign Money and the Press: Three Soundings," *Political Science Quarterly* 102 (spring 1987): 25–42.

13. Gregory Caldeira, "Neither the Purse Nor the Sword: Dynamics of Public Confidence in the Supreme Court," *American Political Science Review* 80 (December 1986): 1209–1228.

14. Robert E. Drechsel, *News Making in the Trial Courts* (New York: Longman, 1983), 19–22.

15. David Pritchard, "Homicide and Bargained Justice: The Agenda-Setting Effect of Crime News on Prosecutors," *Public Opinion Quarterly* 50 (spring 1986): 143–159. Jon Bruschke and William E. Loges, "Relationship Between Pretrial Publicity and Trial Outcomes," *Journal of Communication* 49(4) (autumn 1999): 104–120; Dorothy Imrich, Charles Mullin, and Daniel Linz, "Measuring the Extent of Prejudicial Pretrial Publicity in American Newspapers: A Content Analysis," *Journal of Communication* 45(3): 94–117.

16. Doris A. Graber, *Processing Politics: Learning from Television in the Internet Age* (Chicago: University of Chicago Press, 2001), 137–139.

17. A detailed account of coverage of crime and justice system news is presented in Doris A. Graber, *Crime News and the Public* (New York: Praeger, 1980); also see Roy E. Lotz, *Crime and the American Press* (New York: Praeger, 1991); and Gregg Barak, ed., *Media, Process and the Social Construction of Crime: Studies in Newsmaking Criminology* (New York: Garland, 1994).

18. Richard L. Fox and Robert van Sickel, *Tabloid Justice: Criminal Justice in an Age of Media Frenzy* (Boulder: Lynne Rienner, 2001), chap. 2.

19. Ibid., chap. 3.

20. Susanna Barber, *News Cameras in the Courtroom: A Free Press-Fair Trial Debate* (Norwood, N.J.: Ablex, 1987), especially 18–19.

21. Fox and Sickel, *Tabloid Justice,* chap. 4; Fred Graham, "Doing Justice with Cameras in the Courts," *Media Studies Journal* 12(1) (winter 1998): 32–37.

22. Ben H. Bagdikian, *The Media Monopoly,* 3d ed. (Boston: Beacon Press, 1990), 174. Also see Richard Campbell, *Media and Culture,* 3d ed. (Boston: Bedford/St. Martin's, 2002), 288–303.

23. Frederick Fico and Stan Soffin, "Fairness and Balance of Selected Newspaper Coverage of Controversial National, State, and Local Issues," *Journalism and Mass Communication Quarterly* 72(3) (autumn 1995): 621–633; Janet A. Bridges and Lamar W. Bridges, "Changes in News Use on the Front Pages of the American Daily Newspaper, 1986–1993," *Journalism and Mass Communication Quarterly* 73(4) (winter 1997): 826–838.

24. 1998 Media consumption questionnaire, http://www.people-press.org/med 98que.htm.

25. Jane B. Singer, "The Metro Wide Web: Changes in Newspapers' Gatekeeping Role Online," *Journalism and Mass Communication Quarterly* 78(1) (spring 2001): 65–80.

26. The term was coined by James N. Rosse. See note 4 in James M. Bernstein, Stephen Lacy, Catherine Cassara, and Tuen-yu Lau, "Geographic Coverage by Local Television News," *Journalism Quarterly* 57 (winter 1990): 664.

27. Phyllis Kaniss, *Making Local News* (Chicago: University of Chicago Press, 1991), 5.

28. http://www.naa.org/info/facts00/02.html.
29. See Bernstein et al., "Geographic Coverage by Local Television News," 671.
30. William R. Davie and Jung-Sook Lee, "Sex, Violence and Consonance/Differentiation: An Analysis of Local TV News Values," *Journalism and Mass Communication Quarterly* 72(1) (spring 1995): 128–138; also see David C. Coulson, Daniel Riffe, Stephen Lacy, and Charles R. St. Cyr, "Erosion of Television Coverage of City Hall? Perceptions of TV Reporters on the Beat," *Journalism and Mass Communication Quarterly* 78(1) (spring 2001): 81–92; and Guido H. Stempel III, "Where People Really Get Most of Their News," *Newspaper Research Journal* 12 (fall 1991): 2–9.
31. Daniel Riffe and Eugene F. Shaw, "Ownership, Operating, Staffing and Content Characteristics of 'News Radio' Stations," *Journalism Quarterly* 67 (winter 1990): 684–691.
32. Daniel M. Shea, "All Scandal Politics is Local: Ethical Lapses, the Media, and Congressional Elections," *Press/Politics* 4(2) (spring 1999): 45–62.
33. Kaniss, *Making Local News*, 175–179.
34. Ibid.
35. Martin Linsky, *How the Press Affects Federal Policymaking* (New York: Norton, 1986), 236.
36. Dan Berkowitz and Douglas B. Adams, "Information Subsidy and Agenda-Building in Local Television News," *Journalism Quarterly* 67 (winter 1990): 725.
37. Judy Van Slyke Turk and Bob Franklin, "Information Subsidies: Agenda-Setting Traditions," *Public Relations Review* 13 (1987): 29–41; Dan Berkowitz, "TV News Sources and News Channels: A Study in Agenda-Building," *Journalism Quarterly* 64 (autumn 1987): 508–513.
38. Thad Beyle and G. Patrick Lynch, "The Media and State Politics" (Paper presented at the annual meeting of the Midwest Political Science Association, Chicago, April 1991), 5.
39. Roza Tsagarousianou, Damian Tambini, and Cathy Brian, eds., *Cyberdemocracy: Technology, Cities and Civic Networks* (London: Routledge, 1998).
40. Claire E. Taylor, Jung-Sook Lee, and William R. Davie, "Local Press Coverage of Environmental Conflict," *Journalism and Mass Communication Quarterly* 77(1) (spring 2000): 175–192.
41. Kaniss, *Making Local News*, 107.
42. News selection criteria are discussed in Camilla Gant and John Dimmick, "Making Local News: A Holistic Analysis of Sources, Selection Criteria, and Topics," *Journalism and Mass Communication Quarterly* 77(3) (autumn 2000): 628–638.
43. Kaniss, *Making Local News*, 118–120.
44. Ibid., 126–127.
45. The term is used in Kaniss, *Making Local News*, 126.
46. Ibid., 76.
47. This discussion is based on Stephen Hess, "Levels of the Game: Federalism and the American News System" (Paper presented at the Hofstra University Conference, Hempstead, N.Y., April 1992).
48. For a discussion of state news in the *New York Times,* see Doris Graber, "Flashlight Coverage: State News on National Broadcasts," *American Politics Quarterly* 17 (July 1989): 277–290.
49. Pew Research Center for the People and the Press, "Media Report," http://www.people-press.org/media00rpt.htm. 2000.

50. Ibid.
51. Kaniss, *Making Local News,* 102.
52. Hess, *Live from Capitol Hill,* 49. Also see Taylor et al., "Local Press Coverage of Environmental Conflict," 175–192.
53. Bernstein et al., "Geographic Coverage by Local Television News," 668, 670; for similar results, also see Stephen Lacy and James M. Bernstein, "Daily Newspaper Content's Relationship to Publication Cycle and Circulation Size," *Newspaper Research Journal* (spring 1988): 49–57.
54. Hess, *Live from Capitol Hill,* 53.
55. Mark J. Rozell, "Local vs. National Press Assessments of Virginia's 1989 Gubernatorial Campaign," *Polity* 24 (fall 1991): 75.
56. Mark J. Rozell, "Campaign Press Coverage in the 'New Dominion': The 1991 Fairfax County (Virginia) Board of Supervisors Chairman Election" (Paper presented at the Eighth Citadel Conference on Southern Politics, Charleston, S.C., 1992), 18.
57. For a report on gubernatorial election studies in progress, see Beyle and Lynch, "The Media and State Politics."
58. Byron St. Dizer, "The Effects of Newspaper Endorsements and Party Identification on Voting Choice," *Journalism Quarterly* 62 (autumn 1985): 589–594.
59. A. Lichtenstein, "Differences in Impact between Local and National Televised Political Candidates' Debates," *Western Journal of Speech Communication* 46 (1982): 291–298; also see Dianne Bystrom, Cindy Roper, Robert Gobetz, Tom Massey, and Carol Beall, "The Effects of a Televised Gubernatorial Debate," *Political Communication Review* 16 (1991): 57–80.
60. Betty H. Zisk, *Money, Media, and the Grassroots: State Ballot Issues and the Electoral Process* (Newbury Park, Calif.: Sage, 1987), 28.
61. Ibid., 246.
62. Ibid., 109.
63. Ibid., 247–248.
64. James M. Bernstein and Stephen Lacy, "Contextual Coverage of Government by Local Television News," *Journalism Quarterly* 69 (summer 1992): 338.
65. John McManus, "How Local Television Learns What Is News," *Journalism Quarterly* 67 (winter 1990): 678.
66. Quoted in McManus, "How Local Television Learns What Is News," 672.
67. Bernstein and Lacy, "Contextual Coverage of Government by Local Television News," 339.
68. Kaniss, *Making Local News,* 90–91.

Readings

Barak, Gregg, ed. *Media, Process and the Social Construction of Crime: Studies in Newsmaking Criminology.* New York: Garland Publishing, 1994.
Chiasson, Lloyd, Jr. *The Press on Trial: Crimes and Trials as Media Events.* Westport, Conn.: Greenwood Press, 1997.
Davis, Richard. *Decisions and Images: The Supreme Court and the Press.* Englewood Cliffs, N.J.: Prentice Hall, 1994.
Fox, Richard L., and Robert van Sickel. *Tabloid Justice: Criminal Justice in an Age of Media Frenzy.* Boulder: Lynne Rienner, 2001.

Kaniss, Phyllis. *Making Local News.* Chicago: University of Chicago Press, 1991.
———. *The Media and the Mayor's Race: The Failure of Urban Political Reporting.* Indianapolis: Indiana University Press, 1995.
McManus, John H. *Market-Driven Journalism: Let the Citizen Beware?* Thousand Oaks, Calif.: Sage, 1994.
Slotnick, Elliot E., and Jennifer A. Segal. *Television News and the Supreme Court.* New York: Cambridge University Press, 1998.
Surette, Ray. *Media, Crime and Criminal Justice: Images and Realities,* 2d ed. Belmont, Calif.: Wadsworth, 1998.
Thaler, Paul. *The Watchful Eye: American Justice in the Age of the Television Trial.* Westport, Conn.: Praeger, 1994.

Foreign Affairs Coverage

WHEN ISRAEL AND JORDAN PREPARED TO SIGN a peace agreement in the fall of 1994, they scheduled the ceremony for midday at a barren desert patch two miles north of the Gulf of Aqaba. The place was subject to sudden desert sandstorms and the appointed hour was at the hottest time of the day. Why the location and the time? The answer is simple: It provided an excellent photo opportunity. As Israeli officials explained it, midday at the Arava (near the Jordan border) is time for morning news in America—just the right time to show Americans that their president, depicted in a dramatic setting, was the godfather of the Jordanian–Israeli peace settlement.[1]

Is television coverage really important enough to make major sacrifices to schedule an important diplomatic event to meet broadcasting schedules? Do the mass media shape the political dimensions of the world? What, if any, are the links between the mass media and the process of creating foreign policy and producing policy outputs? How are the media used by governments to further their policy objectives around the world? Does television play any active roles separate from those of other media in the shaping of American foreign policy? In this chapter we will try to answer such provocative questions, to shed light on the role played by the mass media in the shaping and conduct of American foreign policy.

We will first focus on the overall significance that American media and American citizens assign to news about foreign countries. Then we will point out the significant differences between the production of foreign and domestic news. We will consider the qualifications of foreign correspondents and the unique problems they face in collecting news and shaping it to meet newsworthiness criteria while heeding the canons of journalistic ethics and independence. Securing high-quality foreign news is an extraordinarily difficult task, and we shall note how well it is currently carried out and give examples of past accomplishments and failures.

The Foreign News Niche

Newspeople commonly assume that the American public is interested primarily in what goes on in the United States. Reports about the public's ignorance about foreign countries and foreign affairs lend credence to these assumptions. When asked, Americans themselves profess modest interest in foreign news, but when given a choice, they do not seek it out. When survey researchers asked a randomly selected sample of 3,002 people about the types of news that they watched routinely, or only when the story seemed especially important or interesting, only one-third of the respondents (34 percent) claimed to watch international news routinely while two-thirds (63 percent) said they watched only selectively. The figures for watching news about the local community were almost the exact reverse.[2] In a fifteen-year survey of attention to major news stories, reports about international events ranked dead last among stories that people claimed to follow "very closely." Fewer than 10 percent of the sampled public paid close attention to stories about the expansion of NATO (the North Atlantic Treaty Organization) to include Poland, Hungary, and the Czech Republic; stories about ethnic conflict in Kosovo and between the Yugoslav republics; and accounts of the 1997 visit by Chinese President Jiang Zemin to the United States and the 1997 Helsinki summit meeting between President Clinton and Russian President Boris Yeltsin. Major stories about internal politics, such as the inclusion of a neo-Nazi party in the Austrian government or Britain's Labor party ousting the Conservatives in 1997, also fell into the low-interest group, as did the debate over U.S. policy concerning global warming.[3]

Although foreign news lacks attraction for many Americans, it receives a considerable amount of coverage in print and electronic media. A four-month analysis of coverage in 1995 showed that the *New York Times,* the most ample source of foreign news, averaged twenty-six stories per day. Regional newspapers, such as the *Buffalo News* or the *Houston Chronicle,* carried an average of twelve foreign stories daily. The television networks, including CNN, averaged between two and three.[4] Compared with major domestic news stories, foreign news normally receives brief space and time and modest display. Elite newspapers like the *New York Times* and the *Washington Post* are exceptions. Selection criteria are also more rigorous. To be published, foreign news must have a more profound impact on the political, economic, or cultural concerns of the United States than domestic news. It must involve people of more exalted status, and entail more violence or disaster.[5] During crises, particularly prolonged ones that endanger American lives, foreign coverage often doubles or even triples; it may even drown out most other news. Conversely, the number of stories and their length shrinks when times seem unusually calm, as happened right after the Cold War ended with the collapse of the Soviet Union.[6] Public interest in foreign news fluctuates in similar fashion.

When the spotlight shifts away from foreign news, the number of foreign correspondents usually declines. There were 637 accredited U.S. correspondents in South Vietnam in 1968. By mid-1974 only 33 remained. Even though this small corps of correspondents filed relatively few stories from Vietnam, editors often balked at running them in daily newscasts and papers because the public had presumably lost interest. A spiral effect then sets in. Presumed lack of interest leads to less coverage. Reduced coverage further lessens interest in foreign news. An upward spiral of domestic news takes up the slack. This pattern prevails in most of the country's newspapers and television newscasts whenever foreign crises subside.

The country's foreign policy elites, including government officials, depend heavily on foreign news covered by prestigious media. As a State Department official attests, "The first thing we do is read the newspaper— *the newspaper—the New York Times.* You can't work in the State Department without the *New York Times. "*[7] Members of the U.S. Congress, particularly those concerned with foreign affairs, and foreign officials in the United States have made similar comments. All feel that elite newspaper reports keep them informed better and often faster than their own official sources.

Making Foreign News

Although news making for domestic stories and for foreign stories differs substantially, there are many similarities. To make comparisons easier, we will follow the organization of domestic news making and reporting described in Chapter 4. First we will consider the gatekeepers—the corps of foreign correspondents who are the front-line echelon among gatherers of foreign affairs news. Then we will discuss the setting for news selection, the criteria for choosing stories and the means of gathering

Reading Up on Foreign News

It is so easy to sing songs of doom and gloom about the news media. Domestic news is bad enough, but news about foreign affairs is even worse. Foreign news reports are altogether too brief, too superficial, and too limited in scope. So what happens to these claims of unrelieved disaster when one looks at the foreign affairs coverage by a good newspaper on a randomly chosen Sunday, a day when people have above-average leisure time to enjoy their favorite newspaper?

I picked up the *Chicago Tribune* on Sunday, August 12, 2001, to find out. Here is what I discovered. A major trouble spot of perennial interest to Americans—the fighting between Israel and the Palestinians—was amply covered by two long stories, including photographs. A *Tribune* staff reporter wrote three page-long columns about a motley group of foreigners who had positioned themselves as human shields between Israeli riot police occupying a PLO building and angry Palestinians. A second two-column story described what life in a state of siege is like for ordinary people in Israel. These articles contradicted the complaint that stories always ignore the lives of common people abroad.

The conflict in Northern Ireland, the other major trouble spot where U.S. diplomats have been heavily involved, rated one long story. It described Britain's ongoing efforts to encourage peace in the area. It, too, had a large, emotion-arousing photograph showing a good Samaritan aiding a man wounded in a restaurant bombing. A somewhat briefer story reported on efforts by the current Bush administration to renew ties with the Indonesian military despite its record of human rights abuses. The story presented a short history of U.S. relations with Indonesia and explained the objectives of the new policy.

Several brief stories—less than a full column long—reported on international events without explicitly tying them to U.S. policies. These included an Associated Press story about a visit by Japan's Prime Minister Junichiro Koizumi to a war memorial shrine. The visit to honor the dead was controversial because the shrine includes the graves of World War II war criminals. Other stories covered an anti-U.S. speech by Fidel Castro delivered in

(Box continues, next page)

Venezuela, a fight between Macedonian police officers and ethnic Albanians rebelling against the Macedonian government, and
the quest of a woman married to a Zambian Catholic archbishop
to have her husband released by Vatican authorities opposed to
the marriage. Two brief stories dealt with natural disasters, including deadly floods in Thailand and Iran.

History and international relations received ample coverage.
Three long stories covered the Holocaust and the controversies
surrounding the flood of books written by survivors and their lawsuits claiming reparations. Reporters discussed conflicting views
about how much attention such books should still receive and
how international law should deal with claims of war crimes.
Three other international legal issues were explored in an article
authored by University of Chicago scholar Adelle Simmons. Simmons condemned the Bush administration for defying international norms by refusing to accept the Kyoto Treaty on Gobal
Warming as well as conventions banning biological weapons,
nuclear weapons tests, and landmines. The article constituted a
counterweight to prior *Tribune* articles in which the Bush administration had explained its reasons for abstaining from these
widely accepted international agreements. The Simmons critique
demonstrates that the administration's foreign policies are not
always sacrosanct.

On the lighter side, an extensive map and picture story, covering more than a full page, told about the pleasures awaiting
travelers who visit the French Riviera. A shorter story extolled the
virtues of Chinese foods prepared by restaurants in Toronto.
Finally, Chicagoans were encouraged to visit their Field museum
to enjoy the "Cleopatra of Egypt: from History to Myth" exhibit.
There they would be able to see Egyptian antiquities from the
world's leading museums that would give visitors hitherto unavailable insights into centuries of Egyptian history and culture.

So what is the final score? The *Tribune* carried a total of seventeen stories spanning Europe, Asia, Africa, and Latin America.
Among the fourteen stories that raised serious issues, nine covered the problems in depth. Most stories provided context and
critiques. That's not bad for one day's foreign affairs lessons.
Such riches certainly are not the rule, but neither are they the
exception. Critics take note!

them, the constraints on news production, and finally the effects of gate-keeping on foreign affairs coverage.

The Gatekeepers

Concentration of Control. A striking aspect of foreign news coverage is the high degree of concentration of news gathering. Most news about events happening throughout the world is collected by four major wire services. They are the American-owned Associated Press (AP), Britain's Reuters, France's Agence France-Presse (AFP), and ITAR, which replaced the Soviet news agency Tass in 1992.[8] Among these world-class wire services, AP is by far the largest. It maintains ninety-five international bureaus from which it relays news by modern electronic means to subscribers in all parts of the world. For television, pictorial materials are also collected by two television news services: Visnews and WTN. They are owned by British companies, primarily Reuters, the British Broadcasting Corporation (BBC), and Britain's Independent Television News.

The wire services station reporters in nearly half the countries of the world. North American and Western European countries are most likely to have resident reporters; Africa and the Eastern bloc are least likely to have them and are, instead, covered by visiting reporters. The wire services ferret out the stories that make up the pool from which other gate-keepers select complete reports or find leads to pursue stories more fully. Because wire service reporters work for a vast variety of clients throughout the world, their news must be bland so that it does not offend people whose views span a wide political spectrum. Wire service news therefore emphasizes fast and ample reports of ongoing events, not interpretation, which then falls to other foreign correspondents.[9]

Besides these worldwide organizations, the American market is also served by syndicated news collected by major American papers, like the *New York Times,* the *Washington Post,* and the *Chicago Tribune.* These papers have their own correspondents stationed abroad, a luxury enjoyed by barely 1 percent of all American dailies. Because of the advent of television, the print press foreign correspondent corps has been joined by foreign correspondents from the major television networks and CNN.

Since the 1980s, CNN, the twenty-four-hour Cable News Network, has become a major player in the international news game. Its more than four thousand reporters scattered throughout the world collect and report news in multiple languages to audiences throughout the world. The striking feature about CNN, besides the comprehensiveness of its news-gathering apparatus, is its continuous coverage of major crises such as the 1985 hijacking of a TWA jetliner, the 1991 war against Iraq, or the standoff between the United States and mainland China over the downing of a U.S. surveillance aircraft and the detention of its crew on the Chinese island of Hainan in 2001. As is typical of live coverage, the reports are a mixed bag of events and interviews ranging from the trivial to the significant, with less time given to analysis and expert commentary than is typical for network television news.[10] The emphasis is on taping whatever is readily and inexpensively available so that viewers are the first to see a breaking news event at close range.

The stories gathered by the small corps of initial gatekeepers reach huge audiences. Although subscribers generally use only a limited portion of the coverage made available by these sources, what they do use reflects the story patterns and interpretations of the initial gatekeepers. However, given the fact that reporters carry the baggage of their cultures and subcultures in their heads, they transform the same story raw materials into different endproducts. For instance, faced with the same information about global warming before, during, and after a 1997 international conference in Kyoto, Japan, American reporters focused on American stances on the issue, slighting international views; German reporters privileged international views over European opinion. The American media split attention about evenly between the substance of the debates at Kyoto and the strategies used by negotiators; the German media focused more heavily on policy substance at the expense of strategy issues.[11] Once established, story stereotypes become fixed; countries, leaders, and specific policies that gatekeepers have evaluated in particular ways may be characterized that way long after the reality has changed.

Surveillance of the Foreign Scene. The total number of full-time American foreign correspondents has fluctuated over the years, rising during international crises and falling afterward. Overall, the trend has been downward since its peak during World War II. Several reasons account for this. The ability to dispatch correspondents quickly from an American home base to foreign countries is one. Air travel has made it possible for each American correspondent to reach and cover many more countries than ever before. NBC's Andrea Mitchell, for example, between March 1995 and February 1996 reported from Canada, England, Haiti, China, and Vietnam. Her ABC colleague Sheila MacVicar covered Iraq, Zaire, Bosnia, and Ireland. But physical mobility is not matched by the psychic mobility that would allow reporters to feel at home in more countries. Nor is it accompanied by sudden spurts in knowledge that would permit such "parachute" reporters to cover a new area with insight.

High costs also have forced a steady decline in the number of foreign correspondents. In the 1990s it cost as much as $300,000 a year to keep one correspondent abroad, a steep price considering the limited demand

TABLE 11-1   Distribution of Foreign Correspondents: 1991 (in percentages)

Major regions	American correspondents abroad		Foreign correspondents in United States[a]		U.S./foreign comparison[b]
Western Europe	777	40%	687	45%	−5%
East Asia	313	16	307	20	−4
Latin America	249	13	140	9	+4
Middle East	187	10	116	8	+2
Southeast Asia and Pacific	125	7	62	4	+3
Soviet Union	90	5	39	3	+2
Sub-Sahara Africa	66	3	27	2	+1
Eastern Europe	50	3	28	2	+1
South Asia	41	2	28	2	0
Canada	28	2	45	3	−1
Other/International agencies	—	—	46	3	—
Total	1,926		1,525		

SOURCE: For U.S. data, Ralph Kliesch, from the E. W. Scripps School of Journalism, Ohio University of Athens, Ohio; for foreign data, *Editor and Publisher International Yearbook, 1991* (New York: Editor & Publisher, 1991).

[a] The figure is for correspondents based in New York and Washington, D.C.
[b] The figure reflects distribution differences between the American and the foreign corps of correspondents, when column four is subtracted from column two.

for foreign affairs stories. Because it is much cheaper, many papers use stringers instead of regular employees and rely on reports produced by local foreign news media. Stringers, who are usually citizens of the country from which they report, are paid for each story a newspaper publishes. At best, they may have keener insight into local problems than American reporters sent to the country. But they often fail to meet the news-gathering standards prized by American media, and may be unable to tailor news stories to the concerns of American audiences.

U.S. correspondents abroad are unevenly distributed. More are stationed in friendly locations than in neutral or hostile areas. Locations and numbers shift frequently and therefore are difficult to ascertain. Table 11-1 depicts the regions in which American foreign correspondents were stationed in 1991, and the regions whose correspondents were stationed in New York or Washington to report about the United States. The rank orderings of the two groups were mirror images and probably still are. Although the numbers of correspondents have fluctuated from year to year, the proportions have remained fairly constant for regional distributions as well as locations in particular countries. Correspondents are thinly spread over relatively few capital cities, leaving huge gaps in coverage. In 1995, for example, the *New York Times* had thirty-six correspondents in twenty-five capital cities. They were Berlin, Bonn, Frankfurt, Paris, Brussels, Geneva, Madrid, Rome, London, Dublin, Warsaw, Zagreb, and Moscow in Europe; Tokyo, Beijing, Hong Kong, and Shanghai in Asia; Beirut and Jerusalem in the Middle East; Johannesburg and Nairobi in Africa; Buenos Aires and Rio de Janeiro in South America; and Toronto and Mexico City in North America.

The Paris Bureau was the largest, with four correspondents, followed by Tokyo and Moscow with three each. Besides covering their city, correspondents travel to other locations to cover breaking news. When major events happen, additional reporters as well as prominent anchors may fly in for more extensive coverage. Critics appropriately call this "hopscotch" journalism because it leaps over vast, potentially important areas. The work of American reporters is supplemented through news from Reuters, the British news agency, and Agence France-Presse, the French news agency, which have more ample representation in their former colonial regions where American reporters tend to be especially sparse.

What kinds of people are these journalists who select the foreign news for American elites and publics? What are their biases? And how do they compare with the correspondents who cover the United States for the benefit of foreign nationals? A typical American journalist abroad is a white male in his forties, college educated, with more than ten years of reporting news under his belt. Like staff people generally in prominent American news organizations, most foreign correspondents are politically liberal, taking positions to the left of mainstream views. Nonetheless, they rarely challenge the U.S. government's stance on foreign policy issues, unless prominent leaders question the policy. When that happens, the media often rush to join the attack on official policies.

Many foreign correspondents remain at the same locations for several years, so they become fully familiar with their area of coverage. This does not necessarily mean that they are fluent in the local languages. In one survey, more than 80 percent of American reporters stationed in Western Europe and Latin America claimed to read and speak the native languages fluently or with easy facility. But in Eastern Europe and Africa, these figures were cut in half. The poorest showing was in Central and East Asia, where only 9 percent of American reporters could read the intricate written characters and only 18 percent could speak the languages well. Deficient reading skills hamper American reporters in local interviews and investigations. They must depend on translated newspaper reports and on handouts to the foreign press.[12] This sharply curbs their effectiveness as reporters, especially because contacts with local people and personal ties that may supply good insights also tend to be sparse, judging from survey data. In some countries translators are supplied and controlled by the government. Presence of government officials during interviews dampens the free exchange of ideas that might otherwise take place.

Public relations agencies hired by foreign countries to promote their images provide one very important, usually overlooked, additional source of news about foreign countries. Steadily growing numbers of countries are contracting for professional image management. Citizens for a Free Kuwait, a front organization for the government of Kuwait, for example, spent nearly $11 million with just one public relations firm to burnish Kuwait's image in the months after it had been invaded by Iraq.[13] By either stimulating or suppressing media coverage, public relations agencies can improve their client's media image. Presumably this then affects elite and mass opinion so that the country in question enjoys improved relations with American politicians and the American public.[14]

Surveillance of the American Scene. Altogether, 1,548 correspondents from foreign countries covered the United States in 2000. The largest contingent, 695, was stationed in New York City; the Washington contingent had 593 reporters. The remainder were in Florida (25) and Chicago (15). Just as Americans receive the most news about friendly foreign countries, so most news about America goes to its friends.[15] The poorer regions of the world find it too costly to send their own correspondents. In 1991, for instance, when a total of 1,525 correspondents worked in the United States, the corps included a mere 6 correspondents from Nigeria, Africa's largest nation, compared to 39 from Israel. Japan topped the list of U.S.-based correspondents with 213 journalists compared to 39 from China and 22 from India, the world's most populous nations. Neighboring Canada had 45, and neighboring Mexico had 9 correspondents. West Germany sent 129, and East Germany dispatched 5. Italy had a puzzlingly large contingent of 117 correspondents and Belgium made do with 7.[16]

Foreign reporters are an extremely well-educated group. A survey conducted in the mid-1980s found that nine out of ten were university trained, and about half of these had advanced degrees. That included 22 percent who had earned a doctorate. Seventy-eight percent were fluent English speakers, and a majority were fluent in a third language as well. On the average, they spoke three languages. Nevertheless, close contacts with Americans were limited. Only 7 percent said that their best and closest contacts were Americans. In political orientation, foreign newspeople covering the United States were further to the left than most American reporters. Seventy percent claimed to be left-leaning, 14 percent preferred a middle position, and 17 percent leaned to the right.[17]

It is difficult for foreign reporters to cover the whole United States adequately. Most correspondents are kept busy in Washington and New York. They rarely travel to other parts of the country, except to cover special events such as major sports competitions or presidential nominating conventions. Thus the impressions that foreigners receive about Americans' opinions and politics are largely the views of official Washington. The leftward orientation of most reporters from foreign countries produces a substantial amount of criticism of America's economic, military, and foreign aid policies and often makes the conduct of foreign relations rocky. Hostile coverage is only partially balanced by the influx of news from American media and government broadcasts, such as Voice of America (VOA) or WORLDNET, an Internet program sponsored by the United States Information Agency (USIA). WORLDNET enables reporters in foreign capitals to have direct access to news relevant to their country from an official U.S. perspective.

The Setting for News Selection

Cultural Pressures.   American correspondents abroad, like domestic journalists, must operate within the context of American politics and American political culture. Besides reflecting the American value structure, stories also must conform to established American stereotypes. For example, once the stereotype of Iraq's leader Saddam Hussein as "another Hitler" had captured the public's imagination, stories depicting him as a caring benefactor of sick children would have had a false ring.[18] Nonetheless, foreign correspondents abroad have greater leeway than their domestic counterparts to evaluate and interpret the news that they report because there is less likelihood that the domestic audience—ordinary citizens or powerful interest groups—will be offended.

Intraorganizational norms and pressures also influence news selection. Foreign news is gathered by a small enough group of reporters to allow for much personal contact and cooperation. Because the wire services perform the initial gatekeeping tasks for most newspapers and electronic media, topic selection is quite uniform. In the United States, elite papers then take the lead in framing the stories, and editors and reporters throughout the country follow suit.

Political Pressures.   Overt and covert political pressures to publish or suppress news stories play a greater role in foreign news production than on the domestic scene. Foreign correspondents often must do their host country's bidding. Many host governments are politically unstable and fear for their survival if they receive unfavorable publicity. Hence, foreign correspondents, like the native newspeople in unstable countries, are heavily censored. If foreign correspondents want to remain in the country, they must write dispatches acceptable to the authorities. Otherwise they face severe penalties—expulsion, confiscation of their notes and pictures, closure of transmission facilities, refusal of contact by public officials, and the like. This has led to a strange phenomenon: The most undemocratic countries often receive the least criticism whereas more open societies are freely reproached.

Scores of countries have barred foreign reporters entirely from entering or have expelled them after entry. Cambodia, Laos, Vietnam, Nicaragua, El Salvador, Albania, the Soviet Union, and South Africa provide vivid examples from recent decades. Britain kept foreign reporters away from the embattled Falkland Islands in 1983. Israel has repeatedly imposed tight censorship on coverage of its activities in Lebanon and in the occupied West Bank and Gaza Strip. During the Iran–Iraq hostilities in the early 1980s, reporters were permitted at the front only whenever the host country thought it had won an engagement. Large areas of Central America and of the former Soviet Union have been closed to reporters, making it almost impossible adequately to cover hostilities there. Bureaucratic hurdles abound, ranging from difficult visa requirements, to failure to provide transportation to outlying areas, to hurdles in transmitting the news to one's home base. In some countries reporters face physical danger. Not infrequently, they have been jailed, assaulted, and sometimes murdered. In 2000, twenty-six journalists were murdered in seventeen countries. Colombia, Russia, and Sierra Leone were the most dangerous countries with three fatalities each. Hundreds more journalists were arrested and often tortured.[19] The Helsinki Accords of 1975, in which many countries promised free and safe access to each other's newspeople, have done little to improve the situation.

When countries previously closed to foreign journalists suddenly open their borders, journalists may be totally unprepared for insightful coverage. The opening of the People's Republic of China in 1972 is an example. Reporters arrived with President Richard Nixon and Secretary of State Henry Kissinger. During their short stay in China, they dutifully reported those stories that the Chinese arranged for them to report. Not surprisingly, their American audiences were treated to a romanticized travelogue rather than solid political analysis.

Media Diplomacy. A recent development in foreign news production is media diplomacy—attempts by U.S. and foreign leaders to use news media to further their causes and attempts by correspondents in the United States and abroad to inject themselves directly into the political process. As media scholar Eytan Gilboa points out, media reports about political leaders' foreign policy pronouncements are traditional journalism. But media-broker journalism, for which journalists intentionally become direct participants in the political process, runs counter to the tradition of a politically neutral press.[20]

The Middle East situation presents the most dramatic example of media-broker journalism. CBS anchor Walter Cronkite became a peacemaker in 1977 when, during a television interview, he drew from Egypt's president Anwar al-Sadat a promise to visit Jerusalem if this action would further peace. In a separate interview, Cronkite secured a pledge from Israeli prime minister Menachem Begin that he would personally welcome Sadat at Ben Gurion airport. With such mutual commitments, the scene was set for the historic meeting.[21]

When Sadat arrived in Israel, flanked by anchors from the three American networks, two thousand journalists from all over the globe were part of the welcoming crowds. This was media diplomacy in the broadest sense. The event was covered live on American television and radio, giving the principals a chance to woo American audiences. In the weeks that followed, more than thirty million people in America and millions more worldwide watched and judged the peacemaking process. Television alone devoted twenty-four hours of broadcasts to the spectacle, supplemented by radio and print news.

When Arab–Israeli peacemaking moved to the United States the following spring, more traditional media diplomacy continued the efforts to achieve peace. President Sadat, fully aware of the importance of courting the American public, made himself available for a television interview immediately after arriving for the 1978 Camp David meeting. The next day in his address to the National Press Club, he accused the Israelis of stalling the negotiations. Israel countered this propaganda move by promptly dispatching Foreign Minister Moshe Dayan on a ten-day speaking tour of major American cities to garner favorable publicity for the Israeli side. The media reported it all with relish, proud of the role they had played in bringing about encounters between Israeli and Egyptian officials. Little thought was given to the political ramifications that ensue when foreign heads of state readily use the American press as their public relations tool.

The lesson that media diplomacy can succeed where more ordinary government-to-government contacts fail has not been lost on other world leaders. For instance, in 1979 Iran's revolutionary leader, Ayatollah Ruhollah Khomeini, rebuffed official emissaries from the United States who were sent to negotiate the release of the American embassy personnel held hostage by Iranian students. Instead, he arranged a series of interviews with American television correspondents, requiring prior approval of questions so that he could control the discussion. To ensure maximum exposure for the Ayatollah's views, Iranian leaders permitted an especially lengthy interview for the popular CBS program *60 Minutes*. At the same time, they assigned low priority to an interview to be aired on low-audience public television. The Iranian embassy also bought full-page advertisements in the *New York Times* and other American newspapers to offer the American public Iran's version of the hostage story.

Even when diplomatic relations are carried out through normal channels, reporters often become part of the political process by choosing the issues to be aired during interviews with political leaders and by covering selected activities during negotiating sessions and when leaders travel abroad. They report these events as they see them.[22] In the long-standing conflict in Northern Ireland, reporters have given voice to formally excluded parties, like Sinn Fein, the political wing of the Irish Republican Army (IRA), by publicizing their views about ongoing negotiations.[23]

Although media diplomacy is often helpful, it also is fraught with disadvantages and dangers. Government officials, who have far more foreign policy expertise than journalists, may be maneuvered into untenable positions. They may have to react to unforeseen developments with undue haste, especially when twenty-four-hour newscasts may also arouse interest groups who see peaceful or disruptive protests in front of television cameras as a way to promote their causes worldwide. That has been a common occurrence at the annual economic summit meetings of world leaders.[24] Also, journalists may inadvertently provide a propaganda forum for foreign leaders. This is why CNN's Peter Arnett was harshly condemned by many Americans when he engaged Iraqi president Saddam Hussein in a long television interview during the Gulf War. The interview permitted the Iraqi leader to broadcast accusations against his antagonists to a worldwide audience.

Economic Pressures. Economic considerations, like cultural and political factors, strongly influence foreign news selection. First, there is the usual pressure to present appealing stories that attract big audiences and keep the media profitable. This pressure is even more burdensome for foreign correspondents than for their domestic counterparts because their stories must be exceptionally good to attract large audiences. Second, there is the pressure to avoid or minimize huge production costs. Reporting events such as President Nixon's trip to China or Israel's Yom Kippur War cost each network in excess of $3 million per event. Leasing cables for news transmission is expensive and so is telephone communication. Satellite transmission is also costly, especially for short messages. Some stories therefore may be shut out because they cannot be transmitted cheaply, and others may be included merely because transmission is comparatively inexpensive and convenient.

Gathering the News: The Beat

The international beat system is quite similar to local beats. Newspapers initially established their foreign news bureaus in major capitals of the world, primarily in Western Europe. From there, correspondents covered entire countries rather than particular types of stories; London, Paris, Bonn, and Rome were the main news-gathering spots. In the wake of the Vietnam War, Saigon, Tokyo, Hong Kong, and other points in that region became important news centers. China moved into focus with the opening of diplomatic relations in 1972.

The average newspaper bureau abroad has one or two correspondents, one or two film crews staffed by foreigners, perhaps a radio correspondent, and a few stringers. Correspondents from these bureaus jet to spots within easy flying range whenever big stories break. For local news, they rely heavily on national news services that exist in two-thirds of the countries of the world. Countries without such services, and without satellite transmission facilities, are far less likely to receive coverage than countries that have them.

The bulk of foreign affairs news for American media actually originates in Washington from various beats in the executive branch, especially the White House, the State Department, and the Pentagon. The president's views tend to dominate whenever situations are controversial. However, the media put their imprint on the news by deciding which opposition views to feature favorably or unfavorably. Foreign policy stories are often hard to cover because officials are reluctant to talk whenever delicate negotiations or the prestige of the United States is at stake. Stories from Washington rarely involve exciting pictures that will provide dramatic images on television. Foreign correspondents, like their domestic counterparts, prefer to report predictable events, such as elections or summit conferences, so they can plan coverage in advance. The decision to film particular foreign stories abroad is usually made in the United States because the media's home offices think that they know best what will interest American audiences. Foreign bureaus do the actual filming.

Foreign news bestows unequal attention on various regions and countries of the world just as domestic news covers regions of the United States unequally. Neither is there any correlation between size of population and amount of coverage. In general, beats cover the countries with which the United States has its most significant diplomatic contacts. In recent years, that has usually meant England, France, West Germany, Italy, and Russia in Europe; Israel and Egypt in the Middle East; and, more recently, the People's Republic of China and Japan in the Far East. Aside from Canada and Mexico, the Western hemisphere is covered lightly, except when Americans become concerned about production and export of illicit drugs, civil strife, or international business issues. Asian coverage was light until the Vietnam War, when it replaced stories from other parts of the world for several years. Overall, coverage has dropped off sharply in all types of media since the end of the Cold War. It averages just over 5 percent of the total story pool.

TABLE 11-2   Network Coverage of World Regions: October 1, 2000–
November 4, 2000

Region	Period total	Number of stories with visuals	Linkage to the United States
Eastern Europe	51	38	14
Middle East	180	131	101
Asia	49	27	12
Western Europe	18	12	0
Africa	12	7	4
Caribbean	1	0	0
Latin America	11	5	3
North America	21	11	5
Australia	2	2	2

SOURCE: Author's research compiled from Vanderbilt Television News Archives data.
NOTE: $N = 345$.

Similar to domestic news, traditional political content is fading and social and economic news is becoming more plentiful.[25]

Table 11-2 provides data on network television coverage of major regions of the world from October 1 to November 4, 2000. Clearly, coverage is unevenly distributed. Heaviest coverage goes to areas involved in bloody conflicts, including massive injuries to civilians. If it bleeds, it definitely leads. Stories about the Middle East conflict were most abundant during that period, followed by tales of woe from Eastern Europe and Asia. Western Europe, once the mainstay of foreign news, has slipped into limbo, joining Latin America, the Caribbean, and Australia, which have always been there. Attention to North America was a bit above average in 2000, largely because of increased U.S.–Mexican dealings. In general, stories with visuals are more attractive to viewers than stories that are purely verbal. Obviously, when roughly two-thirds (67 percent) of foreign stories lack pictures, the chances are small that they will be noticed and remembered. Audiences are also more likely to pay attention to stories that are linked explicitly to U.S. interests. In the waning months of 2000, only 40 percent of the stories made that linkage, making the stories even less attractive for average Americans. Linkage to a U.S. concern is especially important for regions with which average Americans are least familiar, such as Africa and Asia, and even Latin America and the Caribbean.

Criteria for Choosing Stories

Foreign news, like domestic news, is selected primarily for audience appeal rather than for political significance. This means that stories must have an angle that interests Americans. Sociologist Herbert Gans examined foreign affairs news in television newscasts and in news magazines and identified seven subjects that are covered frequently.[26] First in order of frequency of coverage are American activities in foreign countries, particularly when presidents and secretaries of state visit. Second are events that affect Americans directly in a major way, such as wars, oil embargoes, and international economic problems. Third are relations of the United States with communist and formerly communist states. Internal political and military problems of these countries are emphasized. Fourth, elections in other parts of the world are covered if they involve a change in the head of state. There also is a sentimental attachment for following the major (and minor) activities of European royalty. Fifth are stories about dramatic political conflicts. Most wars, coups d'état, and revolutions are reported; protests, as a rule, are covered only when they are violent. Left-wing coups receive more attention than right-wing coups. Sixth are disasters, if they involve massive loss of lives and destruction of property. There is a rough calculus by which severity is measured: "10,000 deaths in Nepal equals 100 deaths in Wales equals 10 deaths in West Virginia equals one death next door."[27] In general, the more distant a nation, the more frequently a newsworthy event must happen to be reported. Seventh are the excesses of foreign dictators, particularly when they involve brutality against political dissidents (for example, genocide in Rwanda and Bosnia). Noticeably absent from American broadcasts and papers are stories about ordinary people and ordinary events abroad. These would be news to Americans, but, except for occasional special features, they are not *news* in the professional dictionary of journalists.

Foreign news stories also must have an appealing format. Emphasis on violence, conflict and disaster, timeliness or novelty, and familiarity of persons or situations are the major selection criteria. Stories from areas that are familiar because of ample prior stories or because they are common travel destinations are more likely to be published than stories from more remote parts of the world. When news from countries with unfamiliar cultures is published, the rule of "uncertainty absorption" comes into play. Only plausible stories are acceptable, and they must be cast into a familiar framework, such as the battle against poverty and racism or the moral bankruptcy of military dictators.[28] Such biases make it very difficult to change images of culturally distant countries. Far-off parts of the world are rarely covered except when sensational events such as violence and disaster occur or there is negative news about top-level public officials. Moreover, the high costs of covering news abroad force news organizations to limit the sites where they can maintain full-scale news operations.

The media's preference for news about current happenings has led to concentration on rapidly breaking stories in accessible places. More sig-

ANOTHER WORLD PLAYER COOLS *his* HEELS *while the* MONICA GAME GOES ON...

Reprinted with special permission of King Features Syndicate.

nificant long-range developments, such as programs to improve public health or reduce illiteracy or efforts to create new political parties, do not fit the bill if they lack a recent climax. Pressure for timeliness and novelty also fragments news presentation and usually precludes a follow-up. This gives major events an unwarranted air of suddenness and unpredictability. They have neither a past nor a future—merely a brief presence in the parade of current events.

At times coverage errs in the opposite direction. The story of Americans held hostage in Iran from November 4, 1979, to January 20, 1981, was vastly overcovered. During the first six months of the crisis, nearly one-third of each nightly network newscast was devoted to the story.[29] A similar situation developed during the 1991 Gulf War, when 57 percent of the foreign news focused on the Middle East. Much of that coverage was repetitious and uninformative. With media attention riveted on one international trouble spot, most other foreign news is slighted.

News Production Constraints

The problems of producing domestic news are magnified for foreign news making. Staffs are smaller, research facilities are more limited, language barriers are troublesome, and transmission difficulties may be enormous. For television news, which presents the bulk of foreign news for average Americans, the quest for good pictures is often frustrated by restrictions on access or because facilities for taking and processing pictures are inadequate.[30] The ability to use computers to transmit pictures almost instantaneously has made it much easier to supply pictures for breaking international news. Pictures are especially important for foreign news because they bring unfamiliar sights, which might be hard to imagine, directly into viewers' homes. Starvation in India or Somalia, the lifestyles of tribes in New Guinea or Australia, or street riots in Spain or China become much more comprehensible if audiences can experience them visually. Still, not even words and pictures combined can tell a whole story if the audience is unfamiliar with the setting in which the reported events are happening. Ugly street scenes of protesters attacking police, torching buildings, and looting stores may be misinterpreted if the audience does not know even uglier events that might have provoked the protest.[31] Such misinterpretations often have major policy consequences because audiences, including public officials, tend to side with the party that is seemingly in the right.

Space and time limitations are particularly troubling for foreign correspondents because foreign events are often unintelligible without adequate background information or interpretation. Complexity therefore becomes a major enemy and avoidance or oversimplification the defensive strategy. Stories must be written simply and logically even if the situation defies logic. Usually a single theme must be selected to epitomize the entire complex story. The dominant theme of the story about China's detention of the downed American plane and crew in 2001, for example, was that innocent Americans were held hostage by a dictatorial, anti-American regime—a gross oversimplification of a multifaceted situation. The complexities of China's internal politics, particularly the influence of its military institutions, received little attention because they could not be easily incorporated into a dramatic, visually appealing story.

Effects of Gatekeeping

Foreign affairs coverage is dramatic and up to date, but it lacks depth and breadth. It stereotypes and oversimplifies, and it often distorts facts by failing to embed them in a realistic context. Analysis of forty-six years of news coverage of the Soviet Union between 1945 and 1991 revealed that the lion's share went to military aspects of the Cold War while economic and science issues were neglected (see Table 11-3). It was no wonder,

TABLE 11-3   Soviet News Story Topics in the U.S. Press: January 1945 to January 1991 (in percentages)

Topic	Press conference themes	Editorial themes
Soviet foreign relations	23%	14%
Soviet military policy	18	9
U.S. attitude about Soviets	21	33
U.S./Soviet meetings	14	5
U.S. military policy	5	6
Soviet attitudes about United States	4	7
U.S./Soviet comparisons	5	4
Human rights issues	3	11
Soviet leaders' quality	2	4
Communism as ideology	2	3
U.S. policy about Soviet Union	1	2
Soviet technology	1	1

SOURCE: Author's research.

NOTE: $N = 2{,}636$ press conference themes and 5,310 editorial themes.

then, that most Americans, including political leaders, were taken by surprise when economic deficiencies led to the disintegration and ultimate collapse of the Soviet Union in the 1990s.[32] Similarly, a twelve-year study of international terrorism stories led to the conclusion that "network coverage bore little relationship to actual patterns of occurrence. On the whole, the limitations of production and presentation, concerns over audience share, and the narrow focus of journalistic notions of professionalism result in coverage more notable for its erratic nature than for its systematic biases."[33]

Choosing Frames for Friends and Foes.   The fact that foreign news reported in the American press is based primarily on American sources who stay closely to the mainstream line explains why pro-American perspectives dominate. As the saying goes, outcomes are judged by whose ox is gored. Coverage of the downing of two planes, one by Soviet fire and the other by American fire, illustrates the principle.

In 1983, a Soviet fighter plane shot down Korean Airlines Flight 007 with a loss of 269 lives. Five years later, in 1988, the *Vincennes,* a U.S. Navy ship, shot down Iran Air Flight 655 with a loss of 290 lives. The Soviets claimed that the shooting was justified because the Korean plane had been identified as a hostile target; the Americans made the same claim for their action. Though the cases differed in detail and in the context in which they occurred, they were sufficiently alike to expect rough similarity in coverage. That did not happen, judging from coverage of the events in *Time, Newsweek,* the *New York Times,* the *Washington Post,* and the *CBS*

Evening News. The manner in which the news was framed, including the language and pictures used in the stories and the overall context into which the stories were placed, cast the Soviet action as a moral outrage and the American action as a regrettable technological failure.[34]

For example, almost twice as much coverage was given to the tragedy caused by the Soviets than to its American counterpart, even though the loss of life was greater in the Iran Air case. Following the Korean Airlines crash, *Newsweek* proclaimed on its cover "Murder in the Air"; *Time*'s cover read "Shooting to Kill: The Soviets Destroy an Airliner." *Newsweek*'s cover on the 1988 crash was headlined, "The Gulf Tragedy: Why It Happened," omitting any reference to a suspected villain. In the same way, *Time,* in a small insert on its cover, said innocuously, "What Went Wrong in the Gulf." The stories inside the magazines repeatedly accused the Soviets of knowingly destroying a civilian plane, whereas the Americans' actions were excused as pardonable ignorance. The Soviets' action was characterized as typical behavior for that country and guilt was attributed to its leaders. Not so for the Americans.

The stories about the Korean airliner dwelled on the human tragedy; the Iranian airliner story de-emphasized that aspect. When Soviet actions were described, words like "atrocity," "crime," "massacre," and "murder" abounded. For the Americans, the emphasis was on the accidental nature of the event. When, during the investigation of the action of the *Vincennes,* some doubts were raised about the innocence of the American crew, these facts were mentioned inconspicuously. So was commentary that suggested the Soviet action might have been accidental.

There is no evidence that the distortions that spring from such chauvinistic framing are deliberate. Rather, the framing reflects the actual perspectives of the journalists, based on their choice of sources and the predispositions with which they approach stories involving countries identified as friend or foe. Nonetheless, this type of coverage has political consequences. In 1983, it heightened anti-Soviet feelings among members of Congress and the public, sharply reducing the momentum of the nuclear freeze movement that had been gaining ground.[35] In the Iran Air case in 1988, coverage defused potential pressure for withdrawal of American forces from the Persian Gulf region. Instead of seeing the tragedy as an example of harm caused by America's presence in the area, warranting reconsideration of the policy, the incident consolidated American support behind the Reagan administration's foreign policies in the Gulf.

Based on a study of media frames in stories about the 1993 peace agreements between Israel and the PLO, Gadi Wolfsfeld concluded that the Israeli press covered both government and opposition views adequately. Whether government or opposition frames were depicted depended on which claims

TABLE 11-4   Competing Government and Opposition Frames of the 1993 Oslo Peace Agreement between Israel and the PLO

Published frames / Cultural meta-frame	Rabin government viewpoints / Territorial compromise	Opposition viewpoints / Israel's lands are indivisible
Package		
Core frame	A chance for peace	National disaster
	The issue is whether we can achieve peace with our neighbors through compromise	The issue is whether we are willing to surrender our national rights to our enemies and risk the destruction of Israel
Core position	Israel must give up land in order to achieve peace with our neighbors. The Israel–PLO agreement is just such a compromise	Israel's agreement with the PLO constitutes a grave danger to Israel's existence. Israel should cancel the agreement
Metaphors	Dove/Time bomb	Suicide
Historical exemplars	Peace with Egypt/Algeria	World War II (Chamberlain/Vichy government)/Yom Kippur War
Catchphrases	Give peace a chance/Enough blood, enough tears/Let the sun rise/Peace is my security	The Land of Israel is in danger/The Land of Israel is not for sale/Rabin is a traitor
Depictions	PLO as the more moderate force among the Palestinians/The settlers as opponents to peace/Israel as a democratic country who cannot rule over another people	The PLO as terrorists who kill women and children/The left as stupid, naive, or traitorous for giving up Israel's security
Visual images	Signing of accords in Jerusalem and Washington/Palestinians celebrating peace accords	Dead and wounded from terrorist attacks/Arafat's face/Palestinians wearing kefiyas as masks/Rabin in kefiyah
Roots	New willingness of Palestinians to accept Israel's right to exist	A Palestinian state/Destruction of Israel
Consequences	Peace and prosperity for the entire Middle East	A Palestinian state/Destruction of Israel
Appeals to principle	Israel's eternal striving for peace/The end of oppression of another people	The right of the Jewish people to the Land of Israel/The survival of the Jewish state

SOURCE: Adapted from Gadi Wolfsfeld, *Media and Political Conflict: News from the Middle East* (Cambridge: Cambridge University Press, 1997), 106.

seemed most in tune with evolving political events. Table 11-4 presents an outline of the competing frames. It demonstrates how diametrically opposed such frames can be and how each suggests a different policy scenario. Wolfs-feld also points out that reporters commonly ignore opposition frames, leaving the government's interpretation of events uncontested.[36]

Wars in the Television Age.   In the wake of the Vietnam War, many politicians and other political observers believed that fighting lengthy wars had become nearly impossible for democratic societies in the age of full-color, battlefront television. When battle scenes are broadcast nightly in bloody colors, public support for wars is likely to vanish. To avoid such damages, in the 1982 Falkland Islands War, Great Britain and Argentina both resorted to the kind of censorship usually associated only with authoritarian regimes. Like the Soviets in Afghanistan or the Syrians in Lebanon, the British and the Argentines curbed and delayed pictorial coverage of the war to forestall adverse consequences at home. In the same way, no reporters were permitted to witness the first phases of the U.S. invasion of Grenada in 1983. The military is preoccupied with fighting during these initial stages and is disinclined to take time out to deal with reporters. Moreover, it wants to keep its action plans secret. Journalists, on the other hand, want to be at the scene of action from the start with full access to the troops.

The press complained loudly about its exclusion from initial coverage in Grenada. In response to these complaints, a small rotating group of reporters was created to record initial military operations. The system failed miserably when it was first tried in Panama in December 1989 in a mission designed to depose Panamanian president Manuel Noriega. The fourteen reporters in the pool reached Panama four hours after the fighting began and were not allowed to file stories until six hours later. Then their movements were restricted to tours under military escort.[37] The situation was not much better during the 1991 Gulf War, even though the rules had been revised again to permit journalists more freedom of movement. The pool system allowed only 100 of the more than 1,600 American reporters in the area access to some 500,000 troops. Reporters who went to the front without authorization were arrested and detained. The upshot was sanitized coverage of the war. Flawlessly executed precision maneuvers were shown but not failures or pictures of the dead and wounded, friend or foe. Although military censorship was to blame for glamorizing the battlefield, journalists must share in the blame for inadequate coverage. Most of them failed to familiarize themselves with the history and politics of the peoples of the region and with the policies of various outside powers interested in the area, including the United States. Had they done so, their coverage could have been far more insightful.[38]

After the war, executives from the major American media filed a report with Defense Secretary Dick Cheney, complaining about the pool system and efforts to sanitize and delay the news. "By controlling what reporters saw and when they saw it, the military exerted great power to shape and manage the news."[39] The complaints led to yet another revision of the rules, which was endorsed by the journalism community. Under the new rules, pools—which should be as large as possible—will be used only in the initial stages. They will be disbanded within twenty-four to thirty-six hours. The military retains control over the rules, but has promised to smooth the progress of reporting, including facilitating transportation on military vehicles. No agreement was reached on the right of the military to ask to review reporters' work for security purposes.[40]

It is unlikely that the time will ever arrive when the military and the press will be fully satisfied with each other's conduct. Their respective goals are much too antagonistic. War is a dirty business that will never be photogenic when shown in all its brutality. As long as "just" wars for "good causes" (whatever they may be) are condoned and even celebrated by the world community, full coverage remains a sensitive issue. If it does, indeed, discourage military actions, the world community's ability to defend its interests will diminish. Ruthless members of the community can then use the threat of military action to advance their own goals. Peace at any price may be too costly.

Shortcomings and Distortions. Just like domestic news, foreign news neglects major social problems, particularly political and economic development issues. The reasons are readily apparent. Social problems are difficult to describe in brief stories, pictures are scarce, and changes come at a glacial pace. Some social problems are extremely complex; most reporters are ill equipped to understand—let alone describe—them. When they do describe them, the focus is on their dramatic negative aspects: shortages, famines, conflicts, and breakdowns. As Rafael Caldera, former president of Venezuela, told a press conference at the National Press Club in Washington, D.C., "The phrase 'no news is good news' has become 'good news is no news.' . . . Little or nothing is mentioned in American media about literary or scientific achievements" or "about social achievements and the defense against the dangers which threaten our peace and development." Instead, "only the most deplorable incidents, be they caused by nature or by man, receive prominent attention."[41] It is small consolation for such ruffled feelings that news selection criteria for events in developing nations are typical for news from everywhere.[42]

Negative and conflictual news is more prevalent in the U.S. media than in the media of many other societies. Comparisons of news coverage in the United States and in Canada, societies that are culturally close, are revealing. The rate of violence on Canadian television news is half the U.S. rate.[43] When the people of Quebec voted in 1980 on the question of separatism from Canada, the *Washington Post* warned that civil war might erupt. American papers featured stories about serious rioting by separatists in English sectors of Montreal. By contrast, the *Toronto Globe and Mail* buried a small story about minor unrest in Quebec in the back pages. The prospect of civil war was never mentioned and was characterized as "ludicrous" by knowledgeable observers.[44] During the Iranian hostage crisis, *New York Times* coverage featured stereotypical portrayals of Muslims and tales of violence. Far more peaceful images emerged from reading the French paper *Le Monde*.[45]

By and large, Western news media feature more conflict than do media in authoritarian and totalitarian societies. In part this happens because government-controlled news organizations find it comparatively easy to shun dramatic negative news, since government subsidies relieve them of the need to secure large audiences. Regardless of the reasons for the difference, the approach used by American news media draws attention to conflict rather than to peaceful settlement and makes much of the world outside of the United States seem chaotic. Ordinary foreign news languishes in the back pages or is condensed into the briefest broadcast accounts, whereas stories concerned with civil disorder and revolutions are featured prominently. Usually the issues are oversimplified and instead of interpreting what the conflict means to the country and its people, the dominant focus is on what, if anything, the conflict portends for American politics.

Distortions also plague domestic news coverage, but they are less deceptive because American audiences can see the situation more clearly; past experiences and socialization provide corrective lenses.[46] The foreign scene, by contrast, must be viewed without correction for myopia and astigmatism. Americans may be skeptical about the accuracy of the images, but they lack the yardsticks to judge the nature and degree of distortion.

Finally, the thrust of most foreign news stories, like their domestic counterpart, provides support for government policies. The media usually accept official designations of who America's friends and enemies are and interpret these friends' and enemies' motives accordingly. Whenever relationships change, media coverage mirrors the change. Coverage of the Soviet Union's attack on Korean Airlines Flight 007 is a good example of the approach used for disfavored countries. In the same way, a comparison of *New York Times* coverage of strife in Cambodia and East Timor and of elections in Nicaragua and El Salvador showed that "communist-tainted" Cambodia and Nicaragua were judged unfavorably. By contrast, comparable events in East Timor and El Salvador, countries deemed friendly to the

United States, were cast in a favorable light.[47] Because the president and executive branch are the prime sources of foreign affairs news, they can, most of the time, set the agenda of coverage and frame stories to reflect official perspectives.[48]

If the media are generally supportive of government policies, how can their adverse comments about the Vietnam War be explained? The answer is that the media emphasized the government's positions until many respected sources voiced their strong dissent. To use a term popularized by political scientist Lance Bennett, the media index their coverage to the degree of disagreement by powerful political leaders with the government's position.[49] When respected opposition forces publicly express their concerns, the media coupled their Vietnam stories, which were based on government accounts, with coverage of the growing dissent in America about the merits of Vietnam policies. They gave ample attention to antiadministration voices and to antiwar demonstrations. Even when protest was featured, stories primarily featured "respectable" dissenters, not political and social outcasts.[50]

Tests of the indexing hypothesis in the post–cold war era suggest that it may apply only in situations when major national security interests are at stake, as was the case with the cold war or the Persian Gulf War.[51] However, the evidence on that score remains unclear.[52] Different reasons may underlie the indexing phenomenon—reporters' customary reliance on government sources either because they are easiest to locate or because their pronouncements may portend political actions. Or reporters, uncomfortable with their dependence on government sources, may seize every safe opportunity to express their independence by siding with the voices of dissent.[53]

Support of the Status Quo. On the whole, despite some coverage that challenges the official version of international policies and American foreign policies, the tenor of news stories supports prevailing stereotypes about the world. Preoccupation with the developed powers reinforces many Americans' beliefs about the importance of these nations. In the same way, portrayal of less developed countries as incapable of managing their own internal affairs makes it easy to believe that they do not deserve higher status and the media attention that accompanies it.

Newspeople usually are willing to withhold news and commentary when publicity would severely complicate the government's management of foreign policy. For instance, the media suppressed information about America's breaking of Japanese military message codes during World War II, and refrained from sharply criticizing Iranian leaders during the 1979 hostage crisis to avoid angering them. Both are examples in which major political interests were at stake. Likewise, news of delicate negotiations among foreign countries may be temporarily withheld to avoid rocking the boat before agreements are reached. When an invasion of Haiti by U.S. troops was in the offing in 1994, CNN and the three major television networks pledged to refrain from showing any pictures that might put the troops at risk.[54]

The Unique Impact of Television

We have already mentioned that television has vastly broadened the American audience for foreign affairs coverage and that television anchors have repeatedly assumed roles formerly reserved for diplomats. But the medium has done even more.[55] With satellite transmission, its audience has become global. Millions throughout the world, including government leaders, watched unfolding events like CNN's direct broadcasts from Iraq's capital city during the Gulf War in 1991 or saw protest demonstrations against the world's richest nations at an economic summit in Italy in 2001. The publicity glare surrounding modern political actors sharply reduces their freedom to act, often forcing them to make decisions to please a variety of public opinions. The political consequences can be substantial. As Zbigniew Brzezinski, President Carter's national security adviser, pointed out in a retrospective analysis of the Teheran hostage crisis:

> First, TV transforms essentially a political confrontation into a personal drama. The result is you cannot deal with it coldly in terms of the national interest but you must focus on the personal aspects. Secondly, as the confrontation becomes a personal drama, the bargaining capacity of the kidnappers is enhanced. Concentration on accommodation by the American government becomes more important. Thirdly, it humanizes the enemy. Therefore, you begin to make equations and equivalences, which dulls the sharpness of the possible response.[56]

Televised crisis coverage may pressure the president to react hastily to avoid appearing weak and vacillating. As Lloyd Cutler, White House counsel to presidents Carter and Clinton, put it, "If an ominous foreign event is featured on TV news, the President and his advisers feel bound to make a response in time for the next evening news program."[57] This may leave no time for investigation of the news report or for explanation of the event by officials of the foreign country. Normal diplomatic discourse becomes preempted by the media. Madeleine Albright, President Clinton's Secretary of State, put it somewhat differently in an interview in 2001. She commented that the twenty-four-hour news cycle had changed things but saw advantages along with the disadvantages. "Some of it is very good, because you know what's going on and there is a real-time sense about things. . . .

But, in other ways, it makes you have to respond to events much faster than it might be prudent. . . . So it's a double-edged sword. . . ."[58]

Public officials are fully aware that television coverage can affect their actions in major ways. In a survey of ninety-five officials serving in policy-related jobs, 53 percent attributed great influence to the media in the early stages of the policy cycle when the issues are initially framed.[59] Media influence is far less potent later on. Roughly 80 percent of the officials thought that positive and negative media attention enhanced the salience of an issue for the bureaucracy and the public, and that television brings new players into the game of international politics, particularly nongovernmental groups. Most (71 percent) also believed that television coverage speeds up the pace of policy decisions.[60] President Kennedy waited eight days in 1961 before commenting on the erection of the Berlin Wall; President George Bush had to respond overnight to its destruction. As Patrick O'Heffernan put it, "Television plays a special role in the American foreign policy process, but that role is limited and diffused. However, when it plays that role . . . it exerts a power over events and decisions that surpasses all other media combined."[61] Nonetheless, the public officials cautioned against considering television as omnipotent. Impact hinges on the nature of the issue and the prevailing political environment, including official predisposition to act.[62] Thus, pictures of starving Kurdish refugees in the mountains of Iraq would not have spurred relief missions by the Bush administration in 1991 had emergency food aid not already been a policy alternative.

Appraising Foreign News Making

In 1978, the United States, along with 145 other nations, signed a United Nations Educational, Scientific, and Cultural Organization (UNESCO) Declaration on the Media. Among other things, the Declaration stated that "the mass media, by disseminating information on the aims, aspirations, cultures and needs of all people, contribute to eliminate ignorance and misunderstanding between peoples." The media also "make nationals of a country sensitive to the needs and desires of others," thereby ensuring "the respect of the rights and dignity of all nations, all peoples and all individuals." The media also foster "the formulation by states of policies best able to promote the reduction of international tension and the peaceful and equitable settlement of international disputes."[63]

Clearly, foreign news in the American press, or in any other press, does not meet the high standards that UNESCO has set for it. It does not "eliminate ignorance and misunderstanding between peoples." It is too sparse and unbalanced, focusing on the wealthier and more powerful countries. It assesses foreign countries largely in terms of U.S. interests, with little attempt to explain their culture and concerns from their own perspective. It does not sensitize Americans to "the needs and desires of others" nor foster "respect of the rights and dignity of all nations." Rather, it reinforces Americans' preexisting assumptions and stereotypes.

These deficiencies must be assessed in light of the basic philosophy of news in a free society. As discussed in Chapter 1, American journalists by and large do not see themselves as extensions of the government, carrying out and keeping in tune with public policies. Although they may sympathize with UNESCO's goals, their first priority is to report exciting news to the American public.[64] In a society that firmly believes in the independence of the press, this is a tolerable consequence.

Just as the press does not serve UNESCO's objectives, it fails to serve many objectives of the American government and many needs of the American public. Reporting of foreign news usually lacks a sense of history and a sense of the meaning of successive events so that it often confuses the public. The news does not provide sufficient information to permit most Americans to understand the rationale for major foreign policies such as support of the North American Free Trade Agreement (NAFTA) or the limitations of humanitarian interventions. Some stories, even those directly involving U.S. security, are ignored until events reach crisis proportions or until there is a precipitating incident. *New York Times* correspondent James Reston put the problem this way:

> We are fascinated by events but not by the things that cause the events. We will send 500 correspondents to Vietnam after the war breaks out . . . meanwhile ignoring the rest of the world, but we will not send five reporters there when the danger of war is developing.[65]

If one assumes that better information leads to better policies, then deficiencies in news coverage are grave. But that assumption is partly flawed, especially with respect to the public's knowledge and impact on foreign affairs. Although the media are exceedingly important in providing the context for foreign policy and are used widely as the information base for policy formation, their influence is generally weaker than the influence of formal government agencies. When policy failures are not readily apparent and the president alleges that all is going well, contrary media claims are not likely to be believed by officials and the mass public.

Exporting News

Although the American public seems reasonably content with the foreign news it receives, developing nations are unhappy with their coverage by U.S. media. Their disappointment about the world images presented to Americans is compounded by resentment that these images are exported to other countries throughout the globe. In the years since most of these nations gained independence, most of the non-Communist world's political and economic news has come from only four huge American enterprises: the Associated Press (AP), United Press International (UPI), the *New York Times* News Service, and the *Los Angeles Times-Washington Post* News Service. The remainder has been produced largely by news agencies based in Britain, France, and Russia. Four countries thus have dominated the world's news supply. However, some confusion in dividing stories by country of origin has arisen from the fact that many stories about developing nations are transmitted through communications centers, such as London or New York. For example, most news from Latin America is relayed via New York.

Concentration of international news dissemination has given rise to charges of media imperialism—the dependence of domestic media systems on dominant foreign media systems.[66] Dependence on foreign news resources is particularly galling for developing countries because they believe that the flow of news is primarily one way—into the developing world but not out of it. Western news purveyors slight the happenings and the information needs of people in developing nations. Critics in developing nations also decry the corrupting effects of Western news and entertainment programs that feature violence and sexually explicit episodes. Western programs allegedly damage the cultural identity of developing nations, especially those that are vulnerable because colonialism has sensitized them to foreign values.[67] Imported news and entertainment offerings draw people away from their own heritage and create the false expectation that it is easy to become rich. People in developing nations are tempted into materialism for the benefit of industrialists in the United States who are eager to sell their merchandise through television. Buyers of luxury goods then drain the resources of the developing countries.

Such interpretations of the motives and role of Western media are widely believed in developing nations. The interpretations seem quite plausible because the international news market is dominated by a few giant Western corporations that sell news, as well as more tangible goods, for profit. However, scientific proof is lacking that Marxist interpretations are correct in explaining the causes and consequences of Western dominance of the news and media entertainment of developing nations. As we noted in Chapter 7, people do not automatically learn new ways of life from the media, even when offerings are designed to educate. Certain relatively rare conditions must first be met to provide an appropriate context. Hence, claims that exposure to Western news automatically indoctrinates the audience are false.[68]

Content analyses of Western media, including wire service news, also show that many of the charges of deliberate discrimination against developing nations are either groundless or exaggerated.[69] The emphasis on problems and failures, rather than successes, and lack of attention to many small nations appear to be natural consequences of applying customary news selection criteria to developing nations. Although the treatment is the same, its negative impact is likely to be greater in developing than developed nations.[70] The media's emphasis on disasters and conflicts in developing nations reflects the reality that these countries are undergoing major social changes and therefore bear a disproportionate burden of pain and suffering.

Early entry into the media business has given the major news producers an economic edge of size and scale that makes it well-nigh impossible for developing nations to set up viable competing enterprises. Current structures and patterns of telecommunications give price advantages to large producers and consumers. News transmission rates are cheaper when volume is high, making it extremely costly for poor countries to broadcast their messages. It also costs more to transmit news from developing countries than to receive it. In fact, all the economies of scale benefit the rich and hurt the poor.

The high costs of television programming and the comparatively low costs of purchasing foreign television entertainment—roughly one-tenth of the cost of original programming—also have discouraged developing countries from creating their own television industries. Many developing countries still lack facilities for producing television shows. Those that have them nonetheless import an average of more than half of their programs, particularly those shown in prime time.[71] That may be changing. In recent years, local cultural programs have multiplied in Asia, Latin America, and Africa. They are often exchanged among developing nations.

Because they are dissatisfied with the status quo and see news as a powerful political force, developing countries have lobbied UNESCO to place strict controls on the influx of foreign news. It has been largely a dialogue of the deaf. The United States and other Western countries have strongly resisted these attempts, deeming them infringements of the right to a free press guaranteed by the 1948 Universal Declaration of Human Rights. The trend toward controlled news in the developing world is making headway nonetheless. Even the European Community issued a directive in 1989, urging members to reserve the majority of their airtime for broadcasts originating in Europe.[72] When UNESCO developed a code of journalistic ethics that defined *responsible* reporting and investigated ways to make journalism a government-licensed profession, the United States withdrew from the organization.

Developing countries are also contesting the control of the United States and other Western powers over world radio and satellite facilities. Scarce international frequencies have been allocated on a first-come, first-served basis, giving the developed nations nearly 90 percent of the broadcast spectrum and the bulk of satellite facilities. Developing nations want to change this; they want to divide the spectrum equally among all nations and to bar radio and television satellite transmissions across national borders unless the receiving country has given permission. They have also demanded more control over satellites. The U.S. government has resisted demands by the developing nations, believing that countries with current capability to use advanced telecommunications facilities should control these facilities.

Summary

The quality of U.S. foreign policy and the effectiveness of U.S. relations with other countries are crucial to the welfare of people throughout the world. Sound policy and relations require a solid information base. As this chapter has shown, the foreign affairs information base on which Americans depend leaves much to be desired. The causes are complex and cannot be changed readily. They involve the structure of the foreign correspondent corps, the sociopolitical setting in which correspondents must work, and the audiences to whose world views and tastes the news must cater.

Foreign correspondents for the most part are well trained and able. But there are too few of them to cover the world. They work within a narrowly controlled organizational structure consisting of a handful of giant news-gathering institutions that supply the news and entertainment needs of the United States and much of the rest of the world. If one distrusts giant information conglomerates that collect and shape the news for much of the world, the present situation is frightening.

Most Americans are reasonably well satisfied with the foreign news produced by these conglomerates. Live satellite television provides vivid images of breaking news, from American military personnel detained in China, to terrorist bombs killing Israeli civilians, to the Pope visiting Fidel Castro, Cuba's communist leader. Many of the foreign clienteles, particularly political leaders in developing nations, are not pleased. They complain that agents of monopoly capitalism are guilty of "electronic rape" of their people through decadent entertainment and Western political propaganda.

Foreign affairs news often must be produced under trying conditions. Strange locations and inadequate technological facilities can make nightmares of the physical aspects of getting to the scene of the action, collecting information, and transmitting it. These technical difficulties are compounded by political difficulties. They include the reluctance of officials in the United States and abroad to commit themselves publicly on foreign affairs matters and the harassment of correspondents venturing into places where they are unwanted. Expulsion, imprisonment, and physical harm are common. With so much territory to cover and such limited personnel to cover it, newspeople frequently avoid areas where news is hard to get and devote their efforts instead to areas where public attitudes are supportive. This effectively removes many regions from media scrutiny and contributes to unevenness of news flow from various parts of the world.

How good is the foreign affairs news that reaches the United States and other clients of Western international news transmission facilities? The picture is mixed. Foreign correspondents must produce news that is at once timely, exciting, personalized, and brief, yet understandable for an American audience that is not intensely interested in most events abroad. Given the problems of foreign affairs news production, correspondents dwell heavily on negative and sensational news. They write stories mostly from an American perspective and usually follow the current administration's foreign policy assumptions and the American public's stereotyped views of the world. They open the journalistic gates primarily with America's national interests and policy objectives in mind. Despite these shortcomings, Americans can obtain a reasonably accurate view of salient political events abroad, particularly if they turn to several elite newspapers that generally give thorough exposure to controversial American foreign policies. However, these papers rarely challenge the objectives of foreign policies, though they may question the effectiveness of executing them.

In recent years television commentators occasionally have become active diplomats through interviews that set the stage for subsequent political developments. Aside from these adventures, media influence on foreign policy has been largely indirect, exercised primarily through surveillance activities, the power to choose what to report and what to omit, and the ability to interpret the meaning of events. There has been little investigative or adversary journalism except when foreign affairs were obviously going badly and therefore became highly controversial. Most of the time, political controversy has largely stopped at the water's edge.

Notes

1. Clyde Haberman, "Ceremony Will Be Hot, Windy, and Made for TV," *New York Times,* October 26, 1994.
2. Pew Research Center for the People and the Press, "1998 Media Consumption Questionnaire," 1998, http://www.people-press.org/med98que.htm.

3. Pew Research Center for the People and the Press, "Pew Research Center Database: Public Attentiveness to Major News Stories, 1986–2000," 2000. Data Archive. http://www.people-press.org/database.htm.

4. Times Mirror Center for the People and the Press, "A Content Analysis: International Coverage Fits Public's Ameri-Centric Mood," News Release, June 25, 1995.

5. Pamela J. Shoemaker, Lucig H. Danielian, and Nancy Brendlinger, "Deviant Acts, Risky Business and U.S. Interests: The Newsworthiness of World Events," *Journalism Quarterly* 68 (winter 1991): 781–795.

6. Pippa Norris, "The Restless Searchlight: Network News Framing of the Post Cold-War World," *Political Communication* 12(4) (1995): 357–370.

7. Bernard C. Cohen, *The Press and Foreign Policy* (Princeton: Princeton University Press, 1963), 164–165.

8. William A. Hachten, with the collaboration of Harva Hachten, *The World News Prism: Changing Media of International Communication*, 3d ed. (Ames: Iowa State University Press, 1992), 41–53. Other important international news suppliers are Germany's Deutsche Press Agentur (DPA) and Japan's Kyodo News Service, as well as China's Xinhua News Agency. United Press International, once second only to the Associated Press, has been teetering on the brink of bankruptcy for many years.

9. For a brief description of how the Associated Press is adjusting to the Internet age, see Brent Cunningham, "The AP Now," *Columbia Journalism Review* (November/December 2000), http://www.cjr.org/year/00/4/ap.asp.

10. For an analysis of the contents of *CNN World Report*, see Charles Ganzert and Don M. Flournoy, "The Weekly 'World Report' on CNN, an Analysis," *Journalism Quarterly* 69 (spring 1992): 188–193.

11. Brigitte L. Nacos et al., "New Issues and the Media: American and German News Coverage of the Global-Warming Debate," in *Decisionmaking in a Glass House: Mass Media, Public Opinion and American and European Foreign Policy in the 21st Century*, ed. Brigitte L. Nacos, Robert Y. Shapiro, and Pierangelo Isernia (Lanham, Md.: Rowman and Littlefield, 2000), 41–59.

12. Leo Bogart, "The Overseas Newsman: A 1967 Profile Study," *Journalism Quarterly* 45 (summer 1968): 293–306. Judging from more recent profile studies of American journalists in general, these early profiles are still reasonably accurate; see Chapter 4. In the United States, the needs of foreign correspondents are served by the United States Information Agency (USIA). It maintains foreign press centers in major U.S. cities and arranges high-level briefings by government officials and news-gathering tours on major economic, political, and cultural themes. It also provides extensive information services and even helps with arranging appointments and filing facilities at international summits. Washington, D.C., United States Information Agency, *Foreign Press Centers* (January 1996); also, Lori Montgomery presents a brief first-person account of the life of a foreign correspondent in "Foreign Correspondent's Notebook," http://www.freep.com/jobspage/academy/foreign.htm.

13. Jarol B. Manheim, "Strategic Public Diplomacy: Managing Kuwait's Image During the Gulf Conflict," in *Taken by Storm: The Media, Public Opinion, and U.S. Foreign Policy in the Gulf War*, ed. W. Lance Bennett and David L. Paletz (Chicago: University of Chicago Press, 1994), 131–148.

14. Jarol B. Manheim and Robert B. Albritton, "Changing National Images: International Public Relations and Media Agenda-Setting," *American Political Sci-*

ence Review 78 (September 1984): 641–657; Robert B. Albritton and Jarol B. Manheim, "Public Relations Efforts for the Third World: Images in the News," *Journal of Communication* 35 (spring 1985): 43–59; Jarol B. Manheim, *Strategic Public Diplomacy and American Foreign Policy: The Evolution of Influence* (New York: Oxford University Press, 1994).

15. Shailendra Ghorpade, "Foreign Correspondents Cover Washington for World," *Journalism Quarterly* 61 (autumn 1984): 667–671; and *Editor and Publisher International Yearbook, 1991* (New York: Editor & Publisher, 1991).

16. *Editor and Publisher International Yearbook,* 1991 and 2000 editions.

17. Ghorpade, "Foreign Correspondents," 667.

18. Gadi Wolfsfeld, *Media and Political Conflict: News from the Middle East* (Cambridge: Cambridge University Press, 1997), chap. 8.

19. Freedom Forum, "Journalists in Peril" and "Basic Press Freedoms Still Denied in Most of World, Report Says," http://www.freedomforum.org/templates/document.asp, Documents 4044 and 5592.

20. Eytan Gilboa, "Media Diplomacy: Conceptual Divergence and Applications," *Harvard International Journal of Press/Politics* 3(3) (1998): 56–75.

21. Ibid.

22. For a full discussion of reporting on the Middle East peace negotiations between Israel and the Palestinians, see Wolfsfeld, *Media and Political Conflict.*

23. Kirsten Sparre, "Megaphone Diplomacy in the Northern Irish Peace Process: Squaring the Circle by Talking to Terrorists through Journalists," *Harvard International Journal of Press/Politics* 6(1) (2001): 88–104.

24. Patrick O'Heffernan, "Mass Media and U.S. Foreign Policy: A Mutual Exploitation Model of Media Influence in U.S. Foreign Policy," *Media and Public Policy,* ed. Robert J. Spitzer (Westport, Conn.: Praeger, 1993), 187–211.

25. Garrick Utley, "The Shrinking of Foreign News: From Broadcast to Narrowcast," *Foreign Affairs* 76(1) (1997): 2–10. Also see Brent Cunningham, "The AP Now," *Columbia Journalism Review* (November/December 2000), http://www.cjr.org/year/00/4/ap.asp.

26. Herbert J. Gans, *Deciding What's News: A Study of CBS Evening News, NBC Nightly News, Newsweek and Time* (New York: Pantheon Books, 1979), 30–36. See also H. Denis Wu, "Systemic Determinants of International News Coverage: A Comparison of 38 Countries," *Journal of Communication* 50(2) (2000): 110–130; and Wolfsfeld, *Media and Political Conflict,* chap. 6.

27. Edwin Diamond, *The Tin Kazoo: Television, Politics, and the News* (Cambridge, Mass.: MIT Press, 1975), 94.

28. Daniel C. Hallin, "Hegemony: The American News Media from Vietnam to El Salvador: A Study of Ideological Change and Its Limits," in *Political Communication Research: Approaches, Studies, Assessments,* ed. David L. Paletz (Norwood, N.J.: Ablex, 1987), 17; Robert M. Entman, "Hegemonic Socialization, Information Processing, and Presidential News Management: Framing the KAL and Iran Air Incidents," in *The Psychology of Political Communication,* ed. Ann Crigler (Ann Arbor: University of Michigan Press, 1996).

29. William Adams and Phillip Heyl, "From Cairo to Kabul with the Networks, 1972–1980," in *Television Coverage of the Middle East,* ed. William C. Adams (Norwood, N.J.: Ablex, 1981), 26.

30. Barry Rubin, "International News and the American Media," in *International News: Freedom under Attack*, ed. Dante B. Fascell (Beverly Hills, Calif.: Sage, 1979), 227.
31. Wolfsfeld, *Media and Political Conflict*, chap. 4.
32. Author's research.
33. Michael X. Delli Carpini and Bruce A. Williams, "Television and Terrorism: Patterns of Presentation and Occurrence, 1969 to 1980," *Western Political Quarterly* 40 (March 1987): 45–64.
34. Robert M. Entman, "Framing U.S. Coverage of International News: Contrasts in Narratives of the KAL and Iran Air Incidents," *Journal of Communication* 41 (autumn 1991): 6–27.
35. Ibid., 22–23.
36. Wolfsfeld, *Media and Political Conflict*, 104–123.
37. David R. Gergen, "Diplomacy in a Television Age: The Dangers of Teledemocracy," in *The Media and Foreign Policy*, ed. Simon Serfaty (New York: St. Martin's, 1991), 47–63.
38. Stephen S. Rosenfeld, "In the Gulf: The Wars of the Press," in *The Media and Foreign Policy*, 241–255. For a detailed account of news coverage before and during the war, see Bennett and Paletz, eds., *Taken by Storm*.
39. Hachten, *The World News Prism*, 165–166.
40. Robert Pear, "Military Revises Rules to Assure Reporters Access to Battle Areas," *New York Times*, May 22, 1992. Also see Philip Seib, *Headline Diplomacy: How News Coverage Affects Foreign Policy* (Westport, Conn.: Praeger, 1997).
41. Quoted in Fernando Reyes Matta, "The Latin American Concept of News," *Journal of Communication* 29 (spring 1979): 169.
42. Gary D. Gaddy and Enoch Tanjong, "Earthquake Coverage by the Western Press," *Journal of Communication* 36 (spring 1986): 105–112. For a conflicting analysis, see William C. Adams, "Whose Lives Count?: TV Coverage of Natural Disasters," *Journal of Communication* 36 (spring 1986): 113–122.
43. Benjamin D. Singer, "Violence, Protest, and War in Television News: The U.S. and Canada Compared," *Public Opinion Quarterly* 34 (winter 1970–1971): 611–616; and Chris J. Scheer and Sam W. Eiler, "A Comparison of Canadian and American Network Television News," *Journal of Broadcasting* 16 (spring 1972): 156–164. For another comparative perspective on media coverage, see Richard Gunther and Anthony Mughan, *Democracy and the Media: A Comparative Perspective* (Cambridge: Cambridge University Press, 2000).
44. James P. Winter, Pirouz Shoar Ghaffari, and Vernone M. Sparkes, "How Major U.S. Dailies Covered Quebec Separatism Referendum," *Journalism Quarterly* 59 (winter 1982): 608.
45. Edward W. Said, *Covering Islam: How the Media and the Experts Determine How We See the Rest of the World* (New York: Pantheon Books, 1981), chap. 2; also see Gunther and Mughan, *Democracy and the Media*.
46. Hanna Adoni and S. Mane, "Media and the Social Construction of Reality: Toward an Integration of Theory and Research," *Communication Research* 11 (July 1984): 323–340; see also Doris Graber, *Processing Politics: Learning from Television in the Internet Age* (Chicago: University of Chicago Press, 2001), 82–91.
47. Edward S. Herman, "Diversity of News: 'Marginalizing' the Opposition," *Journal of Communication* 35 (fall 1985): 135–146. See also W. Lance Bennett, "An

Introduction to Journalism Norms and Representations of Politics," *Political Communication* 13(4) (1996): 373–384.

48. John A. Lent, "Foreign News in American Media," *Journal of Communication* 27 (winter 1977): 46–50. See also Jyotika Ramaprasad and Daniel Riffe, "Effect of U.S.-India Relations on *New York Times* Coverage," *Journalism Quarterly* 64 (summer/autumn 1987): 537–543; Hallin, "Hegemony"; and David Altheide, "Media Hegemony: A Failure of Perspective," *Public Opinion Quarterly* 48 (summer 1984): 476–490.

49. Bennett, "An Introduction to Journalism Norms and Representations of Politics."

50. Daniel C. Hallin, "The Media, the War in Vietnam and Political Support: A Critique of the Thesis of an Oppositional Media," *Journal of Politics* 46 (February 1984); also see Jonathan Mermin, *Debating War and Peace* (Princeton: Princeton University Pres, 1999); and John Zaller and Dennis Chiu, "Government's Little Helper: U.S. Press Coverage of Foreign Policy Crises, 1946–1999," in *Decisionmaking in a Glass House*, 61–84, for many examples.

51. Zaller and Chiu, "Government's Little Helper," 74–81.

52. Mermin, *Debating War and Peace.*

53. Zaller and Chiu, "Government's Little Helper," 81–84.

54. "TV Networks Say Coverage Would Not Endanger Troops," *New York Times,* September 19, 1994.

55. The discussion that follows is based on James F. Larson, "Television and U.S. Foreign Policy: The Case of the Iran Hostage Crisis," *Journal of Communication* 36 (autumn 1986): 108–130; and Joseph Fromm, "TV: Does It Box in President in a Crisis?" *U.S. News & World Report,* July 15, 1985, 23–24. Also see Robert M. Entman, "Declarations of Independence: The Growth of Media Power after the Cold War," and Martin Shaw, "Media and Public Sphere Without Borders? News Coverage and Power from Kurdistan to Kosovo," both in *Decisionmaking in a Glass House,* 1–26 and 27–40, respectively.

56. Quoted in John Corry, "The Intrusion of Television in the Hostage Crisis," *New York Times,* June 26, 1985.

57. Quoted in ibid.

58. Madeleine Albright, "Around-the-Clock News Cycle a Double-Edged Sword," *Harvard International Journal of Press/Politics* 6(1) (2001): 105–108.

59. O'Heffernan, *Mass Media and American Foreign Policy,* 40.

60. Ibid., 75.

61. Ibid., 77.

62. Ibid., 48. Nicholas O. Berry in *Foreign Policy and the Press: An Analysis of the New York Times' Coverage of U.S. Foreign Policy* (Westport, Conn.: Greenwood Press, 1990) makes the same argument.

63. Article III, UNESCO Declaration on the Media.

64. Timothy E. Cook, "Afterword: Political Values and Production Values," *Political Communication* 13(4) (1996): 469–481.

65. James Reston, *Sketches in the Sand* (New York: Knopf, 1967), 195; for supporting evidence in the Gulf War, see Gladys Engel Lang and Kurt Lang, "The Press as Prologue: Media Coverage of Saddam's Iraq, 1979–1990," in *Taken By Storm,* 43–62.

66. For a discussion of media imperialism, see Herbert I. Schiller, *Culture, Inc.: The Corporate Takeover of Public Expression* (New York: Oxford University Press, 1989); and René Jean Ravault, "International Information: Bullet or Boomerang?"

in *Political Communication Research: Approaches, Studies, Assessments*, ed. David L. Paletz (Norwood, N.J.: Ablex, 1987), 245–265.

67. The impact of foreign television is assessed in Alexis S. Tan, Sarrina Li, and Charles Simpson, "American TV and Social Stereotypes of Americans in Taiwan and Mexico," *Journalism Quarterly* 63 (winter 1986): 809–814.

68. Ravault, "International Information: Bullet or Boomerang?"; Glen Fisher, *American Communication in a Global Society* (Norwood, N.J.: Ablex, 1987), 15–18; and Michael B. Salwan, "Cultural Imperialism: A Media Effects Approach," *Critical Studies in Mass Communication* 8 (1991): 29–38. For a contrary viewpoint, see Herbert I. Schiller, "Not Yet the Post-Imperialist Era," *Critical Studies in Mass Communication* 8 (1991): 13–28.

69. W. James Potter, "News from Three Worlds in Prestige U.S. Newspapers," *Journalism Quarterly* 64 (spring 1987): 73–79.

70. Wilbur Schramm and L. Erwin Atwood, *Circulation of News in the Third World: A Study of Asia* (Hong Kong: Chinese University Press, 1981); and David H. Weaver and G. Cleveland Wilhoit, "Foreign News Coverage in Two U.S. Wire Services," *Journal of Communication* 31 (spring 1981): 55–63. For a contrary view, see Daniel Riffe and Eugene F. Shaw, "Conflict and Consonance: Coverage of Third World in Two U.S. Papers," *Journalism Quarterly* 59 (winter 1982): 617–626.

71. One exception is Brazil, which supplies its own domestic market and exports programs worldwide. Omar Souki Oliveira, "Brazilian Media Usage as a Test of Dependency Theory," *Canadian Journal of Communication* 13 (1988): 16–27.

72. Duncan H. Brown, "Citizens or Consumers: U.S. Reactions to the European Community's Directive on Television," *Critical Studies in Mass Communication* 8 (1991): 1–12. For a book-length discussion of worldwide press freedom issues, see Douglas A. Van Belle, *Press Freedom and Global Politics* (Westport, Conn.: Praeger, 2000).

Readings

Bennett, W. Lance, and David L. Paletz. *Taken by Storm: The Media, Public Opinion, and U.S. Foreign Policy in the Gulf War.* Chicago: University of Chicago Press, 1994.

Dayan, Daniel, and Elihu Katz. *Media Events: The Live Broadcasting of History.* Cambridge: Harvard University Press, 1992.

Edwards, Lee. *Mediapolitik: How the Mass Media Have Transformed World Politics.* Baltimore: The Catholic University of America Press, 2001.

Galtung, Johan, and Richard C. Vincent. *Global Glasnost: Toward a New World Information/Communication Order?* Cresskill, N.J.: Hampton Press, 1992.

Hess, Stephen. *International News and Foreign Correspondents.* Washington, D.C.: Brookings Institution, 1996.

Manheim, Jarol B. *Strategic Public Diplomacy and American Foreign Policy: The Evolution of Influence.* New York: Oxford University Press, 1994.

Mermin, Jonathan. *Debating War and Peace.* Princeton: Princeton University Press, 1999.

Nacos, Brigitte L., Robert Y. Shapiro, and Pierangelo Isernia, eds. *Decisionmaking in a Glass House: Mass Media, Public Opinion and American and European Foreign Policy in the 21st Century.* Lanham, Md.: Rowman and Littlefield, 2000.

O'Heffernan, Patrick. *Mass Media and American Foreign Policy: Insider Perspectives on Global Journalism and the Foreign Policy Process.* Norwood, N.J.: Ablex, 1991.

Wolfsfeld, Gadi. *Media and Political Conflict: News from the Middle East.* Cambridge: Cambridge University Press, 1997.

Trends in Media Policy

"THE FUTURE OF JOURNALISM ISN'T WHAT IT USED to be." So wrote the editors of a recent issue of *Media Studies Journal* that explores trends in American journalism. "As recently as the mid-1960s, few would have predicted the shocks and transformations that have swept through the news business in the last three decades: the deaths of many afternoon newspapers, the emergence of television as people's primary news source and the quicksilver combinations of cable television, VCR's and the Internet that have changed our ways of reading, seeing and listening."[1] The issue, titled "What's Next?" opens with two prognoses, one of them optimistic, the other pessimistic.

Geneva Overholser, a syndicated columnist and former editor of *The Des Moines Register*, postdates her positive "Letter From the Future" to May 1, 2025. She writes about the new media scene where every serious news story includes lists of links to other media; these, in turn, lead to additional printed or audio information that put the story into its appropriate context. The reporters who guide the audience have already used these links to make their story far more accurate and complete than was possible twenty-five years earlier. By 2025, the worst features of the turn-of-the-century journalism will have been remedied: "our failure to serve readers and customers well, our cheapening of what we did, our desertion of our ethical underpinnings, our finger wagging and sanctimoniousness and generally getting too big for our britches."[2] News media will have returned to their tradition of solid, fact-based journalism, attractively presented, that covers the news that citizens need and want to know.

Overholser's colleague, Elizabeth Weise, a technology writer with *USA Today,* sees the future much more darkly. Journalism in 2025 is not pretty, as pictured in her "Letter from the Future."[3] It is a world where greed rules. Instead of analyzing the news, journalists and media owners infer audience tastes from the mass of electronic traces that modern Americans, stripped of their privacy, leave behind. After classifying audiences according to their tastes for information, media industry minions select and report stories designed to please various groups of news consumers and expose them to potentially attractive advertising messages. "There's just no possibility of a national consensus on much of anything these days, because the nation doesn't have any one single reference point. They get so much junk thrown at them they have the illusion they're well informed. We've done such a good job of giving people what they want that they won't even glance at something that isn't in their 'interest area'. . . . It was the Web news sites that did it . . . suddenly you had ad managers deciding what played because it would sell the most ads."[4]

Who is reading the tea leaves correctly, Overholser or Weise? Are current trends so confusing that two experienced journalists can see them moving in opposite directions? What conclusions can we draw from the trends and developments recorded in this book? Those are the questions that we will tackle in this final chapter. We will highlight the forces pushing for major changes in communications policies and the obstacles that lie in the way. We will also explore some of the areas of disenchantment with mass media performance that have fueled demands for reform and the steps taken by dissatisfied communicators and audiences to improve and supplement the existing information supply. The potential impact of major new technologies on politics and policy alternatives will be examined. Finally, we will try to discern the shape of future communications policies that will shape the interaction between the mass media and the American political system in the twenty-first century.

Dissatisfaction with the Media

Dissatisfaction with American mass media runs deep and wide. The public feels it, the pundits give it voice, and journalists have lately become very self-critical. According to a 1999 survey by the Pew Research Center for the People and the Press, news professionals working for print, television, radio, and Internet organizations complain about neglect of complex issues and say that the lines between commentary and reporting and between entertainment and news have become unduly blurred. Many think that news reporting is increasingly sloppy and full of errors and that the watch-

TABLE 12-1   News Professionals' Agreement with Press Criticism (in percentages)

Major criticisms	National professionals	Local professionals
Too little attention paid to complex issues	71%	72%
Improper mix of reporting with commentary	69	68
Undue focus on entertainment to gain audiences	68	66
Journalists are too eager for scoops and peer praise	58	65
Journalists are out of touch with their audiences	57	51
The press is too cynical	53	51
Journalists use watchdog role to create controversies	49	56
Increased bottom line pressure hurts news quality	49	46
The press covers positive developments inadequately	49	44
News managers skimp on error corrections	41	43
Sloppy reporting, factual errors in news reports	40	55
The press is more adversarial than necessary	34	33

SOURCE: Adapted from the Pew Research Center for the People and the Press, "1999 Journalism Survey: Overview," http://www.people-press.org/press99rpt.htm.

dog role has gone awry. Press reports about misdeeds by public officials are geared to presenting sensational audience-grabbing exposés, rather than bringing about reforms in public life. These flaws, which journalists blame largely on bottom-line pressures, have undermined the public's trust in the news media and have contributed to the shrinking of media audiences.[5]

The sample of 552 news professionals tapped by the Pew Research Center survey was broadly based. It included individuals working at the top, middle, and bottom levels of national and local newspapers, magazines, wire services, news services, television, cable, radio, and Internet organizations. Table 12-1 presents their reactions to twelve major criticisms leveled against the press.[6] While the differences between local and national professionals are insignificant, it is noteworthy that each group is internally split about the validity of particular complaints. Two out of three journalists in each group do not consider the press to be more adversarial than necessary, for example. Such split appraisals are common in media analyses because the appropriate political role of journalism remains contested.

For example, media orientations toward politics have been criticized as both too liberal and too conservative. Sniping from the left about the media's subservience to the establishment and insensitivity to the concerns of the politically powerless and economically deprived has been balanced by criticism from the middle and the right. Conservatives accuse the media of demeaning the status of American business and industry and of devaluing respected professions such as medicine and law. The media, they argue, are unduly romantic about the woes and virtues of the poor, the disadvantaged, and racial minorities. In the process, the media allegedly undermine the nation's economy and hurt its prestige at home and abroad. Liberals charge that the media perpetuate a society that caters to the interests of economically privileged elites at the expense of the concerns of average Americans. Liberals and conservatives alike accuse the media of invading individual privacy and impairing the fairness of the judicial process. The gist of these charges is that the media do not serve the public interest and that they fail to nourish a viable democratic political order. These elusive concepts are always measured by political yardsticks of questionable accuracy and validity.

Putting Criticism into Perspective

Most of the charges made by media critics have been echoed in the pages of this book. Nonetheless, a blanket indictment of the media for failure to nourish democratic life adequately is not supported by the evidence.[7] First and foremost, the collective noun *news media* covers a broad range of institutions. It does not refer only to newspapers and news magazines and various forms of television and radio as groupings of news media types; it also refers to individual institutions within these broad categories. In terms of supplying information essential for citizens in a democracy, there is a wide gulf between the *New York Times* on the one hand and the scores of tabloids and small-town newspapers that highlight local society news on the other. There is a great deal of journalistic wheat as well as chaff in U.S. media, and the proportions of each vary widely in individual media. In fact, I contend that any citizen willing to make the effort to get essential current information about a broad array of major issues of the day can find it more readily than ever before in U.S. media, especially in the traditional media's Internet versions.

Any fair indictment of the news media must also consider mitigating circumstances. This does not mean that the charges are invalid; it means that they must be put into context to assess the degree of guilt. The pressures under which journalists do their work must be considered. These have been discussed in the chapters dealing with domestic and foreign news production under normal and crisis conditions. Besides the economic constraints to produce profits for the parent organization that account for excesses of negativism and voyeur journalism, they include major journalistic conventions of news production. The zeal to rush to publication with breaking news, for example, fosters mistakes and misinterpretations; the beat system privileges newsworthy events occurring on regular beats over important happenings that occur beyond these beats; and pack journalism homogenizes criteria for news selection so that most media become rivals in conformity.

Economic developments have heightened pressures. The multiplication of news channels in the United States and elsewhere, and the ease with which they can be tapped, have forced electronic as well as print media to compete more fiercely for audiences and for advertisers. Shrinking profit margins in individual enterprises have forced cutbacks in staffs that put additional workloads on the survivors. While databases that could be used to provide context for stories have grown exponentially, the time available to individual reporters to search them has shrunk. The traditional media find their news turf eroded by the new media's ability to publish breaking stories immediately. Accordingly, print media must abandon the lure of featuring freshly breaking news for other ways to attract audiences. But when they turn to more analytical and interpretive reporting, they are accused of improperly straying into the terrain of editorial commentary. The upshot has been that the public increasingly perceives newspaper reporting as unduly biased.

Finally, one must put complaints about the media into historical perspective. They are occurring at a period in history when regard for most major institutions in the United States is at a low ebb. Nonetheless, when people were asked in 2000 how satisfied they were with television, 80 percent were either very or fairly satisfied.[8] Satisfaction rates with newspapers are equally high when people are asked about the newspapers that they actually read, rather than about newspapers in general. History also shows that politicians and the general public are fickle and schizoid in their condemnations as well as their praise. The Founders of our Republic were the first to complain about its venal, lying press on the one hand and on the other the first to agree that, warts and all, it was the bedrock on which democratic freedoms rest.

Channels for Voicing Complaints

Given the public's and politicians' penchant to take the media to task for their many serious shortcomings, what forms do these complaints take? Informal criticism has come from within the journalism profession as well as from the general public. Specialized journals that frequently review media performance, such as the *American Journalism Review* and the *Columbia Journalism Review,* publish criticism by media professionals. But the circulation of these reviews is so limited, and the pocketbook effects of adverse criticism so negligible, that their pressure on the industry to alter journalistic practices is minimal. Informal criticism has also come from various public interest groups. In many cases these have been institutions organized for other purposes, such as the national Parent and Teacher Association (PTA) or the American Medical Association (AMA). Special media action groups have voiced their concerns publicly. The National Citizens Committee for

Broadcasting and the Washington-based Center for Media Education are examples. Complaints by public interest and media action groups, like most other forms of informal criticism, have been largely ineffectual. The critics may disturb the news profession momentarily, but they rarely induce major and permanent changes in media policies.

Formal protests about media performance can be lodged with the FCC's Broadcast Bureau in Washington or at FCC hearings. The commission holds such hearings before granting new broadcast licenses or when licenses have been challenged. Hearings provide real opportunities to counter the pressures brought by the media industry and balance the pro-industry biases that public regulatory bodies often develop. Regrettably, the licensing powers of the FCC were diminished by the Radio Preservation Act of 2000, which shifted final control over radio licenses to Congress where broadcast lobbies are most influential.[9] The new radio law may herald a trend of weakening FCC control over the broadcasting industry, leaving future policies more vulnerable to the political tides within Congress. When Republicans hold the reins of power, they show a preference for deregulation.

A number of serious problems impair the usefulness of public complaints. Most importantly, resources are lacking to ascertain whether complaints represent general views or merely the opinions of a tiny, highly vocal group. The squeaky wheel may get the grease, colloquially speaking, at the expense of the welfare of the silent majority. A few examples illustrate the problem of determining what constitutes the "voice of the people." Broadcasts about the Holocaust that dramatize Nazi atrocities have been loudly opposed by groups claiming that such programming generates anti-German feelings and hatred between Jews and gentiles. Yet these programs attract large audiences and receive wide acclaim. Millions of people watched and praised each episode of *The Sopranos,* a television series featured at the turn of the twenty-first century about a Mafia-connected dysfunctional family. Yet thousands of Italian Americans have denounced the show as slandering Italians. Stories about abortion, homosexuality, drug addiction, the activities of religious cults, or the successful ventures of discredited politicians have often been suppressed or toned down because of the flood of protests they might invite. Media policies can also be challenged in the nation's courts. However, most lawsuits involving claims about harmful television programming have failed.[10]

Specialized Media

Hundreds of specialized media address information needs that are neglected or poorly served by the regular media. They are a partial antidote for the general mass media's failure to cover many important groups and issues. Ethnic media are examples. There is an abundance of foreign language newspapers and broadcasts catering to dozens of ethnic groups. Numerous professional and trade journals, newsletters, and Web sites are devoted to a multitude of concerns such as religion, sports, fine and popular arts, automobiles, health issues, and bird watching. Some specialized media, such as the *New Republic, Mother Jones,* and New York's *Village Voice,* and cable and Internet broadcasts like CNN, Fox News, MSNBC, and the *Drudge Report,* are primarily devoted to political commentary. The Internet enables many special interest groups to keep in touch simply and cheaply and to publish and distribute magazines, newsletters, and audio- and videotapes on controversial political issues. Environmental groups, for example, have used these means of communication, as have supporters of fringe candidates for political office. If audiences numbering into thousands and even millions of people constitute a "mass," these special media are, by definition, mass media, no matter how widely dispersed their audiences are.

The demand for targeted information has increased in recent years so that more than ten thousand magazines are now published in the United States. Cable channels are multiplying and specialized Web sites are mushrooming. Specialized media also encompass the politically radical, iconoclastic, and counterculture media that flourish in times of social and political stress such as the late 1960s and early 1970s. These media feature the flagrant opposition to government policy that is permitted in the United States but often forbidden in other countries. At the height of underground press popularity, during the Vietnam war era and its aftermath, readership was estimated at ten million, with most issues read by several people. The rise of the underground print and electronic press during troubled times demonstrates that mass media can be started and operated with modest means. The media of the 1960s were financed mostly through advertising for items such as counterculture records, music productions, pornographic movies, and classified advertisements requesting services such as sex partners, nude models, or hallucinogenic drugs. Staffs were paid meager salaries or no salaries at all.[11] At one time there were nearly one thousand underground newspapers and four hundred counterculture radio stations. Such vitality attests to the vigor and flexibility of the mass media system.[12] The abrupt decline of underground media with the end of the Vietnam War also shows that the system is able to prune its unneeded branches when the demand ends.

The tolerance of the U.S. government for underground media demonstrates that government control over media content, however offensive, has had a light touch. Few countries equal and none exceeds the freedom to express radical viewpoints enjoyed by American media. In fact, some of the causes pressed by underground news sources ultimately became part of mainstream politics. In the end, waning public support rather than official censorship has led to the steep decline in this genre of journalism. Neither technical nor legal barriers block a revival should social or political conditions provide enough incentives. In fact, the Internet has already spawned thousands of vitriolic antigovernment sites that urge opposition to established authorities and their policies and often suggest ways to implement radical ideas.

The Impact of New Technologies

Marshall McLuhan, the television guru of the 1960s, predicted that the world would become a global village where humanity would partake of a global culture via television.[13] His vision of shared audiovisual news and entertainment has largely come to pass, but the reality is quite different and, in many respects, far richer than even McLuhan imagined. The vast amounts of diverse information produced by new technologies permit people to create their own, individualized information diet. The new age of personalized mass media has arrived. Political scientist W. Russell Neuman predicted this development at the start of the 1990s when he pointed out that we now "have the opportunity to design a new electronic and optical network that will blur the distinction between mass and interpersonal communications . . . . A single high capacity digital network will combine computing, telephony, broadcasting, motion pictures and publishing."[14] The new media confront audiences with growing arrays of choices of program content, format, and timing, and with opportunities for private or public interactive telecommunication.

Broadening the Public's Options

The new technologies have reduced the public's dependence on traditional media. The store of information made available through new radio, television, cable, and Internet channels, through communication satellites, and through round-the-clock news programs has grown by leaps and bounds.[15] Small as well as large communities share in this bounty, reducing the dangers of monopoly control over local information and opening up hitherto closed communication ghettos. Even newspapers can be printed and transmitted electronically, making it easier to bypass local media and rely on distant news sources. Cable television systems now can offer broadcasts from hundreds of separate channels, vastly increasing consumer choices of channels, if not content. The large number of radio and television programs available from satellites can be received by television stations over the air or through cable channels. Individual consumers can tap directly into these offerings through backyard satellite dishes. Space for various types of electronic transmissions, including television, can be rented by public and private parties from the satellites' owners.

Videotape recorders, videotapes, and videodiscs store electronic fare, allowing people to watch broadcasts that they would have missed otherwise because of schedule conflicts. Annoying commercials can be readily suppressed. Nearly half of America's households have at least one video recorder, a phenomenal number considering that it takes a bit of sophistication to operate VCRs. Pay cable and pay over-the-air television provide special entertainment or special interest programs at moderate costs. People pay solely for those programs they choose to watch. Public access cable channels and government Web sites keep citizens in closer touch with various public institutions and political leaders. They also permit these leaders to address the public directly without having their pronouncements mutilated by hostile journalists.

When programs are interactive, average people can transform themselves into broadcasters who address their messages to audiences of their choice, including journalists. In addition to flourishing talk shows on radio and television, two-way channels have become commonplace on cable television and the Internet's chat rooms. Viewers can interact with others while watching the same programs. But, given the explosive growth of Internet use, the competition for gaining attention has become extraordinarily fierce. Two-way communication technologies using radios, telephones, and the Internet have been useful in integrating outlying areas with social service systems in more populated centers. In Alaska and northern Canada, for example, these technologies deliver educational and health services and give people a greater voice in government.[16]

The way in which news about the party conventions in Los Angeles and Philadelphia during the 2000 presidential elections reached the public illustrates the nature of ongoing changes in the dissemination of political news. In past elections, the major networks offered many hours of convention coverage during prime time. Not so in 2000, when they limited coverage to a minimum because the major cable companies—CNN, C-Span, MSNBC, and the Fox News Channel—had by then become the dominant source for the public's political news. During the party conventions in 2000, cable news networks devoted up to 90 percent of their time to convention coverage, much of it filmed while events were in progress. When Democratic and Republican presidential candidates debated each other, all but two out of twenty debates were broadcast on cable.[17] On each primary election night throughout the campaign, the cable channels offered round-the-clock coverage, while the networks presented only brief snippets during their regular broadcasting hours. Even at the height of the campaign, network coverage rarely exceeded four or five minutes per night. While all types of political coverage have shrunk on the networks, quality has remained high. Networks with their own Web sites, like NBC, also regularly air reports by their top-notch correspondents on these sites, and routinely refer their viewers to these Web sites for information to flesh out broadcast stories.

Audiences like cable broadcasts. Cable's narrowcasting capabilities suit viewers' growing preference for news tailored to their special likes and needs. Aside from the Internet, cable television is the only political news venue whose audiences are growing. Viewers now name it most often as their source of political information, ahead of network or local news. Nonetheless, cable's reach of audiences remains puny compared to the reach of the networks. On Super Tuesday during the 2000 campaign, when primary results were reported from sixteen states, including giants like New York and California, an estimated 2.3 million households watched the three all-news cable channels between 8 and 11 P.M. That compared to roughly 10 million viewers each for the evening newscasts on ABC, CBS, and NBC. Moreover, the networks could reach nearly all households while only seven in ten households subscribe to cable.

Transforming Journalism

Thanks to the new technologies, the mass media business has made noteworthy advances on three fronts: news gathering, news processing, and news dissemination. Access to computer databases and satellites has put an enormous store of usable information within reach of average journalists wherever they may be. Even foreign countries kept off limits by hostile rulers can be explored by satellites, as can remote areas of the globe and even the private retreats of powerful elites. The ability to search databases electronically for specific bits of information and to combine these data in a variety of ways opens up countless new possibilities for creating news stories and providing valuable contextual information for fast-moving current developments.

When it comes to the distribution of news gathered at various locations, the array of available channels for immediate or delayed transmission has multiplied far beyond the range deemed possible a scant twenty-five years ago. Stations can even use satellites to supply other stations with live videos of stories that the station has covered locally. These offerings reduce dependence on current network programming, enable local stations to put a local spin on national news, and vastly expand television

Getting a Makeover for the Twenty-First Century

How does an old lady, more than a century and a half old, get spruced up to meet the challenges of the twenty-first century? Here's an amazing story that proves that it can be done successfully. The old lady is the Associated Press, the world's largest news-gathering organization. The Associated Press was founded in 1848, spurred by the product of a new technology—the telegraph—that made it possible to quickly distribute news gathered in far-off places. Who would do that job? Six New York newspapers decided to share the costs of news gathering and do it jointly. Their cooperative became known as the Associated Press, AP for short.

AP has remained a not-for-profit cooperative since that time, and now serves nearly all U.S. dailies through its domestic and international bureaus. In addition, all 1,550 members must provide copies of their breaking news stories to the AP. All members thus can draw on an extremely rich and far-flung pool of stories. In addition to daily newspapers, members now include some five thousand radio and television stations. Broadcasters are associate members who subscribe to the service but do not have voting rights. Policy is made by a board of directors which includes print and broadcast enterprises of varying sizes and interests.

To survive in the new multimedia environment, organizations need their own niche of expertise—services that they can provide better and faster than any of their competitors. What is the AP's niche? It used to be furnishing breaking news to its members quickly from the four corners of the earth and each of the fifty states. But that function has been usurped by nonstop cable news services like CNN. AP also could transmit pictures faster than its competitors. Today, anybody can do that from a home computer using inexpensive software. So what is left?

Most important, AP still covers news throughout the world more systematically and completely than any of its competitors. AP has 241 bureaus around the world, 146 in the United States, and 95 abroad. That is more than twice the number of bureaus

(Box continues, next page)

owned by the *New York Times,* the *Washington Post,* and the *Los Angeles Times* combined. It also has 56 more bureaus than Reuters, AP's strongest competitor, and can trump Reuters's expanding U.S. services and financial news services offered by Bloomberg. Most important, AP has a lock on the all-important state and local news with bureaus in every state. The AP has also stayed abreast of the speed-up in news gathering and dissemination. It took just six seconds for the AP to transmit the entire Starr Report, 130,000 words long, to its members in 1998. To move that many words when the Watergate story broke in 1972 would have taken more than thirty hours.

With breaking news no longer its unique forte, the AP is trying to break new ground. In recent years, it has ventured into investigative journalism and even garnered a Pulitzer prize for investigative reporting in 2000 for its story about the massacre of civilians by U.S. troops at No Gun Ri in the Korean war of the 1950s. Previously, AP had shied away from investigative stories because they arouse controversy; it did not wish to offend members who might disagree with a particular investigation. But the necessity of diversifying its journalistic mission to survive helped AP overcome its scruples. Because other wire services provide more original stories, AP has hired more staff to develop more original stories at its many bureaus, in addition to covering spot news. New staff has also been added to do niche reporting in areas that interest members—such as science, sports, health, and entertainment. This is a far more aggressive type of journalism than the journalism of old. The old lady is really swinging it.

AP has managed to develop its own operations in cyberspace without competing with its members—a difficult task. Members gather Internet news on their own, but only AP has the credibility and the staff to systematically gather reliable Internet stories throughout the world. AP has replaced its morning–evening news cycle with a twenty-four-hour cycle geared to the patterns on the Internet. Its stories posted on the Web now have links so that members can explore them in greater depth, as well as through using AP's new Internet databases.

AP has teamed up with CNET, an online round-the-clock news gatherer, for additional computer and technology information. It has also beefed up its delivery of photographs and graphics by using computer transmissions instead of sending prints and by creating an online archive of television graphics. In 1998, AP bought Worldwide Television News, which supplies mostly raw video footage with natural sound and scripts. In 2000, it set up AP Digital to sell AP's national and international—not state and local—stories to non-member Internet customers like AOL and Yahoo, raising money for operating AP. Increasingly, AP is making its money outside its traditional markets, largely in cyberspace—which puts it on a possible collision course with some of its members who are also competing for that market. Future troubles may be brewing, but the rejuvenated AP seems quite capable of handling them. Never sell the feisty old lady short! She is rolling with the punches and coming out on top.

SOURCE: This story is based primarily on an account by Brent Cunningham, "The AP Now," *Columbia Journalism Review,* November/December 2000; http://www.cjr.org/year/00/4/ap/asp.

programming options. The dependence on network programming has been reduced even further by round-the-clock news programming by CNN and other cable and Internet television news venues.

New broadcasting and narrowcasting technologies usually produce problems along with their benefits and require new policies. High-definition television (HDTV) technology is a case in point. Besides requiring consumers to buy new television sets to receive digital television signals, most television stations will have to spend millions of dollars for new equipment and transmitting towers. In view of these major and costly changes, the FCC conceived a fifteen-year transition plan. Established broadcasters would receive a second channel free of charge to duplicate their analog programs in digital versions on this second channel. At the end of the fifteen-year period of airing both analog and digital versions of their programs, the broadcasters would return their original channels to the government while retaining the digital channel as their sole outlet. The plan immediately became embroiled in major political battles.

Although the 1996 Telecommunications Act has embraced the principle of awarding digital channels free of charge, influential members of

Congress wanted the channels auctioned off to the highest bidders. The telephone companies, which pay the government for the right to transmit information over the public airways and who fear potential competition in data transmission from the broadcast industry, joined the lobby against free channels for broadcasters. Naturally, broadcast industry leaders strongly opposed any changes in the current rules. They were eager to get high-definition television under way, as were the manufacturers of the new television sets. In fact, supporters of the plan wanted to shorten the transition period to seven years—a window of time that some experts considered far too short to complete the many required equipment changes. PBS, ABC, NBC, CBS, and Fox began digital broadcasting in major television markets in 1998. They are committed to relinquish their analog broadcast spectrum and broadcast digitally exclusively by 2006.[18]

Another major problem exacerbated by the new technologies concerns the safeguarding of individual privacy. Ever smaller cameras and microphones permit reporters to spy with little chance for detection. Today reporters and other people can assemble scattered bits of information in seconds to derive a comprehensive portrait of an individual's past. Unless individual privacy becomes more fully protected, the computer age could well turn into an Orwellian nightmare—with individuals living in glass cages and exposed to instant public scrutiny.[19] Likewise, the new information-gathering techniques will make it far more difficult to protect national security information from prying eyes. Congress and the courts will be hard put to strike a sound balance between a free press and a secure society. All this is happening at a time when damaging information can spread through private or public channels faster and more widely than ever before.

The Internet

The technology with seemingly the largest impact on the way the traditional media conduct their business is interactive computer communication via the Internet and its features, such as e-mail, Usenets and List serves, and the World Wide Web. The Internet presents the stiffest competitive threat to traditional over-the-air and cable television because it duplicates many of their news and entertainment offerings. It tends to split off large chunks of their audiences and it competes, often successfully, in the battle for advertising revenues. The defining feature of Internet technology is open, nearly unrestricted access. Most people can receive its messages and broadcast their own at relatively small costs. The political consequences have been substantial, although observers measure them with diverse scales and therefore disagree about the magnitude and significance of changes. Assessment of the precise impact of the Internet is also difficult because it is a technology in progress. Its hardware, software, types of uses, and applicable government regulations remain in flux.

As the Internet matures, the directions in which it might turn political life are becoming clearer. The Internet has diminished the traditional news media's tight control over access to large mass audiences. Politicians, for example, who have felt victimized by journalists who paraphrased their comments and boiled them down to meaningless nuggets, can now reach audiences directly via e-mail and Web technology, and they often do. They can customize their messages to fit the needs of various target populations. Politicians who have found it difficult to win access to a media platform—third-party candidates and candidates for local offices are examples—now have alternative channels at their command. But to what extent political leaders and followers will ride the currents of change to supplement or even replace familiar practices, remains uncertain. Major changes in ingrained social behaviors are rarely swift.

The Web makes it possible for average individuals, who have long been ignored by the traditional news media, to make their voices heard in the public arena. Individuals and groups with modest intellectual and economic resources can now reach widely dispersed audiences throughout most parts of the world. Their messages can be constructed to inform or deceive, to rally people for good and bad causes, or to entertain them in socially approved or condemned ways (censorship has not yet come to the Internet, though it may be looming in the wings). Whether audiences will choose to receive these messages remains to be seen and will probably vary considerably depending on government policies, the identities of the senders and potential receivers, and the contents of these messages. By 2002, most Americans were already using the Internet to send and receive messages; socioeconomic and demographic barriers to Internet access were shrinking. Internet users thought that it was the most up-to-date medium, the easiest to use, and the most enjoyable. Nonetheless, when asked to express a preference among media, television was still the first choice at the turn of the century. It is deemed just as accurate as the Internet.

Much Internet use is nonpolitical, of course. The vast majority of users, especially among lower socioeconomic groups, access the Web for e-mail, shopping, and entertainment. Still, 91 percent of Internet users watched the exciting final phases of the 2000 presidential election online. Two out of three (67 percent) said that they had used the Web to look up information about the disputed vote counts in Florida.[20] Table 12-2 records the major ways in which the Web became an important information source during the final phases of the 2000 presidential campaign.

TABLE 12-2   Using the Internet as Presidential Campaign Information Source

How the Web was used	Percentage of users
To follow the news about the presidential campaign	60%
To explore candidates' issue positions/backgrounds	52
To visit a presidential Web site	34
To send supportive or critical e-mail to candidates	10
To discuss election status with chatroom users	5
To send donations to candidates or campaigns	4

SOURCE: Adapted from Gallup Poll Releases, November 30, 2000, http://www.gallup.com/poll/releases/pr001130.asp.

NOTE: Responses are based on a sample of 623 adult e-mail users drawn from randomly collected telephone samples of American adults.

The table shows that noninteractive uses still are far more common than interactive ones.

There is, as yet, no widely available solution to the problem of finding one's way through the Internet's lush jungles of information. It is easy to get lost for hours, sampling usable and unusable intellectual growths without knowing whether one has actually reached the most important specimens. Moreover, the stock of information is doubling every few months! Journalists remain essential, therefore—in fact they may be more essential than earlier—because they are trained to ferret out what seems "most important" within their cultural milieu and to present it in language that average people can understand. Unlike the often unknown dispatchers of Internet information, journalists and major media institutions are deemed reasonably trustworthy. This is why most people, for much of their political information, continue to turn to traditional media most of the time, either in their old formats or their Web site incarnations. Major newspaper and television Internet sites are the most heavily used political information sources on the Web, especially for general information.

Information made available through Internet sources is likely to trickle down to publics who did not encounter it themselves on the Web, through journalists who use the Internet. In fact, journalists and other elites stand to gain most from the new riches, although everybody benefits. Information on the Web reaches journalists faster, from more diverse sources, and in modes that allow reporters to question sources quickly with the expectation of a prompt response. The ample competition for audiences by Internet participants as well as the many other new dispensers of political information is apt to raise standards overall—though pessimists might argue that competition will force news quality to drop to the lowest common denominator. Be that as it may, the potential for producing excellent news has grown by leaps and bounds, which is good news for Americans.

Barriers to Development

A look at technology may tell us what is possible rather than indicate what is likely to happen, particularly in the short run. A number of psychological, political, and economic barriers block the full development of new mass communication technologies. Most people are reluctant to change their media use habits, particularly when there are costs in time, attention, and effort to master new technologies. Many new developments never get off the ground because bureaucracies impose too many regulations to guard against abuses. Unrealistically high standards are frequently prescribed, raising costs beyond economically feasible levels. For example, to stop satellite companies from effectively competing with cable companies at the local level at the turn of the century, the cable companies lobbied for imposing several costly requirements. They wanted to compel the satellite companies to carry all local channels, not just a few, at a price for rebroadcast rights that would be controlled by the satellites' competitors.[21]

State and local rules, piled on top of federal regulations, complicate the picture even further. Not only do they add more requirements, but rules issued by various jurisdictions often conflict. Every major technological revolution—and the information transmission revolution *is* major— has brought about economic and political dislocations. Such massive changes are fought by those whose knowledge and equipment will be made obsolete. Some of the new mass media offerings endanger current jobs. For instance, teachers may lose their jobs when long-distance learning programs transmit a master teacher's lessons to faraway classrooms. Medical programs that teach people better medical self-care methods may be unwelcome competition for the health profession. Televised programs featuring outstanding practitioners and facilities may establish standards for professional performance that average institutions cannot match.

Communications technologies involve large investments so that their sudden obsolescence becomes a crushing financial blow. Business entrepreneurs often try to derail innovations. Early entrants in a technological field frequently develop a squatter's mentality about rights they have acquired, such as the right to use certain broadcast frequencies or particular technologies. Newcomers, on the other hand, are eager to reallocate facilities in line with their special interests. They want to mandate the use of more advanced technologies, even before they can guarantee that a market for these technologies and services will develop. This could wipe out proven interests in favor of new claimants whose prospects for success are uncertain. Obstacles also arise because competing new technologies benefit various groups unevenly. Power struggles, which may be prolonged, are fiercest before the status quo is determined. Meanwhile, technology continues its advance, raising problems that further delay the green light for implementing new systems.

The Cable Television Case

Cable television's rocky history in the United States illustrates the obstacles faced by technical innovations. It also illustrates the many political decisions that must be made to fit a new information technology into existing legislative and administrative structures.

When cable television first became available in 1949, established broadcasters viewed it as a serious threat. They feared that the availability of numerous television channels would lead to a large menu of programs similar to the variety then offered by radio shows. This would splinter television audiences. Smaller audiences would mean smaller advertising revenues and smaller profits for existing stations. In turn, this might mean poorer programming because reduced revenue would necessitate curtailing expenditures. Television networks were also concerned that cable operators would pirate, rather than buy, their signals and broadcast the programs they had produced at high cost. When satellite technology evolved, fears mounted. The networks might be destroyed entirely if stations could pick up programs directly from satellites to broadcast nationwide via cable television.

The initial response of the FCC to cable technology was typical. Prodded by established interests, the commission protected the status quo with regulations that prevented the newcomers from harming these interests. These regulations sharply limited the types of programs that cable television stations could broadcast when they competed with established network services. Consequently, the growth of the cable industry was stunted.

Cable industry groups ultimately persuaded public officials that cable technology was needed because it could reach people in locations inaccessible to regular television signals. The idea of breaking the near monopoly enjoyed by the networks over broadcasting also became attractive. So did the possibility of opening up many new channels for broadcasting to groups hitherto shut out by a limited spectrum. By 1972 these pressures were sufficiently strong to convince the FCC to ease its regulations on the types of programs that cable television could broadcast. The cable system had a new lease on life. However, as usual when new technologies arise, the FCC imposed several very costly regulations to force cable television to serve public needs that had never been met in the past. The industry would have to offer a minimum of twenty channels, including outlets for the general public, educational institutions, and local governments. There were also requirements for two-way capabilities and for carrying signals of local broadcasters.

These rules, which hampered rapid development of cable television, were eased in 1976. Service requirements were eased further after successful legal challenges by cable operators who questioned the propriety of regulating cable television as if it were using scarce airwaves when cable transmission channels were plentiful.[22] In 1979 the FCC issued a lengthy research report on the economic impact of cable broadcasting. It concluded—erroneously, as it turned out—that cable was only a minor economic threat to the established television industry and that it did not endanger the industry's "ability to perform in the public interest." In the wake of these findings, the federal shackles were removed from the industry, one by one.[23] With the passage of the Cable Communications Policy Act of 1984, deregulation was complete.[24] The act deregulated rates and made renewal of cable franchises nearly automatic in areas with ready access to over-the-air television—roughly 90 percent of the cabled areas.

Meanwhile, the resistance of the established industries to this new competition softened gradually. In fact, a number of them, heeding the old adage, "If you can't lick 'em, join 'em," invested heavily in cable facilities once the FCC eased controls regarding cross-ownership and admission of the networks to the cable market. By 1993, broadcasters had full or partial control in nearly half (47 percent) of the top fifty cable systems; newspaper and magazine publishers participated in one third (34 percent). These systems reached 56 percent of the nation's homes that had cable. Fearing that oligopoly might become the dominant cable pattern, Congress provided for cable rate regulation in 1992 to protect consumers from price gouging. Cable rates had risen by more than 60 percent in the preceding five-year period.[25]

Figure 12-1 illustrates the rapid explosion of the cable industry in the 1970s and 1980s and the slower growth thereafter. By 1999, 67 percent of the nation's television households were linked to cable systems. Cable television had become the main source of breaking news. When pollsters asked a national sample of people where they would go to get information about breaking news, such as a terrorist attack on a large American city, 57 percent said they would turn to cable television, mostly to CNN. Nine percent would turn to network television news and most of the rest would turn to other audiovisual sources, including radio. Only 5 percent would turn to print news.[26]

FIGURE 12-1   The Cable TV Explosion

Year	Penetration rate (percent of households with cable)	Cable subscribers (in thousands)
1965	3.3	1,760
1970	7.5	4,498
1975	13.3	9,197
1980	22.6	17,671
1981	28.3	23,219
1982	35.0	29,341
1983	40.5	33,794
1984	43.7	37,291
1986	47.4	41,000
1988	53.8	48,600
1990	54.9	50,000
1991	60.6	51,000
1993	61.0	54,200
1999	67.3	64,170

SOURCE: Compiled from *The Television and Cable Factbook,* 1994 and 2000 editions.
NOTE: The last figure for cable subscribers covers 1998 data.

FCC rules and the opposition of the established industries were not the only hurdles faced by the cable industry. There were and are numerous local political hurdles as well. Laying of cables requires permission from local authorities. To avoid undue duplication of facilities, cable enterprises needed franchises. The franchising process has been highly political, in terms of both the selection of a particular company and the determination of the conditions of the franchise. Many small enterprises were squeezed out because they were unable to pay the costs of bidding for a contract.

In the absence of national rules, local franchising policies have been diverse.[27] Franchisers and franchisees have had to agree on the time to be allowed for constructing the system and the life of the franchise (usually fifteen years). They also needed agreement on requirements regarding public service and open-access channels and service for outlying areas where costs exceeded profits temporarily or permanently. Service to rural areas posed daunting economic problems, particularly in the western plains and the Rocky Mountain states. Alternatives to cable, such as microwave relays, satellite broadcasts, or transmission over telephone wires, had to be considered. Difficult decisions had to be made in choosing appropriate government agencies to supervise the execution of cable contracts and to ensure that programming serves the public interest. Finally, major controversies had to be settled regarding the nature of the fee structure and the manner in which government would exact its tribute.

Regulatory Options

Governments have several policy options for dealing with broadcast systems. First, they can play a hands-off, laissez faire role, allowing the system to develop as its private owners please.[28] The precedent for this policy is the traditional American stance toward the print media. If one believes that government should regulate information supply only when transmission channels are scarce, as happened with early radio and television, then it makes sense to leave the current rich crop of information transmission systems unregulated. When broadcast and narrowcast outlets are plentiful, market forces presumably come into play so that necessary services will be supplied in a far more flexible way than is possible when government regulations intervene. The only restraints that may be needed are safeguards to protect national security and maintain social norms and privacy.

Second, information transmission systems can be treated as common carriers, like the telephone or rail and bus lines. Common carrier status makes transmission facilities available to everyone on a first-come, first-served basis. Under common carrier rules, the owners of cable facilities would not broadcast their own programs as they do now. Instead they would lease their channels to various broadcasters for fees regulated by government or by market forces. As common carriers they would not be allowed to selectively exclude certain programs.

The FCC and many local governments like the common carrier concept. It has been adopted for dealing with communications satellites. But the U.S. Supreme Court decided in 1979 that cable could not be considered a common carrier under federal laws.[29] However, the ruling does not bar state and local authorities from designating the industry as a common carrier. Congress, too, has repeatedly imposed some common carrier features on the cable television industry. In the mid-1960s, for instance, it ordered cable systems to broadcast all local over-the-air programs. The industry brought suit and won judgments in 1985 and again in 1987 that the "must carry rule" violated the First Amendment rights of cable companies.[30] The victory for cable systems was a defeat for champions of broad public access rights to the media.

Third, the government can confer public trustee status on communication enterprises. Owners then have full responsibility for programming but are required to meet certain public service obligations. Examples are adherence to equal time provisions, limitations on materials unsuitable for children or offensive to community standards of morality, and rules about access to broadcast facilities. Access rules are designed to ensure that there are channels available to governments and various publics to broadcast information about public issues such as education, public safety, and medical and social service programs.

The rationale for conferring trustee status on broadcasters has been twofold. In the past, the scarcity argument has been powerful but it has lost validity. The other argument for trustee status is that television is a highly influential medium. There must be assurance that valuable programs are broadcast and harmful ones avoided and that canons of fairness are observed. This is a powerful argument with strong support in much of the world. It is the argument that underlies the treatment of over-the-air television in the 1996 Telecommunications Act. But it is not the primary argument on which the American system was built, and it may clash with the First Amendment.

Paying the Piper

Whether new technologies are treated like any private enterprise, like a common carrier, or like a trustee, their costs have to be paid. There are three possibilities for financing, each with different policy consequences: advertiser support, audience payments, and government subsidies. Various combinations are also possible. Print media, for example, are financed by their audiences, supplemented by advertisements and some mailing subsidies.

Advertiser support requires programming that has mass appeal. Such programming is bound to share the strengths and weaknesses of current mass media. Sponsor influence may increase in the age of medium proliferation because competition for sponsors becomes keener when media multiply. Many outlets—particularly those with small audiences or audiences that lack attraction for advertisers because they represent small markets—may even find it impossible to attract enough sponsors to pay for their operations.

Many new broadcast facilities, along with cable television, rely heavily on *audience payments*. These have generally taken the form of a monthly service charge for the facilities, to which an installation or equipment charge has often been added. Additional programming may be available for a flat monthly rate or on a per-program basis. Service charge financing for broadcasting has been quite popular in many foreign countries. In the United States, however, it initially met with resistance because good broadcast services are available throughout the United States free of charge.

By the mid-1980s, much of the initial resistance to paying for television had vanished. Half of America's households had been cabled, and many were paying for special programs in addition to their standard monthly fees. The worst fears of old-line broadcasting entrepreneurs had not materialized. While cable television had captured a solid slice of the networks' turf, they remained financially viable and even expanded into Web enterprises. News-sharing arrangements, involving major companies, became one of several ways to cut costs. One typical sharing arrangement included NBC, MSNBC, the Washington Post Company, and Newsweek.[31] As had been the case with past innovations, the new media had not mortally wounded their predecessors. When established enterprises could not throttle the newcomers in infancy, they joined them in droves by setting up Web ventures themselves.

A major social drawback of service charges for broadcasts is that poor families who most need many of the specialized programs are least able to pay to receive them. Middle-income families, who already enjoy many social advantages, benefit most from the information resources available through cable and other programs; low-income folks fall further behind.[32] This problem could be reduced through *government subsidies* paid to cable and Internet companies on a basis similar to financing public television, or government could pay subsidies directly to the poor. The latter system seems preferable to avoid making media enterprises financially dependent on the government, thereby endangering their freedom of action.

The Shape of the Future

Rather than projecting images of mass communication in the opening decades of the twenty-first century—always a chancy enterprise—I will sketch out areas of likely major changes and identify looming problems. The shape of the future will hinge on how Americans cope with these issues. The here-and-now sets the stage for what will ensue.

Regulation Versus Deregulation

New communications technologies require a complete rethinking of the scope and purpose of federal regulation of broadcast media. The Telecommunications Act of 1996, although moving beyond some of the outdated assumptions of its 1934 predecessor, still falls far short of matching the revolutionary technological changes with appropriate policy innovations. The difference in treatment between the unregulated print media and the regulated electronic media has become highly questionable. It was based on the assumption that there would be numerous competing newspapers while broadcast channels were scarce, encouraging monopoly. In reality, competition has been rising among broadcasters while it has been falling among daily newspapers. Besides, many newspapers—the *New York Times, Wall Street Journal, Chicago Tribune,* and *the Los Angeles Times* are examples—are now available in broadcast formats. To bring some logic to the regulatory scheme, proponents of regulation could conceivably extend regulations to include the print media in the future. The price of progress in electronic transmission of printed news could be the loss of freedom from government regulation.

The other alternative, total deregulation of all media and reliance on traditional First Amendment values, is still a distant goal, though piecemeal skirmishes and full-scale assaults on regulatory policies continue apace. Opponents of extensive deregulation of all mass media have argued that the age of electronic plenty remains a far-off vision because multiplying broadcast channels does not automatically mean more diversity in programming.[33] Opponents also contend that the impact of television on public life in America is so profound that the public interest requires controls. Even when competition is ample, it may be necessary to mandate access to neglected viewpoints and provide programming for ignored audiences, such as children, as well as protecting children from unwholesome information.

Dissatisfaction with the services supplied by private entrepreneurs, including complaints about price gouging, have further fueled opposition to deregulation. The wave of mergers since the 1980s, which placed most major media enterprises under the control of big corporations, rekindled fears that the media might become the mouthpieces of narrow special interests, and that financial returns would be their programming lodestar. Plummeting revenues and sharp cuts in news division staffs heightened these fears. Calls for regulation to prevent misuse of power by the media, rather than deregulation, once again became the battle cry for champions of a free press.

At the international level, pressures by developing nations are also strong to increase government control and responsibility for media performance. A great challenge therefore faces broadcast policymakers. They can yield to domestic and international pressures and make government the arbiter of what is good and safe news and entertainment for the public, whose voices deserve to be heard on channels controlled by media companies. Or, policymakers can leave these decisions under private control, at the mercy of nonelected media tycoons. Given these alternatives, I

A Merger or an Evolution?
The Big Corporate Fish Are Spinning Off
Multiple Specialized Channels

©ERIC DROOKER
"Media Monopoly"

From the *New York Times*, Op-Ed section, September 9, 1999. Reprinted by permission of Eric Drooker.

cast my vote for the latter option, believing with Thomas Jefferson that "error of opinion may be tolerated where reason is left free to combat it."[34] Venal or not, a press independent from government and free to criticize the government and its policies is still the bedrock of democracy.

Fragmentation of the Broadcast Audience

The multitude of broadcast channels and the even broader options created by videotape technology and the Internet have prompted fears that the national political consensus will become fragmented in the age of multimedia. When people turn to specialized fare in news and entertainment, their attention to politics may diminish. Without national media, there may be no national political consensus.[35] As discussed in Chapter 7, nationwide dissemination of similar news has fostered shared political socialization. When news becomes fragmented, people are likely to be socialized in disparate ways. If political programming becomes available only on channels dedicated to politics, will people choose to watch it? Will government leaders be able to convey their messages to the public? Will they be able to move the nation to agree with new policy directions, accepting equal treatment for racial minorities, the disabled, and people with divergent sexual orientations? A music fan, tuned in to an all-music station, may watch music programs only; an African American or Hispanic person may tune in only to stations concerned with African American and Hispanic affairs. Many citizens thus may become prisoners of their special interests and may miss out on happenings in the broader culture. The country may be carved up into mutually exclusive, often hostile enclaves.[36]

On the positive side of the ledger, specialization raises the possibility of a better fit between audience needs and public messages. Government programs may operate more successfully, given ampler opportunities for one- and two-way communication with selected audiences. The electoral chances of minority candidates and parties may improve with increased ability to target their messages to selected audiences. The possibilities for change are staggering but are still too undefined to hazard predictions.

Fears that fragmentation of the broadcast audience will lead to political balkanization are not shared by everyone, of course.[37] Many people point out that the national consensus was not ruptured when alternative media were used in the past. They argue that fragmented interests create the demand for fragmented media rather than the reverse. If there is political and social consensus, people will seek out information pertaining to the larger community. Others point out that commercially oriented media will always try to attract large audiences by offering programs with wide appeal. That means sticking to the same tried and true formulas. Programming on cable television, which has become uniform and similar to network television, is a vivid example. Even if the new media increase fragmentation, many people do not find this objectionable, believing that pluralism is preferable to earlier melting-pot ideals.

Media pluralism does herald more local programming. Most local governments eagerly use cable channels and their Web sites to broadcast local political news. Many local school systems and police and fire departments air their concerns on the new media. Since publicity means power, the new communications media tend to enhance the power of local institutions, frequently at the expense of national ones. The two-way capacity of the new media makes local programming more attractive for local audiences even when it lacks the polish of professional programs.[38] Although the possibilities for strengthening local communities through increased publicity are good, the new narrowcasting technologies also can deflect interest away from the local scene and produce global villages of like-minded people. As usual, major changes have their dark sides along with the bright ones.

Public Television

Yet another issue brought to the fore by the age of broadcast plenty is the fate of public television. Many political leaders would like to abandon it and save the costs of public subsidies. They point out that its audiences, except for its children's programs, have been quite small. In fact, the disadvantaged groups to which the public broadcast system targets its programs largely ignore it. Instead, its audience tends to be upscale. As discussed in Chapter 2, public television was organized to provide an alternative to the typical programming available on the commercial networks. It also was intended to be an outlet for programs geared to minorities. These are the very services that cable television and other narrowcasting services now can and do perform on a commercial basis.

The hitch in the arguments favoring disbanding public television is the presumption that the mushrooming commercial television enterprises will be willing and able to use their facilities to fill the niche occupied by the public broadcasting system. A glance at any weekly television schedule raises serious doubts. Most of the new outlets provide clones of the offerings that are familiar from network television.[39] Sophisticated cultural and educational programming is scarce and has not been commercially viable because audiences have remained small and the commercial channels show no sign that they are eager to serve the poor and disadvantaged. The difficulty of keeping the public broadcasting system solvent may sound its death knell, nonetheless. The European practice of funding public broadcasting principally through consumer fees has never been considered a realistic option in the United States.

The Consequences of Change

The concerns outlined thus far are not the only ones ahead. Many others will require decisions that go far beyond solving technical issues. The direction of communications policy is at stake and with it the tone and possibly the direction of American politics in general. John M. Eger, a former director of the White House Office of Telecommunications Policy, once remarked that the United States was "moving into a future rich in innovation and in social change." But this meant that the country was also moving into a storm center of new world problems. The new technologies are "a force for change throughout the world that simply will not be stopped, no matter how it is resisted." And then he asked, "Are we ready for the consequences of this change? Are we prepared to consider the profound social, legal, economic, and political effects of technology around the world?"[40]

Currently, the answer is "no." In the communications field, the structure for policymaking at all government levels is fragmented and ill-suited to deal with the existing problems, to say nothing of those that must be anticipated.[41] Policies are improvised when pressures become strong, yielding in a crazy quilt pattern to various industry concerns, to public interest groups, to domestic or foreign policy considerations, to the pleas of engineers and lawyers, and to the suggestions of political scientists and economists. Narrow issues are addressed, but the full scope of the situation is ignored. As political scientist W. Russell Neuman notes, "the concept of a comprehensive industrial policy or even a broadly focused reformulation of communications policy for the information age is political anathema in the centers of power."[42] The struggle over passage of the 1996 Telecommunications Act, and the compromise measure that is now the law of the land, proves that this assessment is unfortunately correct.

Summary

Many people are dissatisfied with the performance of the mass media, especially television. They can and do air their dissatisfaction through various formal and informal channels, but criticism usually has had limited success in bringing reforms. To fill the gaps left by the major mass media, many alternative media have been created. These media are organized either to serve demographically distinct populations or to cater to particular substantive concerns or political orientations. The mushrooming of underground print and broadcast media during the Vietnam War era showed that dissent is allowed to flourish in the United States even in wartime. It also demonstrated that, in a business dominated by giants, small enterprises can operate successfully on a shoestring budget.

In this chapter we explored the social and political consequences of technological advances in mass media and outlined the areas in which new public policies are needed. We briefly sketched the political roles played by the medley of print media, over-the-air and cable television, and the Internet. We discussed the economic consequences of mega mergers and splintered audiences. We also outlined several major looming problems and hailed to the arrival of the age of broadcast plenty. The impact of these changes on life and politics in the United States could be enormous unless resistance to the pace of change slows progress. Fragmentation of the broadcast audience has raised fears of political balkanization and breakdown of the national political consensus that has been deemed essential for successful democratic governance. But the extent and implications of the danger remain disputed.

Various changes in regulatory policy are in progress to integrate the new broadcast and narrowcast technologies into the existing mass media regulatory structure. But a total overhaul of the current policy regime is unlikely. The forces favoring greater government control of media content continue to be strong because the public sees the media as powerful instruments of social and political control. Whatever the outcome, the debate about media regulation needs to focus more clearly on the merits of the First Amendment in the century that lies ahead. Complete media freedom may be risky, but as the *Washington Post*'s Alan Barth put it: "If you want a watchdog to warn you of intruders you must put up with a certain amount of mistaken barking."[43]

Notes

1. "Preface: What's Next?" *Media Studies Journal* 13(2) (spring/summer 1999): xi–xii.
2. Geneva Overholser, "Letter from the Future—II," *Media Studies Journal* 13(2) (spring/summer 1999): 6–11; quotation from p. 8.
3. Elizabeth Weise, "Letter from the Future—I," *Media Studies Journal* 13(2) (spring/summer 1999): 2–5.
4. Ibid., 5.
5. Pew Research Center for the People and the Press, "1999 Journalism Survey: Overview," http://www.people-press.org/press99rpt.htm.
6. Ibid. The survey was conducted from November 20, 1998, through February 11, 1999.
7. For an excellent comparative analysis of these issues, see Pippa Norris, *A Virtuous Circle: Political Communications in Postindustrial Societies* (Cambridge: Cambridge University Press, 2000).
8. Pew Research Center for the People and the Press, "The Questionnaire and Overall Breakdown," 2000, http://www.people-press.org/media00sec5.htm.
9. Stephen Labaton, "Congress Severely Curtails Plan for Low-Power Radio Stations," *New York Times,* December 19, 2000.
10. A widely publicized case about media responsibility for copycat crimes committed by young adults is *Olivia N. (a minor) v. National Broadcasting Company,* 74 Cal. App. 3d 383 (1978), 126 Cal. App. 3d 488 (1981).
11. John W. Johnstone, Edward J. Slawski, and William W. Bowman, *The Newspeople* (Urbana: University of Illinois Press, 1976), 157–179.

12. They are described more fully in Johnstone, Slawski, and Bowman, *The News-people*, 157–181; Laurence Leamer, *The Paper Revolutionaries: The Rise of the Underground Press* (New York: Simon and Schuster, 1972); and Jack A. Nelson, "The Underground Press," in *Readings in Mass Communication,* ed. Michael C. Emery and Ted Curtis Smythe (Dubuque, Iowa: W. C. Brown, 1972), 212–226.
13. Marshall McLuhan, *Understanding Media: The Extensions of Man* (New York: McGraw-Hill, 1964); and Marshall McLuhan and Quentin Fiore, *The Medium Is the Message: An Inventory of Effects* (New York: Bantam Books, 1967).
14. W. Russell Neuman, *The Future of the Mass Audience* (New York: Cambridge University Press, 1991), ix–x.
15. Thomas F. Baldwin, D. Steven McVoy, and Charles Steinfeld, *Convergence: Integrating Media, Information and Communication* (Thousand Oaks, Calif.: Sage, 1996); W. Russell Neuman, Lee McKnight, and Richard Jay Solomon, *The Gordian Knot: Political Gridlock on the Information Highway* (Cambridge, Mass.: MIT Press, 1996).
16. Heather E. Hudson, "Implications for Development Communications," *Journal of Communication* 29 (winter 1979): 179–186. Also see Bella Mody, Joseph D. Straubhaar, and Johannes M. Bauer, *Telecommunications Politics: Ownership and Control of the Information Highway in Developing Countries* (Hillsdale, N.J.: Erlbaum, 1995).
17. Peter Marks, "Networks Cede Political Coverage to Cable," *New York Times,* April 7, 2000.
18. PBS Online, "Digital Broadcast Timeline," http://www.pbs...hcourse/hdtv/timeline.html. Also see Jon Van and Tim Jones, "Digital Promises an Unclear Revolution," *Chicago Tribune,* April 7, 1996.
19. Vincent Mosco, "Une Drôle de Guerre," *Media Studies Journal* 6 (spring 1992): 57–58.
20. Gallup Poll Releases, "Two-thirds of Internet Users have monitored the Florida Controversy Online," November 11–30, 2000, http://www.gallup.com/poll/releases/pr001130.asp.
21. William Neikirk, "Satellite TV Ready to Soar," *Chicago Tribune,* November 25, 1999.
22. *Home Box Office, Inc. v. FCC,* 567 F.2d 9 (D.C. Cir.), *cert. denied,* 434 U.S. 829 (1977); and *FCC v. Midwest Video Corp.,* 440 U.S. 689 (1979).
23. Pay television had been freed from federal controls in 1977. Remaining federal controls were dropped by 1979. Benjamin M. Compaine, Christopher H. Sterling, Thomas Guback, and J. Kendrick Noble, Jr., *Who Owns the Media? Concentration and Ownership in the Mass Communications Industry,* 2d ed. (White Plains, N.Y: Knowledge Industry Publications, 1982), 381, 407.
24. "Cable TV," *Consumer Reports* 52 (September 1987): 547–554.
25. Edmund L. Andrews, "Hopes of Cable Industry Ride on Veto by Bush," *New York Times,* July 25, 1992. Also see *Television and Cable Factbook,* 2000.
26. Pew Research Center for the People and the Press, "The Questionnaire and Overall Breakdown," 2000, http://www.people-press.org/media00sec5.htm.
27. FCC regulations prevail over conflicting state regulations. *Capital Cities Cable v. Crisp,* 104 U.S. 2694 (1984). Federal law may preempt state laws. See William E. Hanks and Stephen E. Coran, "Federal Preemption of Obscenity Law Applied to Cable Television," *Journalism Quarterly* 63 (spring 1986): 43–47.

28. Henry Geller, "Mass Communications Policy: Where We Are and Where We Should Be Going," in *Democracy and the Mass Media,* ed. Judith Lichtenberg (New York: Cambridge University Press, 1990), 290–329.

29. *FCC v. Midwest Video Corp.,* 440 U.S. 689 (1979).

30. "Cable TV," *Consumer Reports,* 555.

31. Felicity Barringer, "Leading Media Companies Forming Joint Web Venture," *New York Times,* November 18, 1999.

32. Mosco, "Une Drôle de Guerre," 56–60.

33. Don R. LeDuc, "Deregulation and the Dream of Diversity," *Journal of Communication* 32 (autumn 1982): 171.

34. First inaugural address, March 4, 1801. See Andrew A. Lipscomb, ed., *The Writings of Thomas Jefferson,* Vol. 3 (Washington, D.C.: Thomas Jefferson Memorial Association, 1905), 319.

35. James G. Webster, "Audience Behavior in the New Media Environment," *Journal of Communication* 36 (summer 1986): 77–91.

36. Lawrence K. Grossman, *The Electronic Republic: Reshaping Democracy in the Information Age* (New York: Viking, 1995).

37. W. Russell Neuman, *The Future of the Mass Audience* (New York: Cambridge University Press, 1991), 58–63.

38. Use of cable television is compared with use of other media in Gerald L. Grotta and Doug Newsom, "How Does Cable Television in the Home Relate to Other Media Use Patterns?" *Journalism Quarterly* 59 (winter 1982): 588–591, 609. Also see "Cable TV," *Consumer Reports.*

39. The reasons for this situation are explained by David Waterman, "The Failure of Cultural Programming on Cable TV: An Economic Interpretation," *Journal of Communication* 36 (summer 1986): 92–107. Also see Robert M. Entman and Steven S. Wildman, "Reconciling Economic and Non-Economic Perspectives in Media Policy: Transcending the 'Marketplace of Ideas,' "*Journal of Communication* 42 (winter 1992).

40. John M. Eger, "A Time of Decision," *Journal of Communication* 29 (winter 1979): 204–207.

41. William A. Lucas, "Telecommunications Technologies and Services," in *Communication for Tomorrow: Policy Perspectives for the 1980s,* ed. Glen O. Robinson (New York: Praeger, 1978).

42. Neuman, "The Future of the Mass Audience," x.

43. Alan Barth, "If the Press Didn't Tell Us, Who Would?" (Chicago: Sigma Delta Chi, 1987).

Readings

Aufderheide, Patricia. *Communications Policy and the Public Interest.* New York: Guilford Press, 1999.

Becker, Ted, and Christa Dayl Slaton. *The Future of Teledemocracy.* Westport, Conn.: Praeger, 2000.

Grossman, Lawrence K. *The Electronic Republic: Reshaping Democracy in the Media Age.* New York: Viking, 1995.

Heap, Nick, Ray Thomas, Geogg Einon, Robin Mason, and Hughie MacKay. *Information Technology and Society.* Beverly Hills, Calif.: Sage, 1995.

Kessler, Lauren. *The Dissident Press: Alternative Journalism in American History.* Beverly Hills, Calif.: Sage, 1984.

Neuman, W. Russell, Lee McKnight, and Richard Jay Solomon. *The Gordian Knot: Political Gridlock on the Information Highway.* Cambridge, Mass.: MIT Press, 1996.

Norris, Pippa. *Digital Divide? Civic Engagement, Information Poverty, and the Internet in Democratic Societies.* Cambridge: Cambridge University Press, 2002.

_____. *A Virtuous Circle: Political Communications in Postindustrial Societies.* Cambridge: Cambridge University Press, 2000.

Pool, Ithiel de Sola. *Technologies without Boundaries: On Telecommunication in a Global Age.* Cambridge, Mass.: Harvard University Press, 1990.

Sunstein, Cass. *Republic.com.* Princeton: Princeton University Press, 2001.

Tehranian, Majid. *Technologies of Power: Information Machines and Democratic Prospects.* Norwood, N.J.: Ablex, 1990.

Index